Uniting Europe

Europe Today
Series Editor: Ronald Tiersky

Europe Today: National Politics, European Integration, and European Security
Edited by Ronald Tiersky

Uniting Europe: European Integration and the Post–Cold War World
By John Van Oudenaren

Uniting Europe

European Integration and the Post–Cold War World

John Van Oudenaren

ROWMAN & LITTLEFIELD PUBLISHERS, INC.
Lanham • Boulder • New York • Oxford

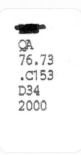
ROWMAN & LITTLEFIELD PUBLISHERS, INC.

Published in the United States of America
by Rowman & Littlefield Publishers, Inc.
4720 Boston Way, Lanham, Maryland 20706
http://www.rowmanlittlefield.com

12 Hid's Copse Road
Cumnor Hill, Oxford OX2 9JJ, England

British Library Cataloguing in Publication Information Available

Library of Congress Cataloging-in-Publication Data

Van Oudenaren, John.
    Uniting Europe : European integration and the post-cold war world / John Van
Oudenaren.
        p.   cm.—(Europe today)
    Includes bibliographical references and index.
    ISBN 0-8476-9032-6 (alk. paper)—ISBN 0-8476-9033-4 (pbk. : alk. paper)
    1. Europe—Economic integration.   2. Europe—Politics and government.
    3. Post-communism.   I. Title.   II. Europe today (Rowman and Littlefield, Inc.)
    HC241 .V352   2000
    341.242′2—dc21   00-038270

Printed in the United States of America

♾ ™ The paper used in this publication meets the minimum requirements of American
National Standard for Information Sciences—Permanence of Paper for Printed Library
Materials, ANSI/NISO Z39.48-1992.

Contents

List of Tables

List of Boxes

List of Abbreviations

ACP	African, Caribbean, and Pacific
APEC	Asia Pacific Economic Cooperation
CAP	Common Agricultural Policy
CFSP	Common Foreign and Security Policy
CIS	Commonwealth of Independent States
CMEA	Council for Mutual Economic Assistance
CSCE	Conference on Security and Cooperation in Europe
EAGGF	European Agricultural Guidance and Guarantee Fund
EBRD	European Bank for Reconstruction and Development
EC	European Community
ECB	European Central Bank
ECJ	European Court of Justice
ECOFIN	Council of Ministers (Economics and Finance Ministers)
ECSC	European Coal and Steel Community
ECU	European Currency Unit
EDF	European Development Fund
EEA	European Economic Area
EEC	European Economic Community
EFTA	European Free Trade Association
EIB	European Investment Bank
EMS	European Monetary System
EMU	Economic and Monetary Union
EP	European Parliament
EPC	European Political Cooperation
EPU	European Payments Union
ERDF	European Regional Development Fund
ERM	Exchange Rate Mechanism
ERT	European Roundtable of Industrialists
ESC	Economic and Social Committee
ESCB	European System of Central Banks
ESDI	European Security and Defense Identity
ESPRIT	European Strategic Program for Research and Development in Information Technology
FRG	Federal Republic of Germany
FYROM	Former Yugoslav Republic of Macedonia
GATS	General Agreement on Trade in Services
GATT	General Agreement on Tariffs and Trade
GDR	German Democratic Republic
HST	High Speed Train
ICAO	International Civil Aviation Organization
IFOR	Implementation Force
IGC	Intergovernmental Conference
ILO	International Labor Organization

ILSA	Iran-Libya Sanctions Act
IMF	International Monetary Fund
JHA	Justice and Home Affairs
KLA	Kosovo Liberation Army
MEP	Member of the European Parliament
MFN	Most Favored Nation
MRA	Mutual Recognition Agreement
NAFTA	North American Free Trade Agreement
NATO	North Atlantic Treaty Organization
NIS	Newly Independent States
NTA	New Transatlantic Agenda
NTB	Non-Tariff Barrier
OECD	Organization for Economic Cooperation and Development
OEEC	Organization for European Economic Cooperation
ONP	Open Network Provision
OSCE	Organization for Security and Cooperation in Europe
PCA	Partnership and Cooperation Agreement
PHARE	*Pologne et Hongrie: Actions pour la Reconversion Économique*
PTT	Post, Telephone and Telegraph
QMV	Qualified Majority Voting
SEA	Single European Act
SIS	Schengen Information System
TABD	Transatlantic Business Dialogue
TAC	Total Allowable Catch
TACIS	Technical Assistance to the Commonwealth of Independent States
TAFTA	Transatlantic Free Trade Agreement
TEN	Trans-European Network
TEP	Transatlantic Economic Partnership
TRIMS	Trade-Related Investment Measures
TRNC	Turkish Republic of Northern Cyprus
UK	United Kingdom of Great Britain and Northern Ireland
UNFCCC	United Nations Framework Convention on Climate Change
UNPROFOR	United Nations Protection Force
USSR	Union of Soviet Socialist Republics
VAT	Value-Added Tax
VER	Voluntary Export Restraint
WEU	Western European Union
WTO	World Trade Organization

Chronology

World Events	European Integration
August 1945 U.S. drops atomic bombs on Japan; war in Pacific ends	
October 1945 United Nations established	
December 1945 29 countries sign Articles of Agreement establishing International Monetary Fund	
	June 1947 Marshall Plan announced
August 1947 British rule in India ends; India and Pakistan gain independence	
January 1948 GATT comes into force	
February 1948 Communist coup in Czechoslovakia; Soviet hegemony in Eastern Europe fully established	
	March 1948 Brussels Treaty establishing Western European Union enters into force
	April 1948 OEEC established to coordinate Marshall aid
May 1948 State of Israel established	
	April 1949 North Atlantic Treaty signed
	May 1949 Council of Europe established

October 1949
Communists triumph in China; People's
Republic established

May 1950
Schuman announces plan for coal and
steel pool

June 1950
Korean War begins

April 1951
ECSC treaty signed

May 1952
European Defense Community treaty
signed

July 1952
ECSC established

March 1953
Stalin dies, leading to "thaw" in East-
West relations

May 1954
French suffer defeat at Dien Bien Phu,
leading to independence for North and
South Vietnam

August 1954
French National Assembly defeats EDC
treaty

November 1954
Algerian war of independence against
France begins

May 1955
Warsaw Treaty Organization formed

June 1955
Six convene Messina conference to consider next stage of integration

July 1956
Egypt seizes Suez Canal; followed by
October war between Egypt and Israel,
France, Britain

March 1957
Treaties of Rome establishing EEC and
Euratom signed

October 1957
USSR launches *Sputnik I*

January 1958
EEC and ECSC established

July 1958
Basic principles of the CAP agreed

January 1959
Fidel Castro takes power in Cuba

January 1959
First tariff reductions and lowering of quotas toward the establishment of the customs union

May 1960
EFTA established

June 1960
Belgian Congo becomes independent

October 1960
Nigeria gains independence from Britain

December 1960
OECD established, replacing the OEEC

July–August 1961
UK, Ireland, and Denmark apply for membership in the Community

November 1961
President Kennedy steps up U.S. military involvement in Vietnam

January 1962
CAP established

July 1962
Algeria becomes independent

October 1962
Cuban missile crisis; India-China war

January 1963
De Gaulle vetoes British application for membership

July 1963
EC signs Yaoundé Convention with 17 African countries

August 1964
U.S. Congress passes Gulf of Tonkin resolution, paving way for escalation of the Vietnam War

July 1965
France precipitates "empty chair" crisis to protest supranational tendencies in the Community

September 1965
China calls for a "people's war" in Africa, Asia, and Latin America

July 1966
Luxembourg Compromise agreed

January 1967
Cultural Revolution rages in China

June 1967
Israel wins Six Day War against Egypt, Jordan, Syria, and Iraq

July 1967
Merger Treaty comes into effect

July 1968
Customs union achieved

August 1968
Warsaw Pact troops invade Czechoslovakia to reverse the liberalization of communism

March 1969
Sino-Soviet clashes on the Manchurian border

July 1969
U.S. astronaut Neil Armstrong lands on moon

December 1969
Hague summit sets ambitious goals for the Community in the 1970s, including the start of European Political Cooperation

April 1970
Council agrees on introduction of the own-resources system

August 1971
Nixon suspends the convertibility of the dollar into gold

December 1971
India defeats Pakistan in war that results in creation of an independent Bangladesh

April 1972
Agreement to establish the "snake," a form of currency cooperation

May 1972
Nixon becomes first U.S. president to visit Russia; signs arms control agreement

August 1972

Arab terrorists kill Israeli athletes at Munich Olympics; international terrorism emerges as a serious challenge to governments worldwide

January 1973

United States, North Vietnam, South Vietnam, Viet Cong sign Paris agreements ending war in Vietnam

March 1973

Group of Ten finance ministers agree to float currencies, ending Bretton Woods system of pegged exchange rates

October 1973

Fourth Arab-Israeli war, followed by Arab ban on oil exports to the United States and huge increases in the price of oil

July 1974

Turkey invades Cyprus

April 1975

South Vietnam collapses, after North, violating Paris agreements, invades

January 1979

Shah of Iran overthrown by Islamic revolution

January 1973

UK, Ireland, and Denmark become members of the Community

December 1974

Paris summit establishes European Council

February 1975

Lomé Convention signed with African, Caribbean, and Pacific countries

March 1975

European Regional Development Fund established

July 1978

Bremen European Council agrees plans to establish European Monetary System (EMS)

March 1979

EMS begins to operate

June 1979

First direct elections to the European Parliament

December 1979
NATO decision to install medium-range nuclear missiles in Europe; USSR invades Afghanistan

August 1980
Solidarity established in Poland as an opposition trade union

January 1981
Greece becomes a member of the Community

November 1981
Germany and Italy present Genscher-Colombo plan for institutional improvements

December 1981
Communists impose martial law in Poland, crushing Solidarity

April 1982
Falklands war between Britain and Argentina

June 1983
Leaders sign Solemn Declaration on European Union at the Stuttgart European Council

July 1983
Council adopts resolution on an EC framework program for research

December 1983
Council agrees to Common Fisheries Policy

June 1984
Member states reach agreement on British rebate at the Fontainebleau European Council

January 1985
Jacques Delors becomes Commission president

June 1985
Commission submits white paper on the completion of the internal market by 1992; five member states sign Schengen Agreement on elimination of border controls

July 1985
Member states decide to convene inter-governmental conference (IGC) to amend the treaties

January 1986
Portugal and Spain become members of the Community

February 1986
Single European Act establishing single market goal for 1992 signed; also strengthens power of the European Parliament and provides a treaty basis for EPC

April 1986
Chernobyl nuclear accident in Ukraine

September 1986
GATT signatories launch Uruguay Round of trade talks

July 1987
Single European Act enters into force after ratification by the member states

June 1988
Hanover European Council establishes committee to examine prospects for economic and monetary union; EC and Council for Mutual Economic Assistance establish relations

October 1988
Council adopts decision establishing the Court of First Instance

February 1989
Roundtable talks begin between Solidarity and the government begin in Poland, after economy languishes through the 1980s

June 1989
Partially-free elections in Poland

July 1989
G-7 agrees to provide economic restructuring aid to Hungary and Poland

November 1989
Berlin Wall opened; communism collapses in central and eastern Europe

December 1989
Strasbourg European Council agrees to convene IGC on EMU

June 1990
Dublin European Council decides to convene an IGC on political union, to run in parallel with the IGC on EMU

July 1990
Stage 1 of EMU begins

August 1990
Iraq invades Kuwait

December 1990
IGCs agreed at Strasbourg and Dublin are launched

January 1991
U.S.-led coalition begins war to liberate Kuwait

December 1991
Soviet Union dissolved

December 1991
Maastricht European Council reaches agreement on draft of the Maastricht Treaty on European Union; Europe Agreements signed with Poland, Hungary, and Czechoslovakia

February 1992
Maastricht Treaty signed

May 1992
Agreement on European Economic Area signed

June 1992
Voters in Denmark disapprove ratification of the Maastricht Treaty

August 1992
Crisis in the European Monetary System

December 1992
Edinburgh European Council paves way to a second Maastricht ratification referendum in Denmark

January 1993
Single European market enters into effect

November 1993
Maastricht Treaty enters into force; formally establishing the European Union and creating the legal basis for the achievement of a single currency by 2002

January 1994
North American Free Trade Agreement comes into effect

January 1995
World Trade Organization established

January 1994
Stage 2 of EMU begins; European Economic Area agreement enters into force

November 1994
Norwegian voters reject EU accession

January 1995
Austria, Finland, and Sweden become members of the Union

March 1995
Schengen Agreement enters into force among seven EU member states

July 1995
Member states sign Europol Convention

November 1995
Euro-Mediterranean Conference in Barcelona establishes a comprehensive partnership with countries of North Africa and the Middle East

December 1995
U.S.-EU Transatlantic Declaration signed

March 1996
IGC to revise the Maastricht Treaty opens in Turin

June 1997
IGC concludes with agreement on a draft Treaty of Amsterdam

July 1997
Commission issues *Agenda 2000* containing evaluations of the candidate countries' membership applications and proposals for reform of the EU

October 1997
Treaty of Amsterdam signed

December 1997
European Council meets in Luxembourg and approves start of enlargement negotiations with six candidate countries

March 1998
Conference in London kicks off enlargement negotiations

May 1998
India and Pakistan test nuclear weapons

May 1998
Special session of the European Council decides that eleven countries have qualified to adopt the euro; Wim Duisenberg selected to head European Central Bank

January 1999
Stage 3 of EMU begins; euro officially launched

March 1999
NATO begins war against Yugoslavia over Kosovo

March 1999
Collective resignation of the Santer Commission following charges of mismanagement; special summit in Berlin establishes budget for 2000–2006

May 1999
Treaty of Amsterdam enters into force

June 1999
Cologne European Council endorses a post-Amsterdam IGC focused on institutional reform

December 1999
Seattle WTO ministerial fails to launch Millennium Round of trade talks

December 1999
Helsinki European Council agrees to establish European military force for peacekeeping, endorses start of enlargement negotiations with six more countries

February 1999
Enlargement negotiations begin with second wave of applicants; IGC on institutional reform convenes

March 2000
Lisbon European Council adopts new economic strategy and goal for 2000–2010

EU member states
Candidate states negotiating accession
Candidate state, not negotiating

Possible Dates of Accession

2003–2007	Cyprus
	Czech Republic
	Estonia
	Hungary
	Latvia
	Lithuania
	Malta
	Poland
	Slovakia
	Slovenia
2008–2010	Bulgaria
	Romania
2010–?	Turkey

FINLAND

Helsinki

DEN

ckholm

BALTIC
SEA

Tallinn

ESTONIA

Moscow

nhagen

Riga

LATVIA

RUSSIA

LITHUANIA

Vilnius

BELARUS

erlin

Warsaw

Minsk

POLAND

Kiev

Prague

UKRAINE

CH. REPUBLIC

SLOVAKIA

enna

Bratislava

Moldova

Chisinau

STRIA

Budapest

VENIA

HUNGARY

ROMANIA

Ljubljana

Zagreb

CROATIA

BLACK SEA

BOSNIA

Belgrade

Bucharest

Sarajevo

SERBIA

ADRIATIC
SEA

MONTENEGRO

BULGARIA

Sofia

Skopje

Tirana

MACEDONIA

Ankara

ALBANIA

GREECE

AEGEAN
SEA

TURKEY

ILY

Athens

ta

IONIAN SEA

Nicosia

MALTA

CYPRUS

LEBANON

Beirut

CHAPTER 1

Introduction
PEACE, PROSPERITY, AND THE CHALLENGES OF EUROPEAN INTEGRATION

Beginnings: 1945–1949

European economic and political integration began in part as an attempt by European leaders, strongly supported by the United States, to overcome the national rivalries that had led to two world wars in the first half of the 20th century. The main victors on the Western side, the United States and Great Britain, ended the war committed to promoting democracy and political reform in the defeated Axis powers, Germany and Italy. They also sought to establish a more open international economic system to replace the prewar order, which had been characterized by protectionism, competitive currency devaluations, and other policies by which the major powers sought to gain economic and political advantage at the expense of their rivals.

At a series of diplomatic conferences in 1944 and 1945, the United States and Britain agreed to establish a new monetary system based on stable currencies pegged to the value of gold, an international bank to promote reconstruction and development in poor and war-torn countries, and an international organization for negotiating lower tariffs and eliminating other barriers to international trade. These understandings led to the establishment, in 1946, of the International Monetary Fund and the World Bank, informally known as the Bretton Woods institutions after the small New Hampshire town in which the most important of these economic conferences took place. The following year 23 countries concluded the General Agreement on Tariffs and Trade (GATT), under which the signatories pledged to lower barriers to trade through negotiations conducted in accordance with the "most favored nation" (MFN) principle.

The design of the postwar international economic order reflected what has been called the "universalist" tendency in the American approach to foreign policy—the idea that a single set of rules should apply to all countries and that discriminatory economic behavior and zones of preference be abolished.[1] In the monetary sphere, universalism meant the convertibility of all currencies into each other and, indirectly, into gold. In trade, it meant application of the MFN principle, under which each country agreed to grant trade conditions to every other country no worse than those granted to the most favored nation. In both areas,

1

the postwar approach was intended as a break with the 1930s, when Germany and other dictatorships created special economic zones based on exclusive trading relationships and government manipulation of currency values, and when even traditionally free-trade–oriented Britain resorted to Imperial Preference—a system of special trade relationships that encouraged trade within the British Empire at the expense of the rest of the world—to combat unemployment at home.

Whatever its merits in principle, the universalist approach proved difficult to apply in economically crippled postwar Europe. The war had resulted in widespread dislocation of peoples and destruction of factories and infrastructure. Germany was divided, with its western part cut off from traditional supplies of grain in the east. As they attempted to rebuild their economies, the countries of Western Europe mainly needed to obtain new machinery and goods from the United States, which they lacked the dollars to buy. They were less interested in trading with neighbors who were struggling with the same shortages and reconstruction problems.

Under these conditions, it was all but impossible for European countries to apply the universalist principles espoused by the United States and by some Europeans at the end of the war. They were simply too weak to participate in a new international economic order. Britain announced in 1946 that it was prepared to convert sterling into dollars and other currencies, but it was forced to abandon this policy after a mere six weeks, as demand for dollars led to the collapse of its currency. Throughout Europe, governments maintained tight controls on currency flows and strictly regulated foreign trade. Businesses had to secure licenses to obtain foreign currency to buy goods from or invest in other countries, and trade took place in the context of bilateral agreements in which, for example, one country would agree to sell a certain number of tons of coal to another country which in turn would commit to selling so many bushels of wheat. Moreover, in all European countries there were powerful groups—ranging from communist-controlled trade unions to private corporations shielded from international competition by cartels and protectionism—that did not accept the philosophy of openness and wanted to retain or even strengthen the autarkic features of the wartime and prewar economic orders. Shortages and difficult economic conditions tended to strengthen the hand of these forces, and to weaken the case for freer trade and economic liberalization.[2]

For its part, the Soviet Union declined altogether to participate in the IMF, the World Bank, or the GATT, choosing instead to pursue the same policies of economic isolation that it had followed in the 1930s. Instead of building "socialism in one country," Stalin's prewar slogan, the Soviets in effect were building "socialism in one empire," as they established exclusive trading links with countries of central and eastern Europe that they had overrun in the last year of the war. At least initially, these links were highly exploitative, as the Soviet Union imposed one-sided economic deals on its partners in order to obtain raw materials and equipment badly needed for the reconstruction of the Soviet economy.

THE MARSHALL PLAN

By early 1947 the Truman administration had concluded that the United States needed to take decisive action to stabilize the economic and political situation in Europe. In a speech at Harvard University in June 1947, U.S. Secretary of State George C. Marshall proposed a program of aid designed to pull Europe to its feet. The United States offered to provide Europe with money and goods, but only if the Europeans themselves came up with a plan for using the aid, and only if the plan was designed as a joint effort rather than a hodgepodge of national requests.

After a series of preliminary meetings, in April 1948 sixteen European states founded the Organization for European Economic Cooperation (OEEC). Based in Paris, this organization helped to administer Marshall aid and provided a forum in which the member states negotiated arrangements to lower intra-European trade and currency barriers. The European Recovery Program (ERP), as the Marshall Plan formally was known, provided a powerful external stimulus to intra-European trade. Under OEEC auspices, in 1948 the member countries began to remove quotas and restrictions on the imports of manufactures and foodstuffs.

The ERP also financed the European Payments Union (EPU), which was established in mid-1950 under OEEC auspices. The EPU was intended as a temporary solution to the problem of currency convertibility in Europe—a halfway house between the full dollar convertibility mandated in the Bretton Woods system and the rigid bilateralism that characterized trade and exchange in the late 1940s. The EPU was based on an elaborate system that summed up a country's surpluses and deficits with all of the other countries of the union and converted them into a single surplus or deficit position that could be settled by dollars, gold, or limited credits. The EPU restored a large measure of currency convertibility within Europe, although it did not entail convertibility of the European currencies into the dollar. In monetary affairs as in trade, Western Europe, with support from the United States, was finding regional solutions to its economic problems. These solutions were a far cry from fulfillment of the universalist aspirations of 1945, but they represented a step towards integration on the regional level and played an important role in reviving the European economies.

Between 1948 and 1951 the United States provided $12.4 billion in grant aid to the European Marshall Plan recipients, the equivalent of over $70 billion in 1999 prices. This aid was important not only for its direct assistance to the economies of Europe, but also for its indirect effects—within and among countries—in promoting a postwar order in which economic growth could be revived and sustained. As Barry Eichengreen has remarked, "The Marshall Plan was a source of US leverage to prompt liberalization and stabilization on the part of European governments and to encourage their adherence to the norms and standards of what might be called the Bretton Woods regime. It strengthened the hand of European leaders seeking to control the levers of economic policy and rebuff the opponents of the market economy."[3] In this sense, the Marshall Plan played an enormous role in placing Europe on the path toward integration along market-oriented principles that was to culminate in the establishment of the European Union.

The Soviet Union at first showed interest in receiving reconstruction aid from the United States, but it was unwilling to participate in a cooperative plan that would have required it to give information about its economy and to yield influence over economic policy-making to outsiders. It thus declined to participate in the plan, as well as blocked participation by its east European satellites. Instead, it established, in January 1949, the Council for Mutual Economic Assistance (CMEA, also known as Comecon) to organize trade in the Soviet sphere of influence and to serve as a political and propaganda counterweight to the integration efforts of the West.

As the cold war deepened, the Marshall Plan became the linchpin of an increasingly determined American strategy to block the expansion of Soviet power. This in part helped to explain the strong political support for the plan in the United States. As Secretary of State Dean Acheson later wrote in his memoirs, "what citizens and representatives in Congress alike always wanted to learn in the last analysis was how Marshall aid operated to block the extension of Soviet power and the acceptance of Communist economic and political organization and alignment."[4]

THE BRUSSELS TREATY AND THE COUNCIL OF EUROPE

In addition to the Marshall Plan, there were several specifically European attempts at closer economic, political, and security cooperation in the late 1940s. In 1947 Belgium, the Netherlands, and Luxembourg formed a common customs union, known as the Benelux. In the same year, France and Britain signed the Treaty of Dunkirk, in which they pledged to come to each other's assistance if either was attacked in Europe. This was followed, in March 1948, by the signing by France, Britain, and the three Benelux countries of the fifty-year Brussels treaty "for collaboration in economic, social and cultural matters and for collective self-defense."[5] The treaty established the Brussels Treaty Organization, which later became the Western European Union (WEU).

For some in Europe, these initial steps toward economic and political cooperation did not go far enough. They wanted to leapfrog the cautious process of intergovernmental negotiation and to create a fully fledged United States of Europe directly based on the popular will of the European electorates. Known after the American example as federalists, they included academics, journalists, trade union leaders, and prominent veterans of the resistance to Nazi and Fascist regimes in World War II. At a Congress of Europe in the Hague in 1948, nearly one thousand delegates from twenty-six countries discussed the federalist project and issued a concluding call to convene a European Assembly that would serve as the constituent body for a united Europe.

In response to these demands, the ministerial council of the Brussels Treaty

Organization convened a special intergovernmental conference in London in early 1949 to discuss the various proposals for a federal Europe. In addition to the five Brussels powers, five other countries—Denmark, Norway, Sweden, Ireland, and Italy—participated in this meeting. The London deliberations soon revealed a wide difference of views between Britain and the Scandinavian countries on the one side and the continental countries on the other over the key question of whether integration should be a matter of agreement among sovereign states represented by their governments or whether, as the name European Assembly suggested, it was to be based directly on a movement of peoples with their own representation at the European level. The British Labour government of Prime Minister Clement Attlee took a rather skeptical view of integration and preferred an intergovernmental committee of ministers. The continental countries endorsed the call for establishment of a European Assembly comprised of members not controlled by the member state governments.

In the end, the conference participants compromised by concluding, in May 1949, the Statute of the Council of Europe. This agreement established a bicameral organization that consisted both of a ministerial committee and a Consultative Assembly of parliamentarians. It stipulated that every member "must accept the principles of the rule of law and of the enjoyment by all persons within its jurisdiction of human rights and fundamental freedoms."[6] The objective of the Council of Europe, as stated in the 1949 agreement, was "to achieve a greater unity between its Members for the purpose of safeguarding and realizing the ideals and principles which are their common heritage and facilitating their economic and social progress."[7] The main areas of cooperation specified in the organization's statute were economic, social, cultural, scientific, legal, and administrative matters and "the maintenance and further realization of human rights and fundamental freedoms."[8]

The gap between these sweeping aims and the limited means established to carry them out soon became apparent. The Council of Europe developed mainly as a body in which ministers met to discuss and to conclude agreements for common action on an intergovernmental basis. The Consultative Assembly laid the groundwork for future cooperation among parliamentarians and governments, but the continental federalists never were able to overcome British and Scandinavian resistance to expanding its power at the expense of the ministerial committee.

Although the Council of Europe was a disappointment to the federalist movement that had pressed for its creation, it nonetheless was important as the first permanent, Europe-specific nondefense institution created after World War II. Located in Strasbourg, France, the committee of ministers and the parliamentary assembly contributed to the harmonization of national laws affecting the welfare of Europeans as citizens, with a strong leveling up bias in the areas of social welfare, health, migration, and other areas. The parliamentary assembly had limited powers, but its members were selected directly by national parliaments and not subject to control by national governments. Periodic visits to Strasbourg convinced many parliamentarians of the value of closer ties with their counterparts from other European countries and helped to lay the basis for more ambitious attempts at integration later in the postwar period.[9]

THE ATLANTIC ALLIANCE

The other major institutional development of the late 1940s was the creation of the Atlantic alliance linking Europe and North America. The United States had emerged from World War II committed to promoting economic and political stability in Europe, but it did not intend to conclude a military alliance with West European states. To do so would go against the American tradition of "no entangling alliances" and was opposed by powerful isolationist forces in the U.S. Congress. However, the communist takeovers in eastern Europe and the onset of the cold war led to a shift in American attitudes. In April 1949 the United States, Canada, the five Brussels powers, and four other European states signed the North Atlantic Treaty, in which they pledged to come to each other's assistance in the event of external attack. The signing of the treaty was followed by the creation of the North Atlantic Treaty Organization (NATO) and the establishment of an integrated military command.

Like the Marshall Plan, NATO was an important American contribution to the postwar revival of Europe and to the fledgling process of building a united Europe. It allowed the European countries to concentrate on economic cooperation, leaving sensitive and contentious matters of defense to the transatlantic organization. The early cold war was a time of great tension in Europe, marked by crises over Berlin in 1948–1949 and again in 1960–1961, violent anti-communist uprisings in East Germany in 1953 and in Hungary in 1956, and fear that World War III might break out at any time. The American connection and the guarantee contained in the Washington Treaty combined with strong and decisive leadership by American presidents such as Truman and Eisenhower helped to give Europe the confidence to build, invest, and consolidate the economic and political recovery that began in 1945.

TWO GERMAN STATES

Germany, after the USSR the most populous country in Europe and by far the largest in Western Europe, at first played no direct role in the early postwar steps toward European integration. Indeed, these steps, and in particular the Dunkirk and Brussels treaties, were directed partly against a possible revival of an aggressive German power.

Following the unconditional surrender of the German armed forces in May 1945, Germany had no government. Britain, France, the United States, and the Soviet Union each took responsibility for an occupation zone. Greater Berlin, located deep within the Soviet zone, was divided by agreement among the victors, while large parts of formerly German territory in the east were incorporated into Poland and the USSR.

At the wartime conferences among the allied powers, Churchill, Stalin, and Roosevelt agreed to settle most questions relating to Germany at a postwar peace conference. However, after the war it gradually became apparent that the victors would not be able to reach an agreement on Germany. The Western powers suspected the Soviets of trying to hinder economic recovery in Germany and delaying a political settlement in hopes of facilitating an eventual communist takeover. Much of central and eastern Europe already had slipped into the communist camp, and there was fear that Germany was another target. For its part, the USSR was unwilling to withdraw Soviet forces from the eastern zone of occupation and conclude a peace treaty with a united Germany if this meant the establishment of a westward-oriented state under U.S. and British influence.

In addition to these strategic considerations, the Western powers were increasingly concerned about the economic burdens of occupation. With the German economy languishing, the victor powers were legally and morally obligated to provide food and fuel to the destitute German civilian population. Britain, which was recovering from its own war effort and straining to meet its worldwide military commitments, was especially concerned about the occupation burden. The United States was better placed to help the Germans, but it was unclear how long the Congress and the American taxpayer would sustain subsidies for a defeated power. Western governments thus wanted to promote economic recovery in Germany, although they also were wary of a too-rapid resurgence of German power.

One way to revive German economic life was to encourage trade among the occupation zones and to restore the internal German market that had existed before 1945. In January 1947 the United States and Britain combined their zones under a single economic administration; they later were joined by the French. The Soviets, however, refused to participate in these efforts and accused the Western powers of unilaterally deciding the fate of Germany in contravention of the wartime agreement to seek collective solutions. The Soviets tightened their grip on the eastern zone, expropriating private property and shipping massive amounts of goods and machinery back to Russia as reparations for the war.

With prospects for a diplomatic solution for the whole of Germany waning, the Western powers and the Soviet Union each began establishing separate German states. In June 1948 Britain, France, and the United States agreed on a central government for the western zones, and in September 1949 they altered the Occupation Statute to permit the establishment of a new West German state, the Federal Republic of Germany. West Germany was not yet fully sovereign, however, and the Western powers retained certain legal rights over German foreign and domestic policy, including the right to enforce restrictions on German rearmament and the ultimate decision-making power with regard to a future peace treaty with a united Germany. The West Germans themselves took the view that the new state was provisional and that it might be replaced in the future by a united German state.

The Soviet Union reacted to these developments by working through the German communists to establish a separate East German state. Officially called the German Democratic Republic (GDR), it was proclaimed in October 1949. Henceforth Germany was divided into two countries, each of which became the linchpin of its respective economic and political grouping. West Germany, having participated in the Marshall Plan under the occupation, assumed its place in the OEEC and the EPU alongside the other Marshall aid recipients. Despite misgivings in other countries about German rearmament, it signed the European Defense Treaty of 1952 and became a member of the WEU and NATO in 1955. For its part, the GDR joined the CMEA in 1949, and became a founding member of the Warsaw Pact in 1955. Not until 1990, following the collapse of the Berlin Wall and sweeping political changes in the Soviet Union, were the two German states united in a single Federal Republic of Germany.

The Community and the Union

ESTABLISHMENT

By the end of the 1940s many of the basic outlines of the post–World War II European order had been established. Germany and Berlin were divided. The key West European countries were (or, in the case of West Germany, were soon to be) linked to the United States through the North Atlantic Treaty and cooperating among each other in the OEEC and the Council of Europe. The east European countries were tied to the Soviet Union by bilateral treaties and the CMEA. In both parts of Europe economic recovery was underway, but prosperity still lagged U.S. levels.

As will be seen in the next chapter, however, the perceived shortcomings of the OEEC and the Council of Europe led to the decision, in the early 1950s, by a group of just six countries to found a new set of organizations and to begin a process of deeper integration involving the transfer of sovereignty to new "supranational" institutions (see Box 1.1). This began with the founding, in 1952, of the European Coal and Steel Community (ECSC), an enterprise that was more limited in geographic and functional scope than the OEEC or the Council of Europe but more ambitious in its long-term economic and political objectives. The new organization was largely the idea of two Frenchmen, Jean Monnet and Robert Schuman, who championed a new approach to integration—one that focused on practical steps in the economic field, the building of permanent institutions, and the harnessing of day-to-day economic cooperation to a long-term political vision.

The ECSC was followed in 1958 by the establishment of two other communities, the European Atomic Energy Community (Euratom) and the European Economic Community (EEC), with the same limited membership. While Euratom followed the ECSC pattern of cooperation in a specific economic sector, the key policy goal of the EEC was the eventual elimination of all barriers to the flow of goods, capital, services, and people among its member states. Together with intergovernmental cooperation in foreign policy and cooperation in matters relating to justice and home affairs, the ECSC, Euratom, and the EEC became the basis for today's European Union (EU). (For an explanation of the terminology, see Box 1.2.) Britain initially chose not to join these communities and, together with sev-

---

Box 1.1   Supranationalism and Intergovernmentalism

Supranationalism is an approach to international integration under which national governments cede sovereignty over certain matters to transnational institutions. These institutions then can make laws and policies that are binding upon those governments. Key features of supranationalist (often also known as federalist) integration include an executive authority independent of national government control, decision-making procedures in which national governments can be outvoted, a court empowered to impose decisions on national governments, and a parliamentary body whose members directly represent the voters rather than national governments.

There are several explanations for why governments are sometimes willing to cede powers to supranational institutions. They include ideological commitment to the cause of integration, the desire to create effective institutions able to cope with problems no longer solvable in a national framework, and a perceived need to establish binding rules that govern the behavior of *other* countries, even if it means limiting one's own freedom of action.

Intergovernmentalism is an approach to integration in which national governments establish institutions and procedures to pursue common interests, but in which those governments retain the ultimate authority to pursue an independent policy if they desire. Key features of intergovernmental integration include the retention of the national veto over decision-making (unanimity rather than majority voting) and the absence of a supranational court and executive with binding powers over national governments. Countries tend to pursue intergovernmental integration when they want to reap the benefits of stable international cooperation without surrendering their independence.

The EU is a hybrid of supranational and intergovernmental integration. Compared with other international institutions, however, its distinguishing feature is its high degree of supranationalism, as reflected in the European Court of Justice, the directly elected European Parliament, majority voting in the Council of Ministers, and the European Commission as an independent executive.

---

eral smaller countries that also were wary of supranational integration, formed a much looser organization, the European Free Trade Association (EFTA).

ASCENDANCY

The other European organizations established in the late 1940s—the OEEC, the Council of Europe, and the WEU—continued to exist, but over time they were transformed in one way or another by interaction with what gradually became the mainstream process of integration flowing out of the three European Communities. With the ending of U.S. aid and the return of economic health to Western Europe, the OEEC and its offshoot, the EPU, lost much of their original rationale. By the end of 1958 the ten European OEEC countries had restored full convertibility with the dollar. The EPU was abolished, its mission having been accomplished. In 1961 the OEEC was transformed into a new body, the Organization

> ## Box 1.2   What's In a Name: ECSC, EEC, EC, and EU
>
> The terminology of the European Union (EU) is confusing and reflects the history of the integration process and the nuances of the EU's constitutional and legal order. The European Coal and Steel Community (ECSC) was established in 1952; the European Economic Community (EEC) and the European Atomic Energy Community (Euratom) in 1958. These organizations were referred to collectively as the European Communities. The EEC was by far the most important of these organizations and before 1993 often was referred to simply as the European Community (EC).
>
> The Treaty of Maastricht, which was signed in February 1992 and went into effect on November 1, 1993, formally renamed the EEC the European Community. It also established the EU, which consists of the three European Communities as the EU's first pillar, the Common Foreign and Security Policy as the EU's second pillar, and cooperation in Justice and Home Affairs as the third pillar of the Union. The three pillars have distinct identities and decision-making processes, but they are tied together by a single institutional framework.
>
> In this book, EC generally is used to refer to the historical development of the Community up to 1993; EU generally is used to refer to these organizations after 1993. In some cases, however, it is necessary for the sake of clarity to refer to component parts of the Union.

for Economic Cooperation and Development (OECD), with the United States and Canada as founding members. Japan, New Zealand, and Australia later joined. Located in Paris, the OECD took on a new mission of promoting economic and social welfare in all developed countries through analysis of policy problems and coordination of economic policies.

The Council of Europe continued its work of harmonizing legislation and promoting human rights, as well as expanded its membership. Greece and Turkey joined in 1949, followed by Iceland in 1950, the Federal Republic of Germany in 1951, Austria in 1956, and most of the remaining West European countries in the 1960s and 1970s. In the 1990s the Council of Europe opened its doors to the ex-communist countries of central and eastern Europe and played a role in helping these countries to harmonize their laws with those of Western Europe and to establish protections against political and human rights abuses.

The WEU played an important part in 1955 in bringing West Germany into NATO on terms that satisfied both the demands of the Germans for equality of status and of the other European states that a rearmed Germany still be subject to some international controls. The Federal Republic became a member of both the WEU and NATO, and the former was used as a mechanism to ban or regulate German production of missiles, certain types of ships and aircraft, and chemical and nuclear weapons. In the main, however, the WEU was rendered superfluous by NATO. It ceased to be an important European security institution and was all but moribund by the early 1980s. Only in the mid-1980s was it revitalized by a French initiative designed to give the European Community countries greater potential to deal with security issues outside the NATO system. In the 1992 Maastricht Treaty it was made "an integral part of the development of the [European] Union,"[10] and by the end of the decade its members had agreed in principle to abolish the organization by merging it with the EU.

THE NATO EXCEPTION

In contrast to these other organizations, NATO played an important role in Europe throughout the cold war period and continues to be a key element in the post-cold war European order. As long as the Soviet military threat existed, the West European countries and especially West Germany were unwilling to entrust their security to any organization that did not include the United States. With the end of the cold war, however, even NATO was forced to redefine itself in relation to the EU. Having rendered superfluous attempts by the European powers in 1947–1955 to develop an autonomous defense capability, in the early 1990s NATO itself faced questions about its future role following the collapse of the communist threat that had led to its creation.

At the 1991 Intergovernmental Conference that led to the adoption of the Maastricht Treaty, the major West European countries agreed to develop their own security identity in the new political union. This identity was to exist alongside and complement rather than replace NATO, but many in the United States feared that a newly confident Western Europe was in fact turning away from the Atlantic Alliance. Accomplishing the Maastricht objectives proved far more difficult than was at first assumed, however, and in the course of the 1990s NATO reasserted its centrality for European security. Under U.S. leadership, it organized the peacekeeping force that was sent to Bosnia-Herzegovina in early 1996, conducted the 1999 war against Serbia over Kosovo, and reached out to central and eastern Europe, providing the countries of this region with an early and important link to the West that helped to underpin the process of economic transformation by providing long-term security against external threats.

Poland, Hungary, and the Czech Republic were admitted to NATO in 1999, several years before they were expected to complete the more complicated and politically difficult process of joining the EU. Other central and east European countries continued to press for membership in both organizations, which were seen as providing different but complementary kinds of support for the transition process. Over the longer term, however, the EU is almost certain to emerge as the more important of the two institutions—with a much deeper and more pervasive effect on the lives of ordinary citizens in all parts of Europe. As will be seen in Chapter 9, even in the defense area NATO's future role will be linked increasingly to the efforts by the EU to establish under its own auspices a European pillar of the Atlantic Alliance.

Deepening and Widening

As the OEEC, Council of Europe, WEU and even NATO were transformed or declined in importance, the integration process that began with the signing of the ECSC Treaty has taken on ever greater significance. By the 1990s, the EU had clearly emerged as the most important economic and political (although as yet not security) organization in Europe.

This emergence was the result of more than four decades of development along two dimensions. The first was an increase in the level and scope of integration. Starting with a relatively simple scheme to pool their coal and steel production, the original members of the ECSC went on to create a common market for trade in all goods and common policies for external trade, agriculture, and transport. They later added the single market program, policies in the environmental, social, regional, and other areas, a single currency, shared policies on immigration and related matters, and at least the rudiments of a common foreign and security policy. This process of increasing the range and intensity of integration often is called *deepening*. It is reflected in the institutional and legal evolution from the original "community" to the "union" established by the Maastricht Treaty.

The other dimension has been the expansion of the original six to other European countries, a process often referred to as *widening* (see Table 1.1). The first enlargement took place in 1973 with the accession of Britain, Denmark, and Ireland, effectively ending an attempt by the UK to establish EFTA as a rival to the Community. Greece, an important NATO member, was admitted in 1981. Spain and Portugal joined in 1986, following the establishment of democracy in those countries in the 1970s. The first post-cold war enlargement took place in 1995, as three neutral countries, Austria, Finland, and Sweden, joined what by then had become the EU, bringing the total membership to fifteen. As shown in Table 1.2, ten formerly communist countries of central and eastern Europe, Cyprus, Malta, and Turkey have formally applied to join the Union. A number of other European countries have declared their intention to seek membership, but have not yet been formally accorded candidate status. If all of the countries that wish to join were to complete the accession process, the EU of 2010–2020 would have more than thirty members.

Table 1.1   Enlargement of the EC/EU, 1958–1995

Date of Entry	New Members
Founding Members, 1958	Belgium, Federal Republic of Germany, France, Italy, Luxembourg, the Netherlands
January 1, 1973	Denmark, Ireland, United Kingdom
January 1, 1981	Greece
January 1, 1986	Portugal, Spain
January 1, 1995	Austria, Finland, Sweden

Table 1.2   Candidate and Potential Member States of the Union

Country	Applied	Started Negotiations
Turkey	April 1987	
Cyprus	July 1990	March 1998
Malta	July 1990	February 2000
Hungary	March 1994	March 1998
Poland	April 1994	March 1998
Romania	June 1995	February 2000
Slovakia	June 1995	February 2000
Latvia	October 1995	February 2000
Estonia	November 1995	March 1998
Lithuania	December 1995	February 2000
Bulgaria	December 1995	February 2000
Czech Republic	January 1996	March 1998
Slovenia	June 1996	March 1998
Switzerland	May 1992 (Negotiations suspended in 1994 following defeat of the European Economic Area agreement by referendum)	
Norway	July 1967	January 1972
	November 1992	June 1994
	(Negotiations completed both times but in each case rejected by popular referendum in Norway)	
Albania	Pending	
Croatia	Pending	
Macedonia	Pending	
Bosnia-Herzegovina	Pending	
Ukraine	Pending	

The magnitude of the widening that has occurred or is underway must be seen in a broad historical context. In the years just after the EC was established, Europe was divided into four groups of countries with very different approaches to integration. The six countries of the original ECSC were taking a highly integrationist approach, forging ahead with explicit political goals and plans to merge many areas of economic activity. Led by Britain, the seven-member EFTA was committed to a much looser form of integration that focused mainly on free trade in industrial goods. In southern Europe, Spain, Portugal, and Greece still were largely cut off from economic and political trends in northern Europe and were participating only marginally in the integration process. The countries of central and eastern Europe had been coerced by the Soviet Union into a separate trading bloc organized in accordance with the principles of state ownership and central planning and had even less contact with Europe's core.

Since 1973, however, these separate zones of economic integration have merged into one—a single zone formed around the core six members of the original coal and steel community. In effect, the pattern of integration championed by Monnet and Schuman in the early 1950s has triumphed, albeit with modifications and for reasons that they did not entirely foresee. The result has been a re-widening of the integration process from the original six to all of those countries that were involved in the founding of the OEEC and the Council of Europe and, with the pending enlargement to central and eastern Europe, to countries that never even participated in the Marshall Plan, the OEEC, or, until the 1990s, the Council of Europe.

In looking to the future of the EU, a key question is whether the projected expansion of the Union can go forward without undermining the progress that has been made toward a deeper and more cohesive Union—whether, in effect, deepening and widening can proceed together. There are many aspects to this question, but four are especially important: (1) governance in a larger Union; (2) identity in a more diverse Union; (3) the relationship between European integration and the broader process of globalization; and (4) the goals and endpoints of the integration process and how they may change as a consequence of enlargement.

SIZE AND GOVERNANCE

In January 2000, the EU had fifteen member states and a population of approximately 370 million. If the EU is considered as a political entity—a political union with many statelike characteristics although not itself a state—then only China and India outrank it in size. Enlargement to just those candidate countries currently engaged in accession negotiations will increase membership to twenty-seven countries and population to nearly 500 million. Admission of countries in the Balkans, Turkey, and possibly Ukraine could push the total to more than thirty members and 600 million citizens.

Widening on this scale raises questions about cohesion and the governance. Even in the United States, which is smaller in population and more homogeneous than the EU, there has been a tendency in recent years for power to devolve from the federal to the state and local levels, as voters have lost faith in the efficacy of decisions taken in Washington. Since the early 1990s the EU has had analogous discussions about the drawbacks of centralization. Consistent with the principle of "subsidiarity" enshrined in the Maastricht Treaty, the EU is supposed to take decisions at the Union level only when there are compelling reasons not to leave decisions at the national or local level. But there is not universal agreement on how to interpret or apply subsidiarity.

As the EU expands and becomes more diverse, centralization of decision-making and regulation will become more difficult to achieve and could command less political support from the voters. But leaving decisions at (or devolving them to) the national level will also be risky. If carried too far it would call into question the Union's core achievement of a single internal market. As will be seen in later chapters, one of the reasons why the EU member states have tried to establish EU-wide rules and standards for the environment, competition policy, social policy, and other areas is not to pursue standardization for its own sake, but because failing to have common minimum standards would allow markedly different competitive conditions in different parts of the Union to disrupt the functioning of the single market. The EU thus will have to wrestle with the choice between risking resentment of more and more vigorously enforced EU-level legislation in a large and disparate Union, and scaling back its legislative ambitions in a way that could threaten the coherence of the Union.

IDENTITY

How effective and cohesive the EU proves to be also relates to the question of identity. The original Community had just six members speaking four languages, with a total population of about 170 million. The member countries were all (except for Italy) located in a compact region of northwestern Europe. They were predominantly Roman Catholic (although West Germany and the Netherlands had large Protestant populations) and all occupied territories that had been part of Charlemagne's empire (and for this reason were sometimes referred to as "Carolingian Europe"). They also had a certain economic coherence. Their coal and steel industries were concentrated in a belt stretching a few hundred kilometers from the Ruhr in Germany's northwest to the industrial regions of France's northeast.

In contrast, the EU of today has fifteen members and eleven official languages (using two alphabets, the Greek and Roman). Economically, culturally, and socially it is far more diverse than the Carolingian Europe of 1957. If enlargement proceeds as planned, the future Union will have at least twenty-seven members, speak more than twenty languages, and use three alphabets (with the addition of Cyrillic for Bulgaria). Whether a political and economic entity of this complexity can function and command the support of its citizens is open to question.

For years officials in Brussels referred to the EC and later the EU as "Europe," a practice that irritated politicians in non-member countries and in some member countries such as Britain. As the EU expanded to include nearly all of what traditionally has been called Western Europe, the countries of central and eastern Europe (and Turkey) came to see membership in the Union as the most important sign of their acceptance into "Europe." Such acceptance is important for practical reasons (access to trade, as a bulwark against external pressures, and as an external "pacifier" of internal conflicts), but it also has symbolic significance. For member states and aspirants alike, Europe has come to be seen not as a geographical expression but as a community of values.

It is not self-evident, however, why accepting these values should require having the same agriculture and transport policies or, conversely, why being in a union formed around such policies necessarily means that member states share the same interpretation of those values. "Europe" is a political construction, a myth created to overcome the divisions and conflicts of the twentieth century. The real Europe has enormous cultural, linguistic, and religious diversity. It has never been united on the scale planned for the twenty-first century—from Finland to Portugal and from Ireland to the Balkans.

Diversity on this scale could set limits to the development of a European identity. Opinion polls show that many people in Europe—particularly younger people—increasingly identify with Europe as well as with their own country. But the depth of this identification is open to question and varies greatly from country to country.[11] And without a strong sense of European identity, it may be difficult to sustain the sense of shared destiny and purpose that underpins support for common policies.

A common European defense, for example, will be difficult to achieve if Europeans do not feel enough of a sense of solidarity to come each other's assistance if attacked (however remote such a possibility may seem at present). The same is true on a less dramatic scale with regard to taxation, expenditure, and the redistribution of wealth that occurs as a consequence of government involvement in the economy. In their own countries, most citizens support some redistribution from the young to the old, the employed to the unemployed, the healthy to the sick, and from wealthy to poorer regions (although even this support has declined as enthusiasm for the welfare state has waned). They are less willing to do so on a European scale—precisely because the citizens of the individual member states do not yet (and may never) feel the same sense of community with citizens of other European countries. The extent to which a European identity emerges and whether there are geographical and cultural limits to how far such an identity can be stretched thus will be key questions for the future, the answers to which will determine in part how successful the EU is in managing the conflicting demands of widening and deepening.

THE EU AND GLOBALIZATION

A third issue that will affect the future of the Union concerns how it relates to an international system characterized by globalization and in which the very nature of the nation-state is changing in response to global trends. Globalization is the process by which markets for goods, technology, and capital are spreading worldwide, driven by the lowering of tariff barriers, the activities of multinational corporations, and the declining cost of moving goods, information, money, and people. It means that workers and firms must compete not just with rivals in their own country or region, but on a worldwide basis.

Globalization creates both economic "winners" and "losers." The former tend to be skilled, high-technology workers that are well-positioned to compete in the expanded global marketplace; the latter are unskilled or semi-skilled workers in industries such as textiles and steel that are exposed to low-cost competition from the developing and other developed countries.[12] Globalization also has a cultural dimension. It is often associated with cultural homogenization and Americanization, since it involves expansion by companies in the service and entertainment industries, most of them American (e.g., McDonald's, Microsoft, CNN), that are seen by some as imposing American norms on local culture and language.

Globalization also impinges upon the traditional power and prerogatives of the nation-state. Since countries must compete for investment (not only foreign investment, but investment by their own firms and citizens, which are free to seek higher returns elsewhere), they are under pressure to attract companies by lowering taxes and offering incentives. This in turn weakens their ability to pay for benefits and sustain the welfare state. Given these factors, it is not surprising that in recent years there has been a backlash against globalization, as was seen most dramatically in the protests at the 1999 World Trade Organization meeting in Seattle.

The relationship between the EU and globalization is complex. On the one hand, the EU is in the same position relative to global trends as the individual nation-states. Working with the member states, it must compete harder to attract capital in ways that impinge on its freedom to pursue social, environmental, and other policy objectives. As will be seen in subsequent chapters, the EU's proposals in the 1990s to levy "eco-taxes" to combat global warming and its ambitious plans for expanded social legislation both had to be scaled down in response to concerns about competitiveness.

On the other hand, because the EU is so big, it can present itself as a unified European response to the forces of globalization—one that can equalize the balance of power between international economic forces and the rights and interests of the European citizen. The global economy operates according to rules and standards, and the EU helps to set those rules and standards in forums such as the WTO. It cannot always get its way—it must negotiate with other countries and there are market forces which no government or combination of governments can control—but in the main the EU is better positioned than any of its member states to help shape the international system in directions favorable to Europe (provided those directions can be defined and command consensus).

Increasingly, the EU presents itself as a necessary response to globalization—one that can help the citizens reap more of its benefits while suffering fewer of its negative effects. Not everyone sees the EU in this light, however. For ordinary workers and citizens, the EU can seem as much a vehicle of as a buffer against globalization. For a worker in France who loses his or her job to "foreign" competition, it probably matters little whether the competition came from Asia or from elsewhere in the Union (or from countries in central and eastern Europe that are preparing to become members of the Union). Similarly, while the EU presents itself as a necessary response to global challenges such as increased immigration or drug trafficking, citizens may just as easily regard it, with its focus on free movement of goods, services, capital, and people, as a cause of rather than a response to problems emanating from beyond the familiar borders of the nation.

For regions or countries confronted with the implications of globalization, the EU may be too much of a globalizing and liberalizing force. They may be tempted to reassert the primacy of national and regional solutions rather than to work to strengthen the Union. At the same time, there are those who see the EU and its policies as barriers to the positive effects of globalization. Many business leaders, for example, have warned that too much rule-making and regulation is damaging the EU's position in the global economy, causing it to miss out on the benefits of e-commerce, financial market innovation, and other aspects of the twenty-first-century economy.

How the relationship between the EU and globalization unfolds in the coming years will have a major influence on the development of the Union. Whether the EU will be seen as a necessary response to globalization and its negative effects that therefore should be strengthened, or as a bearer of unwelcome trends from elsewhere in and from outside Europe, and thus weakened, is a key question.

OBJECTIVES AND ENDPOINTS

A final issue that relates to the prospects for uniting Europe concerns the desired endpoint—the ultimate objective—of the European integration process. Today's political leaders generally avoid discussion of ultimate objectives, which is seen as an abstract exercise that can only stir up debates about national sovereignty and identity, particularly in countries such as Britain where there is uneasiness about the loss of national identity to supranational structures in Brussels. Integration is portrayed as an open-ended process toward the "ever closer union among the peoples of Europe" proclaimed in the preamble to the 1957 Treaty of Rome.

But it is difficult to assess the progress of European integration or to evaluate its successes without having at least a general idea of what the desired final outcome is or should be. While it is easy to say that the EC/EU has continued to develop new policies and to strengthen its internal and external identity even as it has added new members—and that this process can be extended into the future—it can be argued that the most ambitious schemes for political integration have already been abandoned and that, to the extent that integration is a success, it is one that has been purchased at the price of scaling down goals that were once far more ambitious.

There is no talk in today's EU about the creation of a "United States of Europe," such as was discussed with enthusiasm in the early postwar period. There are many reasons why the ambitious federalist visions of the 1940s and early 1950s lost their appeal. The idealism of the generations that suffered under Hitler has faded, giving way to more pragmatic concerns about economic competitiveness. Voters have grown more suspicious about distant governments and bureaucracies and the assumption that "bigger is better." National loyalties and identities have proven more resilient than many expected, while the end of the Soviet threat removed an external motive for the creation of a strong federal Europe.

But progressive enlargements also have contributed to the demise of the most far-reaching schemes for political union, as an earlier sense of purpose has been lost by the growing complexity of decision-making, squabbles over budgets, and the accession of new member states that never signed on to the vision of the 1950s. If a future generation of political leaders were to try to revive the visions of the 1940s and to establish something like a "United States of Europe," it would find the task enormously complicated by the size and diversity of the EU wrought by successive enlargements.

As will be seen in Chapter 11, the pressures of enlargement and institutional reform linked to enlargement are giving rise to a new debate in Europe about the ultimate objectives and limitations of the integration process. Some participants in this debate see little choice for the EU but to press forward to build a stronger and more cohesive order, preferably by adopting something like a written constitution. Others believe that such talk is unrealistic and that Europe will continue along its current trajectory, perhaps even evolving toward a looser organization with more diverse patterns of cooperation.

Key Challenges

This book provides an introduction to the European Union and a framework for analyzing how it will address the challenges outlined in the previous section. Following a brief historical overview in Chapter 2, succeeding chapters examine six major topics: institutions (Chapter 3), market integration (Chapter 4), policy integration (Chapters 5–7), external identity (Chapters 8–9), enlargement (Chapter 10), and, by way of conclusion, the future of Europe as it relates to the citizen (Chapter 11).

INSTITUTIONS

The aspect of the EU that most distinguishes it from the other postwar institutions in Europe is its institutions. Whereas other European and international organizations were little more than forums where member states met to pursue agreed goals, from its founding the Community had its own executive, a parliamentary arm, and a court to enforce the founding treaties and Community legislation. The member states were still the key actors in the development and implementation of Community policy, but they no longer enjoyed absolute veto powers over decisions taken in and by the new Community.

The institutional structures established in the 1950s have undergone constant adaptation over time, especially with the transformation of the original Community into the Union. Despite these changes, there is almost universal agreement in the EU that fundamental institutional reform is needed to ensure that the Union can function after enlargement—that it is able to take decisions, see these decisions implemented down to the level of individual citizens and firms, and convince the voters that such decisions should be accepted as fair and democratic.

MARKET INTEGRATION

The single market remains the core achievement of European integration—the cement that holds the EU together. Building upon the initial trade liberalization that took place in the GATT and the OEEC shortly after World War II, this market developed in two concentrated phases: in 1958–1968 with the completion of the common market and customs union, and in 1986–1992 with the single market program.

Maintaining and expanding the single market is a continuing effort, however, one that presents ongoing challenges to the Union. It entails curbing the use by member states and firms of subsidies, hidden protectionism, and cartels that disrupt the functioning of the market. It also means extending the market to sectors such as energy that are still divided along national lines and broadening market integration to new member states and to new industries and technologies.

POLICY INTEGRATION

Since the 1950s, the EU has acquired a wide range of policy responsibilities. Market integration thus has been complemented by extensive policy integration. There are two reasons why this is so. The first concerns the single market. Given the heavy involvement of the member states in their national economies, policy integration has been an essential component to establishing the open and level playing field on which the single market rests. A Europe-wide market based on the free movement of goods, services, capital, and people requires some degree of convergence among the member states with regard to policies for agriculture, transportation, and competition.

The second reason concerns the scale of integration. Many policy problems—missing transportation links, cross-border environmental pollution, international drug trafficking—can only be tackled on an international scale. When the EC comprised only a small portion of the European continent, many of these issues were addressed in broader European forums such as the OEEC/OECD, the United Nations Economic Commission for Europe, or the Council of Europe. As the EC/EU has enlarged, however, it increasingly has become the logical venue for such Europe-wide cooperation.

But policy integration in the EU is uneven, and there is no consensus within and among the member states about the right mix of EU versus national policy approaches. Implementation and enforcement also are problematic. As enlargement proceeds and the EU grapples with increasingly complex economic and social problems, it will be under pressure to improve policy performance in all areas. It also will need to decide when policy problems should *not* be brought within the purview of the Union but left to the member states or lower levels of government.

EXTERNAL IDENTITY

The EU is the world's largest trading power. Along with the United States, it plays the dominant role in the WTO and has special bilateral and multilateral trade and cooperation arrangements with many countries and regions. Since 1999, the EU has had its own currency, the euro. Since the 1970s, it has tried to be a more important political actor, influencing, for example, the Middle East peace process and the human rights situation in countries around the world. Since the 1990s, the EU has been trying to develop a security and defense identity. A "European army" is still a long way off, but it cannot be ruled out as a possibility.

But how cohesive the EU will become as an international actor and the purposes to which it will put its economic and political power are still unanswered questions. Increasing size and diversity and the pressures of globalization could make for a blurring of the EU's external identity. Alternatively, these trends could encourage European leaders to accentuate foreign policy as a way of managing diversity and creating a greater sense of European solidarity vis-à-vis the outside world. Either way, the EU's external policies will have influence far beyond the EU itself and will have implications for the international system as a whole.

ENLARGEMENT

Enlargement cuts across all issues and policy areas in the EU, including the reform of the institutions, the operation of the single market, and the various policies. It is also a process that needs to be examined in its own right—one that is governed by legal provisions in the EU's founding treaties, that draws upon the experience of past enlargements, and that above all is shaped by the particular character of the candidate countries.

Managing enlargement will require deciding when countries are ready to become members of the Union, successfully integrating these countries, and, not least, deciding where enlargement should stop and which countries by what criteria should *not* be considered as potential members.

EUROPE AND THE CITIZEN

EU and national political leaders frequently talk about the need to bring the Union "closer to its citizens." This is a slogan, intended to generate political support for integration among a public that has grown skeptical about what it perceives as a remote bureaucracy based in Brussels. It is, nonetheless, a slogan that expresses an important truth. The public is not very interested in abstract debate about widening, deepening, identity, or the reform of institutions. It does care about concrete issues such as unemployment, the environment, old-age security, food safety, crime, and matters of war and peace.

The ultimate success of the EU and of the European integration project thus is likely to be determined by how relevant the EU is in addressing these concrete problems and issues. Future prospects for the Union as they relate to these problems are discussed throughout the book, but especially in the concluding chapter, which addresses the challenges of reform and how they relate to the everyday concerns of the citizen.

Theoretical Frameworks

The EU affects the interests of people and firms not only in Europe but around the world—through its role in trade, the environment, international finance, aid to the developing countries, and many other areas. It is not surprising, therefore, that sources of information about the EU have proliferated in recent years. Some information can be found in the general and business sections of American newspapers and magazines. More is available in international publications such as the *Financial Times* and *The Economist* (not to mention publications in French, German, and other European languages) and on the Internet. The EU's own web server—http://europa.eu.int—is a vast store of explanatory material, texts of treaties, laws, white papers, statistics, records of parliamentary debates, accounts of meetings, and more.

But information alone is not sufficient to provide an understanding of the EU. It needs to be related to a conceptual framework in which it can be interpreted. Ever since the founding and initial successes of the three European Communities in the 1950s, scholars have developed theories to try to explain the integration process and relate it to other trends in domestic and international politics.[13] Among the earliest and most influential theories was neofunctionalism, developed mainly by U.S. academics such as Ernst B. Haas and Leon N. Lindberg.[14] Neofunctionalism took seriously the "Monnet method," and was based heavily on the concept of spillover. The neofunctionalists argued that two types of spillover operated to propel the integration process forward.

The first was economic spillover. Successful integration in one economic sector would produce pressures for integration in other sectors of the economy. The second was political spillover. The accumulation of integration in economic fields would lead to political integration, as elites would become increasingly disposed toward working politically with their economic partners and as the accumulation of economic integration increased the demand for common decision-making by the political authorities.

As will be seen throughout this book, the experience of fifty years seems to have confirmed some aspects of the spillover concept, especially in the economic field. Establishment of a common market for goods created pressures to harmonize standards and regulations; pursuit of the single market spilled over into calls for a common currency which, once achieved, resulted in further pressures for the harmonization of tax policy and company law. The argument for political spillover has found less support, as national governments and political elites have proven more reluctant than expected to transfer power to joint or supranational institutions in order to manage economic spillover. Rather, the scope of economic integration at times has seemed to foster intense bargaining among national governments as they seek to maximize the gains from the integration process. Neofunctionalism had its heyday in the 1960s. It declined in the 1970s and 1980s, as the integration process seemed to lose momentum, but it has found new adherents (in revised form) in recent years, particularly as economic spillover seems to have accelerated.

Another influential theoretical approach, directly opposed to neofunctionalism, is intergovernmentalism. The intergovernmentalists argued that despite the limited steps toward supranational integration and institutions such as the Commission and the Court of Justice, the member states remained firmly in control of the integration process, which could best be explained as a game of intergovernmental bargaining in which national governments sought to cut the most advantageous deals possible with their partners, based on traditional concepts of national political and especially economic interest.

Intergovernmentalism has always been present in discussions of European integration, and seems to have found its confirmation in the behavior of national leaders such as French President Charles de Gaulle and British Prime Minister Margaret Thatcher, both of whom saw the Community as primarily an arena for the pursuit of national interests. The most prominent intergovernmentalist theoretician in recent years has been Andrew Moravscik, who has argued that all of the most important turning points in the history of European integration can be seen as negotiated bargains among the largest member states, acting overwhelmingly in pursuit of traditional national interests.[15] Critics argue that the intergovernmentalists go too far in exaggerating the acknowledged importance of member state interests and concentrate too much on high-profile events such as summits, with not enough attention paid to the agenda-shaping and the accretion of rules and patterns of behavior that goes on in the bureaucracy and lower levels of government, unnoticed by headline news.

In addition to such grand theories as neofunctionalism and intergovernmentalism, scholars have developed theories that seek to make sense of particular aspects on European integration. The new institutionalists argue that institutions (and not just national governments articulating national interests) matter in the shaping of decisions. They concentrate on the role that institutions play in shaping policy outcomes in particular areas. They look not only at the formal powers and structures of policy-making institutions (the Commission, Council of Ministers, and so forth), but also at informal practices and patterns of interaction that are harder to observe but that go on behind the scenes as policymakers set agendas and cut deals.

Another theoretical approach focuses on policy networks. Such networks form in particular policy areas and comprise all of the institutions and actors interested in a policy outcome. In telecommunications policy, for example, a policy network would include the national telephone authorities, industries that manufacture telephone equipment, user groups, the parts of the European Commission responsible for telecommunications and industrial policy, and relevant ministries in member state governments.[16] These actors would interact with each other to produce a policy outcome. National interests come into play up to a point, but the very concept of "national" is relativized by the role of transnational actors, such as companies working in all EU countries or lobbying associations located in Brussels, and by the formation of cross-national coalitions that are pitted against other cross-national alliances. (For example, user groups in several countries might join together to promote lower telecommunications costs, in opposition to the telephone companies in several countries that might favor less competition and higher prices.)

Many scholars of the EU would argue that there is no one theoretical approach that can organize and lend coherence to the European integration process. Different theories can be applied, alone or in combination, to understand different aspects of a complex reality. Neofunctionalism may help to explain the accretion of responsibilities by the European Central Bank or the growth of environmental legislation, while intergovernmental bargaining would be more appropriate to the study of major institutional and constitutional turning points, such as decisions to admit new members or to reform political decision-making structures.

As an introduction to the EU, this book does not focus heavily on the theoretical underpinnings of current research and writing on the Union. To the extent that theory is relevant, however, the book uses an eclectic approach. Neofunctionalism is given its due, as instances of spillover are highlighted. But the analysis also points to many instances of intergovernmental bargaining among the member states. Other theoretical approaches relating to specific policy decisions are cited in the notes and in the suggestions for further reading.

Notes

1. Richard N. Gardner, *Sterling-Dollar Diplomacy* (New York: McGraw-Hill, 1969).

2. See Lucrezia Reichlin, "The Marshall Plan Reconsidered," in Barry Eichengreen, ed., *Europe's Post-War Recovery* (Cambridge: Cambridge University Press, 1995), 42–47.

3. Barry Eichengreen, "Mainsprings of Economic Recovery in Post-War Europe," in Eichengreen, ed., *Europe's Post-War Recovery*, 6–7.

4. Dean Acheson, *Present at the Creation: My Years in the State Department* (New York: Norton, 1969), 233.

5. *Treaty of Economic, Social and Cultural Collaboration and Collective Self-Defence*, Brussels, May 7, 1948, *Treaty Series No. 1*, Cmd. 7599 (London: HMSO, 1949), 2.

6. *Statute of the Council of Europe*, London, May 5, 1949, *Treaty Series No. 51*, 1949, Cmd. 7778 (London: HMSO, 1949), 2 [Article 3]. The current statute now in force, with all subsequent amendments and protocols, can be found at http:// www.coe.fr.

7. *Statute*, 2 [Art. 1].

8. Ibid. [Art. 1].

9. For reminiscences by a British participant in early parliamentary sessions, see Julian Critchley, "The Great Betrayal—Tory Policy Towards Europe from 1945 to 1955," in Martyn Bond et al., eds., *Eminent Europeans* (London: Greycoat Press, 1996), 85–96.

10. *Treaty on European Union* [Maastricht], in *European Union: Selected Instruments Taken from the Treaties* (Luxembourg: Office for Office Publications of the European Communities [hereinafter, OOPEC], 1995), 38 (Article J4).

11. European Commission, *Eurobarometer: Public Opinion in the European Union*, Report No. 50, March 1999, 59–60, available on the Eurobarometer website: http://europa. eu.int/en/comm/dg10/infcom/epo/polls.html.

12. Dani Rodrik, *Has Globalization Gone Too Far?* (Washington: Institute for International Economics, 1997).

13. For a review of current theories, see Neill Nugent, *The Government and Politics of the European Union*, 4th ed. (Durham: Duke University Press, 1999), 491–519, on which this section draws.

14. Haas, *The Uniting of Europe: Political, Social and Economic Forces 1950–57* (Stanford: Stanford University Press, 1958); Lindberg, *The Political Dynamics of European Economic Integration* (Oxford: Oxford University Press, 1963).

15. *The Choice for Europe: Social Purpose and State Power from Messina to Maastricht* (Ithaca: Cornell University Press, 1998).

16. Volker Schneider, Godefroy Dang-Nguyen, and Raymund Werle, "Corporate Actor Networks in European Policy-Making: Harmonizing Telecommunications Policy," *Journal of Common Market Studies* 32, No. 4 (December 1994), 473–498.

Suggestions for Further Reading

Gori, Francesca and Silvio Pons, eds. *The Soviet Union and Europe in the Cold War, 1943–53*. New York: Macmillan, 1996.

Hogan, Michael J. *The Marshall Plan: America, Britain and the Reconstruction of Western Europe 1947–1952*. Cambridge: Cambridge University Press, 1987.

Kaplan, Jacob J. and Guenther Schleiminger. *The European Payments Union: Financial Diplomacy in the 1950s*. Oxford: Clarendon Press, 1989.

Milward, Alan S. *The European Rescue of the Nation-State*. Berkeley: University of California Press, 1992.

Osgood, Robert E. *NATO: The Entangling Alliance*. Chicago: University of Chicago Press, 1962.

Zurcher, Arnold J. *The Struggle to Unite Europe: 1940–1958*. New York: New York University Press, 1958.

The organizations discussed in this chapter have websites that provide information about their histories and current activities:

Council of Europe
http://www.coe.fr

European Union
http://europa.eu.int

NATO
http://www.nato.int

OECD
http://www.oecd.org

CHAPTER 2

Stages of Development
FROM COMMON MARKET TO POLITICAL UNION

The European Union of today is the result of a process of political and institutional development stretching back to the early 1950s. The most important milestones in this process have been the conclusion of six or seven major treaties among the member states. As summarized in Table 2.1, these treaties generally have included both an institutional and a policy dimension. In them, the member states have agreed to pursue certain policy goals and have set up institutional mechanisms through which these goals are to be achieved. As will be seen in this chapter, the first stage in this process of institutional and political development was the conclusion of the ECSC Treaty in 1951; the most recent was the ratification and entry into force of the Amsterdam Treaty in the spring of 1999, followed by the convening, in February 2000, of an intergovernmental conference (IGC) aimed at concluding a new treaty to prepare the Union for enlargement.

The European Coal and Steel Community

The ECSC was the inspiration of Jean Monnet, a French businessman and government official who had spent the war years in the United States and who had devoted much thought to the problem of bringing about a European union. Monnet believed that the key to peace and prosperity in Europe was reconciliation between France and Germany, which had fought three wars with each other in the span of a single lifetime—from 1870 to 1940. To achieve this reconciliation, Monnet believed it was necessary to create permanent political institutions whose purpose was to advance collective European interests, rather than simply to reflect the national interests of the individual member countries. He also believed that it was more important to achieve concrete results in a few industrial sectors than to formulate grand plans for economic, social, and cultural union that had little chance of being realized. Because of their economic and political importance at the time and their link to the warmaking capacities of the modern state, coal and steel were the obvious sectoral choices.

Monnet managed to convince French Foreign Minister Robert Schuman and other influential political leaders that his plan was workable and that it offered a way for Europe to move beyond the limited intergovernmental cooperation that

Table 2.1 The Founding Treaties and Treaty Revisions

Treaty Signed Entry in Force	Main Institutional Provisions	Main Policy Provisions
ECSC (Treaty of Paris) April 18, 1951 July 27, 1952	High Authority Parliamentary Assembly Council of Ministers European Court of Justice (ECJ)	Coal and steel pool
EEC (Treaty of Rome) March 25, 1957 January 1, 1958	EEC Commission EEC Council of Ministers Parliamentary Assembly and ECJ shared with ECSC and Euratom Economic and Social Committee European Investment Bank	Customs union and common external tariff Common Agricultural Policy
Euratom March 25, 1957 January 1, 1958	Euratom Commission Euratom Council of Ministers Parliamentary Assembly and ECJ shared with EEC and Euratom	Cooperation in atomic energy
Merger Treaty April 8, 1965 July 1, 1967	Merges commissions and councils of the three Communities	
Single European Act January 17–18, 1986 July 1, 1987	Increased powers for European Parliament (EP) Greater use of qualified majority voting (QMV)	Completion of the single market by 1993 Legal basis for European Political Cooperation (EPC) Environmental, regional, and R&D policy
European Union (Maastricht) February 7, 1992 November 1, 1993	Pillar structure Increased powers for EP More QMV European Central Bank Committee of the Regions Links EU with WEU	Justice and Home Affairs (JHA) Common Foreign and Security Policy (CFSP) European citizenship Economic and Monetary Union (EMU)
Amsterdam October 2, 1997 May 1, 1999	Increased powers for EP More QMV High Representative for CFSP Shift of some JHA matters to first pillar	Employment chapter

took place in the OEEC. On May 9, 1950 Schuman formally proposed to the French cabinet Monnet's plan for France and Germany to combine their coal and steel industries under a joint authority. The joint authority was to be independent of the governments of the two countries, and would guarantee each country full and equal access to a common pool of resources. The long-term objective of the plan was as much political as economic, as Schuman made clear in his declaration:

> The pooling of coal and steel production should immediately provide for the setting up of common foundations for economic development as a first step in the federation of Europe, and will change the destinies of those regions which have long been devoted to the manufacture of munitions of war, of which they have been the most constant victims.
>
> The solidarity in production thus established will make it plain that any war between France and Germany becomes not merely unthinkable, but materially impossible. The setting up of this powerful productive unit, open to all countries willing to take part and bound ultimately to provide all the member countries with the basic elements of industrial production on the same terms, will lay a true foundation for their economic unification.[1]

The Schuman Declaration was enthusiastically welcomed by the West German chancellor, Konrad Adenauer. Belgium, Luxembourg, the Netherlands, and Italy also expressed interest in joining the new community. The Benelux countries had already established an economic union among themselves, and were eager to cooperate on a new basis with their larger neighbors. For Italy, joining the ECSC reflected a decision by its postwar leaders to "scale the Alps"—to turn Italy's energies toward northern Europe and away from the disastrous African and Balkan ambitions of the former dictator, Benito Mussolini.

Britain did not become a member of the ECSC. Like the federalists at the 1948 Hague congress, Monnet hoped that Britain would play a leading role in the integration of Europe. But unlike the founders of the OEEC or the Council of Europe, he was not prepared to hold back the ECSC or dilute its supranationalist essence in order to win British participation. The British government participated in exploratory talks concerning the Schuman Plan, but in the end London declined to join the new organization for reasons that were both political and economic. An island nation with a long tradition of parliamentary democracy that had not been occupied or defeated in either of the world wars, Britain still played an important global role through its special relationship with the United States and by leading the Commonwealth of dominions and former colonies. It did not share the political aims of the founding members, who made clear their intention to form a new political entity by pooling and delegating some of their sovereign powers. As British Foreign Secretary Anthony Eden remarked to an American audience, to join a federation on the continent of Europe "is something which we know, in our bones, we cannot do."[2]

In the months following Schuman's dramatic declaration, the six negotiated the treaty establishing the ECSC. It was signed in Paris in April 1951, and the ECSC became operational in July 1952. For the commodities covered—coal, coke, iron ore, steel, and scrap—the ECSC created a common market in which all tariff barriers and restrictions on trade among the six member countries were banned. To ensure the operation of this common market, the ECSC treaty provided for the establishment of four institutions—the High Authority, the Council of Ministers, the Common Assembly, and a Court of Justice—roughly corresponding to the executive, legislative, and judicial branches of government, with extensive legal and administrative powers in the coal and steel sectors. The High Authority was empowered to issue decisions, recommendations, and opinions prohibiting subsidies and aids to industry that distorted trade, to block mergers and acquisitions and other types of agreements among firms, and under certain circumstances to control prices. It could impose fines to ensure compliance with its decisions. Monnet himself became the first head of the High Authority.

The coal and steel pool never functioned as well in practice as outlined in the Treaty of Paris. National governments and producers' cartels continued to intervene in the market, often clashing with the High Authority.[3] But the ECSC contributed to the rapid expansion of steel production in its member states and fostered even more dramatic increases in trade in coal and steel products. The effects of the elimination of national tariffs and quotas were especially marked for border regions. For example, in 1952 the Aachen region of Germany sold 56.7 percent of its coal to other parts of Germany, and only 15 percent to customers in nearby Belgium, the Netherlands, and Luxembourg. By 1959, its sales to other parts of Germany accounted for only 35.5 percent of the total, whereas shipments to the Benelux countries had risen to 34.9 percent of total sales.[4] Similar shifts were seen in steel, iron ore, and scrap, not only for Germany but for all ECSC members. The result was more efficient patterns of production, lower costs, and increased competition among producers that encouraged innovation and investment in new plants and equipment.

While these economic contributions were important, the greatest significance of the ECSC was political. It began the process of reconciliation between France and West Germany. Leaders such as Schuman, Monnet, and Adenauer were idealists who believed in European integration and Franco-German reconciliation, but they were also hard-nosed pragmatists determined to do what was best for their respective countries (see Box 2.1 for biographies of Europe's "founding fathers."). Germany still was trying to overcome the shame and isolation that it had brought upon itself with World War II. It was a divided country, vulnerable to Soviet political and military pressure, dependent on the United States, and badly in need of allies and partners that could anchor its relatively young democracy in the West. Adenauer saw a close relationship with France as the key to embedding the Federal Republic in a broader framework that would allow Germany to regain an equal economic and political status, revive its industry, and in his view ultimately achieve reunification.

The French, in contrast, were wary of a revival of German power, which in

Box 2.1   The Founding Fathers

Konrad Adenauer (1876–1967). As the first chancellor (1949–1963) of the Federal Republic of Germany, Adenauer was responsible for making West Germany a founding member of the EC. A lawyer by training, he was a member of the prewar Roman Catholic Center party and served as the mayor of Cologne from 1917 to 1933. An opponent of the Nazis, he was removed from his post when Hitler came to power. After World War II, he helped to draft the West German constitution and to found a new political party, the Christian Democratic Union. Adenauer believed that the key to restoring Germany's place in the world after its defeat and disgrace under Hitler was reconciliation with France and integration with the other West European democracies. He therefore embraced Schuman's ECSC proposal and later overcame domestic German opposition to the formation of the EEC and Euratom. Adenauer also won the trust of the United States and oversaw West Germany's integration into NATO.

    Alcide de Gasperi (1881–1954). Born in what before World War I was still an Italian-speaking part of Austria-Hungary, de Gasperi was educated in Vienna and served for a time in the Austrian parliament. In 1925, he became a founder of the forerunner party to the postwar Italian Christian Democratic party. Persecuted by Mussolini for his political activities, he was imprisoned and later exiled to the Vatican, where he lived for fourteen years. He served as prime minister from December 1945 to July 1953 and was responsible for bringing Italy into the ECSC, thereby establishing Italy as a founding member of the Communities, a status that Italy continues to emphasize in today's enlarged EU.

    Jean Monnet (1888–1979). Monnet is known as the "father of Europe." Born in Cognac, France, he entered the family brandy business at a young age and traveled widely on behalf of the firm. During World War I he gained experience in international cooperation by serving as a French official on a French-British committee that jointly managed shipping in the war against Germany. He worked in private business in the interwar years, but in World War II was again involved in supply matters, serving the British government as a senior official responsible for purchasing war material from the United States. After the war he headed the French planning agency responsible for modernizing French industry. In 1950 he hit upon the plan for a coal and steel community and managed to sell this idea to Schuman and other leading politicians. When the ECSC was established in 1952, he became the first president of its High Authority. In 1955 Monnet resigned this post to head the Action Committee for the United States of Europe, a group of politicians and trade union leaders that lobbied for further steps toward integration. He is associated with the "Monnet method" of taking practical steps in the economic field to advance the grand vision of a European political union.

    Robert Schuman (1886–1963). Best known for proposing that France and Germany place their coal and steel industries under joint management, Schuman was ideally suited to the task of bringing about a reconciliation between these two former enemies. Born in Luxembourg of French parents, he grew up in his father's native province of Lorraine, which Germany had annexed from France in 1871 after the Franco-Prussian War. A devout Catholic, he spoke French at home but attended German universities. When Lorraine was restored to France after World War I, Schuman became active in French politics. He was elected to the French parliament in 1919, where he served for forty years. In World War II he was a member of the French

(continues)

(continued)

resistance. After the war, he served as prime minister, foreign minister, and defense minister in various governments. As foreign minister, on May 9, 1950 he issued the famous Schuman Declaration, proposing what was to become the ECSC. A passionate advocate of European integration, Schuman later served as the first president of the ECSC-EEC-Euratom joint parliamentary assembly.

Paul-Henri Spaak (1899–1972). Spaak was a prominent Belgian politician who served as prime minister in 1938–1939. After Belgium was occupied by Nazi Germany in May 1940, he fled to London, where he spent four years and was active in resistance circles. He emerged from the war committed to European integration and strong international alliances, which he saw as the best way to prevent yet another world war from breaking out on European soil. He served as prime minister and foreign minister in various postwar governments and was involved in many of the early steps toward building a new Europe: as the first chairman of the OEEC, as president of the Consultative Assembly of the Council of Europe, and as a supporter of the proposed ECSC. His most important contribution to European integration was to chair the IGC that negotiated the treaties establishing the EEC and Euratom.

their view would leave them exposed to the same threat they had faced in 1870, 1914, and 1940. But they had come to realize that Germany could not be held down indefinitely, especially since the Americans, as the leaders of the West and the key victor power, were interested in building up Germany (including a German army) as a bulwark against the Soviet Union. The French thus saw that their best possible course was to embed Germany in a broader European and international framework—one that allowed for a partial revival of German power but that gave France and other countries permanent levers of influence over Germany. The ECSC was the European core of that framework, soon to grow into the EC. There was also a transatlantic component to the framework, namely NATO, which the United States and its allies began building with the 1949 Washington Treaty and which was completed with Germany's admission to NATO in 1955. Together these institutions provided a stable setting in which France and Germany gradually overcame their resentments and suspicions by working toward shared or at least mutually compatible objectives.

Over time, reconciliation came to be based as much on changed attitudes as on the external framework, as leaders such as Adenauer and French President Charles de Gaulle and later Helmut Schmidt and Valéry Giscard d'Estaing developed close personal relationships and as new generations grew up without the wartime memories. As could be seen in the major turning points in the history of European integration, this combination of pro-European idealism and the pragmatic pursuit of national interest has been a key feature of the integration process, one that helps to explain and in turn itself reflects the Franco-German reconciliation that began with the founding of the ECSC.

The institutions of the ECSC also became the first genuinely supranational bodies in Europe, able to act in their areas of competence with a degree of independence from the national governments of the member states. For the first time

European states had transferred sovereignty from the national level to central institutions. This supranationality was to become the decisive feature of European integration after 1950, and remains the aspect that most differentiates today's EU from other regional groupings such as the Association of Southeast Asian Nations (ASEAN) or the North American Free Trade Agreement (NAFTA).

The ECSC continues to exist as one of the three European Communities that was folded into the EU established under the Maastricht Treaty. It exercises authority over the coal and steel industries of the present EU, although its importance has declined with the relative decline of these industries. Indeed, it is ironic that an organization that was founded to manage a pool of what in the early 1950s were very scarce resources by the 1970s had found a new role in managing the decline of parts of Europe's coal and steel industries—by, for example, monitoring state subsidies to loss-making plants and helping unemployed miners and steelworkers with retraining. The historical importance of the ECSC remains, however, and is reflected in the fact that the EU's institutions celebrate May 9 as Schuman Day, in effect the national holiday of united Europe.

The EEC and Euratom

The ECSC's scope of activity was by definition quite limited. It dealt with a single economic sector, and it could not negotiate tariffs with foreign countries. It thus was understandable that the members should try to build upon their initial success and look for ways to broaden the scope of economic integration. After an abortive attempt in 1952–1954 to form a European Defense Community, the foreign ministers of the six ECSC states met in Messina, Italy in June 1955 to consider ways to carry forward the integration process. At the time, two potential courses of action were widely discussed: a further stage of *sectoral* integration based on a proposed atomic energy community, and a plan for *market* integration through the elimination of barriers to trade and the eventual creation of a common market. Those in Europe who saw integration primarily as a process of building up shared institutions and accomplishing common projects tended to stress the importance of the atomic energy community. They included Monnet himself and many of his compatriots. Others, especially in West Germany and the Netherlands, saw European integration more as a process of tearing down intra-European barriers, and emphasized the common market. These two approaches came to be known as "positive" and "negative" integration, and both have played a role in the development of Europe.

At Messina, the ministers agreed to establish a committee charged with studying these options and formulating concrete proposals. The Spaak Committee (named for its chairman, Belgian Foreign Minister Paul-Henri Spaak) presented its report to the May 1956 Venice meeting of foreign ministers. It struck a balance between the two approaches to integration, and proposed that the ECSC member states create both a European Atomic Energy Community (EAEC, also known as Euratom) and a European Economic Community (EEC). Following detailed and arduous negotiations, in Rome on March 25, 1957 the six signed two treaties creating these new entities.

Like the ECSC, Euratom subsequently came to play an important role in a single sector of the economy. It promoted the development of nuclear power and established a common pool of radioactive fuels for Western Europe's growing stock of nuclear reactors. Of the two institutions created in 1957, however, the EEC proved to be by far the more important. The agreement establishing the EEC became known as the Treaty of Rome, and remains in many ways the core constitutional document of today's EU.

The central feature of the EEC was the establishment of a common market among its member states. (For many years the EEC was referred to in the American press simply as the Common Market, even though this was not its official designation.) The Treaty of Rome called for "the elimination, as between Member States, of customs duties and quantitative restrictions on the import and export of goods, and of all other measures having equivalent effect."[5] It provided for the creation of a customs union through the phasing out, in stages, of all tariffs and quantitative restrictions on trade among the member states. This was to be accomplished over a period of a twelve years, from 1958 to 1970.

The treaty also called for the "abolition, as between Member States, of obstacles to the free movement of persons, services and capital."[6] The common market thus was not limited to trade in goods, but was to be built around what became know as the "four freedoms." The treaty further specified that the common market "shall extend to agriculture and trade in agricultural products."[7] However, the founders of the Community recognized that agricultural production and the problems faced by farmers required a separate set of policies from those that applied to the market for industrial goods. A common market in agricultural goods thus was introduced not through the removal of national barriers, but by the establishment of the Common Agricultural Policy (CAP), the general outlines of which were also specified in the treaty.

The external counterpart to the customs union was the establishment of "a common customs tariff and a common commercial policy towards third countries."[8] The ECSC did not have a common external tariff for coal and steel products, which meant that it relied on a complicated system of rules of origin enforced by intra-ECSC border checks to ensure that steel imported from outside the ECSC and destined for a high tariff country could not be imported through a low tariff country and transshipped to its ultimate destination. In contrast, the common external tariff was intended to facilitate the free circulation of goods, both domestic and imported, throughout the Community. Products imported from the United States to, for example, the Netherlands could be shipped to Germany or another member state as if they were Dutch domestic products. The importer would pay the tariff only once, at the port of entry.

Like the customs union, the common external tariff was introduced progressively, with the first stage of harmonization completed by the end of 1962. The level of the common tariff was set by means of a simple arithmetic average. Relatively high French and Italian tariffs were averaged with the lower tariffs of Germany and the Benelux customs union to produce a common external tariff. The level of the tariff varied according to type of good (industrial countries traditionally place low or even zero tariffs on fuel and raw materials needed by their domestic industries, and much higher tariffs on manufactured goods), but the average was around fifteen percent at the end of the first stage. In addition to the common external tariff, the common commercial policy called for the adoption by the member states of uniform practices with regard to such trade-related matters as aid for exports to third countries, nontariff restrictions on imports from third countries, and measures against dumping and unfair trade practices by non-Community members.

The Treaty of Rome used the basic institutional framework established for the ECSC. The High Authority for the EEC was called the Commission. It was granted broad executive powers, including the sole right to initiate Community legislation. A Council of Ministers was to be the main decision-making body of the EEC, in which representatives of the member states would vote on proposals put forward by the Commission. The chairmanship of the Council rotated, with each member state serving as Council president for a six-month period. As in the ECSC, votes in the Council could be made on the basis of unanimity or majority voting. Euratom had its own commission and council of ministers.

The Treaty of Rome also introduced qualified majority voting—a weighted system that assigns votes in rough proportion to the population sizes of the member states and that requires a certain critical mass of votes to pass a measure. France, Italy, and West Germany each were assigned four votes, Belgium and the Netherlands two, and Luxembourg one. Twelve of the seventeen votes were a qualified majority. In practice, qualified majority voting was disliked by some member state political leaders, notably de Gaulle of France, as too supranational and was little used until the 1980s.

The member states agreed that the three communities—the ECSC, Euratom, and the EEC—would share the same Common Assembly and Court of Justice. The ECSC High Authority remained in Luxembourg, but the new European Commission was established in Brussels, which became the de facto capital of uniting Europe. The Common Assembly was situated in Strasbourg, France, already the venue of the Parliamentary Assembly of the Council of Europe. The treaty also provided for the establishment of two other institutions, the Economic and Social Committee and the European Investment Bank, that were to play much lesser roles in Community policy-making.

BRITAIN AND THE FOUNDING OF EFTA

Like its predecessor, the ECSC, the EC was founded on a much narrower membership base than the institutions established in the late 1940s. Monnet and his colleagues were not opposed to participation by Britain and the Scandinavian countries, but they were unwilling to dilute or slow the pace of their ambitious plans to suit British preferences. At Messina, Britain was asked by the six to join the negotiations, but again it declined—for both political and what its leaders thought were valid economic reasons. Although much weakened by World War II and internal problems, Britain still was the largest and most productive economy in Europe. In areas such as banking and finance, aviation, and nuclear and defense technology the British were accustomed to viewing themselves as competitors and partners of the United States rather than as one of the medium powers of Europe.

Britain also had special ties with the Commonwealth that were hard to reconcile with the Community's customs union and the exclusionary CAP. It obtained much of its food from traditional suppliers in Canada, Australia, and New Zealand, who would have been displaced by the Community agriculture policy, which was to be based on the principle of preference for other Community suppliers. Britain also was concerned about the pound sterling, which like the dollar was a reserve currency held by central banks and used by some countries in international transactions not necessarily involving British trade or business. By entering a European customs union, London might have lost the policy flexibility to take measures needed to protect sterling's role in the world.

Declining to participate in the Community but not wishing to lose out on the economic benefits of increased trade in Europe, Britain took the lead in organizing an alternative organization, the European Free Trade Association (EFTA). Proposed in 1959 and formally established the following year, EFTA included Britain, Portugal, the Scandinavian countries, Austria, and Switzerland. Finland became an associate member in 1961. All of these countries had close economic and cultural ties with Britain or were politically neutral and thus unwilling to join a European Community with supranational aspirations and whose members were also all members of NATO. EFTA established a free trade area for industrial goods among its members, but it did not erect a common external tariff or launch common agricultural, transport, or other policies. Above all, it had none of the supranational political institutions that were being established in Brussels, Luxembourg, and Strasbourg.

DEVELOPMENT OF THE COMMUNITY IN THE 1960s

The basic legal and institutional framework of the Community was set in the Treaty of Rome, and there were no major treaty revisions for nearly thirty years. This did not mean, however, that the legal and institutional situation was static. There was ongoing debate within and among the member states about how strong the central institutions of the Community should be relative to the national governments. A series of judgments from the European Court of Justice (ECJ) tended to strengthen the integration process by ruling against national laws and policies that ran counter to the letter or the spirit of the founding treaties.

From 1958 to the mid-1960s, the Community was preoccupied with phasing in the policies outlined, mostly in framework form, in the Treaty of Rome. The Council of Ministers approved the basic principles for the CAP in December 1960. Tariffs and quotas on trade between member states were dismantled in accordance with the treaty. In part because economic growth was strong and incomes were rising, the member states refrained from invoking the various safeguard clauses contained in the treaty, and actually agreed to accelerate the timetable for completion of the common market. In other areas, development of the Community fell short of federalist aspirations. For example, the six did little to implement provisions in the treaty calling for a Common Transport Policy, and they largely ignored the area of social policy—in both cases as a result of member state opposition to strong action.

As the Community developed and proved its economic value, it somewhat paradoxically faced a growing political challenge from within its own ranks. The source of this challenge was de Gaulle, a leader of the French resistance in World War II who had retired from an active role in politics in 1946, but who returned to power in 1958 amid the crisis caused by France's colonial war in Algeria. De Gaulle had pushed through a series of constitutional changes that created a strong presidency, a post he himself occupied for the next decade. The French leader broke with his European partners on the issue of the powers and responsibilities of the Community's institutions. De Gaulle believed that France needed to be strong and independent—to recover the national greatness that she had lost in World War II. He thus was extremely wary of surrendering French sovereignty to the newly created supranational bodies in Brussels. He wanted a strong Europe, able to assert itself against the United States and the Soviet Union, but he wanted it to be a Europe of cooperating states, not a federal Europe in which historic nation-states such as France would lose their political freedom of action and ultimately their identity.

The issue of supranationalism came to a head in mid-1965 over the question of CAP financing. With the phasing in of the common market running ahead of schedule, in the spring of 1965 Commission president Walter Hallstein proposed that the EC acquire its "own resources" (i.e., revenue raised directly by the EC, rather than contributed to the EC budget by the member states) in July 1967, some three years ahead of schedule. Hallstein further proposed a new budgetary mechanism in which the Commission and the European Parliament would have enhanced powers, and the powers of the member states in the Council of Ministers would diminish through the use of qualified majority voting in place of unanimity for certain issues. De Gaulle saw these proposals as a grab for power by a nascent superstate in Brussels, and as an attack on French sovereignty. He responded by announcing the policy of the "empty chair." Throughout the second half of 1965 France boycotted all meetings of the Council of Ministers. The Commission and the other member states deplored this tactic, but for six months Community business all but ground to a halt.[9]

The crisis was resolved in January 1966 with the adoption by the six of what became known, after the site of the meeting, as the Luxembourg Compromise.[10]

The "compromise" was little more than an agreement to disagree. The six pledged that when issues very important to one or more states were to be decided, the Council of Ministers would try to reach decisions by unanimity. France registered its view—not endorsed by others—that when important issues were at stake unanimity *had* to be reached to take a decision. While noting the disagreement on this constitutional point, the six concluded that there was no need to prolong the impasse in Community decision-making. Hallstein retreated from his proposals, France took her place in the Council, and normal business resumed. The effect of the 1965 crisis on the Community was profound. While the other five members would not yield to de Gaulle's attempt to reinterpret the Treaty of Rome by imposing the unanimity requirement, they had no wish to provoke another crisis. They thus tended to make decisions by consensus—a practice that lasted until well into the 1980s. The powers of the Commission were cut back, as it was widely blamed for provoking the crisis by reaching prematurely for more authority. These developments all tended to slow decision-making in the EC and helped to reverse the momentum towards a federal Europe that had built up in the late 1950s and early 1960s.

The second major issue over which France broke with its partners was that of British membership. It took only four years from the signing of the Treaty of Rome for the British government to conclude that it had underestimated the importance and the staying power of the EC and that Britain risked economic isolation by not becoming a member. The composition of British trade gradually was shifting from the Commonwealth to Europe, thereby reducing the importance of the CAP as an obstacle to membership and bolstering pro-European sentiment in British industry. Impressed by early successes in tariff reductions and the continued rapid economic growth in the Community, Britain formally applied for membership in August 1961. It was joined by Ireland, Denmark, and Norway, all of which conducted much of their trade with Britain and had little choice but to follow its lead on integration issues.

While the other member state governments generally were pleased by Britain's change of heart, de Gaulle had reasons for opposing London's application. He was suspicious of Britain's close ties with the United States and committed to a vision of the Community as primarily a Franco-German enterprise, with France playing the leading role in tandem with a politically docile Germany. He and other French officials were concerned that premature entry for Britain would hinder development of the CAP, important for French agriculture, and turn the Community into a loose free trade area rather than a cohesive customs union with emerging common policies and long-term ambitions to play a more assertive role on the world scene. In January 1963 de Gaulle publicly voiced his doubts about Britain's suitability for membership—a move which led to the suspension of accession negotiations with the four applicant countries shortly thereafter. Britain again applied to join in May 1967, followed by the same trio of countries. But it was not until de Gaulle's passing from the political stage in 1969 that negotiations could resume, and not until 1973 that Britain finally achieved what it might have had in the 1950s had it chosen to become a founding member.

THE HAGUE SUMMIT

Completion on July 1, 1968, of the transition period of the EC—the customs union and the common external tariff—and the retirement of de Gaulle from French politics in 1969 set the stage for a further phase of integration. The new French president, Georges Pompidou, was less suspicious than his predecessor of the UK and more interested in bringing it into the EC as a counterweight to the rising power of West Germany. Pompidou got off to a fresh start with Europe by proposing to convene a special meeting of heads of state and government to review developments in the Community and to launch new integration initiatives. Only the fourth such summit in EC history, this meeting took place in the Hague in December 1969.

The Hague summit was the starting point for several ambitious, long-term initiatives that were to preoccupy the Community over the next several decades and that even today are central to the EU's agenda. France lifted its opposition to enlargement, clearing the way to the start of accession negotiations with the four prospective member states in June 1970. At the same time, the leaders of the six adopted several proposals aimed at deepening the Community in parallel with the expected process of widening. They agreed in principle to the gradual formation of an economic and monetary union (EMU) and appointed Pierre Werner, prime minister of Luxembourg, to chair a committee of experts to develop a plan for such a union. They also asked their foreign ministers to prepare a report on progress toward political union, meaning primarily cooperation in foreign policy matters. In addition to these specific initiatives, the summit generated a new atmosphere—the "spirit of the Hague"—and a widespread feeling that the Community again was on the move after the setbacks of 1965–1969.

These decisions both to widen and deepen took place against the backdrop of a changing international situation that heightened the importance of the Community for its member states. The United States had been bogged down in Vietnam since the mid-1960s, turning somewhat away from the primary focus on Europe of the cold war period. In Germany, Willy Brandt, a social democrat and the former mayor of West Berlin, had been elected chancellor in October 1969 and was beginning to pursue his Ostpolitik with the communist countries of central and eastern Europe, based on political agreements and expanded trade and cultural contacts.[11] As West Germany looked east, Brandt saw a need to anchor the country more firmly in the EC, both to dispel concerns among his allies about a more independent and assertive German policy, and to bolster his negotiating leverage with the communist regimes. Along with continued turbulence in world financial markets—downward pressure on the dollar linked to inflation and the economic problems associated with the Vietnam War—these factors all argued in favor of a stronger and wider EC.

Negotiations between the six and all four prospective member states were completed in January 1972 with the signature of individual treaties of accession. The negotiations with Denmark and Ireland were relatively straightforward, although Ireland's neutral status and its desire to protect its right to set national laws on sensitive social and religious issues such as divorce and abortion presented some complications. The talks with Britain were more difficult, and revolved around the import of butter and sugar from the Commonwealth, fishing rights for EC vessels in British waters, and Britain's contributions to the Community budget. With all sides committed to accession, these issues were resolved, but at the cost of storing up trouble for the next generation of British and EC leaders, as Britain's net contribution to the EC budget became a major point of contention in the late 1970s and early 1980s.

Following ratification in the parliaments of the candidate countries and of the six member states (and a March 1972 referendum in France called by Pompidou), Britain, Denmark, and Ireland became full members of all three communities on January 1, 1973. This was to be the first of four Community enlargements—one that set a pattern for subsequent negotiations between existing and aspiring member countries.

Despite its having signed a treaty of accession, Norway did not complete the accession process. In a national referendum held in September 1972, 53.3 percent of the Norwegian electorate voted against membership. In the debate leading up to the vote, farmers, fishermen, and nationalists concerned about preserving Norway's identity led the fight against membership, managing to prevail over the political and business establishment that generally favored joining the Community. The first country to reject membership, Norway was to some extent a special case, owing to its small size and geographic isolation, but in other respects the Norwegian vote presaged localist and nationalist reaction to European integration that was to become more pronounced in many countries in the 1990s.

Although enlargement was a major achievement, the post-Hague optimism about breakthroughs in other policy areas proved short-lived, as Europe fell victim in the 1970s to unfavorable external economic and political conditions: monetary turbulence, the 1973 oil crisis, the 1974–1975 economic recession, and the rise of tensions with the Soviet Union. As a consequence, major policy initiatives were watered down or postponed. In October 1970 the Werner committee delivered its report on EMU, in which it proposed a three-stage plan leading to the completion of economic and monetary union by 1980. The Council of Ministers endorsed the report in March 1971 and the Community took initial steps toward implementation. However, in August of that year U.S. President Richard M. Nixon announced the suspension of the convertibility of the dollar into gold, effectively ending the Bretton Woods par value system and ushering in a new period of global monetary instability. The EC member countries persisted with plans to align their currencies more closely, but diverging inflation rates and different domestic responses to recession led to growing monetary divergences between Germany on the one hand and France, the UK, and Italy on the other. The Community tacitly abandoned the ambitious goals of the Werner report, and it was not until the end of the 1970s that it was able to resume progress toward monetary cooperation.

In accordance with recommendations of the Community foreign ministers solicited by the Hague summit, European Political Cooperation (EPC) was launched in November 1970. Member states agreed to consult on all questions of foreign policy and where possible to undertake common actions on international problems. EPC was to take place on an intergovernmental basis, outside the structures and institutions of the Community. It was based on a political commitment to work together on foreign policy matters, not a transfer of sovereignty to central institutions. But like monetary union, EPC fell short of initial intentions. It laid the groundwork for foreign policy cooperation among the Community member states and was useful in helping to coordinate the European response to changes in east-west relations in the 1970s. The EC countries acted as a unit, for example, in the economic basket of the Conference on Security and Cooperation in Europe (CSCE) launched in 1973. For the most part, however, EPC resulted in verbal statements with no real capability for enforcement, nor did it prevent the member states from responding very differently to such events as the 1973 Arab-Israeli war or the 1979 Soviet invasion of Afghanistan.

INSTITUTIONAL DEVELOPMENTS IN THE 1970S

There were two important institutional developments in the 1970s: the establishment of the European Council in 1974 and the first direct elections to the European Parliament in 1979. The success of the Hague summit and subsequent top-level meetings in 1972, 1973, and 1974 convinced European leaders of the value of periodic, informal summits. Such meetings were the best way to resolve complex issues through bargaining and compromises among the member states that cut across issue areas. They also provided a platform for launching new Community initiatives in a way that ensured political momentum. French President Valéry Giscard d'Estaing, who assumed office after Pompidou's death in 1974, and German Chancellor Helmut Schmidt, who took power in the same year, were both former finance ministers used to dealing on a personal basis with their counterparts in other capitals, and both were strong proponents of the Franco-German relationship built upon the tradition of regular meetings between the leaders of the two countries. At the December 1974 Paris summit, the governments of the EC member states agreed to a proposal by Giscard that they meet at least three times each year. These regular gatherings (later changed to twice per year) came to constitute a new institution, the European Council, albeit one that was not given a formal legal base until the entering into effect of the Single European Act some twelve years later.

While establishment of the European Council tended to push the Community in an intergovernmental direction—highlighting member state leaders as the driving force in the integration process—direct elections to the European Parliament (EP) counterbalanced this tendency by strengthening and giving enhanced legitimacy to one of the central institutions of the Community. Following agreement in the European Council in December 1975, the first direct elections to the EP took place in June 1979. They brought to Strasbourg for the first time a popularly elected body of men and women who could claim to speak for Europe on behalf of the electorate. The powers of the EP were still strictly limited, but its members could claim to represent the wishes of the voters at the European level. On this basis they were able to press for increased powers in the following decade.

The 1970s also saw the completion of a remarkable set of political transitions in southern Europe that paved the way for the Community's second and third enlargements. Greece had concluded an association agreement with the Community in 1961 that was intended to lead to eventual membership. However, in April 1967 the Greek military seized control of the government and suspended the constitution, causing the Community to halt further development of ties with Greece. Military rule collapsed in July 1974, following Greece's disastrous war with Turkey over Cyprus. The new civilian government applied for full EC membership in June 1975. Although there were grave doubts in Western Europe about whether this relatively backward country was ready to assume the responsibilities of membership and to compete with the other member states in a fully liberalized market, European political leaders were keen to bolster the fragile Greek democracy by welcoming it into the European fold. The Community thus initiated accession negotiations with Greece in July 1976.

Political change also took place on the Iberian peninsula. Since the 1940s, Spain had enjoyed rather frosty relations with the rest of Western Europe, owing to lingering resentment about General Francisco Franco's seizure of power during the 1936–1939 Spanish Civil War and his closeness to the Axis powers during World War II. When Franco died in November 1975, Spain was ripe for change. Under Juan Carlos I, the grandson of the last Spanish king, it returned to democracy, becoming a constitutional monarchy, although not without a strong challenge from the newly legalized Spanish Communist Party.

Like Spain, Portugal was ruled by a right-wing dictator, Antonio Salazar. It had traditionally close relations with Britain, but its position in Europe was marginal owing to its poverty and its determination to retain its African colonies long after the French, British, and Belgians had relinquished their empires. In April 1974 a group of left-wing officers seized power with a program to stop the colonial war in Angola and to erect a socialist order. After a political struggle in which moderate socialist and social democratic forces, with financial and organizational support from the German Social Democratic party, rallied to defeat a communist takeover, constitutional government was resumed in April 1976.

As was the case with regard to Greece, the EC countries wanted to bolster the new Iberian democracies against threats from the right and the left by offering economic and political support. Both countries applied for EC membership in 1977, and accession negotiations began with Portugal in October 1978 and with Spain in February of the following year. Meanwhile, Greece signed an accession treaty in May 1979 and became the tenth Community member on January 1, 1981.

It was not until well into the 1980s that negotiations were completed with Spain and Portugal. With a population of over 35 million and a large agricultural sector that competed directly with the farms of southern France, Italy, and Greece in such products as wine and olive oil, Spain presented particular challenges that took time and political will to resolve. Given its smaller size, Portugal posed fewer difficulties, but its relative poverty and the backwardness of its industry also dragged out the negotiations and argued for long transition periods in the phasing in of many EC rules and regulations. Nonetheless, the groundwork for membership had been laid, and Iberian democracy was very much strengthened by its prospect and the rapid development of business and other ties with the Community.

THE EUROPEAN MONETARY SYSTEM

As the 1970s ended, the Community returned to monetary affairs, establishing the European Monetary System (EMS) as the last major achievement of the decade and a building block of the Community's relaunch in the 1980s. At the time, the dollar was falling on world currency markets, largely in response to high inflation and rising oil imports in the United States. This tended to increase monetary instability in Europe (as investors and speculators sold dollars and bought German marks, thereby driving down the franc and lira against the mark), and damaged European exports on world markets. Irritated by what they saw as the "malign neglect" of the dollar in Washington and concerned about Europe's own weakness in the monetary sphere, the EC countries began to look anew at the problem of restoring monetary coherence in the Community.

While there was no question at the time of reviving the overly ambitious scheme for EMU put forward in the Werner report, in October 1977 Commission president Roy Jenkins put forward a proposal for enhanced monetary cooperation. Giscard and Schmidt expressed support for Jenkins's ideas and became the main political backers of a renewed push toward monetary cooperation. Their efforts led to the founding, in March 1979, of the EMS, a system of fixed but adjustable currency rates built around a central unit of account, the European Currency Unit (ECU). The main purpose of the EMS, which operated within the framework of the EC, was to limit and to smooth out divergences among the EC country currencies that had a disruptive effect on the functioning of the internal market. As will be seen in Chapter 6, the relative success of EMS in the 1980s laid the basis for a renewed and ultimately successful effort to reach EMU in the 1990s.

Relaunch in the 1980s

The early 1980s was a difficult period for European integration. With economic recession and stagflation caused by the second oil crisis (precipitated by the 1979 revolution in Iran), governments were in no mood for bold new initiatives. European industry was threatened by intensified competition from Japan and other

Asian countries, as Europe lost competitiveness in traditional industries such as cars, steel, shipbuilding, and textiles, but failed to establish sufficiently strong positions in newer industries such as computers, electronics, and aviation.

Tensions between the United States and the Soviet Union were on the rise, which also led to increased strains across the Atlantic. Ronald Reagan, inaugurated U.S. president in January 1981, toughened the U.S. position toward the Soviet Union. He increased defense spending, was skeptical about arms control agreements, and in March 1983 called for the development of a space-based defense system against Soviet missiles. West European governments, committed to detente with the East and not eager to boost defense spending or cut back economic ties with the communist countries, resisted Reagan's policies. The high point of transatlantic tensions came in August 1982, when the United States imposed sanctions on French and British firms that were supplying equipment to the Soviet Union for the construction of a pipeline to carry natural gas to Western Europe. The United States had tried to block the building of the pipeline, arguing that it would give the Soviet Union economic leverage over Western Europe. The EC strongly protested what it regarded as an "extra-territorial" exercise of U.S. law and even enacted legislation forbidding European companies to comply with the sanctions.

While many of Europe's difficulties could be blamed on external factors over which it had little or no control, there also was a new questioning about the viability of the European welfare state model that in its different national forms had seemed to work so effectively in the 1950s and 1960s, reconciling high economic growth with concern for social justice, but that appeared to be breaking down since the 1970s. Britain had been experiencing economic decline (relative to other industrialized countries) since the 1940s, which usually was attributed to a variety of factors including low investment, strikes and trade union militancy, and stop-and-go government policies that resulted in a cycle of growth followed by inflation leading to recession. Prime Minister Margaret Thatcher was elected in May 1979 on a platform committed to reducing the government's role in the economy, privatizing nationalized industries, and breaking the power of the unions. Thatcher also was rather skeptical of European integration.

On the continent, the major economies fared somewhat better, but they too were under strain. After rapid wage increases associated with trade union militancy in the late 1960s, Italy suffered large trade and budget deficits, high inflation, and a weak lira in the 1970s. Italian governments sought to restructure the economy, but confronted strong resistance from the unions and the Italian Communist party. France and West Germany also struggled to adjust to more difficult economic circumstances by reining in the growth of wages and slowing the growth of the welfare state.

The EC of the 1970s and early 1980s had limited relevance for national governments as they struggled to cope with economic problems at home. To some extent Thatcher even assumed the role once played by de Gaulle—that of a nationalist opponent to Brussels-based integration. Thatcher's only important interest in the EC seemed to be to obtain a rebate of the large sums that Britain was paying into the Community budget, mainly as a consequence of the CAP. In this period, terms like "Europessimism" and "Eurosclerosis" took hold and were widely popularized.

The difficult economic and political circumstances of the early 1980s eventually led, by mid-decade, to a relaunch of the Community, the centerpiece of which was the Single European Act (SEA), the first major revision of the founding treaties since the conclusion of the Treaty of Rome in 1957. The product of an intergovernmental conference in 1985–1986, the first important IGC since the decisive Messina conference of 1955, the SEA had two aspects, one institutional and the other substantive. It reformed and strengthened the EC's institutions, and it set a new list of policy tasks for these institutions to pursue, notably the "1992" single market program.

Reform of decision-making had been under discussion in the Community for some time. In November 1981 foreign ministers Hans-Dietrich Genscher of Germany and Emilio Colombo of Italy presented to the EP a joint proposal for a European act designed to strengthen the external profile of the Community. The key elements of the Genscher-Colombo plan were a proposal to bring the existing structures of the three European Communities and EPC together in a single framework subject to the political guidance of the European Council, a strengthening of the powers of the EP, and a reform of the Community decision-making process by lessening the role of the national veto.[12] This German-Italian proposal was not embraced by all of the member states, but it was an early indicator of the pressures for reform building in at least some national capitals and in the EP.

The directly elected members of the Parliament tended to be strong supporters of European integration, and many of them were unhappy with the bogging down of the integration process that had taken place with the worsening economic conditions in the 1970s. Declaring that revision of the Treaty of Rome was the key to a successful relaunch of the Community, in February 1984 the European Parliament approved a "Draft Treaty establishing the European Union."[13] This was a purely political gesture—the conclusion or amendment of treaties was the prerogative of the member states—but one that reflected the growing sentiment in favor of a new treaty. As indicated in the title of the EP draft, much of the reform focus was on a "European Union," a somewhat vague term that meant not only a closer drawing together of the member states within the Community, but a fusion of the economic side of integration with aspects of cooperation, notably EPC, that took place outside the Community structures. In the view of the proponents of a union, the whole process of integration needed streamlining and rationalization.

Responding to these pressures, at the 1984 Fontainebleau summit the leaders agreed to a proposal by French President François Mitterrand to establish a committee to explore ways to improve the functioning of the Community and of EPC. Known as the Dooge Committee after its chairman, former Irish foreign minister James Dooge, this grouping consisted of one high-level representative from each member state. At the same meeting, the European leaders finally resolved the long-standing problem of British overpayments to the Community budget, thus at least neutralizing Thatcher's opposition to new Community initiatives.

THE SINGLE MARKET

Calls for institutional reform were accompanied by a growing interest in the re-launch of the Community through a single market program—a concerted effort to eliminate the barriers to trade in goods that had remained in place after the completion of the common market in 1968 and to liberalize trade in services and the flow of capital. The parallel development of these two themes—institutional reform and completion of the single market—was important in winning broad support for changes in the founding treaties. Thatcher was wary of surrendering sovereignty to Brussels and suspicious of proposals to strengthen the Community for its own sake, but she was open to institutional reform that might be needed to promote freer trade. As she later wrote in her memoirs: "I had one overriding positive goal. This was to create a single Common Market. . . . The price which we would have to pay to achieve a Single Market with all its economic benefits, though, was more majority voting in the Community. There was no easy escape from that, because otherwise particular countries would succumb to domestic pressures and prevent the opening-up of their markets."[14]

The European business community, concerned about lagging economic growth and high costs, also generated ideas for and became a strong supporter of a program to complete the single market. Upon assuming the presidency of the European Commission in January 1985, Jacques Delors proposed an ambitious single market plan, choosing the end of 1992 as a target date for implementation. Under the leadership of Arthur Cockfield, the British commissioner responsible for the internal market, the Commission produced a white paper outlining 300 measures that would need to be passed at the Community level to eliminate intra-EC barriers. Many of these proposals had been on the table for years, and completing the single market was not in itself a radically new idea. What was new was the sense of urgency, the existence of a comprehensive plan, and a willingness on the part of the member states to contemplate changes in Community decision-making to ensure that plans were transformed into action.

THE INTERGOVERNMENTAL CONFERENCE

Dooge's Ad Hoc Committee on Institutional Reform presented its final report to the March 1985 Brussels summit.[15] It called for both a broadening of the EC's objectives and areas of responsibility and for selected institutional reforms that would strengthen the Community and speed decision-making, particularly in regard to single market matters. To achieve these objectives, it recommended convening an IGC among the member states that would draw up a new Treaty of European Union. The report did not command universal support for all of its points. The British, Danish, and Greek members of the committee declined to endorse its central recommendation for an IGC, and other members dissented on lesser points. But the general thrust of the report was toward significant changes in the Treaty of Rome as a way of restarting the integration process and ensuring that a single market program could be implemented.

The European Council took up the Dooge Report at its June 1985 session in Milan, the same meeting at which it endorsed Delors's plan for the single market. Italy, a founding member and traditionally a strong proponent of closer integration, occupied the Council presidency, and Prime Minister Bettino Craxi was determined to achieve an outcome that would move the Community forward. Under Article 236 of the Treaty of Rome, the member states were empowered to call at any time, by simple majority vote, an IGC to negotiate treaty revisions.[16] This provision had never been invoked, however, in part because there was limited interest in such revisions but also because, following the Luxembourg Compromise, governments invariably took major decisions by consensus, even when the treaties allowed for majority or qualified majority voting. After hours of discussion in which Thatcher argued against convening an IGC, Craxi forced a vote on whether to call a conference. The result was 7–3, with Britain, Denmark, and Greece opposed. Thatcher was furious at what she saw as an unprecedented disregard of the rule of consensus within the European Council and concerned that the more integration-minded states would use the IGC to push forward a strengthening of the EC's supranational powers. But Britain also supported the single market program, the substance of which by then was closely intertwined with the perceived need for procedural reform. Thus Britain as well as the other dissenters approached the IGC ready to play a constructive role, although determined to block the most ambitious reform proposals.

The IGC began during the Luxembourg presidency in September 1985, and over the next six months entailed seven meetings of the Community foreign ministers, numerous other meetings of two high-level working groups, written submissions on the part of national governments, and intense bargaining among the Community leaders at the December 1985 Luxembourg summit. The result was a new treaty that was formally signed in Luxembourg on February 17, 1986.[17] The original proposal to conclude a Treaty on European Union had fallen away during the negotiations. It was Delors who suggested that the treaty be called *L'Acte Unique*—the Single Act or, as it came to be called, the Single European Act (SEA).[18] "Single" was used because the treaty unified the economic aspects of the Community, which had always been governed by the Treaty of Rome (and the founding treaties of Euratom and the ECSC), and European Political Cooperation, which hitherto had been carried out among the member governments outside the Community legal framework.

The treaty came into effect on July 1, 1987, after all member states had ratified. Ten of the member states were able to do so following favorable votes in their national parliaments, but two—Denmark and Ireland—held national referendums in which the treaty was approved directly by the voters.

INSTITUTIONAL REFORM

The SEA both broadened the Community's areas of responsibility and, as had long been suggested by proponents of institutional reform, made important changes in decision-making processes. New policy areas not mentioned in the Treaty of Rome but added to EC competence included environment, research and technology, and "economic and social cohesion" (meaning regional policy aimed at narrowing income disparities between different parts of the Community). The SEA also inserted a new article in the Treaty of Rome that specified completion of the internal market by 1992. This provision made fulfillment of the 1992 program not merely a laudable political goal, but a legal responsibility that the signatories were bound by treaty to achieve.

Changes in decision-making procedures dealt with the Council of Ministers, the EP, and the ECJ. The SEA specified that for certain policy areas the Council was empowered to take decisions by qualified majority vote. These areas included some social policy matters, implementation of decisions relating to regional funds and Community research and development programs and, most important, most measures "which have as their object the establishment and functioning of the internal market." This last amendment, expressed in a new article inserted in the Treaty of Rome, was the crucial change that Delors and others saw as essential to allowing the completion of the single market program by the 1992 deadline.[19]

The SEA also increased the power of the Parliament. Whereas the Treaty of Rome required only that the Parliament be consulted on legislation proposed by the Commission before its adoption or rejection by the Council of Ministers, the SEA added two new procedures that applied to specified areas of legislation. Under the *cooperation procedure*, the Parliament could demand from the Council of Ministers an explanation as to why its proposed amendments had not been adopted. It still could not block or pass legislation on its own, but it was assured a second reading of a bill. Under the *assent procedure*, the Parliament was required to approve, by simple majority vote, certain key actions, including the Community budget and association agreements with other countries and international organizations. These changes expanded the power of the EP and marked a further stage in its transition from a consultative to a genuinely legislative body.

In the judicial sphere, the SEA made one important change, by providing for the establishment of a new Court of First Instance. In the decades since the establishment of the ECSC, the importance of the ECJ had steadily increased, as the Court was called upon to interpret Community law and to adjudicate legal disputes between the Community and its member states, among institutions of the Community, and between private firms and citizens and member state governments. One effect of the growing importance of the Court was a rising workload. To address this problem, the SEA empowered the Council to establish a new Court of First Instance to hear cases of less than constitutional importance.

Finally, the SEA introduced an important change in the foreign policy sphere by creating a legal basis for EPC. Under the terms of the act, the signatories henceforth were bound by legal agreement, rather than just a political commitment, to consult and cooperate with each other in the foreign policy sphere. However, the EPC itself was not (unlike, for example, such new policy areas as environment or regional policy) incorporated into the Treaty of Rome. There thus was no such thing as a Community foreign policy, but only an agreement among the member states of the Community that they would forge a common foreign policy. This meant that foreign policy would remain a matter for intergovernmental cooperation rather than supranational coordination. Community institutions such as the Commission would not have a role in EPC, and foreign policy decisions would not be subject to the jurisdiction of the ECJ. To facilitate foreign policy cooperation, the SEA established an EPC secretariat that was charged with preparing meetings and assisting with policy coordination between meetings of the Council.

The SEA was an uneasy compromise between those in Europe who wanted a major push forward to political union and those, like the British and the Danes, who would have preferred not to convene an IGC at all. It introduced important reforms in the Community's founding treaty and demonstrated that the member states could use the mechanism of an intergovernmental conference to push the integration process forward. Above all, it elevated to the level of a legal principle the key goal—a single market by the end of 1992—that was to preoccupy the Community in the late 1980s and become all but synonymous with the relaunch that Delors had sought to achieve. It also provided added means to achieve that goal through expanded use of qualified majority voting and created the basis for a stronger Community external profile on the eve of what was to become an extraordinary period of international change.

THE IBERIAN ENLARGEMENT

The June 1985 decision to convene an IGC coincided with the conclusion, after many years of negotiation, of accession treaties with Portugal and Spain. The long period of negotiation reflected the many complex issues that needed to be resolved owing to the relative poverty of both countries and to the special characteristics of their economies. Both countries were formally admitted on January 1, 1986, raising the total membership to twelve.

Following accession, the CAP had to adjust to the problems of expanded production of wine, olive oil, and other Mediterranean products. Enlargement also increased the importance of Community-funded development aid. The Community had long provided such aid to southern Italy, but it now was faced with the much more daunting task of trying to raise the two new members as well as Greece and Ireland to the average income level of the rest of the Community. On balance, however, the Iberian enlargement proceeded more smoothly than many experts had predicted, and membership enjoyed strong public support in both countries.

The European Union

By the end of the 1980s the situation in the EC was characterized by a mix of enthusiasm generated by the successes of the single market program and the Iberian enlargement and dissatisfaction in many quarters with what was seen as unfinished business on the Community agenda. The EMS had been functioning quite well for nearly a decade, but the plans for economic and monetary union outlined in the 1970 Werner report had been abandoned. Similarly, the modest institutional reforms of the SEA were a far cry from realization of the ambitious calls for political union discussed in the early 1980s.

For practical reasons, Delors in his first term had focused on the single market program, but he remained a keen supporter of EMU, ready to return to it when political conditions were more favorable. The French and several other member states also were interested in EMU, which was seen as a way of replacing the de facto German dominance over monetary policy in the EMS with a more symmetrical system in which all member states would make decisions in a European system of central banks. German Chancellor Helmut Kohl and Foreign Minister Genscher also were favorable toward EMU, although they had to tread warily in the face of domestic opposition from those afraid of losing the mark, a symbol of German postwar economic stability. Political reform was less prominent in discussions of the Community's future, but it played a certain role, especially since Germany had stated that moves toward economic and monetary union should be accompanied by a strengthening of political union, lest the "democratic deficit" in the Community increase and lead to political alienation on the part of the voters. Prime Minister Thatcher continued to voice skepticism about both further economic and political integration (see Box 2.2) but, as will be seen, she was unable to block progress in either of these areas.

In June 1988 the European Council appointed a committee, comprised mainly of central bankers and chaired by Delors, to propose specific steps that might lead to EMU. The Delors Committee unveiled its report in April 1989.[20] It followed the basic outlines of the earlier Werner Plan, proposing a three-stage process for reaching EMU and stressing the importance of creating favorable economic conditions before a single currency could be launched. While many in Europe remained skeptical about monetary union, new and more favorable conditions gave reason to believe that the Delors recommendations might succeed where Werner's had failed. EMS had created relative currency stability in Europe and the single market program—particularly those elements dealing with free movement of capital and financial services liberalization—included measures that would make EMU both more necessary and more easy to achieve.

Before the member states could proceed with the recommendations contained in the Delors Report, however, the entire project was unexpectedly caught up in the wider political upheavals rocking the continent. These upheavals helped to pave the way to EMU and ensured that it would be achieved in parallel with a revived project for political union.

Box 2.2   Prime Minister Thatcher's Bruges Speech

British Prime Minister Margaret Thatcher was a prominent "Euroskeptic" in the 1980s. In a famous speech at the College of Europe in Bruges, Belgium, on September 20, 1988, she argued her case for a loose union of nation-states against a Brussels-based federation:

"Willing and active cooperation between independent sovereign States is the best way to build a successful European Community. To try to suppress nationhood and concentrate power at the center of a European conglomerate would be highly damaging and would jeopardize the objectives we seek to achieve. Europe will be stronger precisely because it has France as France, Spain as Spain, Britain as Britain, each with its own customs, traditions, and identity. It would be folly to try to fit them into some sort of identikit European personality.

"Some of the founding fathers of the Community thought that the United States of America might be its model. But the whole history of America is quite different from Europe. People went there to get away from the intolerance and constraints of life in Europe. They sought liberty and opportunity; and their strong sense of purpose has, over two centuries, helped to create a new unity and pride in being American—just as our pride lies in being British or Belgian or Dutch or German.

"I am the first to say that on many great issues the countries of Europe should try to speak with one voice. . . . But working more closely together does not require power to be centralized in Brussels or decisions taken by an appointed bureaucracy.

"Indeed it is ironic that just when those countries such as the Soviet Union, which have tried to run everything from the center, are learning that success depends on dispersing power and decisions away from the center, some in the Community seem to want to move in the opposite direction.

"We have not successfully rolled back the frontiers of the State in Britain only to see them reimposed at a European level, with a European super-state exercising a new dominance from Brussels."

THE COLLAPSE OF COMMUNISM

The fall of communism in 1989–1991 came as a surprise to most political leaders and experts in the West. The unraveling of the system began after the coming to power in March 1985 of Mikhail Gorbachev, a would-be reformer who turned out to be the last leader of the Soviet Union. Gorbachev hoped to modernize and strengthen the communist system, not destroy it, but he was unable to control the forces of change that he unleashed. The Soviet economy fell into crisis, some of the non-Russian peoples in the Soviet Union demanded independence, and the Soviet satellites grew restive. By early 1990 Moscow had lost its empire in central and eastern Europe, and by the end of 1991 the Soviet Union was itself had fragmented into fifteen newly independent states.[21]

Change in central and eastern Europe began with popular movements for democracy in Poland and Hungary and soon spilled over into the hardline communist dictatorship of East Germany. In the summer and fall of 1989 the East German communist state began to weaken, as thousands of East German citizens emigrated to the West via Hungary, which had opened its border with Austria. On November 9 the East German authorities effectively lost control of their borders, as the Berlin Wall was thrown open. Germans from both sides of the Wall began to plan a common future. In March 1990 the East German regime was forced to stage free elections in which the voters opted overwhelmingly for the pro-unification Christian Democratic party. Following a set of fast-moving negotiations involving the governments of the two German states and the four World War II victor powers—the Soviet Union, Britain, France, and the United States—Germany was reunited in October 1990. The five states of the former GDR, with some 16 million inhabitants, automatically became part of the Community, making Germany by far the biggest member state but one whose per capita GNP was substantially lower than before unification.

The end of the cold war and the unification of Germany had enormous implications for the Community, both complicating and making more necessary reforms that had long been on the agenda. The EC had developed primarily as an economic institution, but it also had been shaped by the political and ideological conflict on the continent. Strengthening Western Europe against Soviet pressures had always been an important motivation for supporters of the Community, and the division of Germany had helped to facilitate integration by making France and West Germany approximately equal in size and ensuring that the latter looked to its western neighbors for economic and political partnership, rather than to the east and southeast of Europe, traditional spheres of German influence. The collapse of communism thus negated two of the underlying preconditions for European integration—the presence of an external enemy and rough equality between France and Germany—and inevitably raised questions about its future.

Leaders such as Thatcher, Mitterrand, and Dutch Prime Minister Ruud Lubbers had been skeptical about unification and sought by various diplomatic means to block or delay it. Once unification became inevitable, however, Mitterrand in particular was convinced of the need to push ahead with plans to deepen the Community so as to ensure that the new Germany remained firmly anchored in the West and subject to French influence. He was supported in this by the Germans themselves, notably Kohl, and by Delors, who saw in the collapse of communism new and urgent reasons to strengthen the Community.

EMU, already on the political agenda, was a logical vehicle by which to pursue deepening. The European Council received the Delors Report in June 1989, and at the same meeting decided that stage one of EMU would begin in July 1990. Progress toward stages two and three would require an IGC and treaty amendments. At the December 1989 Strasbourg summit the European Council agreed to convene an IGC on EMU by the end of 1990. The leaders also agreed to adopt a social charter—a Community-wide agreement on labor standards that the trade unions, strongly backed by Delors, had pressed for as a concomitant to the single European market. Britain did not sign the social charter and it opposed the IGC, but on both issues it was unable to dissuade the other member states from moving forward.

The changing international situation also gave new momentum to the old project for political union. In a strong signal that France and Germany intended to lead on this issue, in April 1990 Kohl and Mitterrand sent a joint letter to Irish Prime Minister Charles Haughey (in his capacity as president of the European Council), in which they called for new and concrete steps to realize the aspirations to European Political Union already expressed in the SEA. They argued that progress toward EMU called for strengthening the Community's political side. European voters could not be expected to accept the surrender of national authority over economic policy to European institutions that were less subject to democratic control than national governments. Moreover, only by developing a strong external identity and an effective foreign policy could the Community expect to influence the changes occurring on its eastern borders.

The Kohl-Mitterrand letter set the agenda for an extraordinary session of the European Council in Dublin in April 1990, at which the twelve leaders reaffirmed their commitment to political union. Meeting in the same city two months later, the European Council agreed to convene an IGC on political union to begin at the same time as the IGC on EMU and to run in parallel with it. Both IGCs formally opened at the Rome summit in December 1990. Thus after not holding a single such conference in the three decades after 1955, the Community was to have three IGCs in five years, two of which would run concurrently. This extraordinary situation reflected the extent to which, as Delors had phrased it, history was "accelerating," forcing the Community to respond.

THE NEGOTIATIONS

Conducted as formal diplomatic conferences involving regular meetings at the ministerial and working levels, the IGCs focused on strengthening the decision-making process in areas in which the EC already had competence and on extending the range of issues subject to common policy-making. If these were the general goals, there was little agreement among the twelve about how and how quickly they were to be accomplished. Italy and the Benelux countries were the strongest supporters of European integration and pressed for the most sweeping revisions. Britain and Denmark were leery of change, and sought to block many of the most extensive reforms. France wanted a strong Europe, but tended to be skeptical of the transfer of supranational powers to Brussels. It thus favored expanded use of intergovernmental cooperation, along the lines already established in EPC. Germany tended to align its positions with those of France, but on foreign policy and defense matters it was wary of endangering NATO and transatlantic cooperation by building up a European defense alternative. With regard to EMU, only Britain among the major member states was wholly opposed to the project, but the other member states differed widely about how and within what time frame to create a common currency.

The presidency countries—Luxembourg in the first half of 1991, the Netherlands in the second—played important roles in putting forward draft treaties and in searching for compromises among these national perspectives. Commission president Delors was not happy with the intergovernmental approach of many of the member states, but he did welcome the extension of Community competence to many new policy areas (see Box 2.3).

The negotiations lasted a year, and concluded at the December 1991 Maastricht European Council with agreement on the Treaty on European Union (TEU), more commonly known as the Maastricht Treaty. Agreement was achieved only after last-minute negotiations in which Britain and Denmark secured the right to opt out of certain treaty provisions. Neither country was required to adopt the common currency, and Britain refused to go along with a Social Charter, which as a consequence was adopted by the other eleven member states as a legally binding protocol to the treaty. In effect, agreement to disagree was in these cases the most that could be achieved.

Formally signed in Maastricht in February 1992, the treaty nonetheless was by far the most extensive revision of the founding treaties ever attempted. It had three main elements. First, it contained (in the form of amendments to the Treaty of Rome that were inserted by the Maastricht Treaty) a detailed blueprint for the establishment of EMU by the end of the decade. This aspect of Maastricht is discussed in Chapter 6. Second, it formally established the political union through a complicated structure that differentiated between economic matters on the one hand and foreign policy and internal security matters on the other. Third, it included other innovations, such as the Social Charter, EU citizenship, the strengthening of the Parliament, subsidiarity, and other reforms that in themselves were

---

Box 2.3   Jacques Delors, Speech in London, March 1991

Delors, Commission president from 1985 to 1994, was a passionate believer in European integration. In this speech, delivered as the Maastricht Treaty negotiations were in full swing, he expounded his view that European integration had developed its own self-sustaining dynamic:

"It is no longer correct to speak of a 'common market.' We are building a *community* whose member states jointly exercise a measure of pooled sovereignty through fully fledged common policies—such as agriculture and economic and social cohesion; and other less developed ones—such as concerted projects in research and technology, or the environment, or measures associated with the social dimension. . . .

"One thing leads to another. This has been a feature of the Community, which is constantly being taken into new areas.

"Economic and monetary union is another example of this virtuous circle. It is true that it will mean transfers of sovereignty, particularly with the creation of a European central bank. But this is not so much a great leap forward as a logical consequence of the success of the European Monetary System."

not so important but that in combination with EMU and political union increased the overall significance of the Maastricht achievement.

THE PILLAR STRUCTURE

As its formal name indicated, the treaty brought into being a new entity called the European Union, defined as "mark[ing] a new stage in the process of creating an ever closer union among the peoples of Europe."[22] The EU was established as a structure of three "pillars," each of which was to deal with different and partially overlapping policy areas using different decision-making processes. The first pillar was to consist of the three existing Communities—the EEC (renamed the European Community to reflect its broadened and no longer strictly economic areas of responsibility), the ECSC, and Euratom—in which the member states have pooled sovereignty and transferred decision-making powers to the Commission, the Council of Ministers, the EP, and the ECJ, with a powerful guiding role also assigned to the European Council. EMU was to reside in the first pillar, but use a modified decision-making process involving, in addition to these institutions, the European Central Bank and the national central banks of the member states.

The second pillar, Common Foreign and Security Policy (CFSP), replaced and was based upon EPC. Decisions would remain largely intergovernmental, with only a limited role for Community institutions. CFSP was not made subject to the jurisdiction of the Court of Justice or to decision-making by qualified majority voting. The third pillar was to consist of cooperation in the fields of justice and home affairs, including asylum policy, control of external borders and immigration from outside the Union, and combating drug addiction and international crime. Decision-making would also be basically intergovernmental, conducted more or less along the same lines as CFSP. The three-pillar structure established by Maastricht remains valid for the EU today, although some elements of it were modified by the 1997 Treaty of Amsterdam and still others were placed on the agenda of the post-Amsterdam IGC convened in February 2000.

The security aspect of CFSP was among the most controversial issues negotiated in the 1991 IGC on political union. A Europeanist camp led by France supported the creation of a European defense identity and the merging of the EU and the WEU. Adherents of this position argued that Europe had to be prepared to take over responsibility for its own defense from the United States and that a Europe that relied on Washington for its security could never be an independent power exercising influence in the world commensurate with its economic weight and interests. In contrast, an Atlanticist camp led by the UK opposed a defense role for the EU and upheld the primacy of NATO. Mindful of its relations with the United States and France, Germany straddled both camps, but leaned more toward France.

The result was an especially ambiguous compromise. According to a key provision of the articles establishing the second pillar, "the common foreign and security policy shall include all questions related to the security of the Union, including the eventual framing of a common defense policy, which might in time lead to a common defense."[23] In contrast to the provisions on EMU, which specified a detailed timetable and guidelines for realizing monetary union, the treaty left undefined the meaning of such terms as "eventual" and "might in time." The WEU was treated as a bridge between NATO and the EU. NATO's role in European defense was not overtly questioned, but the way was left open to a future EU role. The treaty declared that the WEU, which previously had not been linked to the structures of the EC, was an "integral part of the development of the European Union."[24] It requested the WEU to "elaborate and implement decisions and actions of the Union which have defense implications."[25] The treaty also left unanswered such questions as the role of those member states—Ireland, Denmark, and, after 1995, Austria, Finland, and Sweden—that were not WEU members.

The third pillar was also an area of political sensitivity, marked by sharp differences among the member states. The completion of the single market and the abolition of controls on the movement of people created strong arguments for European-level cooperation in this area. Proponents of cooperation stressed that international crime syndicates had adjusted to the single market, while the police and judges were still very national in their outlook. At the same time, the member states had very different legal traditions that made them reluctant to surrender sovereignty in this area. There were also genuine differences of interest. Germany, located in the center of Europe and the destination of most refugees and immigrants, had an interest in "Europeanizing" immigration policy so as to spread the burden of newcomers to its territory. The UK, an island nation with relatively secure borders, was better served by a national approach.

In the end the twelve compromised by establishing the third pillar on a loose intergovernmental basis. The members committed themselves to collaboration and agreed to certain provisions under which this collaboration could be strengthened over time. They also agreed to establish a new body, the European Police Office (Europol). The overall approach was cautious, however, and on balance disappointing to those who would have preferred stronger collective action with regard to the "people" side of European integration.

OTHER REFORMS

In addition to the three-pillar structure, the Maastricht Treaty codified in the treaties the principle of "subsidiarity," a concept that attempts to define what decisions are to be taken at which levels. Subsidiarity was introduced in part as a response to fears of excessive centralization of power in Brussels. Under the terms of the treaty, the EU was to take action "only if and in so far as the objectives of the proposed action cannot be sufficiently achieved by the Member States."[26] While there was no universally agreed definition of subsidiarity, its incorporation in the Maastricht Treaty meant that the Commission and other EU bodies had to be mindful of the distribution of powers between the Union and the member states.

The treaty established a European citizenship, to exist alongside and in addition to national citizenship. The provisions on citizenship strengthened the rights of EU citizens to move and reside freely on the territory of other EU member states and conferred certain other advantages, such as the right of an EU citizen to be represented by the consulate of any member state while overseas and the right to vote and run in municipal elections in an EU country of residence, irrespective of citizenship. The treaty also established the post of parliamentary Ombudsman, through which citizens could file complaints about the actions of EU institutions.

Perhaps most significantly, the Maastricht Treaty continued the pattern established in the SEA by strengthening the powers of the Parliament in first-pillar matters. It added a new procedure, called *co-decision*, under which the EP for the first time gained the power to block legislation introduced by the Commission and passed by the Council of Ministers. Co-decision was prescribed only for a limited number of policy areas, although one of these—the internal market—was quite important. In another change that strengthened its powers, the Parliament was given a say in the appointment of the Commission and the Commission president, hitherto a matter of exclusive concern for the Council of Ministers. Finally, the Maastricht Treaty established a new institution, the Committee of the Regions, to provide a means by which regional entities in Europe can give direct input to policy-making in Brussels.

The Maastricht Treaty contained a final provision requiring the member states to convene another intergovernmental conference in 1996 to review the treaty. By inserting this requirement into Maastricht, the member states were acknowledging the treaty's inadequacies. In many areas it contained vague compromises and statements of intent that reflected underlying disagreements among the signatories. The 1996 IGC would review the workings of the treaty in the light of several years' experience and, it was expected, clarify and sharpen some of its provisions, particularly as they related to CFSP and the relationship between the EU and the WEU.

RATIFICATION AND BEYOND

Ratifying the Maastricht Treaty proved to be unexpectedly difficult. After nearly a decade of rapid change in Europe, it was perhaps inevitable that reaction to further integration would set in. With Western Europe racing toward union and the old order in eastern Europe rapidly disintegrating, people needed time to digest the changes. After a short-lived economic boom, the costs of German reunification helped to precipitate an economic recession in Europe, bringing to an end the job growth of the late 1980s. The war in the Persian Gulf and the outbreak of civil war in the former Yugoslavia caused added uncertainty. After 1991 the mood in Europe became introspective, more focused on local and national concerns such as crime, immigration, and unemployment and more skeptical of the headlong rush to union.

The first highly visible sign that sentiments had changed occurred in June 1992, when voters in Denmark narrowly rejected the Maastricht Treaty in the national referendum that was required under the Danish constitution. Since all twelve signatories had to ratify the treaty for it to go into effect, the Community was thrown into crisis. By late summer the political crisis had spilled over into the financial markets, threatening the integrity of the EMS, one of the key building blocks of the planned EMU. In Germany, the treaty was challenged in the supreme court, where opponents argued that it contravened the German constitution by transferring powers of the German states to Brussels.

In September 1992 the French electorate approved the Maastricht Treaty, but only by the narrow margin of 51 to 49 percent. The European Council negotiated additional opt outs for Denmark, and in May 1993 the Danish voters approved the treaty by a healthy margin in a second referendum. Legislatures in the other countries approved the treaty, as did the German federal court. Thus in the end the treaty was ratified. It went into effect on November 1, 1993, some ten months later than originally planned. The European Union was born, even though many voters were confused about the new name and uncertain of what it meant for them.

ENLARGEMENT AGAIN

Just as the collapse of communism intensified pressures to deepen the EC, it contributed, if only indirectly, to a further widening. Before the late 1980s, political leaders had come to accept the division of Europe as a more or less permanent feature of international politics. Many believed that some day communism would end, but this was seen as happening in the distant future, without immediate implications for policy.

The sudden collapse of the system in central and eastern Europe dramatically changed the geopolitical landscape, opening possibilities for enlargement that would have been hard to imagine even five years earlier. As a first step, the end of the cold war encouraged the EFTA countries to reevaluate their stances on membership. Austria, Finland, Norway, Sweden, and Switzerland all were affluent, highly industrialized democracies with close economic and political ties to the EC. For political reasons, both international and domestic, these countries had chosen not to follow Britain and Denmark in leaving EFTA for the Community in 1973. All but Norway were neutral states, whose governments were concerned about domestic and Soviet reaction to any moves toward integration with NATO member countries. The success of the Community's single market program and the thawing of the cold war under Gorbachev led to changes in policy. Beginning with Austria in July 1989 and concluding with Norway in November 1992, all five of these countries applied for membership, as did two small Mediterranean states, Cyprus and Malta.

The Community initially was not enthusiastic about taking in new members, and proposed a looser form of cooperation. Building upon earlier economic agreements, in early 1989 EFTA and the EC began to negotiate a European Economic Area (EEA) that would extend the single market to the EFTA countries but hold off on integrating them into the political and decision-making structures of what soon was to become the EU. The member states of the two groupings signed a treaty establishing the EEA in May 1992, to come into effect on January 1, 1994. The agreement extended the four freedoms of the single market to the EFTA countries, which also were required to adjust their domestic legislation to comply with EU single market directives and other important economic laws. The EFTA countries also gained the right to participate in certain EU programs.

The EEA was always an unsatisfactory arrangement, however, containing a mix of obligations and responsibilities that posed problems for both sides. It meant that the EFTA countries, as the weaker parties to the deal, had to comply with rules which they had no say in drafting. It also posed certain constitutional difficulties for the EU, since it established an EEA court for adjudicating disputes that the ECJ later ruled was incompatible with the EU's founding treaties.[27] Swiss voters rejected the agreement in a December 1992 referendum. Switzerland thus did not become part of the EEA and was forced to suspend its application for full EU membership. Austria, Finland, Sweden, and Norway ratified the agreement and entered the EEA as scheduled in January 1994, but they also decided to press ahead with their membership applications.

Accession negotiations with these countries opened in early 1993, and were concluded in June 1994. Voters in Norway rejected accession in a November 1994 referendum, reaffirming their 1972 verdict, but Austria, Finland, and Sweden ratified their accession treaties without major difficulty, becoming full EU members on January 1, 1995. EEA thus operated as a substantial economic grouping for only one year. It continues to exist, but its only non-EU members are Norway, Iceland, and tiny Liechtenstein. (These countries, along with Switzerland, also constitute what remains of EFTA.)

Meanwhile, the former communist countries of central and eastern Europe also began to press the case for membership. For a time after the fall of communism it was unclear whether these countries would become full EU members or whether they would opt for a looser form of association based on free trade and cooperation in other spheres. Increasingly, however, the leaders of these countries ruled out the alternative possibilities that had been discussed, such as a Europe of concentric circles or an expanded EEA, and demanded full EU and NATO membership. In doing so, they were motivated by a strong desire to be fully integrated into the West, to buffer themselves against instability in the former Soviet Union and a possible resurgence of Russian power, and a desire to have influence over the institutions shaping the development of Europe.

Many of the EU countries were unenthusiastic about absorbing a relatively poor region with over 100 million inhabitants, but after a period of debate they concluded that the EU had little choice but to embrace the region. At the June 1993 Copenhagen summit the European Council in principle agreed that these countries could become members after a period of transition in which they prepared their economies and established working democracies. To do so, they would have to meet a set of economic and political conditions that became known as the Copenhagen criteria, and that still are used to evaluate the readiness of candidate countries for membership. The applicant countries were not happy with what they saw as delaying tactics on the part of the existing member states, but it was clear that they needed a period of transition to modernize their economies and to adapt their domestic institutions and regulatory structures to EU norms. To assist in this process, the EU provided grants, loans, and technical assistance under various programs.

As part of the Copenhagen decisions, the European Council stipulated that the *next* enlargement negotiations—that is, those following the as yet uncompleted talks with the EFTA countries—could not begin until at least six months after the completion of the post-Maastricht IGC. This conference was scheduled to convene in the first half of 1996 and to conclude approximately one year later. Under this timetable, the decision to begin enlargement talks with candidate countries could not be taken until late 1997, and the talks themselves could not begin in earnest until 1998. Previous experience indicated that negotiating enlargement treaties took several years, which would be followed by a process of ratification in the EP and the member state parliaments lasting a year or more. Thus under even the most optimistic of scenarios, enlargement could not be expected to occur until well after 2000.

In view of this timetable, the Copenhagen decisions should be seen as a choice by the EU to widen and to deepen, but to deepen first—by completing the transition to EMU and by having another IGC on institutional reform—and only then to admit new members. This choice was criticized by many at the time, in the candidate countries and in the United States, where the Clinton administration urged the EU to speed up the enlargement process and to some extent even used the perception of EU foot-dragging to pursue its own project of expanding NATO. From the EU's perspective, however, the decision to deepen first made sense. Much of the preparation for enlargement had to be accomplished in the candidate countries themselves through an elaborate process of reform and legislative adaptation. It could not have been accelerated in a major way. To have admitted new members in the late 1990s could well have overloaded an already crowded EU agenda, damaged prospects for a launch of the EMU, undermined public support for European integration, and contributed further to the institutional problems that the 1996–1997 IGC was intended to address.

The Treaty of Amsterdam

The prospect of adding ten or more members lent new urgency to calls for the reform of EU institutions, the issue that was in any case expected to dominate the

IGC. At fifteen, the Union was already too large to function with essentially the same set of institutions that had been devised in the 1950s for a community of six. With twenty members, the Commission had lost its collegial character. The EP, with 626 members, was already larger than most national parliaments. Under the rotating system of presidencies, member states could expect to chair the European Council and the Council of Ministers only once every 7.5 years. Thus as 1996 approached, the impending IGC became ever more closely associated with a need to adjust the institutions to the needs of enlargement.

To prepare for the IGC, the European Council appointed a "reflection group" of high-ranking officials from the member states. In addition to proposing institutional reforms and a strengthening of the Union's much-maligned CFSP, the reflection group called upon the Union to win greater popular support by taking action on issues of direct concern to the citizen, for example, unemployment, immigration, and crime. It concluded that the second and third pillars were both ineffective and excessively complex, unable to meet the real situations that Europe had confronted in the 1990s: the civil war in the former Yugoslavia, the flows of refugees associated with that conflict, and rising international crime and drug trafficking.[28]

While they recognized the need for institutional reform, the member states were wary of yet another major revision of the treaties that would have to be explained to the voters and that might be difficult to ratify. Skepticism about European integration had grown in most countries since Maastricht. Moreover, the EU countries all were struggling to meet the convergence criteria for EMU that were stipulated in the Maastricht Treaty. Governments were cutting spending to meet the debt and deficit criteria in a way that was unpopular with the voters. Member-state governments thus approached the post-Maastricht IGC with mixed attitudes. They recognized the importance of change but they also saw a need for caution in the face of increased voter skepticism.

The IGC convened in Turin in March 1996, and concluded in Amsterdam in June 1997 with agreement on yet another treaty. Formally signed in October of that year, the Treaty of Amsterdam amended the Maastricht Treaty and the Treaty of Rome, albeit only modestly. It provided for some strengthening of the Union's CFSP and for closer cooperation in third-pillar matters such as immigration. As in past revisions, the powers of the Parliament were expanded somewhat.

On balance, however, the changes in the Treaty of Amsterdam were modest compared with those agreed at Maastricht. The member states postponed resolving the central question of how the institutions could be streamlined and made to function more effectively in an enlarged EU. Instead, they adopted a legally binding protocol to the treaty which stipulated that at least one year before membership reached twenty, a new IGC would be convened to carry out a review of the institutions and to examine in particular three questions: the size and composition of the Commission, the weighting of votes in the Council of Ministers, and the possible extension of QMV in the Council. The member states subsequently decided to tackle these questions before any enlargement occurred. They thus agreed, at the Cologne European Council in June 1999, to convene the next IGC in early 2000. The Amsterdam Treaty itself went into effect on May 1, 1999, following an uneventful ratification process in the fifteen member states.

In the meantime, enlargement negotiations with the central and east European applicants had gotten underway. In its *Agenda 2000* report of July 1997 the Commission issued detailed opinions on the suitability of the ten candidate countries for membership.[29] Based on the Commission's recommendations, in December 1997 the Council decided that formal negotiations with Cyprus and five central and east European states—the Czech Republic, Estonia, Hungary, Poland, and Slovenia—could begin in March 1998. The five other candidate countries—Bulgaria, Latvia, Lithuania, Slovakia, and Romania—were promised additional aid and urged to redouble their pre-accession efforts with an eye toward beginning negotiations as soon as possible.

The negotiations began with an elaborate screening process intended to determine those areas in which each candidate country had achieved or was approaching EU norms and standards, and those in which further convergence was required. This was followed by the start of actual negotiations regarding the terms and conditions on which each of the six new candidates would enter the Union, and in particular on whether they would be granted transitional periods for phasing in the more expensive and demanding EU policies, for example in the fields of environment and social policy. In the fall of 1998 and 1999 the Commission issued annual reports on the progress of the candidate countries—both those that were actively engaged in negotiations and those that had been put on hold by the Luxembourg summit.

At the December 1999 Helsinki summit, the European Council, acting upon the recommendation contained in the Commission's 1999 report, concluded that the second-tier countries (which by then included Malta, which had joined the list of applicants) had made sufficient progress toward EU political and economic norms to begin accession negotiations. Negotiations with six additional countries began in February 2000. In the addition, the European Council decided that Turkey could be considered as a formal candidate for membership, although it put off any decision on the actual start of negotiations, which was made conditional upon Turkey's making progress in the areas of human rights and political stability, as well as continued economic progress.

The Helsinki summit also reaffirmed the importance of a new IGC to prepare the Union itself for enlargement. This conference got underway in Portugal in February 2000, and was scheduled to conclude at the end of the French presidency in December of the same year. Its importance for the future of the Union is discussed in the concluding chapter.

Notes

1. Text in European Parliament, *Selection of Texts Concerning Institutional Matters of the Community for 1950–1982* (Luxembourg: Office of Official Publications of the EC, 1982), 47.

2. Speech at Columbia University, January 11, 1952, quoted in Richard Mayne, *The Recovery of Europe: From Devastation to Unity* (New York: Harper and Row, 1970), 204. Eden was referring both to the ECSC and to the even more ambitious plan to develop the European Defense Community.

3. John Gillingham, *Coal, Steel, and the Rebirth of Europe* (Cambridge: Cambridge University Press, 1991).

4. Richard Mayne, "Economic Integration in the New Europe: A Statistical Approach," in Stephen R. Graubard, ed., *A New Europe?* (Boston: Beacon Press, 1964), 187, citing Statistical Office of the European Communities data.

5. For the original treaty text, see Intergovernmental Conference on the Common Market and Euratom, *Treaty Establishing the European Economic Community and Connected Documents*, Rome, March 25, 1957, Article 3a. The English version quoted here follows the official English text in *European Union: Selected instruments*. Amended version substitutes "prohibition" for "elimination."

6. Article 3.1.c TOR (ex Article 3c). The Treaty of Amsterdam renumbered the articles of the Rome and Maastricht treaties to account for the many amendments, insertions, and deletions that had been made over the years. The numbered treaty articles in the notes refer to the renumbered versions; the original numbering ("ex") is given in parentheses.

7. Article 32 TOR (ex Article 38).

8. Article 3b.

9. John Newhouse, *Collision in Brussels: The Common Market Crisis of 30 June 1965* (London: Faber & Faber, 1967).

10. *Bulletin of the European Communities* [hereinafter, Bull. EC] 3–1966, 9.

11. Timothy Garton Ash, *In Europe's Name: Germany and the Divided Continent* (New York: Vintage, 1993), 58–83.

12. Bull. EC 11–1981, 87–91.

13. Bull. EC 2–1984, 7–28.

14. Margaret Thatcher, *The Downing Street Years* (New York: HarperCollins, 1993), 553.

15. "Report from the ad hoc Committee on Institutional Affairs to the European Council, Brussels, 29 and 30 March 1985," Bull. EC 3–1985, 102–111.

16. See Thatcher, *The Downing Street Years*, 548–551. Article 236 was deleted from the TOR and is now Article 48 TEU.

17. *Single European Act*, in *Official Journal of the European Communities* [hereinafter, O.J.] L169 (1987).

18. Charles Grant, *Delors: Inside the House that Jacques Built* (London: Nicholas Brealey, 1994), 74.

19. Article 18 of the SEA, inserting Article 100a.

20. "Report of the Committee for the Study of Economic and Monetary Union," Bull. EC 4–1989, 8–9.

21. J. F. Brown, *Surge to Freedom: The End of Communist Rule in Eastern Europe* (Durham: Duke University Press, 1991); Jack F. Matlock, Jr., *Autopsy on an Empire* (New York: Random House, 1995).

22. Article 1 TEU, ex Article A.

23. Ex Article J.4.1 TEU, subsequently amended as Article 17 TEU.

24. Ex Article J.4.2 TEU, subsequently amended as Article 17 TEU.

25. Ibid.

26. Article 5 TOR, ex Article 3b.

27. ECJ Opinion 1/91, December 14, 1991, *Re a Draft Treaty on a European Economic Area*, in *Court of Justice of the European Communities: Reports of Cases before the Court* (European Court Reports) [hereinafter, ECR] I-6079 (1992).

28. *Final Report from the Chairman of the Reflection Group on the 1996 Intergovernmental Conference* (Brussels: Commission of the European Communities [hereinafter, CEC], 1995).

29. *Agenda 2000: For a stronger and wider Union*, Bull. EC Supplement 5/97; country opinions in Supplements 6–15/97.

Suggestions for Further Reading

Bond, Martyn, et al., eds. *Eminent Europeans: Personalities Who Shaped Contemporary Europe*. London: Greycoat, 1996.

Grant, Charles. *Delors: Inside the House that Jacques Built*. London: Nicholas Brealey, 1994.

Mayne, Richard. *The Recovery of Europe: From Devastation to Unity*. New York: Harper & Row, 1970.

Monnet, Jean. *Memoirs*. Garden City: Doubleday, 1978.

Moravcsik, Andrew. *The Choice for Europe: Social Purpose and State Power from Messina to Maastricht*. Ithaca: Cornell University Press, 1998.

Thatcher, Margaret. *The Downing Street Years*. New York: HarperCollins, 1993.

CHAPTER 3

The Institutions and Laws of the European Union

As was seen in the previous chapter, the EU treaties perform two main functions: they define the purposes and objectives of the Union, and they establish institutions and decision-making processes by which these objectives are translated into policy and law. This chapter deals with the institutions of the Union and the main characteristics of EU law.

Five major institutions set policy and make or interpret EU law: the Commission, the Council of Ministers, the European Parliament, the Court of Justice, and the European Council. The Economic and Social Committee and the Committee of the Regions play lesser roles in legislative affairs, while the Court of Auditors monitors expenditure. In addition, the EU system of institutions includes the European Investment Bank, and the European System of Central Banks (ESCB) and European Central Bank (ECB). There is also an array of secondary agencies and offices located throughout the territory of the member states that assist with policy implementation in particular areas such as health and safety, the environment, and law enforcement. These agencies are autonomous, having been established by Council or Commission decision rather than in the founding treaties. As has been seen, the powers of the EU's institutions are different in the first than in the second and third pillars, and even vary within the first pillar, depending upon the issue being decided.

Major Institutions

THE EUROPEAN COMMISSION

The Commission is the executive body of the EU. In the first pillar it enjoys an exclusive right to propose legislation (known as the right of initiative) and works with the member states to implement and enforce EU policy and legislation. It exercises much more limited powers in the second and third pillars, where the EU does not legislate and where responsibility for policy rests with the member states.

The Commission also represents the EU in international trade negotiations. Often called the "guardian of the treaties," it is charged with looking out for the interests of the Union as a whole and warning member states when they are violating, in the Commission's view, their obligations under the treaties. It is empowered to initiate legal action in the Court of Justice against member states perceived as failing to carry out their treaty obligations. The members of the Commission, and above all the Commission president, also provide political leadership for the European integration process and are among the most visible symbols of the Union to the public.

The ECSC, Euratom, and the EEC originally each had separate commissions (the ECSC's was called the High Authority), but the three were merged in the Treaty Establishing a Single Commission of the European Communities (the Merger Treaty) that went into effect in July 1967. The Treaty of Rome defines most of the powers and responsibilities of the Commission, but the Commission also may act under provisions of the ECSC and the Euratom treaties, for example when it deals with problems in the steel industry or proposes legislation to protect workers at nuclear power plants.

The Commission includes at least one national from each member state, which means that it has expanded with successive enlargements. From 1958 to 1972 it had just nine members—two each from France, Germany, and Italy and one each from Belgium, Luxembourg, and the Netherlands. Since the enlargement of 1995, it has had twenty members—two from each of the five large states and one from each of the other ten member states (see Table 3.1)—including a president and two vice presidents. The term of a Commission and of the individual commissioners is five years, and coincides with the term of each European Parliament.

The Commission is formed under the institutional provisions of the Treaty of Rome, as amended by the Maastricht and Amsterdam treaties. In the last year of

Table 3.1   The Member States in the EU Institutions

	Council Votes	Seats in the EP	Number of Commissioners	Population (millions)
Germany	10	99	2	82.1
France	10	87	2	58.7
Italy	10	87	2	57.6
UK	10	87	2	59.1
Spain	8	64	2	39.3
Netherlands	5	31	1	15.6
Greece	5	25	1	10.5
Belgium	5	25	1	10.2
Portugal	5	25	1	10.0
Sweden	4	22	1	8.8
Austria	4	21	1	8.1
Denmark	3	16	1	5.3
Finland	3	16	1	5.1
Ireland	3	15	1	3.7
Luxembourg	2	6	1	0.4
TOTAL	87	626	20	374.5

a Commission's term, the member states nominate by common accord the person that they wish to see serve as Commission president. This nomination then must be approved by the EP. The nominee for president and the member state governments together then nominate the other members of the Commission. The nominees are subject to a vote by the Parliament and, once approved, are appointed by common accord of the member state governments. Although they are selected by the member states, the commissioners are not supposed to take instructions from national governments or to represent the countries of which they are citizens. They are to take an impartial view, based on what they believe are the interests of the Union as a whole and what is consistent with the letter and spirit of the founding treaties.

In the original Treaty of Rome, the president had no formal powers over his fellow commissioners. This changed in the 1990s, as the member states approved treaty amendments that made the head of the Commission more like a national chief executive, able to choose his "ministers" and direct their work. The Maastricht Treaty established a procedure whereby the nominee for president was to be consulted by the member states regarding the selection of the other commissioners. The Amsterdam Treaty gave the nominee for president a theoretical veto over the choices for the other commissioners put forward by the member states. The treaty also states that the Commission "shall work under the political guidance of its President."[1]

Commissioners can be and often are reappointed, but the member states cannot dismiss the Commission or individual commissioners. The EP may vote to censure the Commission if it is dissatisfied with its performance. If a motion of censure on the activities of the Commission is introduced and receives a two-thirds majority of votes cast, the Commission as a body must resign and a new Commission must be formed to serve the remainder of the five-year term. The EP has never voted such a censure motion, although the likelihood that it would have done so led to the preemptive resignation of the Santer Commission in March 1999.

The Commission takes decisions on a collegial basis, usually by consensus but sometimes by simple majority vote. Irrespective of the issue—anti-trust, trade, the environment, agriculture—there is a unified Commission position approved by the body as a whole when legislation is proposed or other formal decisions taken. Although decisions are taken as a college, the individual commissioners have areas of responsibility which they exercise, chiefly by overseeing one or more of the twenty-three directorates-general responsible for particular policy areas (Table 3.2). Most of the Commission staff of approximately 17,000 civil servants is employed in the directorates-general or in the twelve associated services of the Commission responsible for translation, legal affairs, statistics, and other support functions. Each commissioner also has a small personal staff, or *cabinet* (following the French bureaucratic model). Much of the work of the Commission is accomplished through behind-the-scenes coordination among the *cabinets*, which generally are headed by a trusted co-national of the commissioner, brought in from outside the permanent EU bureaucracy.

Table 3.2   Directorates-General and Services of the Commission

Services under the Commission President
  Secretariat General
  Legal Service
  Press and Communication

Directorates-General
  Economic and Financial Affairs
  Enterprise
  Competition
  Employment and Social Affairs
  Agriculture
  Energy and Transport
  Environment
  Research
  Information Society
  Fisheries
  Internal Market
  Regional Policy
  Taxation and Customs Union
  Education and Culture
  Health and Consumer Protection
  Justice and Home Affairs
  External Relations
  Trade
  Development
  Enlargement
  Personnel and Administration
  Budget
  Financial Control

Other Services
  Joint Research Center
  Common Service for External Relations
  Humanitarian Office—ECHO
  Eurostat
  Inspectorate-General
  European Anti-Fraud Office
  Joint Interpreting and Conference Service
  Translation Service
  Publications Office

The Commission's most important responsibilities and greatest powers are in the first pillar, where they relate to legislation. The Commission proposes new laws, usually to advance the general goals expressed in the founding treaties (e.g., completion of the single market or development of a common transport policy), in response to political requests and pressures from the member states (e.g., in response to unemployment), or to meet new challenges posed by changing internal and external circumstances, such as the development of new technologies or the emergence of new environmental problems. The Commission also promulgates on its own authority regulations that are binding as EU law (generally on technical matters needed to implement existing legislation) and plays a key role in the enforcement of EU law. It has primary responsibility for drawing up the EU budget and for spending funds in the manner approved by the Council of Ministers and the EP.

In the second and third pillars, the role of the Commission is secondary to those of the member states, as represented in the Council of Ministers. When EPC first was established, the Commission was totally excluded from foreign policy deliberations by the member states. France in particular was sensitive to possible supranational intrusions into a realm that it regarded as the exclusive domain of national governments. The distinction between foreign economic and foreign policy always was somewhat artificial, however, and over time the Commission came to play a larger if still secondary role in the non-economic aspects of external policy. The Maastricht Treaty granted it the right to submit to the Council of Ministers proposals relating to CFSP. Unlike in the first pillar, this was not an exclusive right of initiative, as the member states could also make such proposals. The Commission was also to be "fully associated" with the external representation of the Union and the implementation of CFSP decisions.

With the end of the cold war and the challenge of increased economic and political instability on the periphery of the Union, the Commission took on new responsibilities and assumed a higher external profile. In 1993 a new directorate-general was established and made responsible for relations with the central and east European countries and the Newly Independent States (NIS) of the former Soviet Union. It managed the EU's substantial aid and technical assistance programs for the transition countries and played an important role in the pre-accession process for those countries seeking to join the EU. Under the reorganization of the directorates-general and services instituted by Commission president Romano Prodi in 1999, a separate directorate-general for enlargement was established, along with a new Common Service for External Relations.

In the third pillar, the Maastricht Treaty gave the Commission a shared right to initiate proposals in six of nine areas covered under the JHA provisions. However, in three areas—judicial cooperation in criminal matters, customs cooperation, and police cooperation for the purposes of combating international crime—all powers were reserved for the member states, with the Commission given no role. As part of an effort to improve EU performance in these areas, the Treaty of Amsterdam moved asylum, refugee, and immigration policy into the first pillar, giving the Commission a shared right with the member states to propose legislation for five years and an exclusive right of initiative thereafter. In 1999 a new directorate-general for justice and home affairs was established, to be overseen by a commissioner with this as his sole portfolio.

The Commission is closely identified with the Union, and its fortunes have tended to ebb and flow with changing levels of enthusiasm for a more integrated

Europe. It reached the height of its powers in the late 1980s under Delors, when it benefitted from enthusiasm for the single market project. In the late 1990s the Commission experienced considerable turmoil as popular enthusiasm for integration waned—making the Commission a lightning rod for broader concerns about integration and the transfer of powers to Brussels—and because the Commission itself made mistakes that alienated even strong supporters of European integration.

The Commission was criticized by the press, member state politicians, and the EP for failing to adequately control and monitor EU expenditure and, in the view of some, for concentrating too much on trying to expand its powers and not enough on effective implementation of policy. The Commission also had difficulty in adjusting to the growing range of EU involvement in new policy areas. Nationality rather than merit became an important factor in determining who got what job within the Commission bureaucracy, and there were many reports of corruption and mismanagement.

These issues came to a head in March 1999, when the Santer Commission, which was supposed to have served the five-year term from January 1995 to December 1999, was forced as a result of a confrontation with the EP to step down almost a year before completion of its term. The Parliament had long been critical of the Commission for the way it managed the EU budget, citing numerous cases of fraud and mismanagement, particularly in EU humanitarian aid and research spending. Members of the European Parliament (MEPs) also expressed concern about nepotism, favoritism, and excessive reliance on outside contractors to administer major programs.

After months of wrangling with the Commission over these problems and the Commission's perceived failure to correct them, in December 1998 the EP refused to approve the final accounts for the EU's 1996 budget, as required under the Treaty of Rome. Subsequently, a committee of independent experts was asked to review the Commission's financial practices and management controls. The committee completed its work on March 15, 1999, issuing a devastating report in which it charged widespread mismanagement and an effective loss of control by commissioners over programs under their supervision.[2] Although the report did not accuse individual commissioners of personal involvement in corruption, its findings seemed to confirm years of public and press sniping at the arrogance and spendthrift ways of the "Eurocrats." Facing a certain loss on a censure vote in the Parliament, the Commission resigned en masse on the same day that the report appeared. As required by the treaties, the commissioners stayed on in a caretaker capacity, but work on new initiatives ground to a halt.

The member states were concerned about weak leadership at a time when the EU was trying to establish the credibility of the euro, negotiating enlargement, and confronting a crisis in Kosovo. They therefore moved quickly to select a new president, choosing, at the Berlin summit in late March, former Italian Prime Minister Prodi. Working with the member state nominees, he began to form his team after the elections to the new European Parliament in June 1999. Striving for political balance among Europe's leading parties and to name at least five women to the Commission, Prodi announced his complete team, by common accord with the member states, in early July (see Table 3.3). The EP approved the new Commission in September 1999, but only after the customary parliamentary hearings with the individual nominees for Commission posts and after Prodi had announced plans for a wide-ranging reform of the Commission's methods of work and the Commission bureaucracy. By agreement with the EP and the member states, the Commission was to serve the remaining four months of the 1995–1999 Commission as well as the five-year term slated to begin on January 1, 2000.

Four of Prodi's commissioners were holdovers from the previous Commission, and most of the commissioners had served as ministers or members of parliament in their home countries. Several had experience in law, business, and academia. This diverse but high-powered team faced the daunting task of regaining the trust of the EP and the public and reforming the Commission's bureaucracy, even as it tackled the EU's massive policy agenda for the first decade of the new century (see Box 3.1).

THE COUNCIL OF MINISTERS

Also known since the Maastricht Treaty as the Council of the European Union, the Council of Ministers is the EU's primary legislative body. It is composed of one minister from each member state. The composition of the Council changes, depending upon the subject under discussion. The General Affairs Council consists of the ministers of foreign affairs and is responsible for a broad range of EU-related issues. For other issue areas, there are councils of economy and finance ministers (the so-called ECOFIN council), agriculture ministers, transport ministers, and so forth.

Each year more than one hundred Council sessions take place. The frequency and importance of the different types of sessions vary depending upon the degree to which an issue area is subject to EU competence. Agriculture is an area in which the member states have transferred most policy-making responsibilities to the EU level. The agriculture ministers thus meet every month to decide such matters as commodity prices and subsidy levels. In contrast, education remains largely a member state responsibility. Education ministers generally meet two or three times a year to discuss those aspects of education policy that may require EU-level action, for example mutual recognition of diplomas or EU-wide student exchanges. Environment, transport, and other areas lie somewhere between these two extremes, and ministers responsible for these areas meet three or four times each year.

The presidency of the Council rotates among the member states on a six-month basis. The presidency country is responsible for preparing the schedule of and chairing Council meetings, not only of the ministers themselves but of the many working groups of experts and civil servants from the member states that

Table 3.3   European Commission, 1999–2005

Commissioner	Portfolio	Background and Previous Positions
Romano Prodi (Italy)	President	Prime minister; industrialist; university professor
Neil Kinnock (UK)	Vice President, Administrative Reform	Transport commissioner, 1995–1999; head of British Labour party
Loyola de Palacio (Spain)	Vice President, Relations with the European Parliament, Transport and Energy	Agriculture minister; MP; lawyer
Mario Monti (Italy)	Competition	Internal Market commissioner, 1995–1999; professor of economics and management
Franz Fischler (Austria)	Agriculture, Rural Development and Fisheries	Agriculture commissioner, 1995–1999; minister of agriculture; farmer
Erkki Liikanen (Finland)	Enterprise and Information Society	Budget commissioner, 1995–1999; minister of finance and interior; MP
Frits Bolkestein (Netherlands)	Internal Market	President of Dutch Liberal party; oil company executive; foreign and defense minister
Philippe Busquin (Belgium)	Research	Leader of the Francophone Socialist party; MP; physicist
Pedro Sobles Mira (Spain)	Economic and Monetary Affairs	Minister for economics and finance; lawyer
Poul Nielsen (Denmark)	Development and Humanitarian Aid	Minister for development aid
Günter Verheugen (Germany)	Enlargement	Minister for European affairs; party official and journalist
Chris Patten (UK)	External Relations	Governor of Hong Kong; MP; Conservative party official
Pascal Lamy (France)	Trade	Former chef de cabinet to Delors
David Byrne (Ireland)	Health and Consumer Protection	Attorney General; lawyer
Michel Barnier (France)	Regional Policy	European affairs minister
Viviane Reding (Luxembourg)	Education and Culture	MEP; MP; journalist
Michaele Schreyer (Germany)	Budget	Berlin senator for environment; Green party politician
Margot Wallström (Sweden)	Environment	Social affairs minister; culture minister; journalist
Antonio Vitorino (Portugal)	Justice and Home Affairs	Constitutional court judge; deputy prime minister; minister of defense
Anna Diamantopoulou (Greece)	Employment and Social Affairs	Junior industry minister; civil engineer

---

Box 3.1   European Commission, Strategic Objectives 2000–2005

The Commission adopts an annual work program of legislation that it intends to introduce and other policy initiatives. The Prodi Commission also adopted a five-year set of strategic objectives called *Shaping the New Europe*.

Promoting new forms of European governance. This means giving people greater say in the way Europe is run; making the institutions work more effectively and transparently, notably by reforming the Commission and setting an example for other bodies; adapting the institutions to the needs of enlargement; building new forms of partnership between the different levels of governance in Europe; and ensuring an active and distinctive European contribution to the development of global governance.

A stable Europe with a stronger voice in the world. As a top priority we will work to make a success of enlargement and to build a real policy of cooperation with our new neighbours. We will also aim at closer cooperation between European institutions and amongst the Member States and at enabling Europe to take a lead in building the new global economy.

A new economic and social agenda. This means modernising our economy for the digital age in a manner which promotes employment and sustainable development, whilst re-modeling our systems of social protection in order to build a fair and caring society.

A better quality of life. Here we must provide effective answers to the issues which affect the daily lives of our citizens, notably the environment, food safety, consumer rights, justice and security against crime.

---

hammer out the technical details of legislation.[3] On contentious or deadlocked issues, the presidency country, often working with the Commission, will come up with compromise positions for presentation to the other member states. By tradition, states holding the presidency are not expected to use this position to pursue narrow national economic and political interests. However, as a rule the presidency country picks one or two themes or policy issues of particular interest that it seeks to highlight in its presidency. During recent presidencies, for example, Spain has focused on EU ties with the Mediterranean, Germany on enlargement to central and eastern Europe, and the UK on employment and bringing the Union closer to its citizens.

The Council is assisted by a general-secretariat. With approximately 2,000 permanent staff members, including technical experts, translators, and specialists in EU law, this Brussels-based office provides continuity and institutional memory for the Council as the presidency rotates. It is headed by a general secretary, who is appointed unanimously by the Council. As one of the reforms intended to strengthen CFSP, the Treaty of Amsterdam stipulates that the secretary-general is also the EU High Representative for the CFSP and assigns the running of the general-secretariat to the newly created post of deputy secretary general.

Another important body linked to the Council is the Committee of Permanent Representatives, or COREPER, which consists of the permanent representatives (ambassadors) of the member states to the EU in Brussels. There is also a second committee, consisting of deputy permanent representatives, that assumes part of the workload. These bodies (COREPER I and COREPER II) meet on a weekly basis and play a key role in working out policy issues before they reach the ministerial level. Many formal acts of legislation in the Council are in fact pro forma ratifications of positions that have been settled in COREPER. This prevents overloading of the agenda of the ministerial meetings and allows the ministers to concentrate on the more difficult issues where political decisions are required.

Unlike the Commission, which is a supranational body in which the member states as such are not represented, the Council combines elements of supranationality and intergovernmentalism. As in other international bodies, member states are represented on and through the Council. On most matters of EU legislation, however, the individual member states do not have a veto. Voting is by qualified majority. In addition, of course, the right to initiate legislation rests not with the ministers on the Council but with the Commission.

Qualified majority voting (QMV) was established in the 1957 Treaty of Rome and was to have been phased in during the 1960s in areas of limited political sensitivity. But, as has been seen, it ran into strong objections from France, with the result that under the Luxembourg Compromise the member states tacitly refrained from its use. In the early 1980s President Mitterrand ceased to insist on the Luxembourg Compromise. Since then, QMV has expanded into numerous areas of policy and law. It is not used in the second and third pillars of the Union (with some minor exceptions), as well as in some policy areas subject to first-pillar decision-making that are especially sensitive politically, such as taxation. Council decisions on admission of new members also require unanimity. In general, however, QMV is the rule.

In today's fifteen-member Union, sixty-two votes out of the total of eighty-seven are required to pass legislation on matters governed by QMV. This means that twenty-six votes constitute a blocking minority. Any three large member states can block a piece of legislation but two alone cannot. Even if they all join together, the ten smaller states cannot pass legislation over the objections of the larger members. Conversely, with only forty-eight total votes, the five largest member states must win the support of at least three small states to pass a measure. In practice, votes rarely if ever break down into small versus large state coalitions. Different voting combinations occur, depending on the matter at issue. But QMV is a device for balancing the requirements of efficiency and supranationality with respect for the sovereignty and the distinctive economic and political circumstances of the member states. It represents a compromise between the kind of decision-making by consensus that is used in many international organizations but that tends to block action on controversial issues and simple majority voting that may be appropriate for a fairly homogeneous federal state such as the United States but that could prove divisive in a body of diverse nation-states such as the EU.

QMV increases the efficiency of Council decision-making. As long as any one state was able to block decisions, the Council often found it almost impossible to pass legislation needed to complete the internal market or to fulfil other policy goals. There almost always was at least one member with an objection to a given piece of legislation. Moreover, the knowledge that each state had a veto tended to encourage obstructionist behavior, as governments knew they had to explain back home why they did not use the veto to block legislation that might adversely affect a national interest. Under QMV, one or two states are unable to block a law favored by the other members. National governments can claim that they were—or would have been—outvoted on a particular measure. QMV thus tends to discourage opposition, as member states which are skeptical about or opposed to a proposed law often are better served by joining the majority and working to modify what they see as its most objectionable parts rather than simply adopting a negative stance in which they are sure to be outvoted.

As shown in Table 3.1, the weighting of votes in the Council is based roughly on population size, but the weights do not fully compensate the larger member states for the size of their populations. Germany, for example, has more than five times as many people as the Netherlands, but it has only twice the number of votes. As the EU has enlarged over the years, the total number of votes in the Council has increased, but the member states have adhered to a general rule that a qualified majority is about 70 percent of all votes.

In addition to being the primary legislative body in the EU's first pillar, the Council of Ministers takes the lead in formulating and implementing policy in the second and third pillars. Under the CFSP provisions of the Maastricht Treaty, the Council takes decisions on joint actions, on the basis of general guidelines from the European Council. As noted, the Treaty of Amsterdam further institutionalized the CFSP role of the Council by creating the post of EU High Representative for the CFSP in the general-secretariat.

Along with the Commission president, the rotating president of the Council represents the EU at important international meetings. Under an agreement signed by the United States and the EU in 1990, for example, the two sides hold summit meetings every six months in which the U.S. president has two interlocutors—the Commission president and the leader of the country holding the presidency of the Council. Similarly, the EU is represented at Group of Seven (G-7) meetings by two leaders, the Commission president and the current president of the Council. If the president is from one of the EU member states that is a part of the G-7— France, Germany, Italy, or the UK—he or she represents both the union and his or her own country. If the presidency country is one of the eleven other member states, the EU is represented by the leader of this country as well.

Qualified majority voting remains a subject of some political controversy in the EU. Those that support a strong, federal Europe, such as the Commission and some of the smaller states (e.g., the Benelux), tend to favor the extension of such voting to areas still subject to national veto. Other states, and especially the UK, have been much more cautious about extending majority voting to sensitive foreign policy and immigration matters. CFSP decision-making, especially as it relates to decisions with defense implications and the use of military force, remains firmly intergovernmental, subject to unanimous voting. However, the Amsterdam reforms, which were intended to increase the effectiveness of CFSP, did introduce more QMV into the second pillar. Once the European Council has adopted a common strategy toward a particular region under CFSP, the Council of Ministers may adopt by QMV joint actions and common positions to implement the strategy.

The Treaty of Amsterdam also increased the use of QMV for certain justice and home affairs questions by moving them from the third to the first pillar. It did so, however, in a rather cautious way. The treaty stipulated that in the first five years after its entry into force, the Council must act unanimously to establish an EU policy on asylum, refugees, and immigration policy. After five years, the Council may use qualified majority voting in regard to these matters, but only after unanimously deciding which aspects of asylum, refugee, and immigration policy may be subject to QMV.

THE EUROPEAN COUNCIL

At first glance the European Council seems very similar to the Council of Ministers, an institution with which it is sometimes confused. In fact, the two bodies are quite different. The European Council consists of the heads of state or government of the member states, along with the president of the Commission. In practice, this means the prime ministers of the fifteen member states, plus the presidents of France and Finland, who under those countries' constitutions have important policy responsibilities as well as a ceremonial role. Foreign ministers are also present at European Council meetings.

The European Council was not one of the original institutions of the EC in the 1950s. It began in 1974 when the European leaders agreed to hold regular summit meetings to discuss Community business and to provide political momentum to the integration process. The European Council convenes twice a year, usually in June and December, near the end of each country presidency. The country that has the rotating presidency of the Council of Ministers also chairs the European Council and hosts the semiannual summit. The presidency country also may convene special sessions of the European Council to address a specific problem or highlight a particular issue, such as the March 1999 Berlin summit to work out the EU budget for 2000–2006, or the crucial April 1990 Dublin European Council that launched the IGC on political union. Meetings are less structured and without the large staff of advisers that attend ministerial meetings. They provide the leaders a chance to work out compromises behind the scenes and to better understand the positions of their counterparts from the other member states.

The European Council was given treaty status in the Single European Act and further constitutional status and responsibilities in the Maastricht Treaty, which stipulates that "the European Council shall provide the Union with the necessary impetus for its development and shall define the political guidelines thereof."[4] The European Council rarely takes a formal vote, and it tries not to get too involved in the details of legislation and policy-making, which are left to the other institutions of the Union. It does set basic goals and ensures that the member states and the Commission are behind these goals. The European Council in fact has made the key decisions with respect to all of the major EU initiatives in recent decades: the single market program, economic and monetary union, political union, and enlargement. These decisions usually are codified in a single document called the presidency conclusions that is adopted at each summit and that usually includes requests or instructions to other EU institutions—the Council of Ministers and the Commission—to study certain matters or to come up with concrete policy proposals and legislative initiatives.

The European Council plays an especially important role in CFSP. It sets the general guidelines for EU external action, from which the Council of Ministers and the Commission take their lead. Its pronouncements on Bosnia, South Africa, the Middle East, and other international issues reflect the consensus view of the member states and inevitably carry greater weight in international settings than would statements by individual governments and leaders. As noted, a common strategy adopted by the European Council—such as the strategies for Russia and Ukraine adopted in 1999—establishes a framework for action by the Council of Ministers and the Commission.

The establishment of the European Council and the codification of its role in the basic treaties have altered somewhat the institutional balance in the Union. The prominence of the institution reflects a shift to a more intergovernmental approach to decision-making than was envisioned by Monnet and the founding fathers. The Commission's role as initiator of legislation to some extent has been downgraded by default, as has the legislative oversight role of the Parliament. The EP has struggled to increase its ability to oversee the activities of the European Commission and to share power with the Council of Ministers, only to see power accumulate in the hands of the European Council, over which it exercises no direct control. On the other hand, it can be argued that the European Council meets a genuine need and that without it the EU would not be evolving along a federalist path but more likely would be stagnating from lack of political leadership and an inability to resolve complex problems. With fifteen highly disparate members and a broad array of policy responsibilities in trade, monetary affairs, foreign policy, and other issues, experience suggests that the Union can only progress through the direct and sustained involvement of national leaders in taking key decisions and setting overall directions.

THE EUROPEAN PARLIAMENT

The European Parliament is the only EU law and policy-making body directly elected by the voters. The others all either represent or are appointed by the member states. The Parliament has 626 members (MEPs) who are elected to five-year terms. Voting takes place within the same four-day period in all of the member states. Seats are allocated according to member state population (Table 3.1), but as with the Council the weighting does not fully compensate for differences in size. Germany has 99 members to represent its 81 million people (one MEP per 800,000), Luxembourg six members for a population of just over 400,000 (one per 60,000).

The powers and responsibilities of the Parliament have increased with successive revisions of the founding treaties, both in response to pressures from the Parliament itself and as the member states have recognized a need to give the process of European integration greater democratic legitimacy based on accountability to the citizens. The Parliament began as the Common Assembly of the ECSC. Its members were appointed by the national parliaments and its role in making legislation was advisory and consultative. It was renamed the European Parliament in 1962, and direct election of members took place for the first time in 1979.

While the Council of Ministers remains the primary legislative body, the EU has been evolving in recent decades toward a genuinely bicameral legislative system, with the Council in effect the upper and the EP the lower chamber of the legislative branch. The legislative powers of the Parliament are uneven—strong in some areas and weak or nonexistent in others—the result of a process in which the member states have ceded powers to the Parliament only gradually, in some areas going quite far while in others holding back to preserve national control or else transferring powers to technocratic bodies such as the European Commission or the European Central Bank. The Parliament also has almost no role in two of the most important areas of first-pillar policy-making, agriculture and foreign trade, and its powers generally do not extend to the second and third pillars, where decisions must result from intergovernmental agreement among the member states.

Expansion of the EP's legislative powers has occurred in stages, with each of the major treaties and treaty revisions adding to its powers. Under the original 1957 Treaty of Rome, the Parliament was a purely consultative body. The Council of Ministers was required to solicit its opinion regarding certain legislation, but it was free to ignore this opinion when passing directives and regulations. The Single European Act established a cooperation procedure under which the Parliament began to share genuine legislative responsibilities with the Council. Under this procedure, the Parliament could reject, by a vote of a majority of its members, a measure passed by the Council. The Council could still pass the measure, but only if it acted unanimously. Because the SEA also greatly expanded the use of qualified majority voting in Council decision-making, the cooperation procedure constituted an important check on the legislative powers of the Council.

The Maastricht Treaty introduced a third legislative procedure, co-decision. Under this procedure, the Council and the Parliament are obliged to agree on legislation for it to pass. If they do not agree, they are required to form a conciliation commission to work out their differences and approve a common legal text. If they cannot do so, the Parliament's opposition blocks passage, even if the Council acts unanimously. Legislation passed under the co-decision procedure is promulgated in the name of both the Parliament and the Council, as it is truly decided by both institutions wielding roughly equal powers. A fourth procedure, the assent procedure, involves a simple yes or no vote by the Parliament. It is used to approve decisions taken on a unanimous basis by the Council of Ministers in areas relating to international agreements and certain politically and constitutionally sensitive matters, such as the admission of new member states.

After the reforms introduced by the Amsterdam Treaty, a simplified version of the co-decision procedure has become the general rule for the passage of EU legislation. The cooperation procedure has almost been abolished, and is still used only in certain matters relating to EMU, where the Parliament has pressed for increased influence but in which the member states and the European central banking community are wary of greater political involvement. The assent procedure is used to approve the accession of new states, the conclusion of association and other international agreements with budgetary implications, certain specialized matters relating to regional aid and the functions of the European Central Bank, and to approve sanctions against a member state regarded as in serious and persistent breach of fundamental rights. There is also a separate approval process for the EU budget.

In addition to its legislative role, the Parliament has come to exercise a growing influence over appointments to key EU posts. It also exercises controls over executive actions, often by uncovering and disseminating information. It can launch investigations, hold public hearings, set up temporary committees of inquiry, and pose oral and written questions to the Commission and the Council.

Originally, the Parliament had no say over appointments by the member states. Under the Maastricht Treaty, it was to be consulted on the choice of the Commission president and on the Commission as a whole, as well as on appointments to the Court of Auditors and the key positions in the European Central Bank. The Commission and the Commission president then were subject as a body to a vote of approval by the EP.

Under the Treaty of Amsterdam, the Parliament must approve the member states' nominee for the president of the Commission, who then works with the member state governments to select the other commissioners. The Commission is then subject as a body to a vote of approval by the Parliament. The Parliament first exercised its new rights under the Amsterdam Treaty on May 5, 1999—four days after the new treaty went into effect—when it voted 392 to 72, with 41 abstentions, to approve Romano Prodi. It held hearings with the other Commission nominees in early September, and on September 15 approved the whole Commission by a vote of 414 to 142, with 35 abstentions.

The Parliament may dismiss the Commission if it passes a vote of censure against the body as a whole. (It may not dismiss individual commissioners.) There were four such votes of censure between 1979 and 1998, none of which was successful. However, the threat of censure is a powerful reserve weapon, and the likelihood that it would have been used successfully accounted in large part for the decision of the commissioners in March 1999 to step down voluntarily following the release of the independent experts' report documenting financial mismanagement and other failures by several commissioners.

The Parliament must approve and has certain powers to amend the preliminary draft budget submitted by the Commission and approved by the Council for the coming fiscal year. This gives it substantial influence over the budgetary process, which it has used to promote programs of special interest to MEPs, such as increased spending for research and development and certain forms of regional and foreign assistance. However, the Parliament's role in budgetary matters is circumscribed by two factors. First, the level of EU expenditures is largely set by the member states. The Parliament thus mainly can shift spending from one priority to another, but it cannot determine the overall size of the budget. Second, much EU spending is "compulsory," meaning it is dedicated to the CAP and the structural funds. In shifting spending priorities in the EU budget, the Parliament's powers apply chiefly to noncompulsory expenditures that are not already mandated by other EU policies.

In addition to approving the budget for the next fiscal year, the Parliament must "give a discharge" to the Commission for its implementation of the previous year's budget. In other words, it must check that in implementing the budget, the Commission has spent the funds allocated in accordance with the categories and purposes established in the budget and without fraud or mismanagement. It bases its decision on the Commission's own financial report and reports by the Court of Auditors. The Parliament has used this power to bring pressure on the Commission to improve its management practices, most notably in December 1998 when it refused to approve the 1996 budget, precipitating the clash that led to the resignation of the Santer Commission early the following year.

In conducting its work, the EP is organized much like a national parliament, although it confronts certain special problems owing to its multinational makeup and the complexity of its relations with other EU institutions.[5] The MEPs elect a president, traditionally from one of the two main political groupings, the Socialists and the Christian Democrats, for a two-and-one-half-year period. The president and the fourteen vice presidents, elected for the same term, form the Bureau of the Parliament, which is responsible for the overall direction of the Parliament's activities. As in national parliaments, the EP conducts its work through committees and subcommittees. There are twenty standing committees, as shown in Table 3.4.

In addition to serving on these committees, most MEPs are attached to political groups that correspond to the main European political parties. In the chamber of the Parliament, members sit by political group, not by national delegations. The two largest groups by far are the Group of the Party of European Socialists and the Group of the European People's Party, or Christian Democrats (Table 3.5). There are also Liberal, Green, radical left, and three other political groups. Each group must have a minimum of twenty-nine members if they all come from one

Table 3.4   Standing Committees of the European Parliament

Committee on Foreign Affairs, Security and Defense Policy
Committee on Agriculture and Rural Development
Committee on Budgets
Committee on Economic and Monetary Affairs and Industrial Policy
Committee on Research, Technological Development and Energy
Committee on External Economic Relations
Committee on Legal Affairs and Citizens' Rights
Committee on Social Affairs and Employment
Committee on Regional Policy
Committee on Transport and Tourism
Committee on the Environment, Public Health and Consumer Protection
Committee on Culture, Youth, Education and the Media
Committee on Development and Cooperation
Committee on Civil Liberties and Internal Affairs
Committee on Budgetary Control
Committee on Institutional Affairs
Committee on Fisheries
Committee on the Rules of Procedure, the Verification of Credentials and Immunities
Committee on Women's Rights
Committee on Petitions

member state, twenty-three if they come from two member states, eighteen if from three member states, and fourteen if they come from four or more member states. A few MEPs are unattached, but in general members have an incentive to join or form political groups, since the groups work with the EP president in organizing the Parliament's work and drawing up its agenda.

Despite the formidable array of powers that the Parliament wields, it suffers from several major weaknesses that have hindered its development into a co-legislative body with powers equal to those of the Council. The first area of weakness concerns the sheer complexity of the Parliament's legislative powers. This has tended to confuse the voters and to create the impression that the member states have carefully parceled out powers to the Parliament, always holding back in those areas about which national governments care most. The Treaty of Amsterdam attempted to address this issue by evening out and simplifying the powers of the Parliament. It effectively abolished the cooperation procedure, making most areas of legislation subject to the stronger co-decision procedure, which was itself simplified. The treaty also extended the power of the Parliament by moving certain matters previously handled in the third pillar, such as immigration and asylum, into the first pillar where they will be subject to parliamentary decision-making procedures. Still, complexity remains a hallmark of the Parliament's role, reflecting as it does the underlying differences among and within the member states about the extent to which the Union should derive its powers directly from the voters as opposed to from the member states acting within the Council of Ministers.

Table 3.5 EP Parliamentary Groups, 2000–2004

		BELG	DK	GER	GR	SPAIN	FR	IRL	ITALY	LUX	NETH	AUST	PORT	FIN	SWED	UK	TOTAL
EPP	Group of the European People's Party	6	1	53	9	29	15	4	32	2	9	7	9	5	7	36	224
PES	Group of the Party of European Socialists	5	3	33	9	24	22	1	17	2	6	7	12	3	6	30	180
ELDR	Group of the European Liberal Democratic and Reform Party	5	6			2		1	1	1	8			5	4	10	43
G	Green Group in the European Parliament	5		7			9	2	2	1	4	2		2	2	2	38
GUE/NGL	Confederal Group of the European United Left/Nordic Green Left		1	6	5	4	6		6		1		2	1	3		35
I-EdN	Group of Independents for a Europe of Nations		4				13				3						1	21
NI		2					5		5			5				1	18
UPE	Group Union for Europe							6	9				2				17
ARE	Group of the European Radical Alliance	2				2			7							2	13
	Not attached		1		2	3	17	1	8							5	37
TOTAL		25	16	99	25	64	87	15	87	6	31	21	25	16	22	87	626

The second area of EP weakness is practical, and concerns location, language, and parliamentary organization. The seat of the Parliament is Strasbourg, but it holds only some of its plenary sessions there. Committee meetings and some plenary sessions take place in Brussels, while most committee staff work in Luxembourg. MEPs and parliamentary staff spend an inordinate amount of time traveling between these cities as well as to their home constituencies, many of which are quite remote given the Union's enlargements of the 1980s and the 1990s. These arrangements in turn result in high costs for travel and duplicate facilities that increase public skepticism about the Parliament. It is difficult to see how the Parliament can function as a truly equal branch in the EU's governing bodies without being located in the de facto capital city of Brussels. So far, however, the member states, and especially France, have resisted such a move. France argues that the Parliament is the only EU institution located on its territory, and that a move to Brussels would be politically unacceptable. Language presents another major challenge. To communicate with and represent their constituents, MEPs must speak in their national languages. But this makes open debate somewhat stilted and artificial as it must be conducted through simultaneous translation.

Finally, sheer size is a problem. The Parliament began in 1958 with 142 members delegated by the national parliaments of the six member states. In 1973, it increased to 198 members with the accession of Denmark, Ireland, and the UK. In 1979, the size of the Parliament was increased to 410 members to create smaller electoral districts for the first direct elections of MEPs. By 1986 the Parliament's size had increased to 518 as a result of the accessions of Greece, Spain, and Portugal. There was a further increase to 567 members in 1994 to account for German unification, and to the present 626 members in 1995 with the accession of Austria, Finland, and Sweden. Few national parliaments are this large, and unchecked further growth would make the EP too unwieldy to serve as a forum for genuine democratic debate. The Treaty of Amsterdam thus includes a provision stipulating that the total number of members of the Parliament will not exceed seven hundred. This leaves some room for growth associated with enlargement, but it also means that if all or most of the candidate countries become EU members there will have to be a reapportionment of seats and some downward adjustment in the number of representatives from current member countries.

THE COURT OF JUSTICE

The Court of Justice is the judicial authority that interprets EU law and ensures that it is applied uniformly throughout the member states. It is composed of 15 judges who are appointed by common accord of the member states. These individuals serve terms of six years, which may be renewed. The judges are assisted by nine advocates-general whose role is to impartially argue cases before the Court. Both judges and advocates-general must be independent and possess the qualifications required for appointment to the highest judicial office in their own countries. The Court is located in Luxembourg.

The Court mainly hears cases brought by the institutions of the Union and the EU member states or that are referred to it by national courts. It is not like the U.S. Supreme Court, in that it is not a forum in which the constitutionality of national or lower court rulings and legislative acts can be appealed. The ECJ can only rule on whether such decisions or acts are consistent with EU law. Since 1954, over 9,000 cases have been brought before the Court, which has delivered over 4,000 judgments. These cases can be divided into two general categories: direct actions and preliminary rulings. Direct actions apply to the parties in a given case. Preliminary rulings have no direct legal effect, but are delivered to courts or tribunals of the member states when they need advice on how points of national law relate to EU law, and especially on whether national legislation is or may come into conflict with EU legislation.

Attached to the ECJ is the Court of First Instance, which was established in 1989 to relieve the ECJ of part of its enormous workload. Its structure and composition is similar to that of the ECJ. It hears virtually all cases brought by individuals as well as competition policy cases and other cases of less than constitutional import, leaving the Court of Justice more time to concentrate on cases with broader implications. The ECJ must hear all cases brought by the Commission against a member state, by one member state against another, or between institutions of the EU.

In interpreting EU law, the Court often has taken an expansive view of its role, pronouncing not just on the appropriateness of measures in narrow, technical terms but interpreting these measures in terms of the broad objectives outlined in the founding treaties. In this way, it has developed a body of EU jurisprudence that underpins the integration process and that influences the work of the Commission as it formulates initiatives and drafts EU legislation. The development of EU law and the important role of the ECJ in deciding landmark cases on which this law is based are discussed later in this chapter.

Other EU Bodies

THE ECONOMIC AND SOCIAL COMMITTEE

This committee was set up under the Treaty of Rome at a time when the Parliament was still very weak and played only a consultative role. It reflects a lingering corporatist tradition in Europe, which holds that different economic interests should have a direct role in economic and political decision-making, in addition to such representation that takes place through parliamentary bodies at the national and European levels.

The members of the ESC are drawn from three groups: employers, workers (mainly trade unions), and a broad category of other interests that includes farmers, small and medium sized businesses, the professions, consumer groups, cooperatives, and ecological movements. Members are appointed by the Council of Ministers for four-year terms from lists of nominees submitted by the member state governments. The ESC currently has 222 members who serve on a part-time basis: twenty-four each from France, Germany, Italy, and the UK; twenty-one from Spain; twelve each from Austria, Belgium, Greece, the Netherlands, Portugal, and Sweden; nine each from Denmark, Finland, and Ireland; and six from Luxembourg.

Numerous provisions of the Treaty of Rome stipulate that the ESC must be consulted before legislation can be adopted. The Committee also can offer opinions on subjects of its choosing that are relevant to the EU. Working through specialized subcommittees and in plenary sessions, it delivers about 200 such opinions a year. The Committee's influence on legislation is quite limited, however, since the Council of Ministers is under no obligation to accept its suggestions and since advice on legislation comes from many other sources, including lobbyists working on behalf of particular interests that have direct access to the Commission, member state governments, and the Parliament.

THE COMMITTEE OF THE REGIONS

The Committee of the Regions was established by the Maastricht Treaty, largely at the urging of the Federal Republic of Germany. As its name indicates, Germany has a federal system of government in which the states—Bavaria, Saxony, Hesse, and so forth—exercise important governmental responsibilities in such areas as education, culture, and regional development. Other EU member states in which subnational governments are especially important include Belgium, Spain, and the UK. Regional governments had long complained that they had no direct input into decisions taken in Brussels that affected areas for which they were responsible.

The establishment of the Committee of the Regions was an attempt to remedy this situation by providing a vehicle through which subnational regions can influence EU decision-making. The Maastricht Treaty requires that the committee be consulted on legislation relating to trans-European networks, public health, education, youth, culture, and economic and social cohesion. The Committee also can give opinions on other matters that affect regions and cities, such as agricultural and environmental policy. The Committee's role is purely consultative, however, and its ability to influence legislation is limited. The Committee has 222 members, the same number as the Economic and Social Committee, distributed in the same way among the member states. These individuals are mostly elected officials from the regions, such as mayors, regional presidents, and chairpersons of county councils.

THE COURT OF AUDITORS

The Court of Auditors monitors the EU budget, both expenditures and the collection of revenues, and draws up an annual report on its findings for the Council of

Ministers and the EP. It also can prepare special reports on financial questions and deliver opinions at the request of other EU institutions. Located in Luxembourg, it has fifteen members, one from each EU state, who are appointed by the Council after consultation with the Parliament. These individuals must have had experience in their national audit bodies or be otherwise especially qualified. They are supported by a staff of accountants, auditors, and other specialists. The importance of the Court of Auditors and its work have been highlighted in recent years by the many cases of fraud and mismanagement in the handling of EU funds, culminating in the Commission's resignation in March 1999.

THE EUROPEAN INVESTMENT BANK

The EIB was set up in 1958 to provide loans to public and private sector projects that advance Community objectives, especially those that contribute to completing the common market. It has since become the world's largest development bank, with over $20 billion in loans each year. It is owned by the member states of the EU. Its excellent credit rating allows it to raise capital on European markets which it relends at favorable rates of interest, usually to co-finance projects with private sector and other governmental lenders and investors. The bank is headquartered in Luxembourg.

The EIB plays a key role in EU regional policy, where its loans to projects in depressed regions and to the poorer member states complement grant aid from the EU's structural funds. EIB loans also support EU environmental projects and trans-European networks, the large cross-border projects in transport, energy, and telecommunications promoted by the Union. More than 90 percent of EIB loans go to projects inside the EU, but a growing share of lending is to nonmember countries made in support of EU developmental and foreign policy. The EIB provides loans to the African, Caribbean, and Pacific (ACP) countries with which the EU is associated, to the countries of central and eastern Europe that are preparing for accession, and to the countries of North Africa and the Middle East that participate in the Euro-Mediterranean Partnership launched by the EU in 1995.

THE EUROPEAN CENTRAL BANK

The newest of the major EU institutions is the European Central Bank, which was formally established in June 1998, taking over the responsibilities of a transitional body, the European Monetary Institute, that was set up under the Maastricht Treaty to assist with preparations for the single currency. Located in Frankfurt, the ECB is the central institution of the European System of Central Banks, the network of national central banks established to conduct a single European monetary policy. The ECB is discussed in detail in Chapter 6.

SPECIALIZED AGENCIES

In addition to the treaty-based institutions that make law and policy, the EU has established an array of specialized agencies that are responsible for monitoring and helping to implement policy in particular fields such as the environment, workplace health and safety, and testing and certification of technical standards. As the range of EU policies has widened and the body of legislation has grown, the need for such agencies has become more apparent. The Commission bureaucracy lacks the staff and expertise to involve itself in all of the technical and administrative aspects of policy implementation and must in any case focus on its key responsibilities of initiating legislative proposals, guarding against infringements of the treaties, and executing major policy initiatives. The member states have been wary of establishing agencies with real powers at the Union level, but they increasingly have recognized the need for bodies that can bring together the different national perspectives. For the most part they have limited the regulatory and inspection powers of these bodies and have stressed that their role is to gather information on policies and standards, many of which are made at the national level in accordance with EU directives. These bodies are dispersed throughout the territory of the Union, as shown in Table 3.6.

The European Environment Agency (EEA) began work in December 1993, and is responsible for coordinating environmental assessments from a network of institutes from throughout Europe and for disseminating the results of these assessments to the Parliament, the Commission, the member states, and the general public. The European Training Foundation is responsible for coordinating and supporting all EU activities in the field of postcompulsory education and training, including those conducted under EU aid programs. The European Monitoring Center for Drugs and Drug Addiction became operational in 1995, based on a Council regulation of February 1993. Its aim is to provide "objective, reliable and comparable information at European level concerning drugs, drug addiction, and their consequences."[6]

Table 3.6   EU Agencies and Bodies

European Agency for the Evaluation of Medicinal Products—London
European Environment Agency—Copenhagen
European Training Foundation—Turin
European Center for the Development of Vocational Training—Thessaloniki
European Monitoring Center for Drugs and Drug Addiction—Lisbon
European Foundation for the Improvement of Living and Working Conditions—Dublin
Office for Harmonization in the Internal Market (Trade Marks and Designs)—Alicante
Community Plant Variety Rights Office—Angers
European Agency for Safety and Health at Work—Bilbao
European Monitoring Center on Racism and Xenophobia—Vienna
European Police Office (EUROPOL)—The Hague

The European Agency for the Evaluation of Medicinal Products was established in January 1995, and is responsible for ensuring the uniform evaluation and labeling of products in the single market. The Office for Harmonization in the Internal Market began work in September 1994. It registers and administers EU trade marks and designs, an important function in the internal market for intellectual property. Other agencies are the Agency for Health and Safety at Work and the Office for Veterinary and Plant-Health Inspection and Control that is to be established in Ireland.

Europol (discussed in detail in Chapter 7) is not technically an EU agency, since it deals with matters falling under the intergovernmental third pillar of the Union. Whereas the other EU agencies were established by Council regulations on the basis of Commission proposals, Europol rests on a separate international convention concluded among the member states. Nonetheless, it functions very much as an EU agency in that it gathers information from the member states and seeks to assist in the coordination of policy.

How these specialized agencies develop and the extent to which new agencies and regulatory bodies are established at the EU level will be important indicators of the future development of the Union. Two conflicting tendencies are at work. On the one hand, the member states and public opinion in general are wary of creating new centralized bureaucracies outside the control of national governments. This argues for a minimalist approach to institution building. On the other hand, the increasing complexity of technical issues involved in regulating the single market, the unevenness of national capabilities to regulate and inspect in certain areas, and the desire of the Commission and some member states to have strong European counterparts to such internationally influential U.S. agencies as the Food and Drug Administration, the Federal Aviation Agency, and the Environmental Protection Agency (EPA) all argue in the direction of stronger central bodies.

The member states have agreed in principle to establish a single agency to monitor aviation safety. Following politically charged controversies over genetically modified organisms, "mad cow disease," and other food- and health-related issues, they also have agreed to establish a European-level food safety agency. Germany would like to see the establishment of a European anti-trust authority to parallel the Federal Cartel Office that operates at the national level. The EP has called for giving the European Environment Agency actual regulatory powers that would make it more like the U.S. EPA. The Commission has raised the idea of a single telecommunications authority to oversee competition in this sector.

All of these proposals reflect the pressures operating in the direction of stronger, more centralized agencies and a certain federalization of regulation in the Union. At the same time, however, they all provoke resistance from those committed to halting the drift in power to Brussels and reasserting the primacy of the member state governments. As these tendencies coexist and interact, the outcome is likely to be a dual system of monitoring and regulation in which powers are exercised at both the EU and member state levels.

The Ongoing Role of the Member States

Before leaving the subject of the EU institutions and turning to EU law, it is important to recall the central role of the member states. The EU is unique among international bodies in the degree to which its members have pooled sovereignty and delegated powers to central institutions. At the same time, however, it is important not to underestimate the role of the member states or the ongoing relevance of national interest and domestic politics in the integration process. There are four reasons why the member states remain prime actors in the EU.

First, they are directly represented in two of the Union's key decision-making bodies, the Council of Ministers and the European Council, and they determine the membership of two other major decision-making bodies, the Commission and the Court of Justice. They also select the president and governing bodies of the ECB. Member state positions in the European Council and the Council of Ministers as well as attempts by national capitals to influence the Commission and the ECB are based on calculations of concrete national economic and political interest, rather than on commitment to the abstract ideal of European unity.

Second, in some EU policy areas, notably CFSP and some areas of justice and home affairs, decision-making remains largely intergovernmental. The member states are committed by treaty to developing common positions and undertaking joint actions, but these are the positions and actions of sovereign states agreeing to work together, not a single position worked out by centralized institutions exercising their own powers. The difficulties that the EU has had in forging a CFSP or in tackling issues such as immigration at the European level underline the persistence of different national traditions and interests among the member states—differences that in some respects have grown wider with each enlargement.

Third, in other policy areas competence either remains entirely with the member states or is shared between the Union and the member states. Education, health, social welfare, and culture are largely matters of national responsibility, while competence for transport, regional development, the environment, and competition policy is shared between the EU institutions and the member states. From the early 1970s through the early 1990s there was a tendency for more and more issues to be transferred at least partially to the European level, but this trend was ended with the signing of Maastricht Treaty and the difficult ratification debate that followed. The subsidiarity concept now guides the member states and the central institutions (especially the Commission as the policy initiator) in determining which issues are to be handled at the Union level and which are better left to the member states.

Fourth, the member states play a key role in implementing EU policies—even those that are subject to EU competence. Whereas in the United States the federal government has a nationwide bureaucracy, a huge budget, and a vast body of federal law on which to rely in implementing federal policy, this is not the case in the EU. It has only 20,000 or so employees in Brussels and Luxembourg and a number of modest-sized institutions spread elsewhere throughout the member states. The member states provide the administrative and legal apparatus to implement EU law and policy. Thus, for example, even when the EU adopts a Union-wide environmental protection measure, each member state usually must adopt or amend national legislation to ensure that the EU standard is reflected throughout the Union. National environmental protection agencies in turn are responsible for ensuring that individuals and industries comply with the legislation. As will be seen, much of the legal action that takes place in the ECJ arises from disputes over implementation of EU directives at the national level. Indeed, the importance of EU law is directly linked to the complexities inherent in a situation in which member states, having pooled or delegated their sovereignty in central institutions, still must use their sovereign powers to implement EU decisions.

EU Law

One of the most important features that distinguishes the EU from other international groupings is the existence of a body of law that constitutes, in the words of the ECJ, a "new legal order."[7] EU law is different from international law, in that it has direct effect on citizens and other legal persons and that it must be obeyed by sovereign states that are members of the Union. At the same time, it has not replaced member state law, which co-exists with and is supposed to be consistent with EU law. The EU legal system is sui generis—without ready parallels elsewhere in the world.

EU law can be divided into two main categories: primary and secondary. The founding treaties constitute the primary law of the Union. Such law is made by unanimous agreement among the member states, generally by means of an intergovernmental conference. Primary law requires ratification at the national level by national parliaments and in some cases national referenda. Treaties of accession, which are concluded between existing member states and new members when they join the EU, also constitute primary law, since they amend the existing treaties.

Secondary law consists of legislation passed by the institutions of the EU. It is used to translate the broadly stated objectives and intentions in the treaties into specific rules and policy measures. Although more detailed than national constitutions, the EU's founding treaties cannot possibly spell out all the details of the common policies in trade, transport, competition, and the many other areas covered in the treaties. This has to be done over time through subsequent action by the EU institutions. Legal measures adopted by and through these institutions constitute the secondary law of the Union.

REGULATIONS, DIRECTIVES, AND DECISIONS

The Treaty of Rome specifies three main types of legislative measures (secondary law): regulations, directives, and decisions. Regulations are binding and are directly applicable throughout the Union. In this respect they are analogous to federal law in the United States, which applies directly to individuals and corporate entities. Regulations do not require legal action by the member states to take effect, although the states may need to take administrative steps to ensure implementation. Regulations can be passed either by the Council of Ministers acting on a proposal from the Commission, by the Council and the EP (where the treaties provide for co-decision) acting on a Commission proposal, or by the Commission alone.

Council and Council-EP regulations tend to be of a general nature, and deal with such matters as administration of the structural funds, rules under the common fisheries policy, or guidelines relating to actions by the European Investment Bank. Commission regulations are more narrow and technical, and are often of an administrative nature. Many are used to administer the Common Agricultural Policy. Commission regulations are in many ways analogous to rules promulgated by federal agencies in the United States that are used to implement acts passed by the Congress but that do not in themselves require specific Congressional action. Regulations are used wherever there is a need for total uniformity throughout the Union on a particular matter of EU law.

Directives are binding, "as to the result to be achieved," upon the member states to which they are addressed (generally all of the member states), "but shall leave to the national authorities the choice of form and methods."[8] Directives specify, usually in considerable detail, an EU-wide result, but allow the member states to achieve this result in ways that reflect national legal and administrative traditions, the structure of local industry, and other factors. Examples of objectives pursued through directives include the introduction of competition in the market for voice telephony, reductions in urban air pollution, and policing money laundering and financial crime in the Union.

Directives are proposed by the Commission, based on its interpretation of what needs to be done to fulfil both the specific provisions and the broader purposes of the founding treaties. In accordance with the co-decision procedures introduced by the Maastricht and Amsterdam treaties, they are passed by the Council of Ministers and the Parliament, after consultation as required with the Economic and Social Committee, the Committee of the Regions, or both. Once directives are passed, it is up to the member states to ensure their implementation. The member states are not required to adopt identical implementing legislation, and laws continue to differ in accordance with national traditions and political preferences. But national legislation must accomplish the main objectives of the relevant EU directive. If a member state fails to transpose a directive into national legislation, the Commission can institute proceedings against that state in the Court of Justice.

Decisions are binding measures that are addressed to specific parties and that do not have general applicability. Examples of decisions include Commission actions in competition cases (blocking a merger between two firms or enjoining a national government from providing aid to a firm or industry), or actions taken with regard to specific TEN projects. Decisions can be addressed to all of the member states, often to assist them in clarifying the details regarding implementation of directives, in which case they function very much like regulations.

EU legislation in many sectors is a mixture of directives, regulations, and decisions. The member states generally have favored reliance on the directive with its greater latitude for national interpretation, and have resisted the use of regulations. Most legislation for the 1992 single market program, for example, took the form of directives. The extensive use of directives has both benefits and drawbacks. On the plus side, it moderates the intrusiveness of Brussels in national life and allows for adjustment to local conditions. On the negative side, it makes for a complicated legal order that imposes costs on firms operating across national borders and that is difficult to enforce. The Commission must check to see that national implementing legislation is adopted in each of the member states and that it conforms with the directives, and it must further check on an ongoing basis to ensure that such legislation is applied in practice.

KEY PRINCIPLES

EU law exists in a broader legal and political context—one that has developed over the years through the interaction of the ECJ and the national courts and that is based heavily on the case law of the ECJ. The two most salient principles of EU law are *direct effect* and the *primacy of EU over national law*. Neither principle is explicitly spelled out in the treaties; both developed over time as a result of court rulings.

In the van Gend and Loos case of 1963, a Dutch trucking firm of that name brought suit in a Dutch court against the Dutch state for imposing increased tariffs on a chemical product that it imported to the Netherlands from Germany. This was during the transition period in which all tariffs among the six were being phased out and in which the Treaty of Rome prohibited member states from introducing new tariffs or restrictions on trade. The action by the Dutch government thus appeared to contravene the spirit and letter of the treaty. The Dutch court referred the case to the ECJ, which ruled that the trucking firm enjoyed rights under the treaty. The Court further declared that the new national duties on chemicals that had harmed the business interests of the firm were a contravention of the treaty and were therefore void. The case established what is known as direct effect—the principle that European law has direct applicability to citizens and corporate bodies, conferring rights and imposing obligations.

In other important cases, the ECJ established that in situations in which European and national law were in conflict, EU law had primacy. In the Costa v. ENEL case of 1964, an Italian shareholder in an electricity company recently nationalized by the Italian government refused to pay his electricity bill on the grounds that the nationalization was illegal under Community law. The Italian national court referred the case to the ECJ for a preliminary ruling. The ECJ used the case to develop the doctrine that Community law had supremacy over national law, arguing that in joining the Community the member states had irrevocably surrendered some of their sovereign powers. The court subsequently elaborated and strengthened its position on this matter, notably in the 1978 Simmenthal decision, in which it starkly concluded: "a national court which is called upon, within the limits of its jurisdiction, to apply provisions of Community law is under a duty to give full effect to those provisions, if necessary refusing of its own motion to apply any conflicting provisions of national legislation."[9]

The supremacy of EU law over national law is a remarkable development in the integration process. It in part explains the extreme care with which member countries—by reputation the UK and Denmark but *all* members to some extent—decide to add competence for sensitive policy matters to the EU's first pillar, and their decision to establish separate intergovernmental pillars, beyond the jurisdiction of the ECJ, for foreign and security policy and justice and home affairs.

The Budget

Apart from law, a second feature that distinguishes the EU from other international bodies and that reflects the depth of the integration process is its budget. Unlike international institutions that receive funding from their member states, the EU is financed exclusively by a system of "own resources." In the early years of the Community, the member states paid into the budget as in a traditional international organization. Under the budget treaties of 1970 and 1975, however, the EC gained an autonomous source of revenue. This consisted of three elements: the customs duties collected under the common external tariff, levies on imported agriculture products, and a proportion of the value added tax (VAT) collected in each of the member states. In 1988 the EC added a fourth own resource, which consists of an automatic assessment of each of the member states based on their total and per capita GNPs.

The member states set the level of own resources—and by extension the overall spending level—by unanimous decision in the Council of Ministers. For much of the period that the own resource system has been in operation, the member states have been quite generous with the budget. It has grown more quickly than national budgets, allowing the EU to expand into new areas of activity such as regional policy, precompetitive industrial research, and extensive foreign aid programs for central and eastern Europe and the Mediterranean countries. In recent years, however, the member states have tried to rein in the growth of the EU budget, especially since their own national budgets have had to be trimmed to meet the Maastricht EMU convergence criteria.

Commitments in the 1999 EU budget totaled 94.796 billion euros, or some $100 billion.[10] In national terms, this is a modest figure, amounting to about 2.5 percent of combined public spending of the member states. By most other standards, it is a substantial sum that provides the means for the EU to pursue its internal and external policies. Just under half of the EU budget goes to agriculture, down from nearly 70 percent in the mid-1980s, and slated to be reduced still further through reform of the CAP. About a third of the budget goes to the structural funds to support economic development in the poorer regions of the Union. Slightly over six percent of the budget is used to pay for EU policies in such areas as research and development, the environment, and trans-European networks, and almost seven percent for external policies (chiefly foreign aid). Administrative expenditure—staff, facilities, and other expenses associated with the EU's institutions—accounts for just over five percent of expenditure.

BUDGETARY PROCEDURE

Under the EU budgetary procedures, the Commission draws up a preliminary draft budget which it presents to the Council of Ministers. The Council may and usually does amend the Commission's draft. It then establishes, by qualified majority vote, the draft budget and sends it to the Parliament, which has the right to propose amendments before approving the final budget. In the event of differences between the Council and the Parliament, the Council makes the final decisions on compulsory spending, that is, spending essential to carrying out the obligations of the treaties, such as the CAP. The Parliament makes the final decisions regarding noncompulsory spending, but it is only allowed to increase such expenditure within a certain percentage that is determined each year on the basis of economic growth, inflation, and increases in government spending in the member states. The Parliament also can reject, by a two-thirds vote, the draft budget as a whole and ask that a new budget be submitted.

The budget frequently has been a matter of contention among the member states. In the early 1980s the Community went through a protracted crisis over Britain's contribution to the budget. Because support for farmers was the largest part of the budget and because Britain's agricultural sector was smaller in relative terms than those in other member countries, it paid far more into the Community budget than it received back, even though its per capita GDP trailed the Community average. Prime Minister Thatcher demanded a rebate to bring UK contributions more into line with payments. The other states were reluctant to meet this demand, which in their view would undermine the supranational basis of the Community and establish a principle that states must receive back the equivalent of what they pay into the budget (a principle known as *juste retour*, used in many cooperative European arms and industrial projects, but inimical to efficient decision-making and incompatible with pursuit of such goals as redistribution among member states at different income levels). Nonetheless, after many acrimonious debates in the European Council, at the Fontainebleau summit of 1984 the other member states agreed to British demands for a rebate.

The accessions of Greece in 1981 and Spain and Portugal in 1986 also led to new budgetary challenges. Led by Spain, these countries and Ireland successfully pressed for transfers from the Community budget (structural funds) to help them cope with the economic and political challenges of joining with more advanced countries in the single market program and later EMU. More recently, the question of enlargement and excessive payments by Germany and the Netherlands into the budget have been points of contention.

DELORS I AND II

To introduce an element of predictability in the budget process, since the late 1980s the EU has adopted a series of multi-year budgetary packages that establish a framework for the annual budgets. This approach eliminates much of the political squabbling over money that used to dominate nearly every session of the European Council. It also began as part of a long-overdue effort to begin reining in agricultural spending. The first such multi-year package, known as Delors I, was concluded in February 1988 and covered the five budget years from 1988 to 1992. The package was a political compromise that contained something for everyone: increased aid for Ireland and the Mediterranean countries, the rebate for the UK, higher overall levels of spending for those committed to developing EC policies in new areas, and the beginnings of a reform of agricultural spending but on a gradual basis that would not bring hardship to farmers. Its basic elements included an increase in total funding up to a ceiling of 1.2 percent of Community GDP, the addition of a fourth own resource to cover the increased spending, a continuation of the British rebate, a doubling of the financial flows to the poorer regions of the Community, and a commitment to hold down the growth in agricultural spending to no more than 74 percent of the growth in EC GDP.

Delors I was followed by the seven-year, 1993–1999 Delors II package, worked out by the member states at the December 1992 Edinburgh European Council.[11] The Edinburgh package followed the basic outlines of the previous budget agreement and even increased funding levels somewhat. The revenue ceiling was maintained at 1.2 percent of GNP for 1993 and 1994, but set to rise by increments to 1.27 percent of GNP by 1999. The 1988 guideline limiting increases in CAP expenditure to 74 percent of the rate of growth of EU GNP was retained, as was the British rebate. The member states agreed to another large increase in structural funds for the poorer parts of the Union, from ECU 21.277 billion in 1993 to 30.000 billion in 1999, or some 41 percent. The Cohesion Fund established by the Maastricht Treaty to help countries with a per capita GNP of less than 90 percent of the EU average was funded at ECU 1.5 billion, rising to 2.6 billion in 1999. Total spending on structural and cohesion funding was to reach 0.46 percent of EU GNP by the last year of the Delors II package. The other noteworthy aspect of the Edinburgh agreement was the rise in spending for external policies, from ECU 4.450 billion in 1993 to ECU 6.200 billion in 1999, undertaken largely in response to the upheavals underway in central and eastern Europe.

THE 2000–2006 BUDGET PACKAGE

The pending expiration of the Delors II package, the start of enlargement negotiations, and political change in the member states all converged at the end of the 1990s to produce a major debate about EU finances. This debate was driven by two factors: on the one hand the member states were concerned about their own financial positions. In the post-Maastricht period of skepticism about integration and EMU-driven austerity, those countries that paid most into the EU's coffers wanted to reduce their net contributions while those that received net transfers from the budget were reluctant to give up this source of income. On the other hand, the EU was faced with potentially vast new demands on its budget as new members joined. As Belgian Prime Minister Jean-Luc Dehaene summed up the dilemma, "nobody wants to pay more, some want to pay less, nobody wants to get less and we have to spend more for enlargement."[12]

In *Agenda 2000* the Commission outlined what was in effect a "Delors III" proposal. It proposed retaining the budgetary ceiling at 1.27 percent of EU GNP, holding increases in CAP at the existing limit of 74 percent of GNP growth, and keeping structural policies pegged at the level of 0.46 percent of total GNP.[13] It claimed that a budget along these lines would be adequate to finance enlargement, provided agricultural and cohesion policies were reformed to improve their efficiency.

Following the crucial December 1997 Luxembourg decisions regarding the start of accession negotiations with Cyprus and five central and east European countries, the June 1998 Cardiff European Council set March 1999 as the target date for the completion of the financial package—a timetable driven by the elections to the EP scheduled for June 1999. The December 1998 Vienna summit reiterated the commitment to reaching an overall agreement on *Agenda 2000* at a special session of the European Council set for March 24–25, 1999, in Berlin.

Despite the effort by the Commission to dampen controversy among the member states by maintaining continuity with past budget packages, the months preceding the Berlin summit were dominated by fierce debate and seemingly irreconcilable positions over financial issues. The analytical basis for this debate was a report issued by the Commission in October 1998, *Financing the European Union*, that offered a sophisticated and detailed analysis that covered revenues, expenditures, and the distributional effects of each of the four own resources and of the various categories of expenditure.[14] The report spelled out the net payment position of each of the member states in a way that was inevitably somewhat arbitrary and misleading, but that was difficult to ignore. Ireland received a whopping 5.1 percent of GNP per year in net payments, while Germany and Sweden each paid in 0.6 percent of GNP more than they received back. In absolute terms, Germany's net "loss" was 11.46 billion euros, or some $13 billion, while Spain was a net beneficiary of 5.54 billion euros, or some $7 billion.

In the early phases of the negotiations, member state governments staked out widely divergent positions on the budget. Germany, Sweden, and the Netherlands wanted their net contributions cut. France wanted to rein in overall spending, but balked at reforms in the CAP that would fall disproportionately on France or French farmers. Britain was for austerity, but not for giving up its own rebate. Spain pressed for high levels of regional aid and no diversion of structural funds to the east.

The Berlin summit ultimately resulted in an agreement in the European Council on a seven-year budget framework, but only after twenty hours of continuous negotiation that saw many leaders back away from earlier positions and the EU as a whole retreat somewhat from its stated commitment to a sweeping financial reform. The framework once again established the own resources ceiling at 1.27 percent of EU GNP, thereby rejecting the position of those member states that would have preferred a freeze on the EU budget (assuming some real economic growth, the budget will grow as well) and left the agricultural guideline unchanged at 74 percent of GNP growth. It reined in growth in structural and cohesion funds for current member states, but stopped short of the freeze on growth in regional aid that some member states favored. It also retained the British rebate.

As shown in Table 3.7, the financial framework assumes that the first enlargement will occur in 2002. Expenditures associated with pre-accession and post-accession costs for the new member states are "ring-fenced" from spending earmarked for the EU-15: "Expenditure reserved for EU-15 cannot at any time be used for pre-accession assistance and, conversely, expenditure reserved for pre-accession assistance cannot be used by EU-15."[15] The significance of the Berlin agreement is that it allowed the EU to go forward with the enlargement negotiations based on an agreed plan for financing the enlargement. To facilitate a compromise, the EU heads of state and government agreed on a budget that, as with Delors I and II, contained a bit of something for everyone. Those who wanted a more sweeping reform were disappointed, however, and over the longer term the EU most likely will have to revisit its budgetary priorities and undertake more fundamental reforms of its agricultural and structural policies to accommodate enlargement.

Enlargement, Institutional Reform, and IGC 2000

The financial decisions at the Berlin summit were only part of the EU's pre-enlargement agenda. Another set of issues concerns the EU institutions. As has been seen, the Maastricht Treaty undertook major reforms that included creating the Union, establishing the three-pillar structure, and expanding the powers of

Table 3.7   The EU Financial Framework (EU-21) (Millions of Euros, 1999 Prices)

	2000	2001	2002	2003	2004	2005	2006
Agriculture	40920	42800	43900	43770	42760	41930	41660
CAP	36620	38480	39570	39430	38410	37570	37290
Rural Development and Accompanying Measures	4300	4320	4330	4340	4350	4360	4370
Structural Operations	32045	31455	30865	30285	29595	29595	29170
Structural Funds	29430	28840	28250	27670	27080	27080	26660
Cohesion Fund	2615	2615	2615	2615	2515	2515	2510
Internal Policies	5900	5950	6000	6050	6100	6150	6200
External Action	4550	4560	4570	4580	4590	4600	4610
Administration	4560	4600	4700	4800	4900	5000	5100
Reserves	900	900	650	400	400	400	400
Pre-Accession Aid	3120	3120	3120	3120	3120	3120	3120
Agriculture	520	520	520	520	520	520	520
Pre-accession Structural Instrument	1040	1040	1040	1040	1040	1040	1040
PHARE	1560	1560	1560	1560	1560	1560	1560
Enlargement			6450	9030	11610	14200	16780
Agriculture			1600	2030	2450	2930	3400
Structural Operations			3750	5830	7920	10000	12080
Internal Policies			730	760	790	820	850
Administration			370	410	450	450	450
Total Appropriations for Payments	89590	91070	98270	10145 0	10061 0	10135 0	10353 0
of which: enlargement			*4140*	*6710*	*8890*	*11440*	*14210*
Payments as % of GNP	1.13%	1.12%	1.14%	1.15%	1.11%	1.09%	1.09%
Own Resources Ceiling	**1.27%**	**1.27%**	**1.27%**	**1.27%**	**1.27%**	**1.27%**	**1.27%**

the Parliament. The Treaty of Amsterdam introduced further institutional reforms, but on balance failed to resolve the key institutional questions raised by enlargement.

Recognizing that these institutional issues must be settled before new member states are admitted, the June 1999 Cologne European Council decided that another IGC was to be convened in early 2000. The Cologne meeting specified three institutional issues, already raised but not resolved at Amsterdam, as the main agenda of the IGC: the size and composition of the Commission, weighting of votes in the Council, and possible extension of qualified majority voting in the Council. The IGC got underway in Portugal in February 2000, and was to be concluded under the French presidency at the end of the year. It is discussed in the concluding chapter, which deals with the future of the Union and the integration process, with particular emphasis on their relationship to the citizen.

Notes

1. Article 219 TOR, ex Article 163, amended.
2. Committee of Independent Experts, *First Report on Allegations Regarding Fraud, Mismanagement and Nepotism in the European Commission*, Brussels, March 15, 1999.
3. *Rules of Procedure of the Council*, December 6, 1993, O.J. L31/14 (1995).
4. Article 4 TEU, ex Article D.
5. *Rules of Procedure of the European Parliament*, December 7, 1995, O.J. L293/1 (1995).
6. Council Regulation (EEC) No. 302/93, February 8, 1993 on the establishment of a European Monitoring Centre for Drugs and Drug Addiction, O.J. L 036, February 12, 1993.
7. *Van Gend en Loos v. Nederlandse Administratie Belastingen*, Case 26/62(1963) ECR 1, quoted in Karen Alter, "The Making of a Supranational Rule of Law," in Ronald Tiersky, ed., *Europe Today: National Politics, European Integration, and European Security* (Lanham: Rowman & Littlefield, 1999), 305.
8. Article 249 TOR, ex Article 189.
9. Quoted in Alter, "The Making of a Supranational Rule of Law: The Battle for Supremacy," in Tiersky, ed., *Europe Today*, 313.
10. "The Community's Revenue and Expenditure," *European Parliament Fact Sheets*, June 1, 1999.
11. "Future Financing of the Community Delors II Package," *The European Councils, 1992–1994*, 63–67.
12. Quoted in Peter Norman, "Europe's Spoils Up for Grabs," *Financial Times*, December 14, 1998.
13. *Agenda 2000: For a stronger and wider Union*, in *Bulletin of the European Union*, Supplement 5/97, 61–69.
14. *Financing the European Union: Commission Report on the Operation of the Own Resources System*, Brussels, October 7, 1998; europa.eu.int/comm/dg19/en/agenda2000/ownresources.
15. *Presidency Conclusions: Berlin European Council, 24 and 25 March 1999*, Doc/99/1, 3.

Suggestions for Further Reading

Borchardt, Klaus-Dieter. *The ABC of Community Law*. Luxembourg: Office for Official Publications of the European Communities, 1994.

Brown, L. Neville and Francis G. Jacobs. *The Court of Justice of the European Communities*. London: Sweet & Maxwell, 1989.

Dinan, Desmond. *An Ever Closer Union? An Introduction to the European Community*, 2nd ed. Boulder: Lynne Rienner, 1999.

Duff, Andrew, John Pinder and Roy Pryce. *Maastricht and Beyond: Building the European Union*. New York: Routledge (for the Federal Trust), 1995.

Nugent, Neill. *The Government and Politics of the European Union* (Fourth Edition). Durham: Duke University Press, 1999.

CHAPTER 4

The Single Market
FROM CUSTOMS UNION TO
1992 AND BEYOND

If institutions and law are the political heart of the European Union, its economic core is the single market. With over 370 million consumers and a yearly GNP of more than $7 trillion, the EU market is rivaled in size and level of prosperity only by the United States and the broader NAFTA area. With enlargement, it will grow by another 110 million consumers. The EEA with Norway and Iceland, a special trade arrangement with Switzerland, and the customs union with Turkey expand the reach of the market, as will projected free trade agreements with Russia, Ukraine, and the Mediterranean countries. The development of this market goes back to the initial post–World War II trade liberalization in the OEEC and to the founding in 1952 of the ECSC, but it really only took off with the founding of the EC in 1958 and the establishment by the Treaty of Rome of the customs union and the common external tariff.

The Customs Union

The Treaty of Rome provided for the creation of a customs union through the phasing out of all tariffs and quantitative restrictions on trade among the member states over a period of twelve years, from 1958 to 1970. Elimination of these barriers went so well that the member states agreed to speed up the process, and the customs union for goods was completed by July 1, 1968, eighteen months ahead of schedule.

The common market was an immediate success. The elimination of intra-EC barriers to trade helped to accelerate growth and to prolong into the 1960s Europe's postwar economic boom. Trade among the members of the Community increased by a factor of six over the transition period, and average GDP increased by 70 percent. Except in special circumstances such as southern Italy, unemployment all but disappeared, as industries in Germany, France, and the Benelux were forced to import workers from southern Italy and from outside the Community to keep up with the demand for labor. Europe's balance of payments problems, so troublesome in the early postwar period, were largely resolved as the European countries began to register surpluses in their trade and to accumulate reserves of gold and foreign currencies (mainly dollars). The Community's economic performance in these years was in part attributable to investments by U.S. multinational companies, which were quick to recognize the advantages of the common market and in many cases built large, efficient plants in one Community country to manufacture a particular product for the whole EC market.

Despite these impressive achievements, in many respects the Community remained segmented into national markets. The Treaty of Rome allowed member states to restrict imports and exports of goods on grounds of public policy or public security, health and safety, and for certain other reasons if such restrictions did not "constitute a means of arbitrary discrimination or a disguised restriction on trade."[1] When member states applied different health and safety standards to products sold within their borders, it had the effect—if not necessarily the intent—of limiting trade, since manufacturers that were forced to make different versions of a product to meet different standards often were deterred from or priced out of operating at the EC level. The treaty allowed the Council to pass legislation to harmonize health, safety, and other standards, but doing so proved to be extraordinarily difficult, both because of its sheer technical complexity and because member state governments often were reluctant to give up the hidden protection that national standards afforded. Government procurement was another area in which the common market for the most part did not operate. Governments and state-owned utilities were major purchasers of everything from paper clips to locomotives, which they generally bought from national suppliers.

The shortcomings of the common market were even more striking in the areas of free movement of services, capital, and people. The service sector was still largely divided along national lines, with little cross-border competition. Public services such as telecommunications and rail transport were regarded as natural monopolies with room only for one supplier that was either state-owned or subject to heavy regulation. In other areas, such as banking and medicine, governments imposed strict licensing requirements to protect the public. Competition based on market principles hardly applied in many service industries even in the national setting; to open these markets to competition from other European countries was even more difficult and was not seen as desirable in most countries.

Capital markets were segmented by country. Controls on cross-border financial transactions remained in place and served as important instruments of national economic policy. Indeed, the breakdown of the Bretton Woods system and the monetary turbulence of the 1970s led some EC countries to strengthen capital controls as a way of protecting their national currencies. There were also barriers to the free movement of persons. Citizens of one EC country still needed passports to enter other Community countries, and checks at border crossings and airports were a constant reminder that flows of people were controlled. The ability of Europeans to work or set up businesses in other Community countries was limited by rules on residency, work permits, and nationally oriented pension and insurance schemes.

During the boom years of the 1960s and early 1970s, there was little motivation to address these remaining barriers to trade. Workers, companies, and consumers enjoyed the benefits of rising incomes, higher productivity, and greater choice of products associated with the common market in goods, but there was no political impetus to take the complex and controversial decisions that would be required to realize free trade in services or the free movement of capital and persons. In the difficult economic conditions of the 1970s momentum toward establishment of a single market slowed still further, and there were even signs of backsliding in the common market for goods, as national governments sought to bolster struggling domestic industries by providing taxpayer subsidies or by imposing rules and regulations relating to health, safety, and consumer protection that kept out competing products from other EC countries. Only a prolonged period of economic difficulty and a series of crippling recessions caused a rethinking and a renewed push to complete the single market.

The Single Market Program

Economic growth in the EC averaged a robust 4.6 percent per year in 1961–1970, but fell to 2.8 percent in 1971–1975 and recovered only slightly to 3.0 percent per year in 1976–1980. The 1974–1975 recession, caused by the dramatic rise in the price of oil, marked the end of the long, postwar economic boom that began with the Marshall Plan. By 1981 Western Europe was back in recession, with economic activity falling by 0.2 percent in that year before registering a weak 0.3 percent gain the following year.[2] Unemployment rates had risen from the very low levels during the postwar boom to 8.6 percent in France, 9.2 percent in West Germany, and 12.4 percent in the UK.[3] European political and business leaders were concerned that Europe was falling behind the United States and Japan, not only in macroeconomic performance but especially in the high-technology industries of the future.

In explaining the causes of Europe's declining performance, many business leaders focused on the high costs of doing business across national borders in Europe and the barriers to trade and the flow of people and capital that still existed in the common market. A 1986 poll of one hundred corporate executives revealed that the majority thought that the fragmented state of the European market was the major factor behind Europe's failure to compete with the United States and Japan in key industrial sectors. Some 42 percent of the respondents said that their firms incurred higher costs because of different specifications set by national laws; 25 percent cited the sheer cost of paperwork as a factor damaging competitiveness; and 20 percent identified extra warehousing and inventory costs due to different product standards as a source of higher business costs in Europe.[4] In 1983 the chief executives of seventeen of Europe's largest companies formed the European Roundtable of Industrialists (ERT) in order to generate ideas and mobilize governmental, parliamentary, and public support for creating a more favorable market climate in Europe. The stated goal of the ERT was to revitalize the EC by preparing a blueprint for completing the single market.

When Jacques Delors became president of the European Commission in January 1985, he chose to make completion of the single market a centerpiece of his presidency. Shortly after taking office, Delors announced, in his inaugural speech to the European Parliament, that the Commission would introduce a program to eliminate all barriers to the internal market by the end of 1992.[5] This concrete program of action with a firm date for completion (see Box 4.1) was to capture the imagination and win the support of business, government, and ordinary citizens and workers. "1992" became the slogan of the late 1980s and early 1990s.

THE 1985 WHITE PAPER

Delors entrusted implementation of the program to Lord Cockfield, the British Commissioner responsible for the internal market. In the first six months of 1985 Cockfield and his staff produced a detailed plan that was presented to the European Council in the form of a white paper outlining the basic program.[6] In an appendix to the report, the Commission listed some three hundred measures that needed to be turned into Community law to complete the internal market. Each measure was assigned a target date, so that the whole program would be implemented by December 31, 1992.

The report identified three kinds of barriers to the operation of the internal market—physical, technical, and fiscal—all of which it proposed to dismantle. Physical barriers included customs posts and paperwork and inspections at borders. (It was indeed the elimination of these barriers that was to become the most visible manifestation of 1992 for the public.) Technical barriers included the vast array of national standards and regulations that did not always have the intent of impeding commerce among EC member states, but that in practice had this effect. They included rules on the content and labeling of foods, chemicals, and pharmaceuticals; car safety standards; different procedures for public procurement (including in important state-owned sectors such as water supply, the railroads, telecommunications, and electricity); different banking and insurance regulations;

Box 4.1   The Commission Proposal

Unifying this market (of 320 million) presupposes that Member States will agree on the abolition of barriers of all kinds, harmonisation of rules, approximation of legislation and tax structures, strengthening of monetary cooperation and the necessary flanking measures to encourage European firms to work together. It is a goal that is well within our reach provided we draw the lessons of the past. The Commission will be asking the European Council to pledge itself to completion of a fully unified internal market by 1992 and to approve the necessary programme together with a realistic and binding timetable.

(*Source:* "Programme of the Commission for 1985.")

national rules on air, rail, road, and water transport; rules on copyright and trademark protection; and many other barriers to the free flow of goods, services, capital, and people. Fiscal barriers related both to types and levels of taxation, including value added and excise taxes, both of which varied widely across Europe.

THE COMMISSION'S STRATEGY

Although the single market program generated enthusiasm throughout Europe, Delors and his team realized from the beginning that it would be difficult to implement. The Community had launched the Werner Plan for economic and monetary union in 1970 but had completely failed to meet its ambitious targets. European foreign policy cooperation, also launched in 1970, had been a disappointment as well. The Community had been through a long period of drift, and success was by no means assured.

Three factors in the way the Commission and the member states approached the single market program were vital to its eventual success. First, as discussed in Chapter 2, the member states agreed, in the SEA, to revisions of the Treaty of Rome that made completion of the single market by the end of 1992 a binding commitment and that permitted the passage of single market legislation by qualified majority rather than unanimous voting. These changes made it easier to pass such legislation as was needed to complete the single market.

Second, the Community reduced the amount and complexity of the legislation that ultimately would be required by changing the way it addressed the problem of divergent national standards. Under the 1992 program, it relied to the maximum extent possible on mutual recognition of national standards rather than on the more difficult process of harmonization to a single Community standard, such as had been attempted in the 1960s and 1970s, and where possible delegated harmonization and standard-setting tasks to nongovernmental, industry-based organizations.

Third, the Commission mounted a successful political and public relations campaign that helped to convince businesses and the general public of the merits of the program. It undertook several important studies that attempted to quantify the expected economic gains from the elimination of intra-EC barriers. The best known of these studies was the 1988 Cecchini report, officially known as *The Economics of 1992*. It tried to estimate, through detailed sectoral studies, "the costs of non-Europe," that is, the economic benefits that the EC would forgo by not completing the single market program. It estimated that compared to what would happen if the program were not implemented, completion of the single market would increase overall Community GDP by 4.5 percent, reduce prices by 6 percent, lower public sector deficits by 2.25 percent, result in a positive swing in the EC's balance of payments position amounting to one percent of GDP, and create 1,750,000 new jobs.[7]

MUTUAL RECOGNITION AND THE NEW APPROACH

Mutual recognition goes back to the landmark *Cassis de Dijon* case decided by the Court of Justice in February 1979. The case involved the German importer of a French liqueur that the German authorities ruled could not be sold in Germany because it did not meet the minimum alcohol content requirements for this type of product specified in German law. The Court ruled that the German law contravened the common market provisions of the Treaty of Rome. National authorities could not block the import from another member state of a product that met the standards of that state, provided those standards offered equivalent levels of protection with regard to such objectives as health, safety, and public security. The Court did allow for continued differences among national standards, but it argued that any additional protection to the German consumer afforded by the German ban was disproportionate to the disruptive effects on the common market.[8] In the course of the 1980s, mutual recognition was firmly established as an underlying principle of the single market. It also came to play a major role in the service sector and in promoting the free movement of workers by, for example, helping to resolve the problem of different academic degrees and licensing standards for professionals in the member states.

For products for which regulatory standards among the member states were substantively different, as well as for many service-sector issues and questions relating to the free flow of capital and people, the Community could not rely on mutual recognition alone to achieve the single market goals. For these areas, the Commission proposed in 1985 what it called the "new approach" to overcoming hindrances to trade resulting from different national regulation.[9] Endorsed by the Council in May 1985, the new approach entailed the adoption of legislative frameworks in the form of Community directives establishing standards for major industrial sectors. In drafting such directives, the Commission limited their scope to essential standards relating to health, safety, consumer protection, and the environment, thereby eliminating the need for much detailed regulation at the Community and the national levels.[10]

Once these directives were in place at the Community level, the member states would be required to adopt or amend national legislation to conform to these essential requirements. European standardization bodies, such as the European Standards Committee (CEN) and the European Electrotechnical Standards Committee (CENELEC), were asked to draw up detailed technical specifications that reflected these essential requirements and that could serve as European standards. Member states then could issue certificates of conformity stating that products manufactured on their territory met these essential requirements. National authorities would be required to recognize that products manufactured in accordance with these standards met the essential requirements established at the Community level and could not be barred from import on grounds of health or safety. In 1990 the certification bodies of the member states also founded the European

Organization for Testing and Certification to coordinate the mutual recognition of certificates of conformity.

For certain products where the nature of the risk to consumers required absolute uniformity of standards, the Community continued to rely on detailed product-by-product or even component-by-component harmonization. Sectors in which detailed harmonization continued to be used included pharmaceuticals, chemicals, motor vehicles, and foodstuffs. But passage of detailed harmonization directives was rendered easier by the introduction of qualified majority voting under the SEA. The single market program thus used an eclectic mix of mutual recognition, new approach legislation, and detailed harmonization—sometimes in combination for a single sector or product.[11]

Implementing 1992

GOODS

The creation of the customs union through the elimination of intra-Community tariffs and the establishment of the common customs tariff was, along with the Common Agricultural Policy and the addition of six new members, the EC's most important achievement during the first thirty years of its existence. In practice, however, free movement of goods as envisioned in the Treaty of Rome had never been fully achieved, and was to some extent threatened by the backsliding of the 1970s. While the member states did very well in removing tariffs and quantitative restrictions (quotas) on trade, they were less rigorous in eliminating what the treaty called measures having an "equivalent effect" as such restrictions. Such measures included rules and regulations that blocked or made more difficult intra-Community trade, divergent tax systems, and national preferences in public procurement.

Even after the elimination of all intra-EC customs duties, member states maintained customs posts and checks on trucks and trains crossing their borders to insure that importers were complying with the relevant national laws on value added taxes (VAT) and on excise taxes on alcohol, tobacco, luxury goods, fuel, and certain other products. The member states traditionally guard their prerogatives in the area of taxation, especially since ministries of finance want a free hand in raising the revenue needed to fund Europe's generous social welfare and other government programs and because politicians are well aware of the sensitivity of taxation as an issue with the voters. Countries also have different practices and traditions with regard to taxation. There thus was great reluctance to harmonize taxation or to turn decision-making in this area over to Brussels.

Nevertheless, the architects of the single market could not ignore the effects of widely disparate levels and kinds of taxation on the functioning of the cross-border market. The 1992 program did not attempt to fully harmonize member state tax policies, but it tried to do away with those discrepancies that most tended to distort the functioning of the single market. Commission and academic experts noted that U.S. states could levy different sales, gasoline, liquor, and other taxes without disrupting the functioning of the single American market. Some differences among jurisdictions were possible, provided they were not too large. The Council eventually agreed to set the standard VAT rate at 15 percent with a reduced rate of 5 percent for a limited list of goods and services.[12] The EC also instituted a new system for collecting VAT that eliminated the need for border controls by making exporters and importers responsible for reporting cross-border transactions to domestic authorities.

With regard to public procurement, before the single market program Community governments rarely practiced what they preached when it came to their own purchases of goods and services. Purchases by governments and state-owned entities such as the postal service and state-owned telephone, airline, and railroad companies accounted for roughly 16 percent of all spending on goods and services in the EC.[13] Because government and state-owned companies were the most important buyers of high-technology and high-priced capital goods such as aircraft, rolling stock, and telecommunications equipment, opening up public markets was vital to the success of the single market.

The 1992 program extended competition to four sectors previously exempt from the common market—water, energy, transport, and telecommunications—and tightened rules on the award of public contracts. In a series of directives dealing with public works, utilities, and public services, the member states were required to open up procurement by national, regional, and local governments as well as other public entities to competition from other Community countries. Contracts were to be announced for bidding in the official journal of the Community, and selection of suppliers was to be based on objective criteria such as price, quality, and qualifications without regard to nationality.

SERVICES

Before the 1992 program, liberalization of trade in services in the Community for the most part was confined to measures needed to facilitate the free flow of goods. Under the provisions of the Treaty of Rome calling for the establishment of a common transport policy, for example, the Community adopted a ban on discriminatory pricing or conditions of transport based on origin or destination. The transport sector itself was not opened to competition, however, and little progress was made toward achieving the Common Transport Policy mentioned in the Treaty of Rome.

Unlike the situation with regard to goods, creating the single market for services (and for capital and labor) required a much heavier reliance on passage of Community directives. Whereas member states could simplify trade by accepting each other's products as safe and environmentally friendly, establishing a single market in such areas as transport, telecommunications, and banking required elaborate and detailed agreement on the rules of the game for competition and consideration at the European level of the same concerns that shaped national policy, for example dealing with natural monopoly and ensuring the interoperability of complex technical systems.

In transport, the Council passed a series of directives gradually opening the major passenger and freight modes to competition. Frontier checks on road and inland water transport were eliminated, effective January 1, 1990.[14] All quantitative restrictions on trucking operations between member states were to be terminated by the end of 1992. Change in the trucking industry was controversial, however, and it was not until September 1993, nine months after the formal completion date of the 1992 program, that the Council passed a directive fully establishing, as of July 1, 1998, the right of a firm from one member state to carry freight between points in another EU country just as if it were a domestic firm (known as cabotage).

In rail transport, the Council passed a framework directive in 1988 requiring member states to begin operating national rail services according to commercial criteria. Management of the rail infrastructure, such as track and signals, was to be separated from management of the trains themselves, and competitors to the national railroad, including from other EC countries, were to be allowed limited access on a commercial basis to the infrastructure in order to operate rail services between member states. Market opening in the rail sector remained a very slow process, however, marked by resistance from national governments and foot-dragging by the powerful national rail authorities.

Civil aviation was one of the most politically sensitive areas in the single market program. Governments had a long history of subsidizing national carriers for reasons of employment and prestige. High costs and chronic overcapacity in the sector meant that some national airlines might be forced to merge with rivals or go out of business if they were fully exposed to competition. In a first set of reforms agreed in 1987, the Council established that from January 1, 1993, carriers would be free to set prices on commercial grounds in order to compete with rivals. Previously, the fares between cities in different member states required approval by both sets of national authorities, a practice that tended to keep prices high as governments sought to protect small and inefficient carriers. Complete liberalization of the EU aviation market was set for April 1, 1997. Henceforth, any EU airline could operate between points in the Union, provided essential safety standards were met. Thus, for example, British Airways began competing on domestic routes in Germany. Such competition was still difficult, however, since new entrants to markets often had problems in gaining slots at major airports serving the most profitable markets. Elsewhere in the transport sector, there were market-opening measures in inland waterway and maritime transport.

Telecommunications competition was introduced through a series of open network provision (ONP) directives.[15] As in the rail industry, ONP was based on the "unbundling" of the infrastructure needed to deliver a service, in this case the national and local telephone network, and the delivery of service through that network. The owners of the networks were the large national post, telephone, and telegraph authorities (PTTs) such as Deutsche Telekom and France Telecom. They were required to allow access to the network on a nondiscriminatory commercial basis to firms desiring to provide new services or to compete with the traditional monopoly supplier. ONP with regard to leased lines for businesses, various data services, 800-type numbers, and other services began on January 1, 1993, in line with the overall single market program. The big leap forward—competition in voice telephony—took longer to negotiate and was established after a long prepa-ration period on February 1, 1998, with additional delays for several of the mem-ber states. Liberalization and market opening under the single market program contributed to and in turn was bolstered by the wave of privatizations to sweep the West European telecommunications sector. In the UK, the Thatcher govern-ment sold a majority share of British Telecom already in 1984. It took more than a decade for governments on the continent to follow suit, but by the end of the 1990s France Telecom, Deutsche Telekom, Telecom Italia, and the PTTs in most the other EU countries had been at least partially privatized or were scheduled be privatized in the near future.

Commission attempts to establish an internal market for energy, another area in which large public monopolies played a key role, were not very successful until the late 1990s. In the 1980s the Commission proposed single market directives that would require member states to enact legislation opening up gas and electricity transmission networks to competing firms. These directives were very much wa-tered down by the member states, however, as major utilities such as Ruhrgas in Germany and Electricité de France opposed liberalization. In December 1996 the Council finally adopted an electricity directive that required all member states to enact legislation within two years (Belgium and Ireland were granted three and Greece four) that opened about a quarter of their national markets to competition on February 19, 1999, followed by additional market opening in 2000 and 2003.[16] This was to be done by the establishment of common rules for the generation, transmission, and distribution of electricity that allow producers and consumers to contract supplies directly with each other after negotiating access to the trans-mission network with its operator. As in transport and telecommunications, the key to making the directive work and to stimulating cross-border trade in electric-ity is the unbundling of prices for generation, transmission, and distribution and the provision of open access to the supply network.

In June 1998 the Council and the European Parliament adopted a natural gas directive that provided for the opening to competition by August 10, 2000, of at least 20 percent of total gas consumption in each national market. This was sched-uled to rise to 28 percent by 2003 and to 33 percent by 2008. These energy direc-tives are expected to increase competition and lead to lower energy prices in Eu-rope. However, their belated adoption, the phase-in periods, and the continued closing off of the majority of the national markets to competition all attest to how difficult liberalization has been in this sector.

In financial services, in 1989 the Council passed the Second Banking Directive, which established an EC-wide banking license effective January 1, 1993.[17] This enables any bank that is legally permitted to operate in one member state to open branches in or provide cross-border services to another member state. The banking authorities of the country where the bank is headquartered have the main responsibility for prudential supervision of the bank, while the regulatory authorities of the country in which the bank has branches can oversee their activities to protect consumers and ensure the soundness of the national banking system.

In professional services, the Council adopted a 1988 directive that deals with the cross-border provision of services requiring a license, such as law, medicine, nursing, and accounting. Following the mutual recognition principle, member states are required to accept as valid diplomas and certificates awarded in other member states. This directive applies to all diplomas requiring three or more years of study.

CAPITAL

Although the Treaty of Rome provided for the free movement of capital, the EC moved very slowly with regard to liberalization of capital movements. Convertibility of the European currencies into each other was restored with the establishment of the EPU in 1950, and in 1958 the European countries restored full convertibility into the dollar and other third currencies, thereby putting into effect the system of fixed exchange rates and full convertibility envisioned in the Bretton Woods agreements. But most European countries continued to use capital controls—restrictions on the movement of money into and out of the country by banks, other financial institutions, and private investors—to protect their currencies against rapid and destabilizing changes in value.

As in services, liberalization occurred mainly where it was needed to facilitate trade in goods, not in order to promote cross-border competition for its own sake. The Treaty of Rome required member states to eliminate all restrictions on the movement of capital "to the extent necessary to ensure the proper functioning of the common market."[18] In 1960 and 1962 the Community adopted directives on capital movement to facilitate payments for goods traded in the common market and the establishment of branches and subsidiaries in other EC member countries.

In May 1986 the Commission put forward a comprehensive plan to create a single Community-wide financial area in which all financial and currency flows would be free of national restrictions.[19] Under a decision taken in 1988, all intra-EC restrictions on the movement of capital were eliminated as of July 1990. This was important mainly for businesses, but it also had implications for individuals. It meant that member state governments could not restrict their citizens from holding their bank accounts or other investments in other EC countries.

Free movement of capital was closely linked to liberalization in the market for financial services, and progress in these areas tended to reinforce each other. Banks, insurance companies, and stockbrokers could begin to operate efficiently across the member state markets only after capital controls were removed; conversely, the activities of banks and financial services wanting to operate at the European level helped to integrate the single market for capital in ways that government action alone could not have accomplished.

Together with the liberalization of the financial services sector, the removal of capital controls made the shift to a single currency later in the 1990s both more necessary and more feasible. Tommaso Padoa-Schioppa, an Italian economist and a member of the Delors committee on economic and monetary union, warned about the futility of trying to pursue an "inconsistent quartet" of objectives—free trade, full capital mobility, fixed exchange rates, and independent national monetary policies—since without controls speculative capital movements would overpower national attempts to hold stable the currency values. With the Community committed to pursuing the first two objectives in the single market program and the third within the European Monetary System, he argued that "in the long run the only solution to the inconsistency is to complement the internal market with a monetary union."[20]

PERSONS

Movement of persons was perhaps the most difficult of the four freedoms to implement and the one on which the least progress was made during the early years of the Community. In 1958 the EC put in place a system, taken over from the ECSC, to reduce the loss of social security benefits by migrant workers. In 1961 the Community adopted its first regulation to facilitate the movement of labor. But these were very preliminary steps and mainly had to do with working conditions and benefits of citizens of EC countries already employed in other member states. The treaty did not create a generalized right for European workers to move about the Community in search of employment and it conferred few if any rights on persons as individuals.

Free movement of labor was achieved, at least in a formal sense, by 1968, based on the principle of national treatment of workers from other EC countries. Such workers had to be granted the same rights and social benefits as those accorded to nationals.[21] As a practical matter, however, movement of labor was hindered by cumbersome administrative procedures relating to residence permits, different national standards with regard to vocational training qualifications, and restrictions on the right to establish businesses by the self-employed. In addition, EC legislation still tended to treat free movement of persons as an economic right, with limited application to those outside the labor force.

The single market program both improved mobility for the employed and extended the free movement of people to broader, noneconomic categories. With regard to the former, for example, it included directives on the mutual recognition of degrees and vocational training certificates and new legislation on the harmonization of income tax provisions for workers employed in another member state.

With regard to the latter, in June 1990 the Council adopted three directives on the right of residence for students, retired people, and any other citizens who could show that they had sufficient means to live in another EU host country.[22]

With the introduction of EU citizenship in the Maastricht Treaty, free movement of persons has become less an economic right, guaranteed as a function of the single market and the roles of individuals as economic actors (workers, consumers), and more a human and political right, guaranteed to people as a function of their citizenship. The citizenship clause introduced by Maastricht states that "every citizen of the Union shall have the right to move and reside freely within the territory of the Member States, subject to the limitations and conditions laid down in the Treaty and by the measures adopted to give it effect."[23] The "limitations" and "conditions" referred to are set by national governments, and relate to such issues as the portability of pensions and welfare payments, residence and labor permits, and other restrictions, many of which have been whittled away by successful challenges in the Court of Justice.

As a practical matter, however, the main barriers to the free movement of persons in the EU are not legal but cultural and linguistic. Some EU citizens take advantage of the free movement provisions of the treaties, but most are content to live and work in their native countries, where they speak the language, own property, and have social and family ties. An increasing number of EU citizens do move, however. They include workers at both ends of the income scale—for example, relatively poor migrants from Portugal who work in Luxembourg and France, and highly paid managers and professionals who move about in search of better jobs or who are transferred by multinational companies. Movement of retirees is also an important phenomenon in Europe, as can be seen, for example, in the large numbers of German, British, Dutch, and other pensioners who have settled on the Mediterranean coast of Spain.

OVERALL RESULTS

Implementing the single market program was (and to some extent still is) a multi-stage process. In areas in which legislation was needed to overcome market barriers, the Commission had to propose EC-level directives. The Council of Ministers then had to adopt these directives as EC law, without watering down the essence of the proposal to secure the necessary qualified majority. Each member state then had to transpose these directives into national legislation. Finally, the member states had to be willing and able to enforce their national laws, without turning a blind eye to restrictive practices that favored domestic firms at the expense of outsiders. Only if all four of these stages were undertaken—the last on a continuous basis—would the single market truly operate. In addition, for areas in which mutual recognition was used to advance single market goals, it had to function as advertised: as a faster and more efficient but no less effective substitute for harmonization by directive.

The record of the EU and its member states in fulfilling these steps was good but by no means perfect. By the target date of December 31, 1992, the Community had completed most of the single market program. The number of single market proposals had been scaled back from 300 to 282, as the Commission backed away from certain controversial issues that were likely to fail in the Council of Ministers. By the end of 1992, 264 of 282 white paper actions had been passed at the EC level, leaving 18 still outstanding. Elements of the 1985 white paper that were not passed included the removal of border controls on persons at internal frontiers, certain tax harmonization measures, and the creation of a European system of company law.

Transposition of single market legislation into national law was also problematic, given the large volume of legislation, the slow pace of legislative action in the national parliaments, and the fact that even those countries that opposed passage of a directive at the European level but were outvoted in the Council of Ministers still had a legal obligation to transpose into national law. By the end of 1993—one year after completion of the EC legislative program—only a little over half of the single market directives passed by the Council had been transposed into national legislation in all twelve member states. Denmark and Britain (ironically both traditional Euroskeptics) had the best records with regard to transposition, while Greece had the worst. Areas in which the member states had the greatest difficulty in meeting their EU obligations were public procurement and veterinary controls.

Despite the obvious slippages in various stages of implementation, the single market program generally is regarded as one of the great successes in the history of European integration. The late 1980s was a period of dynamism and growing optimism in the EC. In 1986–1990 economic growth in the Community averaged 3.1 percent per year, a pace not seen since before the first oil crisis and more than double the 1.4 percent annual rate of 1980–1985. The Community-wide unemployment rate fell from 10 percent in 1985 to 7.5 percent in 1990, as millions of new jobs were created. Good economic performance was partly attributable to favorable trends worldwide, but the enthusiasm generated by the 1992 program also contributed. European and non-European firms increased their investments in the Community to prepare for increased competition as well as the expanded opportunities of the single market. The value of transborder mergers and acquisitions in the Community increased from $8 billion in 1984 to $167 billion in 1989.[24]

Politically, the 1992 program gave the EC and its member states the self-confidence to proceed with political and economic and monetary union in the Maastricht Treaty. It rekindled enthusiasm for integration among the public and made the Community a far greater pole of attraction for potential new members. Austria, Cyprus, Finland, Malta, Norway, Sweden, and Switzerland all applied for membership in this period, in part because of changing political circumstances in Europe but also because they did not want to be left out of the single market program. Perhaps most importantly, the perceived success of the single market project helped to strengthen the EC precisely at a time when West European unity and strength were needed to deal with the challenges and opportunities presented by the unexpected collapse of communism in central and eastern Europe in late 1989.

The single market clearly did not solve Western Europe's economic problems. EU unemployment began to climb in the early 1990s and economic growth slowed from the pace of late 1980s. But political leaders and economists argued that problems such as unemployment and slow growth would have been worse without the 1992 program and that full implementation of the single market program—including strict action against governments that failed to implement single market directives or that distorted the market through new state subsidies to industry—was one of the keys to overcoming the recession of the early 1990s.[25]

In 1995 the EU attempted to quantify the benefits of the single market by commissioning thirty-eight detailed studies dealing with the effects of the 1992 program in six areas: manufacturing, services, dismantling of barriers, impact on trade and investment, impact on competition and scale effects, and aggregate and regional impact. Because so much else was happening as the Community worked to complete the 1992 program, it was hard to measure precisely those economic effects that were due to the single market; even sophisticated econometric models had difficulty in isolating the effects of the 1992 program from other factors such as global trade liberalization in the GATT, German reunification, and the opening of new markets in central and eastern Europe.[26] It was also too early to measure the long-term effects of the single market, many of which would be felt only over time as certain directives were phased in and implemented at the national level, and as investment patterns in the Union shifted in response to the new realities of the single market.

Despite these methodological challenges, in October 1996 the Commission issued a summary report entitled *The Impact and Effectiveness of the Single Market* that drew together all the findings of the 1995–1996 studies.[27] It concluded that the single market had resulted in greater competition among companies in both manufacturing and services, an accelerated pace of industrial restructuring leading to improved global competitiveness of European firms, a wider range of goods and services available to consumers, especially in newly liberalized sectors such as transport and telecommunications, faster and cheaper transborder delivery of goods, and greater mobility of people between member states. In terms of overall economic effects, the study estimated that the single market program had resulted in the creation of 300,000–900,000 additional jobs, an extra increase in EU GNP of 1.1–1.5 percent over the 1987–1993 period, inflation rates of 1.0–1.5 percent lower than they would have been in the absence of the single market program, and further economic convergence between different EU regions.[28] These numbers were below the optimistic projections of the Cecchini report, but they nonetheless represented a substantial gain for the EU economy.

The Single Market Since 1992

Since 1993 the Commission and, with varying degrees of enthusiasm, the member states have continued to plug away at the single market. This has included passing legislation that was not completed before the 1992 deadline, drafting and adopting new legislation in response to technological change and to fill gaps in the original legislative program, and, not least, seeking to improve compliance and implementation, particularly by the member states. As the guardian of the treaties, the Commission plays a special role in these efforts. One member of the Commission is exclusively responsible for internal market matters, and in that capacity oversees the Directorate-General for the Internal Market. Beginning in 1994, this directorate has prepared annual reports on the operation of the single market that highlight areas needing improvement.

PROBLEMS WITH MUTUAL RECOGNITION

Mutual recognition remains an ongoing challenge for the single market, and one that affects the core goal of free trade in goods along with many parts of the service sector. Although it was adopted with great fanfare in 1986 and was one of the key factors speeding completion of the single market program, it has not proven to be a panacea for trade barriers. In various reviews of the single market, the Commission and the internal market ministers of the member states have identified standardization and mutual recognition as among the weakest areas of the single market. National and local authorities often refuse to recognize as valid product standards set by regulatory bodies in other member states. According to a survey of five hundred large companies undertaken by the Commission in 1997, continued failure to implement mutual recognition of national standards, testing, and certification was the most important remaining obstacle to trade in goods in the single market.[29]

MEMBER STATE COMPLIANCE

Under the provisions in the Treaty of Rome that apply to the EU institutions, the Commission and the Court of Justice are obliged to take action to bring member states into compliance with their treaty obligations. These provisions were strengthened by the Maastricht Treaty, which allowed for fines to be levied against member states that persistently failed to meet an obligation about which they have been warned. The Commission relies upon these provisions in its efforts to police the single market.

If the Commission believes that a member state has failed to fulfill an obligation under EU law, it issues a letter of formal notice to that state expressing concerns about the possible infringement. If it does not receive a favorable response about the matter, the Commission delivers a reasoned opinion on the alleged breach of compliance to the state and asks it to give its observations on the matter. If after a certain period of time the member state fails to comply with the Commission's opinion, the Commission may initiate proceedings against that state in the Court of Justice. If the Court finds that the member state has indeed failed to fulfill its obligations, it can order that state to take measures to bring itself into compliance. If the Commission considers that the state in question still has not taken the necessary measures to comply, it issues a second reasoned opinion specifying the points on which the member state has failed to comply with the judgment of the Court. If the member state still does not fulfil its obligations, the Commission returns to the Court, this time proposing a penalty that the Court can impose on that state for its noncompliance.

The Commission initially was somewhat cautious about using its legal powers against member states in regard to single market matters, but it grew more aggressive in the last several years of the 1990s as EMU approached and Commission and independent economists became increasingly concerned about the dangers of launching the single currency in a still-uncompleted single market. In 1995 Internal Market Commissioner Mario Monti signed a total of 218 formal infringement letters regarding possible breaches of single market rules by member states. In 1996 this rose to 283 letters, of which 187 were letters of formal notice to member states about possible breaches of single market obligations, 76 were reasoned opinions on single market matters, 15 were first referrals to the Court of Justice, four were letters of formal notice to member states warning them that it was prepared to make a second referral to the Court, and one was a reasoned opinion prior to a second referral.[30] Of the 283 actions taken by the Commission, about a third involved late transposition of legislation by the member states, a third arose from complaints by businesses and individuals to the Commission or to the European Parliament, and about a third came about because the Commission itself suspected market irregularities in a member state. The fact that the Commission issued many more letters of formal notice than reasoned opinions and more opinions than referrals to the Court reflected both the relative newness of much single market legislation and the readiness on the part of member states to correct or explain alleged violations of single market obligations once the Commission took note of a matter.

THE 1997 ACTION PLAN

In early 1997 the Commission drew up an Action Plan for the Single Market that included stepped up enforcement measures and a more concerted effort to fill gaps in the existing body of legislation.[31] Endorsed by the June 1997 Amsterdam European Council, the plan aimed to improve dramatically the functioning of the single market by January 1, 1999, the date of the introduction of the EU's single currency. At the time the plan was adopted, 35 percent of all single market directives had not been implemented in national legislation in at least one member state. This number fell to 26.7 percent in November 1997 and to 14.9 percent in October 1998, as the action plan drew to its close.[32]

One of the instruments used by the Commission to promote better implementation at the national level is the regular publication of a single market score-board, which shows the record of each member state in the transposition of legis-lation, broken down by category of legislation. (Table 4.1 summarizes the scoreboard findings as of November 1999.) In November 1998, shortly before the action plan was concluded, Finland had the best record in the Union, having failed to transpose only 0.9 percent of all directives, while Luxembourg had the worst, with 6.2 percent. The improvement over the period of the action plan was espe-cially noteworthy for Austria, Belgium, and by far the largest national economy in the single market, Germany. Nonetheless, the objectives of the action plan were not fully met. Of 1,365 single market directives passed at the EU level, in October 1998 203 still were not transposed in one or more member states. Most member states continued to improve their records into 1999, but in a few cases the percent-age of EU directives not transposed into national law increased. This could happen because new directives constantly are being added to the body of single market legislation, making implementation at the national level an ongoing process re-quiring constant political attention.

As part of the action plan, the Commission also stepped up the pace of legal action against member states that failed to implement single market legislation. Table 4.2 summarizes the enforcement record for the period from September 1997 to September 1998. Compared with enforcement in 1995 and 1996, the Commis-sion now was more prepared to take cases to the Court of Justice. As can be seen in Table 4.3, enforcement in the area of telecommunications liberalization was still at an early stage, following the entering into effect in February 1998 of the voice telephony directive, and the twenty-seven letters of formal notice had been fol-lowed by only one reasoned opinion and no referrals to the Court. Areas such as the establishment and provision of services, environment, and taxation had much higher levels of action in the Court. Another element in the action plan involved the improvement of mechanisms by which businesses and individuals could lodge complaints about possible breaches of single market rules. Lacking its own means to monitor such breaches at the national and local levels, the Commission has to rely on such complaints to identify cases where the market is not functioning as intended.

As the tables demonstrate, difficulties in implementing the single market arise in just about every sector of the economy, with the greatest number of problems in the complex and politically sensitive areas of telecommunications, public pro-curement, and transport. A number of high-profile cases illustrate the tug-of-war that sometimes goes on between the Commission and the member states on single market matters. In 1996 the Commission sent a formal letter of notice to France about a local preference clause that ran counter to EU public procurement law in the call for bids to build the new stadium for the World Cup soccer championship, to be held in France in 1998. After failing to receive a satisfactory response from the French government, the Commission decided in June 1997 to refer the case to the Court of Justice. In March 1998 the French Minister for European Affairs for-mally recognized the existence of the infringement and agreed to improve future

Table 4.1 Member State Nonimplementation of Single Market Directives (Percent)

	LUX	IRL	ITA	POR	FRA	GRE	BEL	AUS	UK	SPA	GER	NETH	DK	SWE	FIN	EU
Nov 99	5.7	4.4	3.9	4.9	5.6	6.2	3.5	3.2	2.8	2.2	2.9	2.8	1.3	2.2	5.6	**12.8**
May 99	4.8	3.9	5.5	5.7	4.8	4.2	3.5	4.5	3.3	1.8	2.4	2.4	1.4	2.1	1.3	**12.8**
Nov 98	6.2	5.8	5.7	5.6	5.5	5.2	5.2	4.2	3.8	2.7	2.7	2.1	1.5	1.5	0.9	**14.9**
May 98	5.6	5.4	6.4	5.9	5.6	5.5	7.1	5.2	3.8	3.3	5.4	2.2	2.2	2.0	1.2	**18.2**
Nov 97	6.5	5.4	7.6	5.9	7.4	7.5	8.5	10.1	4.6	4.7	8.5	3.5	3.2	6.2	4.3	**26.7**

Source: European Commission, *Single Market Scoreboard*, Nos. 3, 4 and 4, 4.

Table 4.2 Single Market Infringement Procedures, Sept. 1997–Sept. 1998 (by Member State)

	BEL	DK	GER	SPA	GRE	FRA	IRL	ITA	LUX	NETH	AUS	POR	FIN	SWE	UK	EU
Letters of formal notice	34	8	42	36	37	78	9	60	9	15	24	19	16	17	25	429
Reasoned opinions	25	3	17	15	12	45	5	31	7	9	10	19	2	5	14	219
Cases referred to the ECJ	8	0	3	3	7	13	1	2	1	3	2	4	0	0	1	48
Judgments of the ECJ	9	0	6	6	5	5	0	8	2	1	0	5	0	0	0	47

Source: European Commission, *Single Market Scoreboard*, No. 4, 9–10.

Table 4.3   Single Market Infringement Procedures, Sept. 1997–Sept. 1998 (by Sector)

	Letters of formal notice	Reasoned opinions	Cases referred to ECJ	ECJ rulings
Free movement of goods	116	53	2	20
Free movement of services and establishment	88	62	18	6
Establishment and provision of services	50	34	11	3
Transport	11	27	7	3
Telecommunications	27	1	0	0
Free movement of people	68	24	6	5
Environment	55	35	10	9
Public procurement	52	24	2	1
Taxation	37	17	10	6
Consumers	8	3	0	0
Intellectual and commercial property	5	1	0	
TOTAL	429	219	48	47

Source: European Commission, Single Market Scoreboard, No. 3, 8–9.

performance with regard to public procurement. The local preference clause was eliminated from the contracting document and the Commission dropped its case.[33]

In another case, the Commission singled out Finland for rules it had imposed subjecting imported used cars and trucks to higher safety and pollution standards than those that applied to the resale of domestic vehicles. The Finnish authorities amended these rules to eliminate the discrimination, and the Commission terminated its proceedings. Other infringement cases have related to everything from the marketing of online databases (Belgium, Denmark, Greece, Ireland, Italy, Luxembourg, the Netherlands) to diplomas for psychologists (France) to the sale of nonalcoholic energy drinks (Italy).

In many cases, infringement of single market legislation occurs because local authorities are insufficiently aware of changes in national law that have been made as a result of EU legislation. Many citizen complaints in fact arise out of encounters with police and local authorities. For example, an Irish citizen who entered Sweden as a student complained to the Commission that Swedish immigration authorities asked him about the purpose of his visit to Sweden and stamped his passport with an entry stamp. Since Ireland is a member of the EU, these actions were contrary to EU legislation on free movement of persons. The Swedish national authorities later issued instructions to their police and border authorities to resolve this problem.

Professional qualifications are another area in which local authorities or nongovernmental bodies sometimes frustrate the working of the single market, often without any overtly protectionist motives, but simply because they are not used to recognizing foreign diplomas and qualifications as valid. Recent cases in which the Commission has been asked to intervene on behalf of EU citizens involved a Danish architect in Germany, a British art conservator in Belgium, and German nurses in France.

As part of the stepped-up drive on enforcement—and as many single market infringement cases worked their way through the stages of the enforcement process—in 1998 the Commission for the first time asked that financial penalties be levied against member states for persistent failure to correct shortcomings. In a case involving a 1985 directive on the approximation of laws concerning liability for defective products, the Court of Justice censured France in January 1993 for failing to transpose this directive into national law by the deadline of July 30, 1988. The directive provides that in all member states the manufacturer or importer of a defective product must pay damages and interest for harm caused by the product. Following the initial judgment of the Court that France had failed to enact the necessary legislation, the Commission issued a second reasoned opinion on the case, which was followed by the decision to ask the Court to impose fines—in this case ECU 158,250 for each day the noncompliance continued—on France.[34] Similarly, the Commission asked the Court to impose financial penalties of ECU 39,975 per day on Greece for its failure to respect a 1996 Court ruling censuring Greece for not implementing in national law a 1992 directive on public procurement of services.

Future Challenges

For the next decade and beyond the EU faces two major challenges with regard to the internal market: completing and sustaining the single market in the Union, and integrating the countries of central and eastern Europe into the single market as they prepare for EU membership.

The single market is not a one-time achievement. It requires constant attention to ensure that it keeps pace with political developments and with technological and economic change. Implementation of single market rules at the national level has proven to be unexpectedly difficult even in some traditional industrial sectors that were singled out in the 1985 program or in post-1992 follow-up legislation. In France, for example, where there is deep suspicion about the deregulation and privatization of public services, the national parliament failed to agree on implementing legislation to open the French electricity market to national and international competition.[35] Germany complied with the terms of the EU electricity deregulation directive, but the Commission has expressed concern about the limited competition in the German electricity market, particularly after the country's second- and third-largest electricity producers agreed to merge.[36] In these and other sectors, the single market is by no means complete.

Even where national implementing legislation is in place, member state compliance remains a problem, particularly in cases where powerful domestic political pressures have led governments to conclude that they must defy European rulings. This has been especially apparent in the area of food safety. Austria and Luxembourg enacted blanket national bans on the sale of genetically modified organisms, in clear defiance of EU rules regarding the single market and the Common Agricultural Policy.[37] In December 1999 the Commission threatened to take France to the Court of Justice for failing to allow the import of beef from the UK—after the Commission lifted an earlier ban that had been imposed at the EU level to contain the possible spread of "mad cow disease" from Britain to other countries.[38]

New technologies and the development of whole new industries based on these technologies—for example, biotechnology and electronic commerce—also pose challenges for the single market. National governments have been quick to regulate these industries at the national level, in so doing threatening to fragment the single market in precisely those industries that will be most important in generating future employment and prosperity. To head off this danger, the EU has moved to adopt European legislative frameworks. Examples of such legislation include an electronic commerce directive, a new legal framework to guarantee the security of electronic signatures, and a proposed directive on the legal protection of biotechnological inventions.

Competition policy is another area of challenge for the Union. While cross-border mergers and acquisitions can help to bolster the single market by enabling companies from different countries to compete against each other in the broader EU market, mergers and acquisitions can also be used to segment markets and to stifle competition. The Commission has been particularly concerned about the behavior of car and pharmaceutical manufacturers, both of which it has accused of pursuing anti-competitive practices under which they sell the same products at widely different prices in different member states. State aid to industry also poses a challenge to single market. Government grants and loans that are given to help national industries and to preserve employment distort the market by making it harder for firms from other EU countries to compete. For this reason, competition policy, as it relates both to anti-competitive practices by firms and to state aids by governments, has become a key component of the EU's single market strategy.

While the problems of completing and sustaining the single market in the existing Union are daunting, they pale in comparison to the challenge of establishing the market in the formerly socialist, nonmarket economies of central and eastern Europe. As will be discussed in Chapter 10, countries that wish to become members of the EU must adopt what is known as the *acquis communautaire*—the full range of laws, regulations, and policies concerning trade, competition policy, the environment, and so forth that have developed since the 1950s. While all parts of the *acquis* are in theory equal, as a practical matter its core is the single market. As part of their accession agreements, the prospective member states may secure long phase-in periods for costly environmental regulations or even permanent derogations from certain treaty provisions. But full participation from day one in the single market is likely to be an absolute requirement of admission. The single market is politically too important and affects too many individuals and interests in the existing member states—both consumers and competing producers of goods and services—to be subject to compromise.

The candidate countries had little in-depth understanding of the single market when they applied for membership in the early 1990s and they now are engaged in comprehensive efforts to remake their own domestic economies in the image of the single market. Doing so would be difficult under any circumstances, but it is made more so by the fact that the single market is a moving target. The aspirant countries must adopt not only the market rules in force in the EU at the time of their application, but those that have since been or that will be put into place by the time of their accession, such as those relating to the opening of the electricity and natural gas markets and the new steps to market opening in telecommunications.

To assist the candidate countries in preparing for the single market, the December 1994 Essen European Council asked the Commission to prepare a detailed white paper that would explain the single market and identify all of the relevant EU legislation going back to the 1950s. The Commission delivered its paper in the spring of 1995, and it was quickly translated into Polish, Czech, Hungarian, and all the other applicant country languages and distributed to the government bureaucracies and the offices of parliament.[39]

The paper emphasized the demands that participation in the internal market places on the member states: "An internal market without frontiers relies on a high level of mutual confidence and on equivalence of regulatory approach. Any substantial failure to apply the common rule in any part of the internal market puts the rest of the system at risk and undermines its integrity."[40] It went on to note that "any systematic checks and controls that are necessary to ensure compliance with the rules take place within the market and not when national borders are crossed." It stressed that reliance on the mutual recognition principle placed a heavy premium on the establishment of adequate standards and effective regulatory and inspection bodies in the acceding countries, since any product that the Poles or Czechs would lawfully produce or import after membership would be available to everyone else in the Union. Consumers in the existing member states must be assured that products from the new member states are safe and reliable. For this reason, as the white paper noted, "structures [needed to operate the market]—be they testing laboratories, metrology institutes, or customs posts at the external border of the Community—all need to win the confidence of the Community as a whole if the principle of mutual recognition is to be applied."[41] Similarly, companies in all member states that will compete with producers from the new member countries had to be confident that they would do so on a level playing field: that firms in the new member countries, particularly state-owned firms left over from socialism, will not benefit from open or hidden subsidies, tax concessions, and other advantages that contravene EU norms.

The white paper contained a detailed appendix of some 438 pages that was intended to serve as a "user's guide" for candidate governments as they worked to align legislation and practice with EU norms. It was divided into twenty-three sections, dealing with topics ranging from movement of capital to transport to public procurement to taxation. In each of these sections, the Commission provided an overview of existing legislation, of conditions necessary to operate the legislation (e.g., inspection services), and of key measures that needed to be implemented. Approximation to EU norms remained the responsibility of the applicant countries themselves who, consistent with practice in the Union itself, had a degree of latitude in drafting national legislation to implement EU directives. However, the EU offered help in the form of specialized technical assistance, help in estimating the costs and benefits of different sequences of approximation, and advice in strengthening or setting up monitoring or regulatory bodies. Much of this work was undertaken with financial support from the EU and involved partnerships and "twinning" arrangements with organizations and firms from EU member states.

Conclusion

Assuming that the single market is preserved in the EU-15 and gradually extended to the candidate countries, it will remain the core of the European integration process. It is a key factor in Europe's economic prosperity and its ability to compete in the global economy, as well as a point of leverage in the WTO and other trade forums. It also underpins and in turn is strengthened by the EU's common policies, which are the subject of the next chapter.

Notes

1. Article 30 TOR, ex Article 36.

2. CIA, *Handbook of Economic Statistics, 1986* (Washington: U.S. Government Printing Office, 1986), 39.

3. 1983 figures, in ibid., 60.

4. *Wall Street Journal* poll, March 6, 1986, cited in Carlo De Benedetti, "Europe's New Role in a Global Market," in Andrew J. Pierre, *A High Technology Gap? Europe, America and Japan* (New York: Council on Foreign Relations, 1987), 76.

5. "The thrust of Commission policy," Bull. EC Supplement 1/85.

6. European Commission, *Completing the Internal Market: White Paper from the Commission to the European Council* (Luxembourg: OOPEC, 1985).

7. "The Economics of 1992," *European Economy*, 35 (March 1988).

8. *Rewe Zentral AG v. Bundesmonopolverwaltung für Branntwein*, Case 128/78 ECR 1979.

9. *Technical harmonization and standards: a new approach*, COM(85) 19 final.

10. Bull. EC 5–1985, 11.

11. In a retrospective study of the 1992 program carried out in 1996, the Commission estimated that 76 percent of all intra-EU trade in goods was subject to some kind of techni-

cal regulation with the potential to hinder trade. 25 percent of all such trade was covered by the mutual recognition principle, while another 21 percent was subject to mutual recognition agreements among the member states or some combination of mutual recognition and EU legislation. 14 percent of intra-EU trade in goods subject to technical barriers was covered by new approach legislation, while 25 percent was covered by detailed harmonized requirements. For 15 percent of intra-EU trade subject to technical regulation, barriers had not yet been eliminated by any of these methods. Commission, *The 1996 Single Market Review: Background Information for the Report to the Council and European Parliament*, Commission Staff Working Paper, Brussels, December 16, 1996, SEC (96) 2378, 20.

12. Council Directive 92/77/EEC, October 17, 1992, O.J. L316/92.

13. Loukas Tsoukalis, *The New European Economy Revisited* (New York: Oxford University Press, 1997), 65. With increased competition leading to lower costs and with privatizations, this share had dropped to 11.5 percent in 1994. European Commission, *Green Paper: Public Procurement in the European Union: Exploring the Way Forward*, Communication adopted by the Commission, Brussels, November 27, 1996.

14. Council Regulation (EEC) 4060/89, December 21, 1989, O.J. L390/89.

15. European Commission, *Present Status and Future Approach for Open Access to Telecommunications Networks and Services (Open Network Provision): Communication from the Commission to the Council and the European Parliament*, COM(94) 513 final, Brussels, November 29, 1994.

16. Directive 96/92/EC concerning common rules for the internal market in electricity.

17. Second Council Directive on the coordination of laws, regulations, and administrative provisions relating to the taking-up and pursuit of the business of credit institutions and amending Directive 77/780 [the First Banking Directive], 89/646/EEC, O.J. L386/89.

18. Article 67 TOR (provision later abolished).

19. *Programme for the liberalization of capital movements in the Community*, COM(86) 292 final; summary in Bull. EC 5–1986, 13–16.

20. "The European Monetary System: A Long-Term View," in Francesco G. Giavazzi, Stefano M. Micossi and Marcus Miller, eds., *The European Monetary System* (Cambridge: Cambridge University Press, 1988), 376.

21. Tsoukalis, *The New European Economy Revisited*, 118.

22. Bull. EC 6–1990, 89–91.

23. Article 18, ex Article 8a.

24. Kalypso Nicolaidis and Raymond Vernon, "Competition Policy and Trade Policy in the European Union," in Edward M. Graham and J. David Richardson, eds. *Global Competition Policy* (Washington: Institute for International Economics, 1997), 297.

25. See, for example, Leon Brittan, *Europe: The Europe We Need* (London: Hamish Hamilton, 1994), 84–87.

26. For a discussion of the methodological difficulties and the econometric models used, see Commission, *The 1996 Single Market Review: Background Information for the Report to the Council and European Parliament*.

27. COM(96) 520 final.

28. European Commission, *The Impact and Effectiveness of the Single Market: Communication from the Commission to the European Parliament and Council*, October 30, 1996, at http://europa.eu.int/comm/dg15/en/update/impact.

29. *Single Market: Business Survey Reveals Cautious Optimism*, November 1997, http://europa.eu.int/dg15/en/update/score/99.htm.

30. *Single Market: Overview of Compliance Problems in 1996*, http://europa.eu.int/comm/dg15/en/update.

31. COM(97) 184.

32. European Commission, *Update on the Single Market: Single Market Scoreboard and Related Documents*, http://europa.eu.int/comm/dg15/en/update/score.

33. This and the other cases cited in this section are documented on the home page of the Directorate-General for the Internal Market of the Commission, http://europa.eu.int/comm/dg15.

34. "Liability for defective products: Commission seeks financial penalties against France," http://europa.eu.int/comm/dg15/en/goods/infr/311.htm.

35. "Opening up electricity markets to competition: reasoned opinions to France and Luxembourg," European Commission press release, IP/99/1034, Brussels, December 22, 1999.

36. "Commission opens in-depth investigation into merger between VEBA and VIAG," European Commission press release, IP/00/114, Brussels, February 4, 2000.

37. Simon Coss, "Commission Hints at GMO Rethink Amid Calls for a Ban," *European Voice* 4, no. 37 (October 15–21, 1998) 1.

38. "Commission opens infringement proceedings against France for refusal to lift embargo on British beef," European Commission, Directorate-General for Agriculture, press release, November 16, 1999.

39. European Commission, *White Paper: Preparation of the Associated Countries of Central and Eastern Europe for Integration into the Internal Market of the Union*, COM(95) 163 final, May 3, 1995.

40. Ibid., 8–9.

41. Ibid., 13.

Suggestions for Further Reading

Cockfield, Lord. *The European Union: Creating the Single Market*. London: Wiley Chancery Law, 1994.

Jacquemin, Alexis and André Sapir, eds. *The European Internal Market: Trade and Competition*. Oxford: Oxford University Press, 1990.

Molle, Willem. *The Economics of European Integration*. Aldershot: Dartmouth, 1990.

Tsoukalis, Loukas. *The New European Economy Revisited*. New York: Oxford University Press, 1997.

CHAPTER 5

Common Policies
A MIXED PICTURE

In addition to establishing the common market and common institutions, the Treaty of Rome provided for common policies in a number of areas. The treaty explicitly mentioned three such policies—the Common Agricultural Policy, the Common Commercial Policy, and the Common Transport Policy—and indirectly suggested others by including provisions relating to competition, coordination of economic policy, approximation of national laws to facilitate the common market, and a few references to social policy and labor conditions. The treaty emphasized those areas in which policy integration was closely related to the functioning of the common market. The Common Agricultural Policy was the foremost example of such integration.

Over time, policy integration expanded into new areas that were less directly linked to the market. In this way, the integration process to some extent continued to reflect the sectoral approach championed in the 1950s by proponents of the aborted European Defense Community and Euratom. Legally, the expansion of the Community's role into new policy areas often was based on Article 235 of the Treaty of Rome, which stipulated that "if action by the Community should prove necessary to attain, in the course of the operation of the common market, one of the objectives of the Community and this Treaty has not provided the necessary powers, the Council shall, acting unanimously on a proposal from the Commission and after consulting the European Parliament, take the appropriate measures."[1] This article provided a broad opening to advance new policy initiatives if doing so was seen as essential to the overriding goal of the treaty, the common market. On the basis of this catch-all article, the European Commission began developing Community environmental and regional policies in the early 1970s, long before they were identified as areas for Community action in the Single European Act, claiming that the proper functioning of the common market called for policies that would create a more even playing field among economic competitors and extend the market to all parts of the Community.

The interaction between market integration and policy integration has been a constant theme in the development of the European Union. Market integration focuses on the tearing down of barriers between and within the member states. It often is associated with a smaller role for government intervention, as it requires the cutting back of government rules and regulations that may favor particular firms and because it has led to the privatization of major state-owned industries.

Policy integration, in contrast, means an ongoing role for governments at the national level as implementors of policy, as well as the transfer of powers to European institutions—chiefly the Commission. Too much focus on policy integration can stifle progress towards the single market, while unfettered market integration inevitably limits the scope of member state governments to pursue integrated policies. While at first glance market integration and policy integration seem to be in tension with each other, under certain circumstances they can complement and reinforce each other. This certainly has been the case since the 1980s and the launch of the single market program. In complex industrial sectors such as transport and telecommunications as well as in more traditional sectors such as agriculture, market integration requires policy integration, while policy integration is economically and politically feasible only if it works in tandem with market forces.

Since the 1980s, two things have happened in the EU with regard to common policies. First, beginning with the SEA and continuing with the Maastricht and Amsterdam treaties, many more policy areas have been written into the treaties. Environmental, regional, and other policies and laws that originally were based on the catch-all Article 235 were given their own treaty basis. The change in terminology from European Economic Community to European Community mandated by the Maastricht amendments to the Treaty of Rome reflects the shift from exclusive association with economics to a sense that Europe is an environmental, social, and cultural as well as an economic community. This tendency to "Europeanize" new policy areas slowed dramatically with the subsidiarity discussion of the early 1990s, but the basic trend continued with the addition of an employment chapter in the Amsterdam Treaty. Second, and somewhat paradoxically, the single market became a complement to and in some respects the driving force behind policy integration. To give a concrete example: in the 1960s and 1970s, the Community did very badly in establishing a common transport policy, even though such a policy was mandated by the Treaty of Rome. In the 1980s, however, it made enormous strides toward finally unifying Europe's transport networks and industries, not by concentrating on transport for its own sake, but by treating transport as an essential part of the single market.

This interaction between market and policy integration was seen in the discussion in the previous chapter of the single market program, and will be apparent in the treatment in this chapter of the EU's main sectoral policies: agriculture, competition, transport and infrastructure, social and regional policy, the environment, and industry, research, and development. Like the single market, these are all areas covered within the EU's first pillar, subject to EU legislation that is passed by the Council and the European Parliament, based on proposals by the Commission.

The Common Agricultural Policy

THE COMMUNITY AND THE CAP

The Community put in place its Common Agricultural Policy in 1958–1968, in parallel with the establishment of the common market for industrial goods. In the mid-1950s, about 20 percent of the working population of the six still was employed in agriculture. Average farm size was small (about ten hectares), and many farmers were poor and economically vulnerable. The economic and social need for an agricultural policy thus was apparent. The member states of the new Community already operated extensive national systems of agricultural support and protection. To dismantle these systems to create a common market was politically unthinkable. The alternative was to establish a Community-level system that would be consistent with the goals of market integration but that still would provide the needed support for farmers. The CAP also was at the heart of the political compromises struck in the negotiations to establish the Community. In France there was deep skepticism about free trade in industrial goods and unfettered competition with German industry, but France had a large agricultural sector that needed new market outlets. France thus sought preferential access to the German market for its farm products and extensive agricultural support measures under the CAP as a trade-off for accepting the customs union.[2]

The treaty established five objectives for the CAP: (1) to increase agricultural productivity; (2) to ensure a fair standard of living for agricultural communities; (3) to stabilize markets; (4) to assure the availability of supplies; and (5) to ensure that supplies reach consumers at reasonable prices. These objectives have remained the basis for the CAP to the present, even though they are somewhat self-contradictory and help to explain many of the problems that the CAP has encountered in recent decades. Ensuring supplies to consumers at reasonable prices has tended to conflict with the goal of ensuring farmers' standard of living, which generally has required that they receive high prices for their products. The treaty did not spell out how these objectives were to be pursued. This was done in the first four years of the Community's existence, through passage of legislation by the Council of Ministers, acting on proposals from the Commission.

In early 1958 the Commission and the member states formulated three basic operational principles for the design of the CAP: (1) unity of the market based on common prices; (2) Community preference; and (3) financial solidarity. Unity of the market meant that even though free market principles would not apply in the agricultural sphere, the Community would strive to operate a common market for agricultural goods just as it did for industrial products. Wheat would cost the same in France as it did in Germany (with some allowance for local conditions and transport costs), and governments would not be permitted to segment the Community market through tariffs, national export subsidies, or other devices prohibited under the Treaty of Rome. Community preference meant that member states would import first from each other and only secondarily go out on the world market for supplies. Financial solidarity meant that the costs of the CAP would be pooled and shared on a Community basis. These same goals and operational principles apply in today's EU. However, the Union is undertaking major reforms of the CAP designed to lower costs that many farmers claim are undermining the basis of the system as it has existed since the early 1960s.

The CAP was set up to operate through a complex system of prices and levies, determined not by markets but by the Commission and the member states in the

Council of Ministers. For commodities such as grain, beef, and milk, the EU sets a "target price"—the price that farmers are to receive for their products. This price is determined each year, and is set high enough to guarantee farmers a certain standard of living. Target prices generally are above world market prices, since European farms are on average smaller and less competitive than farms in other parts of the world. The EU also sets an "intervention price" for each commodity. This is the price at which intervention agencies are required to step into the market to buy commodities to ensure that prices on the markets do not fall below the target price. The intervention agencies are designated by the member states, and receive their funding from the European Agricultural Guidance and Guarantee Fund (EAGGF), which was set up in April 1962 to fund the CAP. Finally, the EU sets an "entry price." This is the minimum price at which commodities from outside the Union can be imported. The entry price generally is near the target price, and is designed to keep lower-priced products from North America, Australia, and elsewhere from competing with European farmers. To maintain the entry price, the CAP imposes a levy that is calculated as the difference between the world market price and the entry price. The levy varies, depending upon the level of world market prices. Thus if world grain prices fall because of abundant harvests in major grain-producing countries, the EU increases the levy on grain to ensure high entry prices, allowing EU farmers to maintain their share of the EU market at the same high target price.

With the EU deliberately choosing to maintain its internal farm prices above world market prices, it normally would not be expected to export agricultural products outside the Union. But the CAP also has a mechanism for exports that is in effect the reverse of the variable import levy—a variable export subsidy paid in the form of a refund to EU agricultural exporters. These subsidies enable Europe to sell on the world market products bought from farmers at the uncompetitive target price. To agricultural producers in other countries, this practice constitutes dumping and has been a major source of international trade tensions. Tensions over European export subsidies were particularly acute in the mid-1980s, when an undeclared price war caused by European subsidies and international (especially U.S.) retaliation came to dominate world grain markets. U.S. producers also complained about subsidized sales of cheese, wine, hams, and pasta on the North American market.[3]

The CAP accomplished the basic objective of extending the common market and the common external trade policy to agricultural products by application of the principles of unity of the market, Community preference, and financial solidarity. It did so, however, at a high economic and political price. Most of the financial burden of the CAP was borne by consumers, who were forced to pay higher prices for their food than they would have had they been able to purchase food at world market prices. The CAP also encouraged waste and overproduction. Since farmers were guaranteed a target price, they had no financial incentive to match production to demand. Farmers increased production for sale at the target price and used the higher revenues in part to improve productivity and raise output through investments in equipment, fertilizer, and land.

In the 1960s and 1970s foreign suppliers gradually were squeezed out of the EC market, as the variable levy neutralized the advantages they gained from lower prices. The CAP resulted in increased production and, under Community preference, substitution of intra-EC trade for imports from traditional overseas suppliers. The first major trade dispute between the United States and the EC, known as the "chicken war," arose in 1962 when American suppliers, who traditionally had sold large amounts of frozen poultry to West Germany, lost this market as German importers shifted their purchases to other EC member countries. As domestic production increased, the EC shifted from being a net importer to a major exporter of food. The Community became the owner of "wine lakes" and "butter mountains" that became the object of political derision at home. The EC sought to dispose of these stocks by selling them on world markets at subsidized prices, cutting into sales by U.S. and other exporters and thereby increasing trade tensions. When the CAP was introduced in 1962, the EC produced about 80 percent of its food and imported the remainder. Today, the EU produces about 120 percent of the amount of food that it consumes, leaving a large surplus for export.

The CAP also became a major burden on the Community budget, accounting for over 70 percent of total expenditure by the early 1980s. This was especially problematic at a time when the Community was expanding its activities into industrial research and development, regional policies targeted at poor urban as well as rural areas, and other priority areas. However, the powerful farm lobby, represented both in Brussels and in the member states, strongly resisted changes in an agricultural system upon which farmers had become wholly dependent. France and Germany, each for somewhat different reasons, both resisted major reforms, and without the support of the Community's two leading powers little could be achieved.

Britain, in contrast, had long imported much of its food from its overseas empire and other countries such as Argentina, and it had a much smaller farming sector—measured either by share of agricultural production in GDP or number of farmers relative to total employment—than the other Community countries. This meant that British consumers contributed to CAP financial solidarity by paying high prices for their food, while British farmers received far less back from the Community treasury than farmers in other countries. British governments generally favored reform, but were unable to overcome resistance in other member states.

PRESSURE FOR REFORM

The problems of overproduction and the budgetary burden posed by the CAP led to growing pressures for change.[4] In 1979 the Community attempted to curb excess milk production by introducing a levy on dairy farmers that would be used to help pay for the storage and disposal costs of excess milk. When the levy system failed to cut overproduction, the Community introduced, in 1984, a system of national quotas on milk production that had some effect in holding down supplies.

The first major reform of the CAP came about in 1988, as part of the five-year Delors I budget package. At a special session of the European Council in Brussels in February 1988 the member states agreed that Community spending on agriculture could not increase at more than 74 percent of the rate of increase in Community GNP for the next five years. This meant that agricultural subsidies as a share of GNP and of the Community budget gradually would fall. To effect these savings, the Community put in place several measures to curb production, including a land set-aside scheme and a system of production quotas beyond which farmers would not receive full support payments for their products.

The 1988 reforms signaled a new readiness on the part of the political leadership to tackle the problems of the CAP, even if it meant conflict with the Community's farmers. They were too modest, however, to solve the problems of overproduction and ever-rising costs. The Community thus launched a second round of reforms in 1992.[5] Known as the MacSharry Plan after the Commissioner responsible for agriculture, Ray MacSharry of Ireland, these reforms were undertaken in response to both internal and external pressure. Agriculture had by this time become the main sticking point in the Uruguay Round of the GATT, and without changes in the CAP the successful conclusion of this negotiation would not have been possible. Internally, there were strong pressures to cut costs.

The distinctive element of the MacSharry Plan was a move away from price supports for agricultural products to direct income support to farmers. Price supports were ruinously expensive, encouraged overproduction, benefitted wealthy as well as poor farmers, and were at the heart of the international complaints about the CAP. In contrast, direct income payments did not encourage overproduction and did not disrupt global markets. Farmers had always resisted direct income support as the basis for the CAP, fearing that such payments would be seen as a form of welfare that was demeaning to farmers and potentially more vulnerable than other types of aid to future cost cutting, but they were unable to block the MacSharry proposals.

The reforms left in place the CAP's traditional basic price support mechanisms, but they called for steep cuts in the intervention prices for key commodities such as grain, beef, and dairy products. Grain prices were to be reduced by 29 percent over a three-year period in 1993–1994, beef prices by 15 percent, butter by 5 percent, and price supports for oilseeds eliminated altogether. To compensate for lower overall prices, the CAP instituted a system of compensatory payments to farmers based on the amount of land they had under cultivation and the historic yield level in their particular region of the Community—in other words on their capacity to produce. The CAP also instituted set-aside schemes under which farmers agreed to take land out of production or to reduce herd sizes in exchange for compensation payments. In addition to these core elements related to prices and incomes, the MacSharry reforms included measures to encourage more environmentally friendly farming and to promote the afforestation of land taken out of production.

These reforms were highly controversial among farmers, but in the end they were accepted by the member states and became the basis for the Blair House agreement between the EC and the United States in November 1992. The Community agreed to a 21 percent cut in export volumes over the six years 1993–1999, during which time the United States and the EC would observe a "peace clause" in agricultural trade disputes. These understandings became the basis for the breakthrough in the Uruguay Round GATT negotiations and the completion of the round in December 1993.

Whether the reforms would result in lower costs and reduced international trade tensions became key questions after 1992. For the most part these objectives were achieved. The ceiling of 74 percent of EU GNP in the growth of agricultural spending was renewed in the Delors II financial package for 1993–1999, which meant that the share of agriculture in the EU budget continued to decline even though the absolute level of spending still rose. Agriculture as a share of the EU budget fell to 42 percent in 1999, down from 50 percent in 1996 and 64 percent in 1988. In the course of the 1990s, the EU's vast commodity surpluses largely disappeared, lowering storage costs and reducing the incentive to dump on world markets. The EU remained a major agricultural exporter, but tensions with other agricultural nations were kept in check.

AGENDA 2000 AND THE BERLIN PACKAGE

By the end of the 1990s the CAP was facing new challenges and pressure for reform linked to enlargement. The Commission estimated that the ten candidate countries of central and eastern Europe had some 9.5 million agricultural workers and 60 million hectares of agricultural land—compared with 8.2 million agricultural workers and 140 million hectares in the EU of the fifteen. Over 22 percent of the total workforce in the candidate countries was employed in agriculture, compared with only 5 percent in the EU-15.[6] To extend the existing CAP to this many farmers would be ruinously expensive. *Agenda 2000* therefore called for continuing reform of the CAP in the context of a broader reform of EU finances. In its draft financial package for 2000–2006, the Commission proposed that increases in CAP spending be kept at the existing upper limit of 74 percent of GNP growth, but acknowledged that holding agricultural spending at this level would necessitate further reform.

Building upon the proposals in *Agenda 2000*, in 1998 agricultural commissioner Franz Fischler proposed additional large cuts in the support prices for meat, cereals, and dairy products intended to reduce the costs of the CAP, to be replaced by direct payments to sustain income. Fischler proposed that the cereals intervention price be cut by 20 percent in 2000; beef prices by 30 percent between 2000 and 2002; and dairy prices by 15 percent by 2006. The Commission also suggested that the shift from price intervention to direct income support might make possible the transfer of responsibility for a portion of these direct payments (as much as 25 percent) to the member states.

For the next twenty months debate over CAP reform raged in the EU. Member state ministers of agriculture were nearly unanimous in denouncing the Commission's proposals as damaging to farmers, but could agree on very little else. France was adamantly opposed to any "renationalization" of agricultural support payments, which in its view ran counter to the basic bargain embodied in the 1957 Treaty of Rome. Germany was equally firm that its large net payments to the EU budget had to be cut, and agriculture was the logical place to start. Final agreement was achieved only at the March 1999 Berlin session of the European Council, following a preliminary deal forged by the agricultural ministers the preceding month.

In the final deal negotiated at Berlin, cereals prices were to be cut 15 percent in two equal steps in 2000 and 2001. Ten percent of land devoted to cereals will be taken out of production for each year to 2006. Beef prices will fall 20 percent over three years, beginning in 2000. Dairy prices will be cut 15 percent, but only in 2005–2006. Greece, Spain, Italy, Ireland, and the UK (Northern Ireland) were awarded increases in milk quotas beginning in 2000, equal to 0.9 percent of the EU total. Absolute levels of spending will continue to increase, as they have every year from 1962–1999.

PROSPECTS

The CAP faces three long-term challenges that the Berlin agreements did not resolve. First, enlargement will put enormous strains on the system. Prices will remain above world market levels, which will mean high costs for consumers and could encourage the production of large amounts of unneeded food in the countries of central and eastern Europe under subsidies from the EU budget. These factors suggest that either the CAP will require further reform before enlargement goes forward or that it will be applied only partially to the new member countries.

Second, a new round of international trade talks, which the EU was committed to entering under WTO auspices after the peace clause expired at the end of 1999, again promised to put EU agriculture in the world spotlight. The United States, Australia, and other agricultural exporters charged that the 1999 reforms did not go far enough in reducing export subsidies, certain to be one of the most contentious issues in these talks. The failure of the Seattle WTO meeting in late 1999 temporarily took the spotlight off the CAP, but it did not eliminate rising international tensions over agriculture.

Third, the CAP is facing a new set of environmental, food safety, and animal rights issues that played almost no role when the CAP was established but that increasingly impinge on both the domestic and international aspects of agricultural policy-making.

Increases in agricultural production have been achieved by intensive use of fertilizers, herbicides, pesticides, and machinery, all of which contribute to environmental problems. Agriculture thus has become a priority area for EU environmental policy, and the CAP itself has placed increasing emphasis on environmentally friendly farming and taking land out of production for conservation purposes. New issues related to food safety and the ethical and scientific bases of modern farming also have arisen, bringing new tensions within and among the member states and between the EU and its major trading partners. The outbreak of bovine spongiform encephalopathy (BSE, commonly known as "mad cow disease") caused the Commission in 1995 to ban the sale of British beef to other EU and external markets, which in turn led to a political crisis between Britain and its partners before the ban was lifted. A similar ban was placed on exports of dioxin-contaminated products from Belgium in June 1999, again provoking a political crisis and raising concern about EU food safety regulation. As noted in the previous chapter, France's refusal to lift its ban on the import of British beef, after the Commission had certified British herds as clean and lifted the EU ban, was a contravention of single market rules that prompted the Commission to start infringement proceedings.

Consumer and environmentalist opposition to farming with genetically modified organisms is strong in Europe. Several member states have imposed national bans on the sale of such crops, thereby undermining the unity of the market in a way that would seem to contravene the Treaty of Rome but that the Commission has been reluctant for political reasons to challenge in the Court of Justice. The Commission may seek to tighten regulations dealing with genetically engineered crops at the EU level, but it is also criticized by the United States for imposing politically driven limits on the import of products that scientists regard as safe. To defuse these issues, in December 1999 the European Commission proposed the establishment of a European Food Authority that would provide independent advice on food safety issues.[7]

Animal rights issues also have been thrust on the agenda of the Union. The Amsterdam Treaty contains a protocol on the protection and welfare of animals, adopted largely in deference to British opinion, in which the EU and its member states pledge to pay full regard to the welfare requirements of animals in formulating and implementing EU agriculture (as well as transport, internal market, and research) policy. The protocol itself has no binding force, but it reflects a complex new political environment in which consumer concerns and the attitudes of urban and suburban voters rather than just the interests of producers are shaping the operation of the CAP.

THE COMMON FISHERIES POLICY

The legal basis for a fisheries policy was established in the articles in the Treaty of Rome dealing with the CAP, which defined agricultural products as "products of the soil, stockfarming, and of fisheries." However, the Community did not begin to develop common guidelines for commercial fishing until the 1970s, after the accession of Denmark, Ireland, and the UK, countries with long coastlines and substantial domestic fishing industries. The EC formally adopted its Common Fisheries Policy (CFP) in 1983, shortly before the accession of Portugal and Spain, also major fishing nations whose accession lent new urgency to the issue.

Commercial fishing accounts for less than 1 percent of GNP and employment in most EU countries, but it has become an important area of EU policy concern, both for internal and external reasons. European crews traditionally have fished in the waters off other European countries as well as on the high seas and off the coasts of Africa and North America. Overfishing is a serious worldwide environmental problem, and the member states look to EU action as a way of managing the industry in European coastal waters and of negotiating fishing rights with other countries around the world.

The CFP divides fishing grounds into three categories: coastal waters up to the twelve-mile limit, coastal waters beyond twelve miles, and fishing grounds in international waters or under the jurisdiction of non-EU countries. Within twelve miles, access is reserved for fishermen from local ports who traditionally have fished in those waters. Small fishing boats from other EU countries with claims based on tradition also are allowed some access. EU legislation carefully sets out which boats from which countries and at what times of the year may fish in these waters. The twelve-mile preference is an exception to the EU's single market non-discrimination principle, and it is scheduled to be phased out by the end of 2002.[8]

Beyond the twelve-mile coastal zone, freedom of access for boats from any EU country applies, irrespective of nationality. When Spain and Portugal joined the Community in 1986, the other member states insisted on a ten-year delay in putting this provision into practice for them. Nevertheless, it caused a stir in local communities when, in early 1996, Portuguese and Spanish trawlers appeared off the coasts of Ireland and the UK. Beyond the 200-mile limit, the EU negotiates bilateral agreements with other coastal nations to ensure access by its fishermen to those waters and participates in international regulatory bodies such as the North Atlantic Salmon Conservation Organization and the International Commission for the Conservation of Atlantic Tunas.

Since 1983, fisheries management in EU waters has been based on the concept of a total allowable catch (TAC) for each species in a given area. The EU's Scientific, Technical and Economic Committee for Fisheries (STECF), working with international scientific bodies, annually assesses stock levels with an eye toward conservation. On the basis of this scientific assessment, the Commission makes a recommendation to the Council, which in December of each year sets the TACs that are divided among the member states and their fleets. So far this approach has not solved the problem of overfishing in EU waters. Not all areas and species are covered by TACs, and member state governments in the Council too often have been tempted to avoid short-term political costs at the expense of long-term environmental damage by establishing quotas larger than those recommended by the experts. Overfishing by EU boats in international waters is also a problem, and has led to sharp disputes with other countries, notably in 1995 when Canada impounded Spanish trawlers for exceeding their allowable catches in waters off the Canadian coast.

In 1997 the Council adopted a new plan for the restructuring of the EU fisheries sector for the period 1997–2002, the main objective of which was to achieve a better balance between available stocks and the level of fishing. The financial framework for 2000–2006 allocates 1.1 billion euros to the EU's Financial Instrument for Fisheries Guidance, which supports improvements in the sector, including help to the industry with processing and marketing. As in the agricultural sector, EU policy also aims to assist local communities that are heavily dependent on fishing to develop alternative sources of employment such as tourism.

Although useful up to a point, none of these measures solved the fundamental problem of overfishing. EU fishing ministers finally took decisive action on this matter at their December 1999 session, at which they agreed to large reductions in TACs for 2000. Cuts ranged from 62 percent for cod in the Irish Sea, 40 percent for haddock in the Atlantic west of France, and 20 to 25 percent for lobster in a range of areas. These cuts were bitterly protested by the fishing industry and resisted by some of the ministers, who succeeded in diluting Commission proposals for even more drastic cuts. In the end, however, environmental considerations won out over economic interests, if only because the sheer scale of the problem compelled the Council to action. As the UK minister remarked, "I wish we could give the industry more fish. But the fish are not there."[9]

The Common Transport Policy

Transport is important both as an economic sector in its own right, accounting for about 7 percent of EU GDP and employing more than 6 million people, and as an input to other sectors, notably manufacturing and agriculture.[10] The founders of the Community recognized that it would make little sense to eliminate tariffs and quotas if discrimination against imports in the cost of rail and other forms of transport persisted. The Treaty of Paris establishing the ECSC prohibited member states from using transport rates and policies to favor domestic suppliers of coal and steel at the expense of suppliers from other member states. The Treaty of Rome broadened the principle of nondiscrimination to trade in all goods by calling for the establishment of a common transport policy to support the overall objectives of the treaty. Under Article 80 of the treaty, the common transport policy was to apply automatically to road, rail, and inland waterway transport.[11] The Council of Ministers could extend the CTP to marine and aviation transport—sectors with a more important extra-European dimension—by unanimous vote, as eventually was done in 1974.

In contrast to what happened with respect to agriculture, however, the Community failed to develop a comprehensive transport policy until well into the 1980s. This failure was mainly the responsibility of the member states, which had different interests in the transport sector and could not agree among themselves on key aspects of the policy. The Benelux countries and, after the first enlargement, geographically peripheral states such as the UK and Denmark mainly were interested in free movement by their trucking and barge companies in and through the Community's core—Germany, France, and northern Italy—while the geographically central states wanted to open their domestic markets and transport infrastructures to foreign competition on a basis that would preserve certain advantages for domestic firms. The national railroad companies, state-owned and with proud traditions going back to the 19th century, also resisted opening to foreign competition.

In fulfilment of its responsibilities to propose legislation to implement the goals of the Treaty of Rome, in 1962 the Commission adopted an Action Plan for Transport.[12] It proposed three kinds of measures: (1) anti-discrimination measures to apply to goods shipped from other member states; (2) liberalization measures to allow carriers to supply services across national frontiers in the Community; and (3) harmonization measures with regard to such matters as the size and weight of trucks, road taxes, and safety and working conditions in the transport sector. The Commission also proposed that the EC play a role in coordinating infrastructure investment, particularly with regard to trunk routes of Community importance. Very little of the action plan actually was adopted, however, and the transport sector remained highly fragmented along national lines. Truck transport, for example, was regulated by a series of bilateral agreements among the member states specifying how much freight firms from each country could carry to the other country in a given year. In the aviation sector, governments were mainly concerned with protecting the interests of their flag carriers, while in maritime shipping they continued to protect national fleets from international competition in the face of global overcapacity in the industry.

The Community finally began to develop a comprehensive transport policy in the 1980s. This was mainly the result of two factors. First, in 1983 the European Parliament brought an action in the Court of Justice against the Council of Ministers for failing to adopt a common transport policy, as mandated in the Treaty of Rome. This was an excellent example of how the Court could be called upon to adjudicate disputes among the institutions of the Community, even if it meant challenging the positions of the member states (whose representatives, after all, made up the Council of Ministers). It also reflected the activist, pro-integration stance of the EP after the direct elections of 1979. In May 1985 the Court ruled in favor of the Parliament, and called upon the Council to develop a plan to liberalize transport services within a reasonable time.[13] Second, as was seen in the previous chapter, transport liberalization became an important element in the single market program adopted under the 1986 Single European Act. Trucking, rail and inland waterway, shipping, and air transport now are all at least partially open to competition under a body of EU legislation that aims to harmonize fiscal, technical, and social provisions in member states that affect competition in the transport sector.

In 1992 the Commission issued a white paper, *The Future Development of the*

Common Transport Policy, that became the policy guideline for the remainder of the decade.[14] It specified three main goals: completing the single market in transport by the removal of remaining restrictions on competition; developing a comprehensive transport system able to serve the economic and social needs of the Union; and integrating environmental objectives into the common transport policy. Promoting transport safety was another important objective, added to the transport provisions of the Treaty of Rome by amendment.

Market liberalization continued throughout the decade, and included the opening of air transport in 1997 and continued steps toward open competition in road, rail, and other sectors. This was a slow and difficult process, however, technically complex and resisted by political forces in many of the member states. In road transport, for example, the member states had difficulty in harmonizing standards on maximum driving hours and other safety and employment provisions that affect competition in the industry. Similarly, the Commission and the transport ministers of the fifteen agreed on the need to revitalize rail transport in order to shift freight off Europe's congested roads, but the EU made only slow progress on the implementation of directives calling for the separation of infrastructure and transport operations and other measures to promote competition.

Environmental considerations have become increasingly important in EU transport policy. Traffic congestion has led to concern about a virtual breakdown of transport in key cities and markets. In addition, cars, trucks, and buses are responsible for over 75 percent of the carbon dioxide produced in the EU, and thus a major contributor to the greenhouse effect that is believed to be responsible for global warming. The EU is committed to reducing its carbon dioxide emissions, which can only be done by efficiency improvements and by shifting traffic to more environmentally friendly alternatives such as high speed and commuter rail.

Trans-European Networks

In addition to harmonizing standards and promoting competition, EU transport policy has placed a growing emphasis on the identification and completion of major transport projects known as trans-European networks (TENs). In its 1962 action plan the Commission had called for a Community role in coordinating infrastructure investment, but little was done to ensure that Europe's physical network of roads, track, and airports could accommodate the growing volume of cross-border freight and passenger traffic generated by the common market. The Maastricht Treaty included new provisions that gave the Union powers and responsibilities to promote, through the TENs, the interconnection and interoperability of national networks in the context of the single European market. TENs are intended for transport, telecommunications, and energy infrastructure, but the bulk of spending and political attention has been on the transport sector. The EU does not finance the construction of these networks and it cannot compel national and regional governments or private investors to undertake specific projects, but it does promote the TENs by establishing guidelines and setting priorities for such projects, financing feasibility studies, providing loan guarantees and interest rate subsidies from the EU budget, providing loans from the European Investment Bank, and, for countries that are eligible, offering grant assistance from the Cohesion Fund.

In 1994 the Union selected fourteen major transport projects as priority TENs and called for construction of all of these projects to start by the end of 1996 (see Table 5.1).[15] More than 60 percent of EU spending for transport TENs goes to passenger and freight rail projects that are aimed at improving the viability of Europe's railways and shifting traffic from the roads. Three of these projects are virtually complete, six others have secured financing and are expected to be completed by 2005, while the remaining five have not yet secured financial backing and are only expected to be completed well beyond 2005.[16] Lining up finance for many of these projects has been problematic, especially since banks and investors have

Table 5.1   Trans-European Networks—Priority Transport Projects

Project	Countries	Completion
HST/Combined Transport North-South Nuremberg-Erfurt-Halle/Leipzig-Berlin-Brenner axis (Verona-Munich)	Italy, Austria, Germany	After 2005
HST PBKAL Paris-Brussels-Cologne-Amsterdam-London	Belgium, Netherlands, France, Germany, UK	2005
HST South Madrid-Barcelona-Perpignan-Montpellier/Madrid-Vitoria-Dax	France, Spain	2005
HST East Paris-Metz-Strasbourg-Appenweier with junctions to Metz-Saarbrücken-Mannheim and Metz-Luxembourg	France, Germany, Luxembourg	2005
Betuwe Line Conventional Rail/Combined Transport Rotterdam-Dutch-German border	Netherlands, Germany	2005
HST/Combined Transport France-Italy Lyon-Turin/Turin-Milan-Venice-Trieste	France, Italy	After 2005
Greek Motorways	Greece	2005
Motorway Lisbon-Valladolid	Portugal, Spain	After 2005
Conventional Rail Link Cork-Dublin-Belfast-Larne-Stranraer	Ireland, UK	2000
Malpensa Airport Milan	Italy	2000
Oresund fixed link	Denmark, Sweden	2000
Nordic triangle multimodal corridor	Finland, Sweden	After 2005
Ireland/UK/Benelux road link	Ireland, UK	After 2005
West Coast Main Line (rail)	UK	2005

been burned on previous mega-projects, such as the Eurotunnel between France and Britain. Obtaining environmental approvals also has been difficult and time-consuming, and member states often have differed over the design of particular transnational projects and the border points at which they should connect.

One of the future challenges for EU transport policy is to upgrade the linkages between the territory of the present member states and the candidate countries of central and eastern Europe, as well as to help these countries expand and modernize their own domestic transport infrastructure. Roads, railroads, and airports in these countries were built before or during the communist era and are totally inadequate to support the integration of the region into the single market or to attract the level of investment needed to raise these countries to West European standards of income. A series of pan-European transport conferences that began in 1992 has endorsed the building of ten pan-European corridors that are expected to complete the basic physical interconnection of the continent, but work is only beginning on translating the corridor concepts into actual projects. The European Commission has developed a Transport Infrastructure Needs Assessment for the overall central and east European network within the basic framework of the ten major corridors. This network comprises 18,030 kilometers of roads, 20,290 kilometers of railway line, 38 airports, 13 seaports, and 49 river ports. Completing this network is estimated to cost a total of 90 billion euros in the period to 2015.[17] EU aid funds and loans from the EIB will underwrite a small part of the cost, but most of the investment will have to come from the central and east European countries themselves.

Competition Policy

The Treaty of Rome provided for the establishment of "a system ensuring that competition shall not be distorted in the Common Market."[18] The framers of the treaty recognized that with overt barriers to trade among the member countries no longer available, governments and firms might resort to other actions to frustrate cross-border competition. These concerns were especially valid in view of Western Europe's long history of industrial cartels and the weak to nonexistent role of anti-trust legislation in most member states. Firms might get together to form cartels to set prices or control supplies in all or parts of the common market. Alternatively, governments might be tempted to provide state aid (subsidies, low interest loans, excessively generous grants for training or R&D) to domestic firms that could disadvantage competitors from other Community states.

The ECSC Treaty gave the High Authority the power to block mergers in the coal and steel industries. This power was conceived as one of the ECSC's safeguards against a resurgence of German power, which it was feared might come about through mergers and acquisitions involving German firms. The power to block prospective mergers in these industries later passed to the European Commission by virtue of the Merger Treaty. However, the Treaty of Rome itself did not grant the Commission comparable powers in other industries. Rather, Article 85 banned as incompatible with the common market "agreements, concerted practices, and decisions between undertakings that have as their intention or effect the restriction or distortion of competition and that may affect trade between member states." Article 86 prohibited the abuse of a dominant position by firms that affected the functioning of the common market. Under Article 87, the Council was required to pass within three years of the entering into force of the Treaty of Rome legislation giving effect to the general provisions of Articles 85 and 86.[19] Thus in 1962 the Council passed Regulation 17, which gave the Commission powers to investigate anti-competitive practices and abuses of dominant position and to order a stop to any infringements.[20]

MERGERS

Under a new merger resolution adopted by the Council in 1989, from September 1990 onward the Commission was granted authority to control prospective mergers and takeovers that might restrict competition in the single market.[21] These powers applied only to large deals involving firms with business activities in two or more EU countries. For mergers that were smaller or that involved companies operating largely on a national scale, national legislation alone would continue to apply. In the first five years in which the new resolution was in effect, the Commission received approximately 400 cases for review, but it blocked only one transaction, the proposed takeover of the Canadian commuter-aircraft maker de Havilland by a joint venture of a French and an Italian firm engaged in the same business. However, in many cases in which the Commission did not block a merger, it established conditions—such as divestiture of particular business units—before granting approval.[22] Firms that fail to notify the Commission of intended mergers can be assessed large fines and forced to divest themselves of holdings or take other steps required by Brussels to restore competition in the marketplace.

Commission involvement in policing mergers and acquisitions has increased in recent years, as companies have restructured and combined with each other in response to global economic trends and the anticipated introduction of the euro. In 1997 alone the Commission received 172 notifications of mergers and made 135 final decisions under the merger regulation.[23] By 1999 this had risen to 292 notifications and 270 decisions.[24] It approved nearly all of the deals that it examined, but often only after the companies involved accepted conditions.

The Commission's authority under the Treaty of Rome and the merger regulation is not limited to companies that are based in the EU, but extends to many large mergers between European and U.S. firms and even to third-country firms that are active in the EU market as producers or exporters. The EU thus has become more global in its approach to competition policy. In 1997, for example, the Commission threatened to try to block the acquisition by the Boeing Company of the McDonnell Douglas Corporation. European involvement in a deal between two U.S. firms that had been cleared by U.S. antitrust authorities caused a certain amount of irritation in Washington, but it was justified in Brussels on the grounds that Boeing's dominant position in the worldwide commercial aviation market would be strengthened and could adversely affect European interests. In the end the Commission approved the acquisition, but only after Boeing gave assurances to open up to competition exclusive supply contracts that it had with U.S. airlines. In general, the United States and the EU cooperate quite closely in the anti-trust area, as authorities on both sides of the Atlantic share an interest in protecting consumers from monopolistic practices. Tensions do arise, however, especially when one side suspects the other of using competition policy to advance the interests of its own firms. In the Boeing case, for example, it was widely believed that Commission concerns about competition were in reality a continuation in a different form of the longstanding European governmental support for Airbus Industrie, the European competitor to Boeing in the civil aircraft market.

STATE AIDS

The provisions on state aid in the Treaty of Rome distinguish between permissible aid provided to foster social development in poor regions or for certain other legitimate purposes and aid, the intent or effect of which is to favor particular industries or firms in ways that distort trade among the member states. Aid that distorts or threatens to distort competition in the market is banned. The treaty requires member states to notify the Commission of all state aids to industry or proposals for new aid. The Commission reviews all such notifications and in cases where it finds that such aid is incompatible with the functioning of the market orders the member state to cease or amend the aid and to recover from the beneficiary firm any funds already paid. The treaty recognizes the right of member states to operate public undertakings, for example, utilities or transport firms that enjoy a monopoly position or taxpayer subsidies, but prohibits these firms from interfering with the functioning of the market. In effect, state-owned or -sanctioned monopolies are supposed to behave as much as possible as if they were private enterprises, in business to make profits and pay dividends rather than to carry out governmental objectives such as maintaining employment.

For much of the history of the EC, the record of the member states with regard to notification of state aids was weak, and the Commission often was reluctant to challenge governments seeking to support their national industries.[25] The prevailing wisdom of the day about the importance of developing national champions of adequate size and scope to compete in global markets tended to militate against strict enforcement. As with competition policy for firms, however, there was a sea change in the 1980s as the Commission became more convinced of the benefits of competition (including intra-European competition) and of the threat posed to the single market by state aids, and as the right-of-center governments of the period became more interested, for both ideological and financial reasons, in scaling back aid to industry.

In 1988 the Commission began to publish a regular biannual survey of state aid to industry designed to highlight possible distortions in the single market. The 1998 report indicated that Italy and Greece are the member states that provide the highest subsidies to industry, but that Germany is also above the EU average. Aid to industry is lowest in the UK, Austria, and Sweden. Aid to all industrial sectors averages 3.5 percent of value added across the EU, but reaches a staggering 25 percent of value added (down from 34 percent in the late 1980s) in the shipbuilding sector.[26]

Most of the aid covered in these reports is legal, if not optimal from the standpoint of economic theory. However, in recent years there also have been many clashes between the Commission and the member states over aid to industry that is considered to contravene the Treaty of Rome and secondary legislation designed to regulate state aid in specific industrial sectors such as steel, shipbuilding, and aviation. Much of the focus has been on France and Italy, countries with large state-owned sectors and long records of subsidizing private and state-owned firms to save jobs and bolster international competitiveness. More recently, Germany, with its large subsidies to the sunset industries—coal, steel, textiles, and shipbuilding—has been the target of many Commission actions. The Maastricht Treaty inserted an amendment into Article 92 of the Treaty of Rome that expressly permits aid to the former East Germany to overcome the economic legacy of division, but in some cases the Commission has questioned the size and appropriateness of such aid.

Recent high-profile state aid cases have involved UK government support to British Aerospace for the purchase of the carmaker Rover (subsequently sold by BA to BMW), French government support to Renault, the state-owned car company, and aid to loss-making national airlines such as Air France, Olympic, and Iberia.[27] In cases where the Commission declines to approve an aid allocation, the government in question must recover the money from the company involved. If a member state refuses to comply with a Commission order regarding state aid, the Commission can take that state to the ECJ and, under the provisions introduced in the Maastricht Treaty on enforcing EU law, may levy a fine against it for noncompliance.

Social Policy

Ever since its founding in the 1950s, the EC was vulnerable to criticisms by trade unions, political parties, and various other groups that European integration unduly favored big business to the detriment of workers, small businesses, and ordinary citizens. Critics also argued that integration tended to concentrate wealth in those parts of the Community that were already prosperous, leaving peripheral regions less well off, at least in relative terms. While political opponents of integration tended to exaggerate these negative side effects, even supporters recognized that integration *has* distributional consequences—that it produces gainers and losers—and that social and regional policies designed to offset the negative effects of integration were needed to maintain political support for the Community. Another argument for a Community role in social and regional policy was that highly disparate national approaches to such questions as labor standards or aid to industry in depressed regions can distort competition and disrupt the functioning of the single market.

The Treaty of Rome established a European Social Fund to finance retraining and relocation programs for displaced workers. It also took a strong stand against sex discrimination in the workplace by guaranteeing equal pay for equal work for women and men.[28] This provision was included at the insistence of France, and is a good example of the interaction between social conditions and market competition. The French negotiators were motivated less by concern for the plight of women in other European countries than by a fear that France, which already had strong national equal pay provisions in place, would suffer in competition with other countries whose industries might employ female workers at substandard wages. In addition to these specific provisions, the member states agreed on the need to promote improved working conditions and standards of living for workers. For the most part, however, social welfare, employment policy, and health and safety matters remained national responsibilities, with only a limited role for the Community through the 1960s.

The completion of the common market, the impending first enlargement, and the expectation of monetary union by the end of the decade led to renewed interest in social policy in the early 1970s. European political leaders believed that such policies were needed to defuse the social tensions that were apparent in the strikes and youth revolts of the late 1960s, and that were bound to grow worse, it was thought, as economic competition intensified in an enlarging Community. At the 1972 Paris summit the leaders of the six instructed the Commission to draw up a Social Action Plan aimed at promoting full and better employment, improved living and working conditions, better dialogue between employers, unions, and government, and workers' participation in enterprise management. This burst of activism in the early 1970s resulted in some Community-level social legislation, for example directives mandating firms to consult with their employees before undertaking large lay-offs. For the most part, however, the ambitious objectives formulated in 1972 fell victim to the difficult economic conditions of the 1970s. Pressed by inflation, rising unemployment, and other economic and social problems, member states focused on immediate actions at the national level rather than on building a European social order.[29]

The relaunch of the Community in the 1980s under Jacques Delors led to new developments in social policy, but also to new debates about the proper distribution of European and national responsibilities. Delors was a French socialist who genuinely believed in the values of social solidarity and in promoting a European model of capitalism different from that in the United States. He strongly believed that the launch of the single market program called for the Community to develop a stronger social dimension. To maintain political support for the largely business-driven program of deregulation and market opening, the trade unions and ordinary workers needed to be convinced that European integration offered benefits for them as well as for business.[30] In addition, intensified competition in the single market could be expected to produce a degree of unemployment and worker dislocation. Employment, welfare, and job training policies mainly had to be implemented at the national level, but Delors saw an important role for Europe as well. The Single European Act contained a number of new provisions that strengthened the Community's social policy role, including articles committing the EC to upgrade and harmonize national health and safety standards, to strengthen "economic and social cohesion" through use of the European Social Fund and other Community funds, and to promote dialogue at the European level between business and labor.

At the December 1989 Strasbourg summit, the European Council adopted a nontreaty document, the Community Charter of the Fundamental Social Rights of Workers, that covered such general topics as freedom of movement, living and working conditions, freedom of association and collective bargaining, and equal rights for men and women (see Box 5.1). EC involvement in most of these areas was new, and the significance of the agreement was largely symbolic—a political gesture in the face of continued high unemployment and concern by the trade unions that workers receive a share of the benefits of the economic growth being generated by the single market program. Known as the Social Charter, the agreement was purely declaratory, and had to be followed by Community and national legislation to be translated into binding commitments. The British government of Margaret Thatcher opposed the creeping involvement of the Community in em-

---

Box 5.1   The Twelve Principles of the Social Charter

1. The right to work in the EU country of one's choice
2. The freedom to choose an occupation and the right to a fair wage
3. The right to improved living and working conditions
4. The right to social protection under prevailing national systems
5. The right to freedom of association and collective bargaining
6. The right to vocational training
7. The right of men and women to equal treatment
8. The right of workers to information, consultation and participation
9. The right to health protection and safety at work
10. The protection of children and adolescents
11. A decent standard of living for older people
12. Improved social and professional integration for disabled people

(*Source*: European Commission, *How Is the European Union Meeting Social and Regional Needs?* Brussels, OOPEC, 1996, 7.)

ployment and social policies, and declined to endorse the Social Charter. As part of her effort to revitalize the British economy, Thatcher was committed to rolling back the welfare state and the power of the trade unions in the UK. She did not want to achieve this at the national level, only to see the same "socialist" policies reimposed from Brussels.

The Social Charter became the basis for the protocol on social policy that was appended to the Maastricht Treaty and later incorporated into the amended version of the Treaty of Rome by action of the Amsterdam IGC. John Major, who succeeded Thatcher in November 1990, refused to accept inclusion of a social chapter in the treaty. With the other member states (especially France, Italy, and Belgium) committed to the chapter, this became one of the most hard-fought issues of the Maastricht negotiations. In a last-minute compromise that averted a breakdown of the conference, Britain and the other member states agreed to an arrangement under which all of the member states except Britain signed a Social Protocol that was appended to the treaty and that allowed the eleven to apply Community decision-making procedures to issues covered under the protocol, but with Britain not participating and the voting procedures and weights in the Council of Ministers adjusted accordingly.

The substantive provisions on social policy were included in an agreement among the eleven. It covered the same issues as the 1989 Social Charter, but allowed the EU (minus Britain) to adopt directives setting minimum requirements for implementation of EU standards with regard to workers' health and safety, working conditions, information and consultation of workers, equality between men and women in the labor force, and "the integration of persons excluded from the workforce."[31] The agreement also charged the Commission with promoting dialogue between management and labor at the EU level.

This unorthodox arrangement undermined the constitutional coherence of the EU and set a bad precedent for future à la carte arrangements. It was controversial on the continent, where politicians accused Britain of "social dumping"—competing unfairly for investments and jobs by applying lower labor and social standards—and in the UK itself, where the Labour party attacked Major for failing to go along with a European consensus on basic issues of worker rights and the Conservatives continued to warn against intrusions by Brussels in matters that could affect the British way of life and undermine the competitiveness of British industry.

The anomalous situation of having eleven members observing the Social Protocol and using it as a framework to pass directives and one not (fourteen and one, after the 1995 accession of Austria, Finland, and Sweden) was resolved by a political shift in Britain and the electoral victory of Labour in the spring of 1997. Prime Minister Tony Blair's first weeks in office coincided with the final stages of the negotiation of the Treaty of Amsterdam. Reversing Major's position, Blair announced that the UK would sign the Social Protocol. The protocol thus could be integrated into the amended Treaty of Rome as originally intended by the eleven before Maastricht and made binding on the EU as a whole. Blair also agreed that the UK would accept all of the directives that had been passed by the other member states under the interim arrangement and transpose those directives into national law as required.

With Britain fully on board, the EU remains committed to social policy. However, as is discussed later in the chapter, the EU's largest social problem is by most accounts unemployment. If it could be reduced, particularly among weak and vulnerable segments of the population, many other social problems would be ameliorated. Social policy thus has tended to blend with and even to some extent be made subordinate to employment policy, a new focus of EU activity introduced by the Amsterdam Treaty.

Regional Policy

POLICY DEVELOPMENT

At the 1972 Paris summit the leaders of the six agreed to establish a Community regional policy, to be overseen by a Commissioner responsible for regional affairs and supported by a new European Regional Development Fund (ERDF). The summit thus laid the groundwork for Community-level redistribution from wealthier to the less wealthy member states and for the eventual development a full-fledged cohesion policy.

Cohesion is the term used in the EU for collective efforts to reduce economic and social disparities between the wealthier and the poorer regions of the Union. It has become more important as membership has expanded to include more countries at more disparate levels of development. The economies of the six original EC member states all were roughly at the same level of economic development, with the main exception being southern Italy. The European Investment Bank, the provisions in the Treaty of Rome allowing free movement of labor, and the CAP all provided assistance to southern Italy, as did national programs under which the Italian government transferred massive amounts of money from the north and center to the south of the country. The six did not, however, develop an explicit regional policy for this special albeit important situation.

The enlargement of the Community in the 1970s and 1980s as well as a realization that market integration was leaving behind depressed regions even within the wealthier countries led to a growing emphasis on regional policy. Ireland, Greece, Portugal, and Spain were the countries whose per capita incomes lagged the Community average by a substantial margin. Since the late 1980s these countries have been able to argue, for the most part successfully, that ambitious EC/EU initiatives like the single market and later Economic and Monetary Union would be politically and economically sustainable only if these disparities were narrowed. Building upon the decisions of the 1972 Paris summit and the establishment of the ERDF, the SEA included new articles on cohesion, which henceforth became a treaty-based objective of the EC, to be pursued both through a separate cohesion policy and considered as a factor in the making of other Community policies such as trade, transport, and the environment. The Community's three structural funds—the European Social Fund, the European Regional Development Fund, and the European Agricultural Guidance Guarantee Fund of the CAP—along with credits from the EIB were the main sources of financial support for cohesion policy.

POLITICAL BARGAINING

Making cohesion policy for the most part has involved a process of bargaining between the poorer and the wealthier member countries, in which the former have been able to win concessions by dragging their feet on other issues valued by the wealthier countries, such as the 1992 program and EMU. The poorer countries also have benefitted from a relatively sympathetic attitude in Brussels (both the Commission and the Parliament stand to gain power by exercising control over a large regional aid budget) and from the willingness of Germany essentially to foot the bill for cohesion policy by paying much more into the budget than it receives back.

After becoming a member of the Community in January 1986, Spain emerged as the leader of a group of four states that consistently demanded larger cohesion payments from the Community budget. In February 1988 the twelve agreed to double the size of the structural funds. This decision was the result of a bargain between the poorer member states, led by Spain and its prime minister, Felipe González, and the wealthier north led by Germany and Helmut Kohl. In essence, the poorer countries agreed to go along with implementing the Community's single market program, but only in exchange for larger amounts of aid. This deal was seen as politically necessary, since the adverse effects of heightened competition in the single market were expected to fall disproportionately on countries such as Spain and Portugal, whose industries would be exposed to new competition from the north.

The same dynamic played out in the 1991–1992 IGC. With France and Germany pressing for a Community agreement on EMU, Spain and the other cohesion countries again made the argument that more aid from the north was needed if the economically weaker states were to participate in another major initiative that would intensify competition in the single market and that would require strenuous efforts to meet the convergence criteria for EMU that were being demanded by the Germans and the Dutch. Some of Spain's demands were excessive, but in the end Kohl and González struck a bargain, subsequently endorsed by their counterparts in the other member states, to create in effect a fourth structural fund, a Cohesion Fund that was formally set up in May 1994. Under the terms of a protocol to the Maastricht Treaty, the fund was to make financial contributions to projects in the fields of environment and transport infrastructure. Countries eligible to access the fund were those with a per capita GNP less than 90 percent of the EU average, that is, the four traditional recipients, provided they were making progress on meeting the convergence criteria that were stipulated in the Maastricht Treaty.

The relatively favorable political climate for cohesion policy largely evaporated in the course of the 1990s. With reunification, Germany acquired five new states in which economic and social conditions lagged the EU average. As the federal government began providing large amounts of aid to the former East Germany, it became less willing to bankroll EU solidarity. Governments in the south became increasingly concerned about competition with the east for regional funds, and threatened to veto EU enlargement if it meant the loss of support from the structural funds. Ireland was expected to graduate from the category of a cohesion country as a result of its rapid economic growth in recent years, much of it due to foreign investment and EU infrastructure aid, but it was reluctant to lose an important source of revenue. The stage thus was set for a major debate over the size, composition, and ultimate beneficiaries of regional aid.

THE 2000–2006 PACKAGE

In designing its cohesion policies, the EU has had to manage a tension between concentrating aid in a few regions to maximize effectiveness and dispersing aid over a wider area in a way that dilutes the effect of the aid but that generates broader political support. In the 1990s, the structural funds were targeted at seven objectives: Objective 1 to assist those regions whose per capita GDP was less than 75 percent of the EU average; Objective 2 to facilitate redevelopment in regions seriously affected by industrial decline; Objective 3 to combat long-term unemployment and improve youth employment opportunities; Objective 4 to assist the adaptation of workforces to industrial change; Objective 5a to assist with modernization of agricultural and fishing industries; Objective 5b to help with development and economic diversification of vulnerable rural areas; and Objective 6, created in 1995 to benefit Finland and Sweden, to help sparsely populated Arctic regions. In addition, the Cohesion Fund supports environmental, energy, and transport projects in the four eligible countries.

Although the bulk of the structural funds went to poor regions in poor countries, the Commission's eligibility criteria also channeled aid to many disadvantaged urban and rural regions in the more affluent countries of the Union. The share of the EU population covered by Objectives 1 and 2 in the late 1990s was in fact 51 percent. Regions that received aid included the five eastern states of Germany, rust belt regions of France and Belgium, a sparsely populated part of the Netherlands north of Amsterdam, Scotland and northern England, and of course southern Italy. Additional aid to backward or disadvantaged regions came from funds set aside under the CAP and the Common Fisheries Policy.

In *Agenda 2000*, the Commission tried to move in the direction of more concentration and greater effectiveness. It proposed that the seven objectives be reduced to just three and their management simplified and decentralized. This would reduce the share of the EU's population covered by Objectives 1 and 2 to 35–40 percent. Objective 1 would become the most important component of EU regional policy, but the per capita GDP threshold would be strictly enforced to ensure that regions graduate as their standard of living rises. A new Objective 2 would tackle economic and social restructuring in areas outside Objective 1 regions where unemployment is above the EU average and where help with economic redevelopment is needed. Pockets of urban poverty in otherwise affluent regions could be covered by Objective 2. Objective 3 would be a new program covering human resources and training EU-wide. It would complement activities taken under the new employment chapter of the Treaty of Amsterdam. The Commission also proposed that the Cohesion Fund be retained, but that a review of the 90 percent threshold take place at the halfway point of the 2000–2006 budget period.

The Commission's proposals implied a gradual shift in regional aid from the south to the east and were bound to be politically controversial. In late 1998 the Commission issued a report predicting that eleven regions could lose Objective 1 aid: the whole of Ireland, two regions in France, and one region each in Germany, Spain, Italy, Portugal, Belgium, and the Netherlands. Each of these countries could sustain the loss of one or two regions, but Spain (with eleven Objective 1 regions) and the other cohesion countries were particularly concerned about the impending enlargement to central and eastern Europe, when the addition of more than 100 million people and a very small GDP would lower the EU average that determines the 75 percent threshold.

The Berlin European Council ultimately adopted the main outlines of the Commission's approach, but only after very hard bargaining involving Spain, Germany, and other member states. The 2000–2006 financial framework sets aside a total of 213 billion euros for regional policies for existing member states, of which 195 billion is for the structural funds, and 18 billion for the Cohesion Fund. Allocation of the structural funds is as shown in Table 5.2. The Cohesion Fund, which some member states argued should have been eliminated after the successful launch of the euro, will be continued, but eligibility will be reviewed in 2003. Spain will receive 62 percent of the total, Greece 16–18 percent, Ireland 2–6 percent, and Portugal 16–18 percent.

Looking to enlargement, the 2000–2006 financial framework allocates 3.75 billion euros in regional aid for new member states in 2002, rising to 12.08 billion euros in 2006—in the unlikely event that accession of new member states actually occurs on this timetable. This money will be used to continue pre-accession aid programs funded by the EU, including investment in environmental upgrades and road, rail, and other infrastructure projects, and for tackling the same problems of unemployment and rural and urban poverty that persist in the EU of the fifteen. Considering the scale of the coming enlargement and the relative backwardness of the candidate countries, the envisioned aid for the new members is less generous than the applicants might have hoped. They will not receive, in per capita terms, grant aid at nearly the level that Ireland, Greece, and the Iberian countries received in the 1980s and 1990s. They will have to rely on their own national budgets, for-

Table 5.2   Structural Funds—2000–2006

	Criteria	Funding (billion euros)	Share
Objective 1	Regions with per capita GDP less than 75% of EU average	135.9	69.7%
	Most remote regions (Azores, Madeira, French Overseas departments)		
	Subarctic regions of Finland and Sweden		
Objective 2	Industrial (10%), urban (2%), rural (5%), and fisheries-dependent (1%) areas undergoing economic adjustment	22.5	11.5%
Objective 3	EU-wide "horizontal" programs to promote employment	24.05	12.3%
Other	Cross-border actions, innovative programs	12.6	6.5%

eign investment, and loans—including from the EIB, the World Bank, and the European Bank for Reconstruction and Development—to finance development.

The framework does plan for a peaking of structural funds for the EU-15 in 2000 and a gradual tapering off, as countries and regions in the existing EU raise their level of income and graduate from assistance, freeing resources for the east. The shift is gradual, however, owing to strong resistance from current member state recipients such as Spain and to concerns about the ability of the new member states to absorb large amounts of cash from Brussels on productive projects. In 2006 aid for regions in the current EU-15 is still set at 26.66 billion euros, while assistance for new members will be less than half that level. Given the scale of the economic and social needs in the east, this distribution would appear to make little sense. It reflects, however, the power of incumbency and the ability of the current member states to use their positions in the European Council and the Council of Ministers to head off a more radical redistribution.

EFFECTIVENESS

The effectiveness of EU regional policy has long been a matter of debate. Critics have noted the large amount of waste and fraud in some EU programs and have questioned whether structural and cohesion funds have been spent wisely or should even be spent at all. Other critics argue that the effect of closer European integration is to marginalize the economic periphery, as capital and other resources are attracted from the periphery to the dynamic core of the Union—often defined as inside the London-Paris-Milan triangle that includes the affluent and high-technology regions of the largest EU countries. They claim that regional aid and regional policy in general have not done enough to counter the effects of concentration. How effective regional aid will be in addressing the long-term problems of the accession countries is also difficult to predict.

The Commission argues that regional policy has been effective in achieving its main goal of evening out economic disparities in the Union. Table 5.3 shows that in 1986–1999, the four cohesion countries made gains relative to the EU average. In the 1990s alone, per capita GNP for the cohesion countries rose from 68 percent to 78 percent of the EU average. Progress has been most spectacular in Ireland, which now surpasses the EU average in per capita income, and least impressive in Greece, which was overtaken by Portugal to become the poorest country in the Union and which even lags the per capita income level of some of the most advanced candidate countries, such as Slovenia and the Czech Republic. Progress in leveling disparities among regions within countries has been more mixed. The Commission estimates that nearly 20 percent of EU citizens live in regions where per capita GNP is 25 percent or more below the EU average. (The comparable figure for Americans is 2 percent.) To some extent regional aid may even exacerbate disparities within countries, as it has helped cities such as Dublin and Lisbon rapidly raise their incomes, leaving behind the rural areas and smaller cities.

It also is difficult to determine how much effect regional policy as such has had in closing income disparities and how much importance should be ascribed to other factors, such as market integration and foreign direct investment. In successful cases, these factors all work together. In Ireland, for example, accession to the EC made the country a popular investment location for foreign companies, such as U.S. electronics firms seeking a base from which to manufacture and sell to the broader European market. Regional funds helped to build the roads and other infrastructure needed to accommodate this investment. Whatever the answers to these questions, repeating the Irish miracle—or even the more modest progress of Portugal and Spain—in central and eastern Europe but with less money under more difficult circumstances will be the main challenge for EU regional policy in the coming decades.

Environmental Policy

Environmental policy was not mentioned in the Treaty of Rome, an omission that reflected the relatively low importance accorded environmental issues in early postwar European politics. By the early 1970s, however, national governments and the general public were becoming increasingly aware of environmental degradation as a consequence of urbanization, industrial growth, and intensive farming. In 1972 the member state governments asked the Commission to prepare the first EC Environmental Action Program for the period 1973–1976. Multiyear environmental action programs since have become the blueprint for policy at the European level. The fifth environmental action program covered the period 1993–

Table 5.3 GDP per Capita, Percentage of EU Average (Purchasing Power Parity Basis)

	1986	1987	1988	1989	1990	1991	1992	1993	1994	1995	1996	1997	1998	1999
Greece	59.2	57.4	58.3	59.1	57.4	60.1	61.9	64.2	65.2	66.4	67.5	69.2	68.6	69.3
Ireland	60.8	62.5	63.8	66.3	71.1	74.7	78.4	82.5	90.7	96.8	96.5	96.4	102.1	105.1
Portugal	55.1	56.7	59.2	59.4	58.5	63.8	64.8	67.7	69.5	70.1	70.5	70.7	71.1	71.8
Spain	69.8	71.5	72.5	73.1	74.1	78.7	77.0	78.1	78.1	78.6	78.7	77.8	78.6	79.6

Source: Eurostat.

2000.[32] The sixth environmental program will form the basis for EU environmental policy early in the 21st century.

Acting within the framework of these programs, the EU has adopted over 200 pieces of legislation covering the pollution of air, water, and soil, waste management and recycling, chemical and biotechnology safeguards, product standards, environmental impact assessments, and protection of nature. Initially, the Commission proposed and the Council adopted these laws on the basis of the catchall Article 235 of the Treaty of Rome, or by referring to the single market implications of environmental policy. The SEA established for the first time a treaty basis for environmental policy, specifying three objectives: to preserve, protect, and improve the quality of the environment; to contribute towards improving human health; and to ensure a prudent and rational utilization of natural resources. The Maastricht Treaty added a fourth objective: to promote "measures at international level to deal with regional or worldwide environmental problems."[33] The treaty also introduced environmental considerations into the overall framework of EU economic policy, specifying "sustainable and non-inflationary growth respecting the environment"[34] as one of the fundamental objectives of the Union.

There are two reasons why national governments often try to address environmental problems at an international level rather than simply within a national framework. First, many environmental problems such as long-range air pollution and the pollution of rivers that run through several countries cannot be dealt with effectively in a national context. Second, environmental regulations affect the competitiveness of firms and industries and thus can influence the working of the single market. If one country passes stringent national legislation compelling factories on its territory to dispose of industrial waste in an environmentally friendly manner while other countries do not, firms from the first country will be disadvantaged. Both of these rationales have played a role in the development of EU environmental policy.

Member states differ markedly with respect to the importance of the environment national politics. Germany, Denmark, and the Netherlands are known as traditionally "green" countries with strict national environmental legislation. (The new members of 1995—Austria, Finland, and Sweden—also fall in this category.) The Mediterranean countries, in contrast, had adopted very little environmental legislation before being compelled to do so by Community directives beginning in the 1970s. The pattern has been for the green countries to adopt strict environmental legislation and then to try to "Europeanize" these laws, both in order to deal more effectively with environmental problems and to ensure that industry in all member states bears comparable environmental costs.[35]

The addition of a new environmental policy objective to the Maastricht Treaty—promoting measures at the international level to deal with regional or worldwide environmental problems—reflected the growing awareness in the early 1990s of environmental problems outside the EU and a readiness on its part to try to play a leadership role on global environmental issues. The collapse of communism exposed a huge backlog of environmental and associated human health problems in the countries of central and eastern Europe and the former Soviet Union, including severe air, water, and soil pollution, toxic waste dumps, and ageing and unsafe nuclear power plants. The environmental ministers of all the European countries met for the first time in 1991 at Dobris Castle near Prague in what was then Czechoslovakia, where they commissioned the Dobris Assessment, the first comprehensive, pan-European inventory of environmental problems.[36] Environmental remediation and nuclear safety became important elements of the EU's technical assistance programs for the transition countries, and meeting EU environmental standards became a major challenge for those countries seeking to join the Union.

The EU's most controversial foray into international environmental diplomacy has been its efforts since the Rio Earth Summit of June 1992 to promote a worldwide tax on carbon dioxide emissions to combat global warming. In October 1990 a joint Council of energy and environment ministers adopted a target of stabilizing carbon dioxide emissions by 2000 at their 1990 level. To implement this ambitious goal, the Commission began working on a package of measures that was to include support for renewable energy resources, a climate tax to discourage the burning of fossil fuels, and programs to promote energy efficiency. The package was intended to give Europe a world leadership role at the Rio summit. As this meeting approached, however, several of the member state governments, lobbied intensively by business interests concerned about Europe's global competitiveness, grew increasingly nervous about approving a unilateral tax on energy in the absence of similar action by the United States and Japan. In the end the Council approved the package of global warming measures, but it made actual implementation of a carbon tax conditional upon acceptance of similar taxes by other OECD countries.[37]

The UN Framework Convention on Climate Change (UNFCCC) was signed at Rio by 160 parties, including the EU and its member states. In the course of the 1990s the parties to the convention met in periodic conferences to discuss ways to implement the convention and to reduce greenhouse gases. The United States under the Clinton administration adopted a more positive stance toward binding measures to limit emissions than had its predecessor, which had blocked endorsement of the carbon tax at Rio. Nonetheless, as scientific evidence accumulated that global warming was in fact occurring, there was continued controversy among the developed countries and between the developed and developing countries over how best to combat the problem. Led by China and India, the developing countries were unwilling to shackle their industrial growth to address what they argued was a problem created over decades mainly by the industrialized North.

In December 1997 the parties to the UNFCCC signed the supplementary Kyoto Protocol, which called for the developed countries to stabilize 2000 emissions at 1990 levels. Beyond 2000, the EU committed itself to reducing emissions by 8 percent in 2010 over the base year of 1990 and to showing "demonstrable progress" by 2005. The EU now is struggling to meet these objectives. The 2000 goal more or less was met, but largely because emissions dropped precipitously in 1990–1994, owing to restructuring in the former East Germany, slow overall economic growth, and other factors. Since 1994 emissions again have been rising, and are projected, in the absence of new policy measures, to increase by some 6 percent in 2010 over 1990 levels, meaning that the EU will miss its reduction target by 14 percent.[38]

The Commission and the Council thus are considering new measures to curb emissions, including various taxes. The experience of the 1990s demonstrated, however, that the member states are not prepared to accept a uniform carbon or energy tax with a high degree of harmonization across the EU. Instead, they are looking at a more politically feasible approach that will allow the individual member states more flexibility in deciding how to use energy taxes and other measures to meet the Kyoto targets. The EU also is preparing to implement an intra-EU system of emissions trading, under which companies and countries that exceed emissions reduction targets will be allowed to sell their rights to emit to companies and countries unable to meet their targets.[39] Whatever the ultimate mix of policy measures adopted, meeting the Kyoto targets promises to be very difficult for the EU, especially since many older nuclear plants (which do not emit greenhouse gases) will be phased out and not replaced, thereby contributing further to the burning of fossil fuels.

Research and Development

Community involvement in this area began in the late 1970s, prompted by concern about Western Europe's failure to keep pace with leading U.S. and Japanese firms in information technology, medical and biotechnology, robotics, and other research-intensive industries of the future. In 1979 Internal Market and Industrial Affairs Commissioner Etienne Davignon launched a dialogue with the heads of Europe's leading information technology companies about what could be done collaboratively to accelerate technological progress. This led to the launching, in 1982, of the European Strategic Program for Research and Development in Information Technology (ESPRIT), under which the Commission made available a pool of ECU 11.5 million to fund precompetitive collaborative projects involving partners from several member states. By late 1983 an initial 38 projects involving 600 companies and institutes were underway.[40] Based on its initial success in launching real projects, ESPRIT was funded at the more substantial level of ECU 1.5 billion for the ten-year period 1984–1993. It became the model for an array of programs, usually designated by a catchy French or English acronym, designed to promote collaboration in different technical fields, for example RACE (Advanced Communications Technologies for Europe), COMETT (Community Action Program in Education and Training for Technology), and SPRINT (Strategic Program for Innovation and Technology Transfer).

The SEA for the first time provided an explicit treaty basis for a Community-level R&D policy. The main instrument for this policy has been a series of multi-year framework programs, beginning with the 1984–1987 First Framework Program that incorporated ESPRIT and other sectoral initiatives. The Fourth Framework Program for 1994–1998 was funded at ECU 13.1 billion, consisting of an initial allocation of ECU 12.3 billion in 1994 and a supplementary allocation in 1996 of ECU 0.8 billion of make room for Austria, Finland, and Sweden. It focused on four main themes: research, technological and demonstration projects, cooperation with third countries and international organizations, dissemination of results, and training and mobilization of scientific and technical personnel. Consistent with the EU's focus on improving competitiveness and generating jobs, it stressed research that was precompetitive but that still was expected to have commercial pay-offs down the road.

The Fifth Framework Program for the period 1998–2002 was approved by the Council and the European Parliament in 1998 and began soliciting its first proposals in early 1999. Funded at a level of 14.96 billion euros over the five-year life of the program, or about 3 billion euros per year, it is intended to engage private industry and academic researchers in the key issues facing the EU in the early twenty-first century: jobs, the environment, and the social implications of new technologies. In response to criticisms that the previous framework program was too diffuse, it focuses on twenty-three key actions or top research priorities, including food, nutrition and health, the ageing population and disabilities, new methods of work and electronic commerce, global change, climate and biodiversity, and the city of tomorrow and cultural heritage.[41]

The EU's budget for research is only a small proportion of all such spending by national governments and private industry, but it is an important catalyst for promoting cross-border cooperation among European firms, universities, and research institutes. In 1995, more than 12,000 organizations were involved in EU-funded research programs. These programs usually require organizations from three or more member countries to work together. In writing their proposals, researchers must focus on substance and scientific merit, but they are often also careful to achieve a politically attractive mix of partners from large and small, northern and southern member countries. In addition to running the framework programs, the EU has four of its own joint research centers, located in Italy, Belgium, the Netherlands, and Germany, that work on energy and industrial projects.

Employment Policy

The limited social policy provisions of the original Treaty of Rome focused on the rights of workers, with some attention to the migration of labor in the common market and the retraining of displaced workers in what was essentially a full-employment economy. Unemployment as such was not a Community concern. By the 1990s, however, unemployment had become the EU's most intractable economic problem, and the policy focus shifted to helping those excluded from the workforce. The social chapter of the Maastricht Treaty proposed greater "development of human resources to achieve lasting employment," and the treaty empowered the EU to legislate by QMV on issues dealing with the integration of excluded groups into the labor force. Overall, however, the treaty emphasized EMU and combating inflation and deficits, with far less attention paid to employment.

At the June 1993 Copenhagen summit Delors delivered a special report on the growing problem of unemployment in Europe, claiming that lack of competitiveness with Japan and the United States was a fundamental cause of Europe's failure to generate jobs. Under a mandate from the European Council, the Commission subsequently produced a white paper that proposed to create 15 million new jobs and to reduce the unemployment rate by 50 percent by 2000. The Delors plan called for extensive investment in infrastructure and TENs, training, R&D, and, perhaps most importantly, efforts to hold down growth in the cost of labor to below increases in worker productivity.[42]

The Treaty of Amsterdam inserted into the Treaty of Rome a new Employment Chapter that called for EU involvement in this crucial issue, stipulating that member states "shall regard promoting employment as a matter of common concern and shall coordinate their action in this respect within the Council."[43] Arguing that a new policy in itself would not create jobs—a task that had to be accomplished by a growing private sector—many member states initially were opposed to the employment chapter. But governments increasingly came round to accepting Sweden's position that positive action to generate jobs was necessary to counterbalance the overwhelming emphasis on economic austerity in the run-up to EMU.

The key element in EU employment policy after Amsterdam is a member state peer review process. The Council and Commission are charged with producing a joint annual report on employment in the Union. The European Council then is required to draw conclusions from the report and to establish guidelines for the employment policies of the member states. Each member state in turn is required to provide the Council and Commission with an annual report detailing its actions and policies taken to comply with the guidelines. This process is intended to keep pressure on national governments to make employment a priority policy area, and to encourage the sharing of best practices among the member states.

Following the signing of the Amsterdam Treaty, the EU began a series of high-level political dialogues focused on employment, beginning with the first-ever jobs summit, which took place in Luxembourg in November 1997. Convened at the initiative of French Prime Minister Lionel Jospin, the Luxembourg Jobs Summit was used to begin formulating among the member states the employment guidelines called for in the Amsterdam Treaty. It focused on four pillars of employment policy: employability, entrepreneurship, adaptability, and equal opportunity.

At the Cardiff summit in June 1998 marking the conclusion of the British presidency, the EU adopted further proposals for reform of national labor markets to promote employment. The Cologne summit in June 1999 approved a nonbinding European Employment Pact designed to bring together all of the disparate elements of the EU's new employment policy. Cologne called for closer coordination of member state economic policy and called upon the EIB to release additional funds, such as for TENs, that would generate jobs. As has been seen, the EU's reformed regional policy also had a new emphasis on employment, rather than simply on the elimination of income disparities.

Unemployment began a slow fall in the second half of the 1990s, as labor market reforms and other job-creating policies took hold in some countries and as economic growth accelerated, increasing the demand for labor. At the end of 1999, the unemployment rate for the EU as a whole was 9.0 percent, down from 11.0 percent in 1997 and a peak of 11.6 percent in 1994. (The U.S. rate was 4 percent, down from 7.5 percent in 1992.) Spain still had the highest national rate of unemployment, 15.4 percent, down from well over 20 percent in the early 1990s. France and Germany had rates of 10.5 and 9.1 percent respectively, also down from previous highs.[44] These aggregate figures mask huge disparities in the incidence of unemployment in particular groups such as youth and minorities. Unemployment of workers aged under twenty-five in Italy, for example, was a staggering 30 percent in 1999.

Continuing the recent successes in lowering unemployment and extending these gains to especially hard-hit sections of the population remain the major challenges for the future. To what extent the launching of an explicit EU employment policy actually results in more jobs remains to be seen. Economists and politicians alike recognize that Europe needs reform of labor markets that will bring down the costs of and increase the demand for labor. Entrenched domestic political forces representing those who already have jobs and who benefit from the existing system continue to resist such reforms, although the latter have made some headway in most EU countries.

It is also ironic that as the EU continues to struggle with unemployment and its consequences, it must devote increasing attention to the ageing of its population and the problem of unfunded pension liabilities. For years European governments have encouraged workers to take early retirement to free up jobs for younger workers. While this has had some positive effects, it may contribute to a situation in which fewer workers support a growing number of retirees. This has prompted some political leaders to call for raising the retirement age, as well as for more fundamental reforms of the pension system, such as a shift from the currently favored pay-as-you-go schemes (under which current taxation is used to finance pensions) to funded systems based on savings and insurance plans, such as are more common in the United States.

Other Policy Areas

In addition to the major policies discussed in this chapter, the EU plays a secondary policy role in many other areas, generally by adding a European dimension to what remain essentially national responsibilities. These areas include public health, culture, education, vocational training, and youth, consumer protection, energy, civil protection, and tourism. In health, for example, the Treaty of Rome provides for close coordination among member states and assigns certain special responsibilities to the EU level, for example, setting high standards for the protection of the blood supply and fostering international cooperation with third countries and international organizations. Delivery of health services and medical care to individuals remains, however, a national responsibility. In consumer protection, the Treaty of Rome merely states that consumer protection requirements shall be taken into account in defining other EU policies and activities. In education, vocational training, and youth, the EU promotes cooperation among the member states and seeks to develop the European dimension in education, for example through language teaching and exchanges. EU-funded and -administered programs such as TEMPUS (Trans-European Mobility Scheme for University Students) play an important role in encouraging students and academics to study and conduct research and in other EU countries. As in the health area, however, European action is complementary to that of the member states, which retain full responsibility for organizing and financing their educational systems at the primary, secondary, and higher levels.

Perhaps most importantly, the member states retain responsibility for pensions, health care, and unemployment insurance. These are the big-ticket items that account for the bulk of spending in the modern welfare state and that will loom even larger as populations age and the cost of health care continues to rise. Retention of these responsibilities at the national level sets limits to the share of spending and taxation that takes place at the European level and ensures that national politics will continue to be a primary focus for citizens concerned about their personal interests and welfare.

Conclusions

It is important to stress three general points about common policies in the EU. First, the expansion of EU policy responsibilities has been an uneven and politically controversial process. In some cases, the Commission has pressed to acquire new policy responsibilities at the European level. This has been the case with regard to energy, for example, an area that the Commission sees as difficult to separate from other policies that have a dominant or large European dimension, such as the single market, transport, the environment, and competition policy, but in which the member states have resisted integration. In the face of national opposition to a comprehensive EU energy policy, EU-level action in this area has tended to flow from other policy areas such as the single market, for example, through partial liberalization of the natural gas and electricity markets. In other cases, however, member states have shifted policy responsibilities—or at least the appearance of such responsibilities—to the European level, sometimes in the face of skepticism in Brussels. They have done so for a variety of reasons: to show domestic interest groups that the national government is pursuing their concerns in Brussels, to open the door to harmonization at the EU level, or to secure funds from the EU budget for programs of national concern.

Since the Maastricht Treaty and the debate over ratification, the Commission and the other central EU institutions have become wary of taking on new policy responsibilities in areas where the EU cannot make much of a difference and where EU action is as likely to produce a public backlash against meddling from Brussels as effective policy action. This approach is consistent with the subsidiarity principle enshrined in the Maastricht Treaty. After 1995, the unofficial motto of the Santer Commission was in fact "Legislate Less to Act Better."

The second general point regarding EU policy concerns the all-pervasiveness of the single market. While it is true that the EU has very limited explicit policy-making authority in such areas as health and education—and that in recent years the Commission has been cautious about trying to obtain such responsibilities— the reality of the single market and the growing role of competition policy mean that the member states are no longer completely free to make policy and set rules in these areas. The national governments are responsible for their national health and education systems, for example, but under the free movement of services and people legislation of the single market they must accept the credentials of students, academics, and health-care professionals trained in other EU countries. Similarly, the explicit consumer protection provisions of the Treaty of Rome are very sketchy and there is no mandate to establish the EU equivalent of the U.S. Consumer Protection Agency. Nonetheless, there is a large body of single market legislation and ECJ case law that has the effect of protecting consumers across national frontiers in the Union, if only because doing so is an essential underpinning of the single market. In these areas as in many others, the indirect working of negative integration—of removing barriers to trade in the single market—has had the paradoxical effect of achieving at least a part of what has been sought by the advocates of positive integration, namely common or harmonized standards at the EU level.[45]

The third general point is the pervasive effect—now and even more so in the coming years—of enlargement on both the objectives and the implementation of EU policy. The enormous challenge that the farmers of Poland and the other candidate countries present to the CAP already has been noted. The EU will need to allocate fishing catches to the new member states, extend transport networks into central and eastern Europe and ensure that the new member states harmonize safety and competition regulations for truck, rail, and other transport sectors, and extend environmental regulation in ways that balance the need for improvements with assessments of what central and eastern Europe can reasonably afford.

Harmonizing competition law and policy with EU norms is one of the most important tasks of the pre-accession process in central and eastern Europe, and competition law is likely to remain a challenge even after enlargement. The candidate countries are overcoming a legacy of state ownership and state planning of industry in which Western concepts of competition did not apply, even as their governments are under pressure to maintain jobs in industries such as steel, coal, and shipbuilding that long have been in decline in the West. At the same time, these countries are relatively poor and they cannot afford continued subsidies to loss-making industries. EU regional, social, and employment policies will need to be adapted to the long-term task of raising central and east European standards of living to EU averages, even as they cope with pockets of poverty and high levels of joblessness in the existing Union of the fifteen.

For the most part, the new member countries will be charged with adopting EU policies on an as-is basis—with accepting the *acquis communautaire*. However, the EU also will need to reform those policies to make them more efficient and to cope with the greater diversity of situations within the Union. In addition to pressures to cut costs, there may be a tendency to allow greater flexibility at the national level in implementing EU policies. Sparsely populated areas of eastern Poland, for example, may not need to follow the same waste-water standards as the crowded parts of Germany and the Benelux. Long phase-in periods also will be used to integrate the new member states into EU policies unrelated to the functioning of the single market.

However it is managed, the extension of common policies to the new member countries will pose challenges to the policy coherence of the Union, making what is already a mixed picture even more complex and variegated. It will call for greater flexibility and improved decision-making procedures on the part of the EU's institutions, as well as improved policy implementation at the EU and national levels.

Notes

1. Article 308 in the renumbered TOR.

2. Moravcsik, *The Choice for Europe*, stresses the centrality of agriculture in French thinking about the EC.

3. Timothy E. Josling, "Agriculture in a Transatlantic Economic Area," in Bruce Stokes, ed., *Open for Business: Creating a Transatlantic Marketplace* (New York: Council on Foreign Relations, 1996), 61.

4. "EC Agricultural Policy for the 21st Century (Report of an Expert Group)," *European Economy: Reports and Studies*, 4(1994), 1–147.

5. European Commission, "Reform of the CAP and its implementation," *CAP Working Note 1993*, VI/2024/93-EN.

6. European Commission, *Agenda 2000*, 113.

7. European Commission, *White Paper on Food Safety*, COM (1999) 719 Final, Brussels, January 12, 2000.

8. European Commission, Directorate-General for Fisheries, *The New Common Fisheries Policy* (Luxembourg: OOPEC, 1994), 11–12.

9. Quoted in Michael Smith, "EU Fish Accord Will Prompt Business Failures, Warn Fleets," *Financial Times*, December 18–19, 1999; for the TACs, see Press Release, 2237th Council Meeting, Fisheries, December 16–17, 1999.

10. European Commission, *Moving Forward: The Achievements of the European Common Transport Policy* (Luxembourg: OOPEC, 1999), 62.

11. Ex Article 84 TOR.

12. "Community transport policy: action programme," Bull. EC 7–1962, 14–16; and "Memorandum showing the lines on which the common transport policy should be based," Bull. EC 7/8–1961, 38–44.

13. *European Parliament v. Council of the European Communities: Common Transport Policy—Obligations of the Council*, Case 13/83, ECJ, Report of Cases before the Court, 1985–4, 1513–1603.

14. Bull. EC, Supplement 3/93.

15. *Trans-European networks: Interim report of the chairman of the group of personal representatives of the Heads of State or Government to the Corfu European Council (Christophersen group).*

16. Press Release, European Commission, Directorate-General for Transport, June 3, 1998.

17. Press Release, European Commission, Directorate-General for Transport, June 24, 1998.

18. Article 3, ex Article 3, with "internal" substituted for "common" in the amended version.

19. Articles 85, 86, and 87 became Articles 81, 82, and 83 with the Amsterdam renumbering.

20. "Council Regulation No. 17: First Regulation Implementing Article 85 and 86 of the Treaty," in George A. Bermann et al., eds., *European Community Law Selected Documents* (St. Paul: West Group, 1997), 492–502.

21. "Council Regulation 4064/89: On the control of concentrations between undertakings," *ibid.*, 558–578.

22. Nicolaidis and Vernon, "Competition Policy and Trade Policy in the European Union," in Graham and Richardson, eds., *Global Competition Policy*, 302.

23. *General Report on the Activities of the European Union, 1997*, 231.

24. *General Report on the Activities of the European Union, 1999*, 193.

25. Mitchell P. Smith, "Autonomy by the Rules: The European Commission and the Development of State Aid Policy," *Journal of Common Market Studies* 36, no. 1 (March 1998): 55–78.

26. European Commission, *Sixth Survey on State Aid in the European Union in Manufacturing and Certain Other Sectors*, COM(98) 47, 10, 13–14.

27. *Aid to British Aerospace for its purchase of Rover Group Holdings—United Kingdom*, O.J. 1993, L143/349; *Aid to the Renault Group*, O.J. 1991, C11/c/11/03; *Aid granted to the Volkswagen Group for investments in the new German Laender*, O.J. 1994, L385/1068.

28. Article 141, ex Article 119.

29. David Purdy and Pat Devine, "Social Policy," in M. J. Artis and N. Lee, eds., *The Economics of the European Union* (Oxford: Oxford University Press, 1994), 287–289.

30. Grant, *Delors*, 83–87.

31. Article 137, ex Article 2 of the "Protocol on social policy."

32. European Commission, *The Fifth Environmental Action Program—Towards Sustainability*, Com(92) 23, Vol. 2.

33. Article 174 TOR, ex Article 130r.

34. Article 2 TOR; subsequently amended by the Treaty of Amsterdam, Article 2.

35. Alberta Sbragia, "Environmental Policy," in Helen Wallace and William Wallace, eds., *Policy-Making in the European Union*, 3rd ed. (Oxford: Oxford University Press, 1996), 237–241.

36. David Stanners and Philippe Bourdeau, *Europe's Environment: The Dobris Assessment* (Copenhagen: European Environment Agency, 1995).

37. Jon Birger Skjærseth, "The Climate Policy of the EC: Too Hot to Handle?" *Journal of Common Market Studies* 32, no. 1 (March 1994).

38. *Commission Communication to the Council and the Parliament: Preparing for Implementation of the Kyoto Protocol*, COM(1999) 230, May 19, 1999.

39. Green Paper, COM(98) 353.

40. Peter Stubbs and Paolo Saviotti, "Science and Technology Policy," in Artis and Lee, *The Economics of the European Union*, 154.

41. "Fifth Framework Programme," europa.eu.int/comm/dg12/fp5/.

42. European Commission, *Growth, competitiveness, employment* (Luxembourg: OOPEC, 1994).

43. Article 126 TOR.

44. Press release, Eurostat, January 4, 2000; and IMF, *World Economic Outlook* (Washington: IMF, 1998), 175 (Table 4).

45. Stephan Leibfried and Paul Pierson, "Social Policy," in Wallace and Wallace, *Policy-Making in the European Union*, 200–202.

Suggestions for Further Reading

Grant, W. *The Common Agricultural Policy*. London: Macmillan, 1997.

Majone, Giandomenico. *Regulating Europe*. London: Routledge, 1996.

Mortenson, Jorgen. *Improving Economic and Social Cohesion in the EC*. New York: St. Martin's Press, 1994.

Wallace, Helen and William Wallace, eds. *Policy-Making in the European Union*. 3rd ed. Oxford: Oxford University Press, 1996.

CHAPTER 6

Economic and Monetary Union
THE EURO AND THE EUROSYSTEM

Few developments in the history of European integration will so directly affect the average citizen or have been as politically controversial as Economic and Monetary Union (EMU), the decisive stage of which began on January 1, 1999, with the introduction of a new currency, the euro, in eleven member states of the EU. Under the EMU provisions of the Maastricht Treaty, the euro was to operate alongside the national currencies of these countries until the end of 2001 and be used for checks, credit card charges, transfers between banks and companies, and other paper and electronic transactions. It would not yet circulate as cash. In the first half of 2002, the European Central Bank is to begin the circulation of euro coins and bank notes, and national authorities are to start the process of withdrawing all national money from circulation. From July 1, 2002, at the latest, the euro is to be the only money in circulation in these countries, and national currencies such as the mark, franc, lira, and peseta—most of which have been in use in one form or another for centuries—will have been consigned to history.

Establishing the euro was the EU's number one policy goal of the 1990s, just as completing the single market was the priority of the previous decade. The proponents of the single currency put forward three main arguments in its favor. First, it would complete the single market by eliminating the last remaining major barrier to the free circulation of goods, capital, and services: different national currencies, the values of which could change, introducing price distortions and imposing the transactions cost of converting from one currency to another. Second, it would compel a tremendous leap toward political union, as governments and central banks would be forced to adopt common policies and to create stronger central institutions in order to make the single currency work and as individual citizens came to feel more "European" by having a European money in their pockets. Third, the euro would strengthen Europe's position in the global economic and political system by challenging the dominant role played by the dollar since the 1940s.

Critics of the euro were skeptical about whether these objectives could or should be achieved, and pointed to the enormous political and technical problems likely to arise from the attempt to use a single currency in a region that included such economically disparate countries as Finland and Portugal. Skepticism about EMU was so strong in Denmark, Sweden, and the UK that these countries chose not to abandon their national currencies in 1999. (Greece was the other member state left out of the move to the euro, but this was not by political decision but because Greece had not yet managed to meet the stringent economic criteria needed to join the euro zone.)

Although EMU was an economic project, it was fundamentally about politics. It was carried out by a group of European political leaders, led by Kohl and Mitterrand, who were convinced of the need to keep Europe moving ahead on its path toward "ever closer union"—a position that in their view complemented rather than undercut the pursuit of national economic and political interests. Apart from the original 1957 decision to establish the common market and the customs union, EMU was the most far-reaching act of deepening in the history of European integration. By turning responsibility for money over to supranational bodies in Frankfurt and Brussels, European governments believed they were entering a qualitatively new stage in the integration process—one that would be visible to every citizen in the form of euro notes and coins. The fact that they attempted to do this at a time when, despite the optimism caused by the success of the single market and the collapse of communism, much of the initial political impetus behind the integration process was fading made the achievement of EMU all the more remarkable. It also helps to explain the dogged resolve with which European governments pursued EMU in the 1990s. The single currency was the gamble on which they staked the future of the integration process—a gamble that they were afraid to lose.

By successfully launching the euro in 1999, European political leaders "won" this gamble, at least in the short run. Over the longer term, however, the issue of whether EMU was worth the huge political investment made in the 1990s and that continues to be made as the euro countries strive to make the single currency work will depend on the answers to two questions. First, will EMU prove to be economically sustainable or, better yet, deliver the economic benefits its backers promised? Second, will EMU deliver the political pay-offs envisioned in the late 1980s and 1990s in the form of a deepening of the political integration process and a change in citizen attitudes? Will it mean greater popular identification with European integration as a political project or, as one commentator has suggested, will it simply mean the depoliticization of money, without a decisive shift in loyalties from the national to the European level?[1] These questions are crucial to the future of both EMU and the EU as a whole. They can only be answered in the context of the long road that the EU has traveled on the path to monetary union.

Background

At its founding in 1958, the EC played no role in monetary affairs. These were handled at the national level, by national central banks and ministries of finance, and at the global level through the IMF in Washington. Europe did not have a distinctive monetary identity. There was no need to create such an identity; currencies were stable against each other and against the dollar. This situation began to change in the 1960s, as the U.S. balance of payments deteriorated and as the leading European countries came under pressure from Washington to help to shore up the dollar and to preserve the par value system backed by the convertibility of the dollar into gold. In January 1962 the United States, Canada, Japan, and seven European countries concluded a General Arrangements to Borrow agreement under which they pledged to lend supplemental funds to the IMF in the event of a major financial crisis, most likely involving the dollar, that strained the IMF's own resources. The Group of Ten (G-10) subsequently became the major forum for the discussion of international monetary issues involving the developed countries. The OECD and several of its committees also became important for monetary and financial discussions among member countries.

The EC as such played very little role in monetary matters, as the member states took rather different approaches to the question of the dollar and international monetary stability. West Germany, the chief European military ally of the United States, helped to support the dollar by refraining from purchasing gold, buying large amounts of military equipment from the United States, and by other measures. France, in contrast, followed a diametrically opposite policy, accumulating gold and seeking to reduce the role of the dollar, which de Gaulle saw as an instrument of American hegemony.[2]

The movement toward monetary union was born in the late 1960s, as European leaders saw an increasing need to develop a Community monetary profile in a world in which the dollar was no longer stable and the United States was increasingly preoccupied with the war in Vietnam (itself a major contributor to U.S. balance of payments deficits and domestic inflation, both of which weakened the dollar) and social and political problems at home. Currency stability in Europe also was threatened by internal developments, notably the strikes and student uprisings that rocked France in May 1968, resulting in the weakening of the French economy and enormous pressure on the franc as investors and speculators shifted money into Germany and the German mark. After more than a year of economic and political uncertainty, in August and September 1969 France devalued the franc by 11.1 percent while Germany revalued its currency by 9.3 percent. The outbreak of currency turmoil in Europe threatened to undermine the common market just as it had come into being with the removal of the last intra-EC tariffs on July 1, 1968. It also ruled out progress toward the free movement of capital, even though this was one of the four freedoms proclaimed in the Treaty of Rome.

These developments led to the first ambitious effort to develop an EC economic and monetary union. At the Hague summit in December 1969, the leaders of the six EC countries agreed in principle to the gradual formation of an economic and monetary union and appointed Pierre Werner, prime minister of Luxembourg, to chair a committee of experts to develop a plan. This was the same meeting at which the leaders of the six agreed to launch their foreign policy cooperation and to undertake the Community's first enlargement. As in the 1990s, economic and monetary union was seen as a political step toward deepening the Community that needed to be taken in advance of a projected widening that, while valuable in its own right, had the potential to dilute the Community's identity and undermine its effectiveness.

The Werner committee report called for the completion of monetary union in three stages by 1980.[3] During the first three or so years of the transition, governments would work to coordinate monetary and fiscal policies. In the second stage, exchange rate fluctuations would be narrowed and the Community would set up a monetary cooperation fund to provide balance of payments credits to member states to support their currencies against devaluation. Toward the end of the transition period, the EC countries would fix irreversibly the values of their currencies against each other, abolish all capital controls, and set up a system of European central banks that would take over monetary policy for the Community. The report also called for much stronger fiscal coordination among the member states, including decisions at the EC level regarding the size and financing of national budgets. Many of the ideas contained in the Werner report later were to appear in the Maastricht Treaty provisions relating to EMU—although not the recommendation to determine the size of national budgets at the European level.

The deliberations over the Werner report revealed a gap concerning monetary union between two schools of thought that became known as the "economists" and the "monetarists."[4] The economists, represented chiefly by the hard currency, low inflation countries of West Germany and the Netherlands, argued that monetary union would be feasible only if the participants managed to achieve convergence in their economic policies and, better still, in their actual economic performance. Since Germany had no intention of allowing its rate of inflation to increase, this meant that France, Italy, and the other Community countries had to reduce inflation and bring their main economic indicators into line with those of Germany. The monetarists, in contrast, argued that the Community should take an essentially political decision to proceed with monetary union. The existence of a common currency then would force policy coordination and convergence in the performance of the real economies. The result would be the same—greater uniformity of economic policy and performance—but the order would be reversed. The debate between the "economists" and the "monetarists" was never really resolved in the 1970s, and it was to come back in the late 1980s in the next debate over EMU.

The economic convergence that a successful economic and monetary union required became more difficult after the breakdown of the Bretton Woods system of fixed exchange rates. In December 1971 the United States and its key monetary partners in Europe and Japan announced a realignment of currencies, including a devaluation of the dollar, designed to bolster the U.S. balance of payments. The G-10 countries participating in the Smithsonian Agreement (so-named because the talks took place in the historic castle building of the Smithsonian Institution in Washington) pledged to allow their currencies to fluctuate against each other by no more than 4.5 percent. This attempt to preserve the old par value system was unsuccessful, however. Continued turmoil in the currency markets and economic imbalances among the leading industrial countries led to abandonment of the 4.5 percent band and adoption of a generalized system of floating exchange rates in March 1973.

The EC countries still were officially committed to monetary union by 1980, and they took some steps to advance this goal and to buffer themselves against the broader international trends. In March 1972 the six agreed to limit swings in their currencies to no more than 2.25 percent. This became known as the "snake in the tunnel" system, with the 2.25 percent band the snake and the global 4.5 percent band the tunnel. As long as the tunnel existed, keeping the snake within its narrower band was not all that difficult. Once the snake disappeared, however, as occurred with the global move to floating in March 1973, the snake became all but impossible to maintain, as some EC currencies moved up against the dollar while others moved down.

Germany, the Benelux countries, and Denmark (as well as several non-Community countries, such as Austria, Norway, and Sweden) managed to keep their currencies within the narrow 2.25 percent band, but the other major EC countries—Britain, France, and Italy—all left the snake and allowed their currencies to float freely against each other and against the mark. What survived of European monetary integration was a de facto Deutschmark zone in northwestern Europe. The German Bundesbank set monetary policies for Germany, while the central banks of the smaller countries shadowed German policy to make sure that their currencies did not fall out of the 2.25 percent band. If Germany raised its interest rates, they did likewise; if Germany cut rates, they followed suit—in either case usually within days if not hours.

The Deutschmark zone had no institutional connection with the EC and it was a far cry from fulfilment of the ambitions of the Werner report to create a Community monetary union. While it tightened the economic linkages between Germany and its smaller neighbors, it both reflected and tended to perpetuate a situation of economic divergence among the major Community member states. In 1974–1979, for example, Germany's inflation rate averaged 4.7 percent per year, while the rate in France averaged 10.7 percent, Italy 16.1 percent, and the UK 15.6 percent per year. Comparable rates for the same period were 9.9 percent in Japan and 8.5 percent in the United States.[5] The inflation rates of the European countries thus were diverging more relative to each other than they were against the U.S. and Japanese rates. Since higher inflation generally leads to a falling currency on world markets (since more of the same currency is needed to buy actual goods and services), the dollar could be expected to weaken against the mark but strengthen vis-à-vis the franc, lira, and pound sterling. Europe thus was headed for increasing monetary disunion, a situation that threatened the core achievement of the common market and that ran counter to the plans to use monetary union to relaunch the Community in tandem with the first enlargement.

The European Monetary System

EUROPE RESPONDS TO THE DOLLAR

By the end of the 1970s the EC countries began to look anew at the problem of restoring monetary coherence in the Community. The first major proposal for a

new approach to monetary integration came in an October 1977 speech by Commission president Roy Jenkins, who was looking for ways to lift the Community
out of the doldrums of the 1970s and who, as a former British finance minister,
was acutely aware of the economic and political problems associated with currency
instability. With strong support from French President Giscard and German
Chancellor Schmidt, both also former finance ministers, this led to the founding,
in March 1979, of the EMS.

In the EMS, each national currency had a fixed rate against the ECU, an artificial currency whose value was set by a weighted basket of EC member country
currencies (see Table 6.1). Central rates in ECUs then were used to establish a grid
of bilateral exchange rates. Authorities in member countries were responsible for
ensuring that these rates fluctuated by no more than 2.25 percent (6 percent in the
case of Italy) against each other currency in the grid. This system for regulating
the EMS currencies within established bands was called the Exchange Rate Mechanism (ERM). The central rates were not intended to be set for all time, but they
could only be changed with the consent of the other members of the EMS. The
EMS operated within the framework of the Community, but participation in the
ERM was not mandatory for the member states. The UK chose not to participate.
Greece, Portugal, and Spain, all relatively poor countries that had their hands full
in coping with the demands of the common market, also chose to stay out of the
ERM when they became EC members in the 1980s.

The initial ECU basket was established in March 1979. The weights of the
member state currencies in the ECU were adjusted every five years to reflect
changes in the relative economic performance of the member states. The enlargements of 1981 and 1986 also necessitated changes in the composition of the ECU,
since all member state currencies were represented in the basket. The value of the
ECU fluctuated on world markets as the national currencies in the ECU basket
floated against the dollar, generally in the area of $1.15 per ECU. The general ap-

Table 6.1   Composition of the ECU (Percentage)

Currency	March 1979	September 1984	September 1989
Deutschmark	33.00	32.00	30.53
French franc	19.80	19.00	20.79
Pound sterling	13.60	15.00	11.17
Netherlands guilder	10.50	10.10	10.21
Belgian and Luxembourg franc	9.50	8.50	8.91
Italian lira	9.50	8.50	8.91
Danish krone	3.00	2.70	2.71
Irish punt	1.10	1.20	1.08
Greek drachma	—	1.30	0.49
Spanish peseta	—	—	4.24
Portuguese escudo	—	—	0.71

Source: Eurostat.

proach of using a weighted basket of member state currencies later was adopted to create the euro, with the crucial difference that from January 1, 1999 onward the member state currencies were "irrevocably fixed" against each other and against the euro, thus ruling out the controlled realignments allowed in the EMS.

The EMS worked surprisingly well throughout the 1980s, providing a high degree of at least intra-European monetary stability at a time when the dollar went through several wild gyrations, rising to astronomical heights in the early years of the Reagan administration before falling back after 1985. The relative success of the EMS thus paved the way for the revival, at the end of the decade, of plans to achieve EMU. But EMS most likely would not have survived had it not been for the strong political support that it enjoyed in the key member states, above all France and Germany. This support was reflected not only in the rhetoric of these governments, but more importantly in their willingness to make adjustments in their *domestic* economic policies in order to preserve the EMS and reap its promised benefits.

One of the major turning points on the road to monetary union occurred in early 1983, and involved a key decision by the socialist government of François Mitterrand in effect to subordinate the pursuit of certain deeply cherished domestic economic and political goals to the external disciplines of the EMS. After taking power in 1981, the socialists nationalized many French companies and pursued a policy of Keynesian reflation through high government spending and a permissive attitude toward wage increases. These policies, designed to combat unemployment and appeal to Mitterrand's left-wing political base, led to high inflation and two devaluations of the franc. By 1983 the French currency was under severe pressure from the markets, and the government faced a stark choice between leaving the EMS and pursuing a distinctly French economic path or staying in the system but adjusting France's economic policies to bring them more into line with those of Germany. Without a change in policy, it was unlikely that the franc could stay within the EMS bands without large and repeated devaluations.[6]

At the urging of the minister of finance at the time, future Commission president Delors, Mitterrand chose the latter course. Henceforth, France increasingly gravitated to the so-called *franc fort* (strong franc) policy by keeping its currency closely aligned with the mark in the EMS, even if it meant abandoning politically driven domestic economic priorities, such as the campaign against unemployment or the socialist program to bring much of French industry under state ownership. France's 1983 policy choice prevented the EMS from contracting into another politically marginal D-mark zone as had happened in the 1970s, and kept France and Germany, the two main drivers of European integration, on the path toward an EC-wide economic and monetary union. It also began a new era in the interaction between the external monetary environment and domestic economic reform in France and the other EC countries.

TOWARD A FIXED REGIME

The EMS began as an attempt to achieve at the European level the benefits of the par value, adjustable peg system that were provided at the global level by the Bretton Woods system until its breakdown in 1973. Those benefits are a combination of rigidity and limited flexibility—of externally imposed discipline combined with the possibility to make adjustments as needed. After 1983, however, the elements of rigidity began to dominate the system, with both positive and negative effects for the European economies.

The bugbear of the interwar system had been competitive devaluation. Faced with low internal demand and high unemployment, countries sometimes sharply reduced the values of their currencies relative to the currencies of their trading partners in order to make their exports cheaper and imports more expensive in their home markets. In this way, currency manipulation could have the same beggar-thy-neighbor effects as tariffs, quotas, and other barriers to trade. The postwar Bretton Woods monetary system was designed to rule out competitive devaluations by making changes in par value subject to international rules. At the same time, however, the designers of the system recognized that too much currency rigidity was also undesirable. If a country had higher inflation or lower productivity growth than its main trading partners, it would find that its exports would decline and imports increase as its own goods became more expensive and were priced out of the international and eventually even its domestic market. The result would be large trade deficits and rising unemployment. Along with steps to restore competitiveness (for example, by reining in inflation), the main remedy for such a situation was to devalue the currency so as to make imports more expensive and exports cheaper and thus more competitive on world markets.

After World War II, the European countries for the most part managed to avoid competitive devaluations, but there were several hefty currency realignments designed to restore the competitiveness of lagging national industries. France devalued the franc by 16.7 percent in August 1957 and again by 14.8 percent in December 1958. These devaluations were regarded by some experts as excessive, but they helped to ensure the price competitiveness of French exports during the formative period of the common market.[7] The same pattern of behavior persisted into the 1960s, and was seen even in the early stages of the EMS, when frequent and substantial realignments of the franc, lira, and other currencies against the mark were used to offset the effects on trade and growth of different rates of inflation among the countries of the system. Governments tended to avoid currency devaluations if possible, but when they did choose to devalue they made sure that the devaluation was large enough to give a boost to their domestic industries.

The Mitterrand decisions of 1983 marked a turnabout in intra-European policies with regard to currency adjustments. In the currency realignments of 1979–1983, devaluations generally were larger than inflation differentials. France realigned its currency four times vis-à-vis the mark in this period, each time an average of 7.1 percent to offset a rise in French prices relative to those of Germany of an average of 6.7 percent between devaluations. In other words, all else being equal, France was using currency realignment in the EMS to gain modestly in competitiveness relative to Germany. In the period after 1983, however, France and the other traditional soft currency countries took much smaller currency devaluations. France had only two devaluations against the mark between 1984 and 1989, averaging 4.5 percent each, while in the same time-frame prices rose an average of 8.3 percent more in France than in Germany in the periods between devaluations. Currency devaluation was offsetting only 54.5 percent of France's loss of competitiveness (because of higher prices) relative to Germany in this period, compared with 105.4 percent in the earlier period.[8]

The reason for this change in approach was a rethinking in France and elsewhere about the nature of comparative advantage in the integrating European economy. Governments could not fail to notice that no matter how many times they devalued their currencies relative to the mark, Germany always seemed to have a large trade surplus. In highly integrated economies, devaluation did not necessarily result in a long-term gain in competitive advantage. Firms in countries with weak currencies had to pay more for imported energy and components. Higher prices for imports quickly translated into higher inflation, which in turn resulted in higher wage demands from trade unions and a further loss of cost advantage. (In countries such as Italy, where wages were indexed to inflation, higher import prices automatically led to wage increases.) A weak currency also made foreign direct investment more expensive, precisely at a time when moves toward completing the single market created new opportunities for firms to strengthen their competitive positions by buying or establishing subsidiaries in other European countries. For these reasons, the French and others concluded that their long-term economic interests would be served by breaking the inflation-devaluation cycle and instead following policies to preserve the strength of their national currencies relative to the mark. With France committed to monetary stability and all of the Community countries focused on combating inflation, the EMS began to evolve into a system of nearly fixed exchange rates. During the first four years of EMS, from 1979 to 1983, there were twenty-seven currency realignments in the system, compared with only twelve parity changes in 1983–1989. The changes in the later period also were smaller, averaging 3.8 percent per adjustment compared with 5.3 percent for the earlier period.[9]

Gradually, inflation differentials in Europe converged, as workers and consumers in France and the other traditional high inflation countries were convinced of their governments' commitment to fighting inflation. In effect, other countries "imported" the inflation-fighting credibility of the Bundesbank by their commitment to monetary stability. French and Italian firms were forced to try to maintain their competitiveness by holding down costs at the microeconomic level, rather than depending upon macroeconomic action in the form of a currency devaluation. Much of the work of convergence that had been called for in the Werner report but that had not been accomplished in the 1970s thus took place in the late 1980s through the mechanism of the EMS.

One indication of the relative success of EMS was the increase in its membership. Spain joined the ERM in June 1989, although the peseta was allowed to fluctuate within the wider, 6 percent band used by Italy. In Britain, there was a bitter debate about the EMS that pitted Prime Minister Thatcher against many of her advisers. Ever the Euroskeptic, Thatcher was against joining. She was opposed by members of her cabinet who were concerned about being left out of the accelerating integration process. Britain finally entered the ERM in October 1990, also at the 6 percent fluctuation margin. Portugal joined in April 1992. Greece, which was still struggling to bring down its stubbornly high rate of inflation, was the only member country not inside the ERM.

In the end, however, the increasing rigidity of the EMS almost proved to be its undoing, as the narrow currency bands turned out to be unsustainable. France and Italy lost competitiveness relative to Germany in the late 1980s, as inflation in these countries remained higher than in Germany and as currency devaluations were used more sparingly than in the past to compensate for inflation differentials. In the changing economic conditions of the early 1990s, this trend ultimately led to financial crisis.

Toward EMU

DELORS LEADS THE WAY

Along with the successes of the single market program, the EMS and the economic convergence that it helped to promote created a favorable economic and political climate for the revival of plans to move beyond a mere system of monetary coordination to the establishment of a full-fledged monetary union. Taking this next step was largely the achievement of Commission president Delors, a firm believer in both the political and the economic benefits of monetary union.[10] Already in the fall of 1984, as he prepared the assume the presidency, he contemplated making a push for EMU, but in view of the lack of political support from the British and others instead decided to focus on the single European market. The most that could be achieved with regard to EMU was a reference in the preamble to the Single European Act recalling the Community's 1969 commitment to the "progressive realization of economic and monetary union" and a short chapter in the treaty entitled "Cooperation in Economic and Monetary Policy." However, the SEA also stipulated that any move toward EMU would require another intergovernmental conference—an eventuality that in early 1986 seemed rather remote.

By 1988 talk of EMU again was becoming fashionable in the Community, despite Thatcher's distaste for the idea and the skepticism of many others, including in the powerful central banking community. By this time, the EMS had been operating for nearly a decade and had been quite successful in its original goal of insulating intra-European trade from turbulence in global currency markets and from the wild swings in the value of the dollar that marked the Reagan years. As the EMS evolved toward a de facto fixed rate regime, a growing number of economists and political leaders argued that Europe should take the next logical step and move to full EMU. The single market program also strengthened the case for

EMU. Proponents of monetary union argued that there was an inconsistency between the creation of a single internal market and the maintenance of separate currencies, since changes in the value of these currencies affected the prices of goods and services traded in the internal market and thus constituted a barrier to trade. National currencies also imposed transactions costs on businesses and consumers. The idea that the 1992 program virtually required EMU was later captured in a Commission report entitled *One Market, One Money*.[11]

A further factor strengthening the case for EMU was the elimination of national controls on capital. Free movement of capital had been enshrined in the Treaty of Rome, but it was never put into effect, as national governments relied on controls to influence the exchange rates. However, in 1988 the twelve agreed, as part of the single market program, to remove all such controls by 1990. Economists warned that it would be very difficult to sustain the EMS—a system that retained different national currencies but that sought to limit variations in the value of these currencies relative to each other—in circumstances in which investors had complete freedom to move money across borders to seek the highest rate of return.

Responding to the growing interest in EMU, at the June 1988 Hanover summit the European Council agreed to establish, under the chairmanship of Delors, a committee to propose concrete steps leading to economic and monetary union. Composed mainly of the central bank heads from the member states, the Delors Committee developed a detailed three-stage plan for the establishment of EMU. It did not explicitly call for the creation of a single currency, but it proposed that in Stage 3 exchange rate parities be "irrevocably fixed" and full authority for determining economic and monetary policy be transferred to EC institutions. The report stressed that with the expected completion of the single market and the establishment of competition and regional policies, the Community had already accomplished much of the work toward EMU.

The June 1989 Madrid European Council approved the Delors Committee's three-stage approach and declared that Stage 1 of EMU should begin on July 1, 1990.[12] The key elements of Stage 1 were closer coordination of member state economic policies and completion of plans to free the movement of capital. Stage 1 thus was in part an extension of the single market program. The member states pledged to place all of their currencies within the narrow band of the ERM. They also agreed that another IGC would be held to consider moving to Stages 2 and 3, although they did not yet set a date for convening such a meeting.

There was still considerable skepticism in Europe about the Delors plan. The Bundesbank was at best lukewarm about EMU, and the British were outright opposed to what they rightly believed would be another major loss of sovereign powers to Community institutions. On the other hand, Kohl and Mitterrand both were strong backers of EMU, even though they had differences over its precise form and how it was to be achieved. Their support was crucial, and ultimately ensured that EMU became a reality.

ECONOMIC PROS AND CONS

While the Thatcher government questioned the political desirability of EMU, many economists raised doubts about its economic feasibility. Concerns about whether a single currency could work tended to focus on two considerations: the fact that the EC was not an optimum currency area, and the absence of fiscal federalism in the Community. An optimum currency area is one in which the existence of a single currency does not impose real costs on the economy, particularly as it adjusts to external economic shocks that differently affect different regions of that economy. The optimum currency area is a theoretical construct, developed by economists in the 1960s, and no country or trading bloc fully conforms to the ideal.[13] But economies like the United States that have high internal mobility of capital and labor come much closer to the ideal than does Western Europe, with its still uncompleted single market and its administrative, cultural, and linguistic barriers to internal movement, especially of labor.

In a currency area such as the United States, the economy responds to asymmetric external shocks through the internal redeployment of resources rather than through currency realignments. If, for example, as happened in the 1970s, the world price of oil increases dramatically, it inevitably will have different effects on Texas than on the Midwest. All else being equal, as world oil prices rise economic activity will fall and unemployment will rise in the energy-poor Midwest. In oil-producing Texas, in contrast, employment and economic activity will tend to rise as companies increase energy production and as higher wages and profits diffuse through the economy. In an open, flexible economy such as the United States, workers from the Midwest will head for Texas in search of employment, while capital will flow from other parts of the country into Texas to finance construction and investment. After a time, a new equilibrium will be established. Unemployment rates in the two regions will tend to converge, as labor costs fall in the Midwest and rise in Texas (as least in relative terms), as capital and labor shifts from one region to the other, and as industries in the Midwest increase their "exports" to Texas and other booming parts of the country. That, at any rate, is the theory.

In Europe, where mobility of capital and especially labor are lower than in the United States, currency devaluations rather than movement of factors of production traditionally have played the major role in bringing about adjustments to external shocks. If, for example, Portugal faced a trade deficit and rising levels of unemployment because its domestic manufacturing industry was suddenly exposed to a new low-cost competitor from the developing world while Germany encountered no such increased competitive threat, Portugal might have devalued its currency to restore the competitiveness of its products and thereby bolster employment. As has been seen, France, Italy, and the other traditionally high inflation countries in Europe effected numerous devaluations over the years to assist their domestic industries. Monetary policy and shifts in the external value of the currency in effect were used as a substitute for the kinds of internal adjustments that occurred in the United States, such as the downward adjustment of wages and the movement of workers from one state or region to another. Because French workers always would be unwilling to move to Germany and vice versa, critics argued, Europe could never become an optimum currency area. Countries suffering low growth and high unemployment would be deprived of one of their main means of adjustment, currency devaluation, with the result being further economic problems and ultimately a political backlash against EMU and economic integration as a whole.

Whatever the technical merits of the optimum currency argument, ultimately the question boiled down to one of politics. Proponents of the single currency acknowledged that the EC was not yet an optimum currency area, but that it surely had to become one. In their view, the transition period preceding the introduction of the single currency had to be used to introduce greater wage flexibility and freer movement of labor and capital into the European economy. Increased flexibility and mobility of capital were worth pursuing in their own right, and they were prerequisites to a successful EMU. While the relative success of the single market program argued for EMU, making EMU work in turn called for renewed efforts at completing the single market and the efficiency improvements that it entailed.

The argument about fiscal federalism also drew upon empirical evidence from the United States and from other federal systems using a single currency, such as Switzerland and the FRG.[14] In the United States, the existence of a unified federal budget acts as an automatic economic stabilizer that counters recessions in lagging regions and somewhat dampens economic activity in boom regions, thereby smoothing out economic imbalances among these regions. If the Midwest falls into recession, for example, income and other taxes paid by workers and firms from that region to the federal treasury automatically decline, while payments from Washington for unemployment insurance and welfare increase. If California is enjoying an economic boom at the same time, tax payments to the federal treasury will rise and receipts from Washington for certain programs will fall. If California is in recession and the Midwest is enjoying strong growth, the same processes will occur but in reverse. In either case, the federal budget will act to dampen disparities between regions of the United States. In studies prepared partly in anticipation of EMU, economists calculated that the counter-cyclical effects of the federal budget offset somewhere between 20 and 40 percent of differences in economic performance among regions.[15] Other federal systems use different mechanisms (in Germany, the states transfer money directly to each other and less adjustment is left to the automatic workings of individual income taxes and benefit programs), but all such systems are based on an assumption that a unified fiscal system must exist alongside a single currency and a centrally operated monetary policy.

In the EC of the 1980s, however, fiscal responsibilities were highly decentralized and likely to remain so. Even with the increases in the structural funds since the late 1970s, the Community budget still only amounted to a few percentage points of GDP. The Werner plan had called for closer fiscal coordination among the member states, but these ideas were quietly abandoned as politically impractical and did not reappear when EMU was revived in the late 1980s. Even though European governments tax and spend a much higher proportion of GDP than in the United States (as well as tend to be more overtly redistributional in their fiscal policies), they did so mainly in a national context. EMU skeptics thus argued that the EC was adopting a centralized monetary system and policy, without an accompanying degree of centralization in the fiscal realm. As with regard to the optimum currency area, economists were concerned that governments would be giving up a traditional tool—currency devaluation—for countering recession and unemployment, without gaining any new instruments for dealing with these problems. Ultimately, however, the arguments for EMU were political, and concerns about fiscal federalism were set aside, much as were those relating to the optimum currency area. For Kohl, Mitterrand, and Delors, making the single currency work was a question of political will.

THE MAASTRICHT NEGOTIATIONS

EMU most likely would have gone ahead in any case, but developments in eastern and central Europe lent new urgency to the project. As German unification became all but inevitable following the November 1989 opening of the Berlin Wall, Mitterrand saw a single currency as the key to a deeper process of European integration and deeper integration as the key to anchoring a larger and more powerful Germany in a European framework. Kohl was aware of the economic arguments against EMU and the skepticism that prevailed in Germany about giving up the mark, but he shared Mitterrand's political concerns. With the leaders of France and Germany strongly committed to moving ahead with EMU and most of the other European leaders supportive as well, the December 1989 Strasbourg European Council agreed to convene an IGC on EMU by the end of 1990.

The IGC on economic and monetary union formally began in Rome in December 1990 and ran concurrently with the IGC on political union. In a year of intense negotiations carried out mainly by finance ministry officials from national capitals, the twelve member states thrashed out the design for EMU. The final compromise, as embodied in the provisions of the Maastricht Treaty amending the Treaty of Rome, reflected French preferences with regard to timing and German preferences regarding conditions. The French obtained an iron-clad, treaty-based commitment that the final stage of EMU would begin no later than January 1, 1999. In return for agreeing that EMU was a sure thing—no longer a question of whether but rather a matter of when—Germany gained agreement to a long transition period before the phasing out of the mark and was able to determine the structure of and mandate for the future European central bank.

Stage 2 of EMU would begin on January 1, 1994, and would last as little as three but no longer than five years. In this period, all member states would work to align fiscal and monetary policies. Participation in the single currency was to be limited to member states that successfully used Stage 2 to converge with each other in having lower inflation and reduced budget deficits and levels of national debt. In effect, Germany had reasserted the old "economist" position with regard to convergence and had managed to incorporate its tenets into the Maastricht Treaty.

In Stage 2, the member states also were obliged to ban central bank financing of government debt and to enact legislation to ensure the independence of their national central banks. With the start of Stage 2, the European Monetary Institute (EMI) would be established to undertake the technical preparations for the introduction of the single currency and to help monitor member state performance with regard to the convergence criteria.

Stage 3 would begin no later than January 1, 1999. Its key feature would be the launch of the new currency, provisionally referred to in the treaty as the ECU but later named the euro by decision of the European Council. The new currency was to be managed by a European Central Bank (ECB), which in turn would be part of a European System of Central Banks (ESCB) consisting of the ECB and the national central banks of the countries adopting the euro. In this respect, the European national central banks would become analogous to the regional federal reserve banks in the United States. Modeled on the German system, the ECB and the ESCB were to pursue the primary policy objective of price stability.

The treaty specified that the ECB was to be led by a six-member Executive Board, composed of a president, vice president, and four other members who are appointed by consensus of the member states and serve for eight-year, nonrenewable terms, and a Governing Council comprised of the members of the Executive Board and the governors of the national central banks of those countries participating in the single currency. The members of the Executive Board were to be fully independent in the performance of their duties and not to take instructions from national governments or other EU institutions. The relatively long term in office was intended as a further safeguard against political interference. The ECB would not be established until shortly before the start of Stage 3 and the launch of the single currency.

The UK remained skeptical about the whole enterprise but, as with the social protocol, it chose not to alienate its partners by blocking EMU—as it might well have done given the unanimity required to amend the founding treaties. Instead, it negotiated an opt-out protocol from those sections of the treaty dealing with the single currency. Britain was not required to move to the third stage of EMU, although it had the option to do so if it chose. Traditionally Euroskeptic Denmark negotiated a similar opt-out protocol.

The Mediterranean countries were not opposed to the single currency, but many observers doubted whether they would be able to meet the strict conditions for Stage 3 included in the treaty. Not falling behind the northern members and thereby creating a two-tier union became an important concern for the Mediterranean states. This was especially so for Italy, which carefully guards its status as a founder member of the EC. Spain, ever the champion of redistribution of wealth from the more to the less developed member states, managed to secure, in the form of the Cohesion Fund, additional aid to the poorer member states to help them meet the Stage 3 convergence criteria. The Maastricht provisions on EMU thus were a compromise, similar to many other such deals negotiated in the history of the EC, but with the German imprint dominant and the Franco-German tradeoffs on timing and conditions clearly the essence of the deal.

Before the Maastricht design could be put into effect, however, Europe was to face one final bout of currency instability that for a time called into question many of the assumptions about EMU and seemed to confirm the arguments of those who said that Western Europe was too economically disparate to make a currency union work.

THE CRISIS OF 1992–1993

While German reunification provided a strong if indirect political boost for EMU, the way in which the Kohl government managed the absorption of the five new German states created new and unforeseen challenges for currency stability in Europe. This, combined with the political uncertainties surrounding the Maastricht Treaty ratification process and the accumulating competitiveness problems associated with the *franc fort* policy (and its analogues in Italy and the other traditionally soft currency countries), very nearly derailed the whole plan for EMU in the late summer and early fall of 1992.[16]

In June 1992 the Danish voters rejected the Maastricht Treaty by a narrow vote of 50.7 percent for and 49.3 percent against. A similar vote was scheduled for France in September, and polls suggested that the treaty might be rejected there as well. Although there was no direct connection between Maastricht and the ERM, the difficulties of the former put growing pressure on the latter. Without Maastricht there would be no EMU, and without the prospect of EMU governments would have far less incentive to maintain their links with the German mark in the ERM at a time when doing so was causing real pain to their domestic economies.

Attempting to control inflation amidst the heavy borrowing and spending associated with German reunification, the Bundesbank had raised interest rates in July 1992 to 8.75 percent. With free movement of capital, banks and other investors were able to move their money out of Italy, the UK, and other EMS countries to reap the benefits of high real German interest rates. This put downward pressure on the currencies of these countries, forcing them to raise interest rates in order to compete with the German currency. Alignment with the policies of the Bundesbank had been the pillar of the ERM and the EMS system, but the markets began to suspect that countries such as Italy that were suffering high unemployment eventually would be forced to devalue rather than continue to raise interest rates in a way that further dampened domestic economic activity. Speculators began to sell the franc, lira, and pound in anticipation of devaluation.

In the face of massive selling in the markets, Italy and Britain were unable to maintain the value of their currencies, and both countries left the ERM in mid-

September. Turbulence in the currency markets persisted into 1993, with attacks on the Spanish peseta, the Portuguese escudo, and the Irish and Swedish currencies. In August 1993 the EU effectively put an end to the speculation by widening the currency bands for all of the ERM currencies to $+/-15$ percent (an exception was the Dutch guilder and the mark, which remained within their narrow band). It appeared as if Europe was moving further away from EMU, rather than continuing the quasi-automatic progression from the single market and EMS to monetary union that Delors and other proponents had pictured and had used so effectively to promote EMU.

Ratification of the Maastricht Treaty finally was secured in the fall of 1993, and the twelve, notwithstanding the bitter lessons of the last year, proceeded to implement their now treaty-based commitment to begin Stage 2 of EMU. This was the real hard part of the transition to monetary union—the convergence phase in which states were required to cut their deficits and lower inflation in order to qualify for Stage 3—and there were reasons to suspect that once again the European countries might fail in their quest for monetary union.

Stage 2 and Convergence

Stage 2 of EMU began on January 1, 1994. The ban on financing government debt by national central banks took effect, as did the excess deficit provisions of the treaty. The member states began working in earnest to meet the convergence criteria that would determine whether they would be eligible to adopt the euro in 1999. They also began to implement a common economic policy, with a stress on eliminating government deficits.

Member states began to enact or amend central bank legislation to ensure the political independence of the national central banks that were to become members of the ESCB. The precursor to the ECB, the EMI, was formally established in Frankfurt, and charged with strengthening cooperation among national central banks and beginning the detailed technical preparations needed for the switchover to the single currency. These preparations included the development of new electronic payment systems, arrangements for improved statistical reporting in the euro area, and the design of euro coins and notes. (The timetable for transition to full economic and monetary union is shown in Box 6.1.)

THE MAASTRICHT CRITERIA

By far the most difficult task in Stage 2—and the one that became identified in the public's mind with EMU—was meeting the convergence criteria specified in the Maastricht Treaty to qualify for participation in the currency union. The treaty stipulated four such criteria: the achievement of a high degree of price stability, the sustainability of the government financial position, exchange rate stability, and

Box 6.1   Steps to the Euro

July 1, 1990	Stage 1 of EMU begins. Capital movements among member states fully liberalized.
Nov. 1, 1993	Maastricht Treaty comes into effect.
Jan. 1, 1994	Stage 2 of EMU begins. EMI is set up in Frankfurt. Procedures for economic policy coordination are improved. Member states strive to achieve economic convergence and avoid excess deficits.
May 3, 1998	European Council decides on countries eligible to adopt the euro; appoints leadership of the ECB.
June 1, 1998	ECB established in Frankfurt, replacing the EMI.
Jan. 1, 1999	Stage 3 of EMU begins. Euro becomes a currency in its own right. Member states issue new public debt only in euros. ESCB begins to frame and implement a single monetary policy and to conduct foreign exchange operations in euros.
Jan. 1, 2002	ESCB to put euro notes into circulation and to withdraw national banknotes. Member states to put euro coins into circulation and withdraw national coins.
July 1, 2002	Changeover to the euro to be complete in all participating member states.

the durability of the convergence as reflected in long-term interest rates. To meet the criterion for price stability, inflation had to be not more than 1.5 percent above that of the three best-performing member states in terms of price stability. The standards for government finances were the same as those used in the excess deficit provisions of the section of the treaty on economic policy: gross debt of 60 percent or less of GDP and a budget deficit 3 percent or less of GDP. Exchange rate stability was defined as managing to keep the national currency within the normal fluctuation margins of the exchange rate mechanism of the EMS for at least two years without devaluation. The durability criterion was defined as having an average nominal long-term interest rate that did not exceed by more than 2 percentage points that of the three best-performing member states in terms of price stability.

The actual performance of the member states in meeting the convergence criteria is summarized in Table 6.2. At the beginning of Stage 2, Germany, Ireland, and Luxembourg were the only member states with deficits below the 3 percent threshold. Inflation had been on a downward trend in the EU for over a decade, but rates in 1994 still ranged from over 10 percent in Greece to just one percent in Finland (a member from January 1, 1995). Long-term interest rates also diverged significantly, as lenders to countries such as Greece, Italy, and Portugal demanded higher nominal rates of return to compensate for higher inflation and greater risk

Table 6.2   The Convergence Criteria—Member State Performance, 1994–1998

		Inflation	Long-term Interest Rate	Surplus/ deficit	Gross debt
Belgium	1994	2.4	7.8	−5.3	135.0
	1995	1.4	7.5	−4.1	133.7
	1996	1.8	6.5	−3.2	126.9
	1997	1.5	5.8	−2.1	122.2
	1998	1.0	3.9	−1.3	117.3
Denmark	1994	2.0	7.8	−3.8	75.6
	1995	2.3	7.4	−1.4	71.9
	1996	2.1	7.2	−0.7	70.6
	1997	1.9	6.3	0.7	65.1
	1998	1.3	4.9	0.8	58.1
Germany	1994	2.7	6.9	−2.6	50.2
	1995	1.5	6.9	−3.5	58.1
	1996	1.2	6.2	−3.4	60.4
	1997	1.5	5.6	−2.7	61.3
	1998	0.1	3.9	−2.1	61.0
Greece	1994	10.9	20.8	−11.4	113.0
	1995	9.0	17.4	−9.1	111.8
	1996	7.9	14.4	−7.5	111.6
	1997	5.4	9.9	−4.0	108.7
	1998	3.5	8.5	−2.4	106.5
Spain	1994	4.7	10.0	−6.6	63.0
	1995	4.7	11.3	−6.6	65.7
	1996	3.6	8.7	−4.6	70.1
	1997	1.9	6.4	−2.6	68.8
	1998	1.8	3.9	−1.8	65.6
France	1994	1.7	7.2	−6.0	48.4
	1995	1.7	7.5	−4.8	52.8
	1996	2.1	6.3	−4.1	55.7
	1997	1.3	5.6	−3.0	58.0
	1998	0.3	3.9	−2.9	58.5
Ireland	1994	2.4	7.9	−2.1	91.1
	1995	2.4	8.3	−2.0	81.6
	1996	2.2	7.3	−0.4	72.7
	1997	1.2	6.3	0.9	66.3
	1998	2.3	3.9	2.3	52.1
Italy	1994	3.9	10.6	−9.0	125.4
	1995	5.4	12.2	−7.1	124.9
	1996	4.0	9.4	−6.7	124.0
	1997	1.9	6.9	−2.7	121.6
	1998	1.4	3.9	−2.7	118.7

(continues)

Table 6.2 (Continued)

		Inflation	Long-term Interest Rate	Surplus/ deficit	Gross debt
Luxembourg	1994	2.2	6.4	2.2	5.9
	1995	1.9	7.6	1.5	6.0
	1996	1.2	6.3	2.5	6.6
	1997	1.4	5.6	1.7	6.7
	1998	0.6	3.9	2.1	6.7
Netherlands	1994	2.8	6.9	−3.2	78.0
	1995	1.1	6.9	−4.0	79.7
	1996	1.4	6.2	−2.3	77.2
	1997	1.9	5.6	−1.4	72.1
	1998	2.0	3.9	−0.9	67.7
Austria	1994	3.0	7.0	−4.4	65.2
	1995	2.0	7.1	−5.9	69.0
	1996	1.8	6.3	−4.0	69.5
	1997	1.2	5.7	−2.5	66.1
	1998	0.3	3.9	−2.1	63.1
Portugal	1994	5.2	10.4	−5.8	69.4
	1995	3.8	11.5	−5.1	71.7
	1996	2.9	8.6	−3.2	65.2
	1997	1.9	6.4	−2.5	62.0
	1998	2.7	3.9	−2.3	57.8
Finland	1994	1.1	9.1	−5.8	59.8
	1995	1.0	8.8	−5.2	59.2
	1996	1.1	7.1	−3.3	57.6
	1997	1.2	6.0	−0.9	55.8
	1998	0.9	3.9	1.0	49.6
Sweden	1994	2.3	9.7	10.4	79.7
	1995	2.9	10.2	−8.1	78.7
	1996	0.8	8.0	−3.5	76.7
	1997	1.8	6.6	−0.8	76.6
	1998	0.2	5.0	2.0	74.1
United Kingdom	1994	2.4	8.0	−6.8	50.1
	1995	3.1	8.3	−5.8	54.1
	1996	2.5	7.9	−4.8	54.7
	1997	1.8	7.1	−1.9	53.4
	1998	1.5	5.6	0.6	49.4

Sources: European Monetary Institute, *Convergence Report: Report required by Article 109j of the Treaty establishing the European Community.* Frankfurt: EMI, March 1998; ECB, *Annual Report,* 1998 (ECB: Frankfurt, 1999). 1998 long-term interest rate is the average for the euro area, as reported in ibid., 51.

of currency depreciation. The gross debt position of most EU countries was either beyond or dangerously close to the 60 percent limit in the treaty. Given the disparities in economic performance, there was much talk at this time about a likely inner core EMU of five or six countries that would be ready to adopt the single currency, and even some speculation about possible postponement of the whole project, especially if France, whose participation was a political necessity, was unable to meet the convergence criteria.

Over the course of the next several years, however, the member states did remarkably better than expected in converging towards each other and towards the objective standards for deficits set in the treaty. By 1997—the key year on which the European Council was to base its decisions regarding participation in Stage 3—every member except Greece had met the deficit criterion. In a sign that investors believed in the durability of convergence and the growing likelihood of a successful launch of the single currency, long-term interest rates had converged toward the German rate of 5.6 percent. Lowering the huge stock of government debt as a ratio of GDP was proceeding very slowly, but most member states were moving in the right direction, as lower annual deficits added less each year to the stock of government borrowings and as some debt was redenominated in bonds at lower rates of interest.

There was some grumbling among central bankers and finance ministers about the durability of the shift to fiscal austerity and suspicions about the use of "creative accounting" to embellish especially the debt and deficit figures. Italy levied a Eurotax that it claimed was temporary and would be paid back to taxpayers after the start of EMU, several countries sold gold or other state-owned assets to pay down debt, and France used the pension funds of state-owned France Telecom to strengthen its government accounts. For the most part, however, the Commission, the EMI, and the statistical arm of the EU, Eurostat, kept a sharp eye on such practices and sought to gain assurances that convergence was real.

THE STABILITY AND GROWTH PACT

Convergence in the 1990s undoubtedly was real; whether it was permanent was another question. German Finance Minister Theo Waigel in particular was concerned that some EU states might be making a one-time effort to reduce their deficits in order to qualify for the euro, after which they might revert to high levels of borrowing that could reignite inflation and endanger the stability of the new currency. To guard against such a possibility, Germany demanded the conclusion of a supplemental "stability pact" that would not be a part of but that would strengthen the deficit provisions of the Maastricht Treaty.

The European Council adopted such an agreement at its June 1997 Amsterdam meeting, but only after it was renamed the Stability and Growth Pact in deference to France, Sweden, and other governments worried that the intense focus on fighting inflation might lead to overlooking the issues of growth and employment.[17] The pact clarified how fiscal deficits were to be handled after the launch of euro. Waigel was especially concerned that countries suffering an economic slow-down and rising unemployment might fail to observe the strictures in the excessive deficit procedure. The pact thus specifies how fiscal policy can and cannot respond to economic shocks.

A country that experiences a fall of 2 percent of GDP in one year or that is hit by an unusual event outside its control (for example, a major natural disaster) may run an excess deficit (over 3 percent of GDP) without penalty. A country that experiences a drop of 0.75 percent or less of GDP must adhere to the excess deficit criterion. If it does not, it can be forced to pay a financial penalty. For cases in between—recessions that entail a fall in output of between 0.75 and 2.0 percent of GDP—the finance ministers of the euro countries may decide whether or not to impose a penalty. Penalties take the form of a mandatory, interest-free deposit with the ECB by the offending state totaling from 0.2 to 0.5 percent of GDP, de-pending on the size of the deficit. If the excessive deficit is corrected within two years, the deposit is returned to the member state, although without interest. If the deficit persists for more than two years, the deposit becomes a fine.

THE BIRTH OF THE EURO

1998 was the final year of Stage 2 in which the European Council made its crucial decisions about the leadership of the ECB, the list of countries that qualified to adopt the euro, and, not least, the rates at which the national currencies of the participating states would be "irrevocably locked" to make up the euro. The EMI was abolished and the ECB formally established on June 1, 1998, in order to allow a seven-month shakedown period before the actual start of Stage 3.

The run-up to the May 1998 session of the European Council that was slated to make the key decisions regarding the launch of the euro was marred by an un-seemly battle over the selection of the ECB's first president that for a while boded poorly for the future of the whole enterprise. Germany favored for the post Wim Duisenberg, at the time the president of the EMI and the former head of the cen-tral bank of the Netherlands. With the ECB located in Frankfurt, there was no chance that a German would be selected as the first ECB president. But as the successful guardian of the link over the years between the Dutch guilder and the mark, Duisenberg was, from the German perspective, a satisfactory alternative. He also had strong support from his own government, which had vivid memories of how former Prime Minister Ruud Lubbers had lost in his 1994 bid for the Euro-pean Commission presidency and believed that it was high time for a Dutchman to occupy a top EU post.

While the other ECB members were ready to fall in behind the German-Dutch position in favor of Duisenberg, France chose to go against the tide. In De-cember 1997 President Jacques Chirac announced that he was proposing Bank of France governor Jean-Claude Trichet to be the first ECB president. The other member states were dismayed that France was attaching such importance to the nationality of the ECB president, which seemed to run counter to the principle that he was to be completely independent of national government controls. But Chirac seemed intent on using the presidency issue to underline the French view that the ECB, while independent in the day-to-day conduct of monetary policy, ultimately had to be subject to political control by Europe's elected leaders.

With consensus required, a deadlock ensued between France on the one hand and Germany and the Netherlands on the other. After months of speculation about the possible withdrawal of both Duisenberg and Trichet in favor of possible third candidates, at a special session on May 2–3 the European Council broke the impasse with a compromise. Duisenberg was awarded the post, but only after volunteering that he did not intend to serve for much more than four years of his term.[18] It was assumed that Trichet would take over at that point. Germany and the Netherlands were unwilling to abandon Duisenberg in a way that they believed would cripple EMU from the outset, not least by raising public concerns about political manipulation of the currency that was to replace the mark and the guilder. For his part, Chirac needed to emerge from the dispute with something to show for his efforts, but he was also wary of further alienating Kohl and inflicting damage on the Franco-German relationship, which France valued for other reasons.

Although there was no formal deal, the implication that the member states had engineered a politically based split term seemed to run counter to the spirit of the Maastricht Treaty provisions stressing the independence of the ECB and the deliberate choice of an eight-year term as a safeguard against governmental lobbying. The European Council chose Christian Noyer, a French civil servant with long experience in economic matters, as vice president. The other members named to the Executive Board were a German economist and member of the Bundesbank directorate, the chairwoman of the Bank of Finland, a Spanish professor of economics who was also a member of the executive committee of the Bank of Spain, and an Italian economist with many years of experience with the Bank of Italy. Because the members of the Executive Board are supposed to be independent, nationality in theory should not matter a great deal. But as with the European Commission, when it came to filling these posts member state governments argued strongly for their own candidates.

At the same special summit, the European Council selected the countries that in its view had met the convergence criteria and thus qualified to adopt the single currency. The selections were based on detailed reports by the Commission and the EMI on the progress made by each of the member states in meeting the convergence criteria and in adapting national legislation, including that governing the national central bank, along the lines stipulated in the Maastricht Treaty. The choice of eleven countries was a remarkable achievement that ran against nearly all expectations of the early 1990s, when it was thought that only a few countries would qualify or that the project itself might be abandoned.

After continued technical preparations for the remainder of 1998, the actual launch of the euro went surprisingly smoothly. On December 31, 1998 (a Thursday), the EU finance ministers met in Brussels to set the irrevocable conversion rates between the euro and the national currencies of the eleven participating states (Table 6.3). This translated into a rate of approximately $1.18 per euro at the opening of trading on January 4, 1999.

With New Year's Day falling on a Friday, thousands of employees at banks, stock brokerages, and government agencies worked over the long holiday weekend to be ready to conduct national and international business in the euro on Monday morning. Major tasks included redenominating all outstanding public debt in euros, converting bank balances into euros, redenominating stocks and bonds in euros, and activating euro accounts for customers. They also had to make the final tests of and activate the new computer systems developed to handle the euro, including the TARGET (Trans-European Automated Real-time Gross settlement Express Transfer) system operated by the ECB to make cross-border euro payments among banks in the euro zone. All of the hard work, investment, and testing of the previous months and years paid off, however, as euro trading began on the first business day of the new year with only a handful of technical glitches in the leading financial centers of Europe.

With the euro successfully launched, one of the few unresolved questions for EMU concerned relations between the euro and the currencies of the four EU countries that had not adopted the single currency. To help ensure monetary stability in the EU as a whole as well as to facilitate eventual adoption of the euro by these countries, the EU established a new exchange rate mechanism designed for the euro and the national currencies of non-euro EU member states. Called ERM II, the new mechanism became operational on January 1, 1999. Greece and Denmark chose to participate, thereby linking their national currencies to the euro. The Danish krone would fluctuate against the euro at the pre-1993 band of $+/-$ 2.25 percent, the Greek drachma at the $+/-$ 15 percent rate established after the 1992–1993 crisis. Sweden and the UK came under pressure from the ECB to join ERM II but, still smarting from the devaluations of the early 1990s, at least initially declined to participate. As enlargement proceeds, the new member states are

Table 6.3   Irrevocable Conversion Rates, December 31, 1998

One euro equals:
1.95583 German marks
6.55957 French francs
1936.27 Italian lire
166.386 Spanish pesetas
2.20371 Dutch guilders
40.3399 Belgian francs
13.7603 Austrian schillings
200.482 Portuguese escudos
5.94573 Finnish markka
0.787564 Irish pounds
40.3399 Luxembourg francs

expected to join ERM II, although some conceivably could adopt the euro immediately upon becoming members of the Union.

Following the launch of the euro, Greece continued to make progress in meeting the convergence criteria, especially in lowering its rate of inflation. It thus appeared to be on track to becoming, as early as 2001, the twelfth EU member state to adopt the euro. Denmark and Sweden also moved closer to adopting the euro, as domestic political opposition to EMU diminished. In Britain, Prime Minister Blair was committed to bringing his country into the euro zone but faced a skeptical public and diehard resistance in the opposition Conservative party. He pledged that the UK would adopt the euro only if doing so was approved in a national referendum that would be held only after the next parliamentary elections, likely to take place in 2002.

EMU in Operation

ECONOMIC POLICY

As its name indicates, there are two parts to EMU: economic and monetary. Economic policy coordination was seen as an essential part of the preparations for monetary union (the old "economist" position), but also as valuable in its own right, to be continued after the launch of the euro and to embrace even those countries that were EU members but that did not adopt the single currency.

The Maastricht Treaty required all member states to begin to coordinate their economic policies within the Council of Ministers at the start of Stage 2. The treaty defined the overall objectives of EU economic policies as a "harmonious and balanced development of economic activities, sustainable and non-inflationary growth respecting the environment, a high level of employment and social protection, the raising of the standard of living and quality of life, and economic and social cohesion and solidarity among Member States."[19] The provisions in the treaty on economic policy coordination for the most part apply to Denmark and the United Kingdom, even though these countries were not required to adopt the euro in 1999. They also will apply from the date of accession for new member countries, even though these countries may not at first abandon their national currencies for the euro.

Under the economic policy provisions of the treaty, each year the Council of Ministers (in the composition of ECOFIN) must adopt broad guidelines for the economic policies of the EU and its member states. The Commission provides the first draft of these guidelines, which then are examined by ECOFIN and approved by the heads of state and government in the European Council in a way that gives them added political weight. The Commission is charged with monitoring member state economic policies and performance to ensure that the guidelines are implemented. The guidelines include, in addition to general recommendations that apply to the EU as a whole, country-specific economic guidelines that address particular economic problems or policy failures in member states.

The EU institutions are free to adopt whatever set of guidelines they deem appropriate, consistent with the general objectives set forth in the treaty. However, the treaty assigns a special priority to coordinated action against excessive government deficits and debt, defined—as in the original convergence criteria of 1994–1998—as a deficit of 3 percent or more of total GDP at market prices and a total government debt of 60 percent or more of GDP. If a member state appears to be exceeding the reference values of 3 percent of GDP for deficits and 60 percent for debt, it can be designated as having an "excess deficit" and compelled under the treaty to take remedial action. The Commission prepares a report on the situation in the country, taking into account such factors as whether the deficit is rising or falling, whether it is the result of structural or cyclical economic factors, and whether it is being used to finance current consumption or government investment (e.g., public goods such as roads and schools). The Commission sends its report to the Council of Ministers, which by qualified majority vote may determine that an excessive deficit exists and issue recommendations to the member state for its elimination. If a member state persists in having an excess deficit, the Council of Ministers, again by qualified majority vote, may take concrete measures against that state. These measures include requiring the state to publish additional information before issuing bonds and securities, limiting access to EIB credits, requiring the member state to make a noninterest-bearing deposit with the EU institutions until the deficit has been corrected, or imposing fines of an appropriate size.

When the Treaty of Maastricht came into effect, nearly all of the member states had debt or deficit figures above the reference values. There thus was no particular stigma attached to being in the excess deficit dock. Because the 3 percent and 60 percent reference values were among the criteria established to determine whether a state was eligible to adopt the euro in Stage 3 of EMU, the excess deficit procedures never were put to a politically interesting test in the 1990s, as the Council of Ministers never had to vote to take action against a recalcitrant member state that was not doing enough to reduce budgetary imbalances and thus openly defying the EU's macroeconomic guidelines. Such a situation could occur in the future, however, and concern about such a possibility accounted for the desire of the German government to strengthen the excess deficit provisions of the Maastricht Treaty with the supplementary agreement that later became known as the Stability and Growth Pact.

Although fighting inflation and holding down deficit and debt levels have a special status under the EU legal order, they are by no means the exclusive focus of economic policy under EMU. The Broad Economic Guidelines for 1999, for example, contained three sets of policy recommendations: macroeconomic policy, economic reform, and employment.[20] Under macroeconomic policy, they called for, in addition to ongoing efforts to meet budgetary targets mandated by the stability pact, review of pension and health care systems with regard to the projected ageing of populations, tax reforms to improve incentives for employment, and efforts to restrain wage increases that could generate inflationary pressures. With regard to economic reform, the guidelines called for stricter application and monitoring in all member states of single market and competition legislation, with particular reference to opening up public procurement, liberalizing public utilities, and controlling state aids, as well as for efforts to improve the legal and regulatory framework for business, with a particular emphasis on reducing barriers to starting up businesses. In the employment area, the broad economic policy guidelines reinforced the themes in the EU's 1999 employment policies. In addition to these strictures for the Union as a whole, the Broad Economic Guidelines contain country-specific recommendations that are based on the Commission's analysis of the economic problems and policy setting in each member state. The country-specific recommendations for 1999 are summarized in Box 6.2.

MONETARY POLICY

As noted, the institutional setup of EMU in the Maastricht Treaty was modeled on the postwar German system, which in turn had many points of similarity with the U.S. Federal Reserve System. Before EMU, each of the national central banks was responsible for conducting monetary policy on a national basis. This meant determining the money supply, setting the discount rate (the rate of interest at which the central bank lends to commercial banks), and managing official foreign reserves. For countries adopting the euro, these responsibilities were transferred on January 1, 1999, to the ESCB and its core institution, the ECB, which together were dubbed the "Eurosystem" in the EU's official terminology.[21] The key actors in setting monetary policy for the euro area were the president of the ECB, the Executive Board of the ECB, and the Governing Council of the ESCB. With eleven countries adopting the euro, the latter body began with seventeen members in all.

Under the guidelines established by Maastricht, the ESCB defines and implements monetary policy in the euro area. The ECB establishes the basic short-term interest rate in the euro area, just as the Federal Reserve sets interest rates in the United States. It also imposes reserve requirements on banks and credit institutions. It conducts open market operations to manage the money supply and influence the trend of market interest rates. It operates a European payments system, and has the exclusive right to authorize the issue of banknotes in the euro area, which may be done by the national banks with ECB authorization.

Operating a successful monetary policy in the euro zone promises to be both technically and politically difficult, especially during the early years of monetary union, in which the ECB has to establish its credibility and deal with problems of transition. Measuring and regulating the money supply in the euro area will be an especially complex assignment, given the parallel existence (until mid-2002) of euros and national currencies and the amount of euro-induced financial restructuring underway. Based on estimated real economic growth, inflation, and other

Box 6.2   1999 Broad Economic Policy Guidelines: Country-Specific Guidelines

Country	*Guidelines*
Belgium	• Budgetary discipline (run a primary surplus of 6 percent of GDP in 1999 and beyond) • Improve implementation of single market legislation • Pursue labor market reforms; reform labor laws to allow greater regional and sectoral differentiation of wages
Denmark	• Budgetary discipline and reduction of distortions in the tax system • Stronger application of competition regulations; implementation of reforms in the electricity sector • Implement reforms in the labor market; increase incentives through tax reforms
Germany	• Budgetary discipline; faster progress on medium-term deficit reduction targets • Reduce level of state aids; simplify procedures for establishing small and medium enterprises • Review benefit and assistance schemes to increase incentives to work; implement reforms to reduce labor costs at the lowest end of the wage scale
Greece	• Achieve budget deficit reduction targets for 1999 and 2000; increase the efficiency of the tax system and reform the public sector • Improve implementation of single market legislation; reduce administrative burden of starting new businesses; formulate a strategy to develop venture capital markets • Reform training and education systems; implement part-time contracts and more flexible working hours
Spain	• Meet budget targets • Improve implementation of single market legislation; reduce administrative burden on companies • Place more emphasis on labor market policies, especially training and education; improve possibilities for part-time work and reform labor system to allow greater regional wage differentiation
France	• Respect deficit targets; use improved economic growth to make further progress on deficit and debt reduction • Reduce the proportion of nonagricultural state aid devoted to rescuing firms; accelerate liberalization of network industries (transport, telecommunications, utilities); reduce administrative burden on businesses • Review unemployment benefit schemes to strengthen work incentives; continue policy of cutting taxes at the low end of the wage scale

(continues)

(continued)

Ireland
- Restrain growth of government expenditure
- Improve implementation of single market legislation; strengthen competition authority; liberalize network industries; encourage venture capital and R&D
- Place greater emphasis on measures to get the long-term unemployed into the labor force; improve training and education for low-skilled workers; avoid setting the minimum wage so high as to price low-skill workers out of employment

Italy
- Meet deficit reduction targets; aim for a primary surplus of 5.5 percent of GDP in 2000 to cut past debt levels; increase government investment; reassess reform of the pension system
- Accelerate implementation of single market legislation; reduce state aids; intensify liberalization of the transport sector; streamline process for establishing new businesses
- Improve labor market policies; shift tax burden away from labor to other tax bases; introduce greater regional wage differentiation

Luxembourg
- Monitor government expenditures closely, in particular in the social security system
- Speed up implementation of single market legislation; consider abolition of system of price regulations
- Raise the employment rate of women and older workers through job training and additional childcare facilities

Netherlands
- Limit increase in the 1999 deficit; achieve better medium-term budgetary results
- Step up transposition of single market legislation; remove obstacles to business start-ups and speed liberalization of the transport sector
- Continue efforts to reduce the overall tax burden

Austria
- Meet deficit reduction targets
- Accelerate transposition of single market legislation; put in place an independent cartel office; reform public services; speed deregulation; develop and facilitate access to venture capital
- Review generous conditions of early retirement and reform the tax system in favor of low-wage and low-skill workers

Portugal
- Meet and surpass budgetary targets for 1999
- Improve single market transposition record; implement reform of competition law; liberalize network industries and develop the venture capital market
- Improve education and training; develop an adequate benefit system to enable workers to participate in education and training; enhance labor market flexibility

(continues)

(continued)

Finland	• Increase the government surplus by reducing government expenditure, thus making possible needed reduction in the tax burden, especially on labor
	• Strengthen powers of the competition authorities; improve the competitive environment, especially between public and private enterprises
	• Review benefit assistance schemes with the aim of increasing incentives and job availability; strengthen the retirement system and introduce more flexibility as regards the retirement age
Sweden	• Budgetary discipline; efforts to reduce the high burden of taxation
	• Solve competition problems in certain sectors and strengthen the powers of the competition authorities
	• Use budgetary room for maneuver to reduce taxes on labor, with priority for low-paid workers; review benefit and assistance schemes
United Kingdom	• Budgetary discipline; prompt action to correct any deterioration in the government balance not caused by the business cycle
	• Improve single market transposition record and strengthen the environment for entrepreneurship, innovation, and R&D
	• Continue efforts to lower marginal effective tax rates on low-paid workers; deal with regional unemployment differences

Source: European Commission, *1999 Broad Economic Policy Guidelines.*

factors, the ESCB set 4.5 percent per year as its initial target for annual money supply growth in the euro area. The ECB also set a basic interest rate of 3 percent for open market operations by central banks.[22] Meeting the money supply target was difficult. During the euro's first year growth frequently overshot the ECB's target, raising concerns about a triggering of inflation.

On the political side, the birth of the euro was marked by controversy over the old question of the relative importance of fighting inflation versus the pursuit of higher growth and employment. Even before the euro was launched, the ECB came under a barrage of criticism from political leaders who argued that Europe desperately needed lower interest rates in order to promote growth and combat unemployment. Germany, which under conservative Finance Minister Waigel had been the strongest proponent of a hard euro and the need to combat inflation through fiscal and monetary restraint, ironically became a strong backer of pro-growth policies following the election of the Social Democratic party (SPD)–Green coalition in the fall of 1998. Waigel's SPD successor, Oskar Lafontaine, repeatedly called for the ECB to lower interest rates. Duisenberg brushed aside these calls as flawed on their merits and inconsistent with the independence of the ECB.

Relations between the ECB and Germany settled into a calmer pattern after Lafontaine resigned his post in March 1999, in part out of frustration with the failure
of his German cabinet colleagues to back his economic policy proposals. But the
early squabbling between governments and central bankers took its toll on the
euro, which fell from $1.18 to $1.08 in the first ten weeks of its existence, surprising many experts who had predicted a rapid appreciation of the new currency.

Freed from the visible public lobbying of the German finance ministry, in
April 1999 the ECB cut its bank refinancing rate by 0.5 percentage points, to 2.5
percent. This decision was taken by the ECB's Governing Council, and was intended to head off the threat of deflation and recession. As in the United States,
where the press and financial markets closely follow meetings of the Federal Reserve's Board of Governors for hints about interest rate trends, European and
world markets began scrutinizing statements by ECB officials and press reports
from meetings of the Governing Council for indications of where euro-zone rates
were headed. In November 1999 the Governing Council decided to raise the
ECB's financing rate back to 3 percent. By this time, economic growth in the
euro-zone had accelerated and the ECB was more concerned about inflationary
pressures than recession.

The euro itself continued to show a pattern of relative weakness against the
dollar. By July, it was approaching parity with the dollar at $1.02. European gov-
ernments and central bankers insisted that this fall reflected generally weak economic conditions in Europe, contrasted with the continued economic boom in the
United States, and not something fundamentally flawed in the EMU project. The
currency rallied for a while, but closed the year at near parity with the dollar, a 15
percent drop from the rate established at the end of 1998. In late January 2000 it
broke through the symbolically important one dollar level, closing below 99 cents
in New York on January 27.

THE POLICY DEBATE

Many experts were surprised by the euro's decline against the dollar, but few attributed to it any lasting significance or thought that the EMU project was threatened with collapse. In a world of floating exchange rates, the euro is expected to
fluctuate against the dollar and the yen, and the initial decline was attributed to
relatively stronger growth and investment opportunities combined with continued
low inflation in the United States. The big question seemed to be not whether
governments and central banks could make a single currency work, but whether
the European governments and, insofar as it has a role to play, the EU itself could
devise and carry out the right mix of economic, employment, social, research, and
related policies to deal with unemployment and with the problem Europe has had
in generating self-sustaining growth in the rapidly globalizing economy.

What that policy mix should be was an important topic of debate in the late
1990s, as European political leaders attempted to define national and EU ap-

proaches to the economic challenges of globalization. Prime Minister Blair proposed a "Third Way," an approach to economic policy that in his view combined the economic dynamism of free market capitalism as practiced in the United States (and championed by his Conservative predecessors, Thatcher and Major) with the broad concerns for equality, social justice, and the welfare state favored by the continental social and Christian democratic parties. He was echoed by German Chancellor Gerhard Schroeder, who came to power as an exponent of the *neue Mitte* (new middle), a combination of market-oriented reform and welfare state politics. In France, Prime Minister Jospin, a socialist, took a more traditional left-wing approach, not embracing a third or new way. As a practical matter, however, France under Jospin made important strides in the direction of a more market-oriented economy, through deregulation, privatization of some industries, and a changed attitude towards foreign investment.

In contrast to these positions on the center-left and left of the political spectrum, other leaders and economists dismissed talk of the third way and called for unambiguous efforts to follow the American path. Specifically, they favored cuts in government spending, labor market reforms to encourage higher levels of labor force participation and an end to "well-paid idleness," and policies to promote new information and communication technologies.[23] All sides in the policy debate agreed, however, that while setting interest rates and trying to influence the value of the euro relative to other currencies were important elements of the policy mix, they were only part of a larger and more complex picture that included labor, social security, taxation, information and infrastructure, and other policy areas.

Implications

ECONOMIC BENEFITS

Like the single market, the euro will affect every aspect of economic life in Europe, making the EU a more formidable global competitor with greater influence on international economic and monetary affairs. The major economic benefits of EMU are expected to include greater price transparency leading to a larger and more competitive single market, deeper and more liquid stock and bond markets that will lower the costs of capital for businesses and promote the restructuring of European industry on a continental scale, and more cross-border mergers and acquisitions among European firms leading to stronger global competitors. EMU also will intensify pressures to accelerate integration in other areas such as taxation policy and company law that will bring added economic benefits.

Despite the existence of the common market since the 1960s and the single market since the end of 1992, many product and service markets in the EU are still highly fragmented along national lines. Manufacturers and retailers often charge higher prices in some countries than in others by retaining control of the distribution channels that set market prices or simply by taking advantage of different local expectations as to what constitutes a fair price. Prices for the same car, for example, can vary by as much as 25 percent among the member states while those for everyday items such as toys and clothing can vary by 50 percent or more. EU competition policy aims to break down such segmentation, but the single currency will provide an even more powerful impetus to the evening out of prices across markets. With euro pricing, consumers and business purchasers will be able to recognize instantly the kinds of disparities in pricing that hitherto have characterized the single market. Those companies that respond effectively to the new and more competitive environment will become stronger global players, while those that have survived in the single market by the implicit protection offered by national currencies will be forced to adapt or go out of business. The growth of electronic commerce via the Internet will accelerate this trend.

The euro also will tend to unify the fragmented European stock and bond markets. Cross-border mergers among banks, insurance companies, and stockbrokers multiplied in the run-up to the single currency and can be expected to continue for several years before the shakeout in the financial sector is complete. As in the market for products and services, the euro will facilitate comparisons across national stock markets and lead to a single European market for stock similar to the one in the United States. With the shares of companies all denominated and paying dividends in euros, closer comparison of profitability and other performance measures is inevitable and will lead to greater Europeanization of ownership and new pressures on companies to create shareholder value. Small and medium-sized companies will enjoy lower capital costs as they benefit from lower interest rates and have better chances to issue stock in the broader euro-market for new equities.

There also will be stronger competition among European financial centers for businesses and jobs. London will have to work to maintain its preeminence over Frankfurt, while smaller financial centers such as Lisbon, Brussels, and Vienna may lose out to a combination of electronics and the euro. The arrival of the euro may also help Western Europe to deal with its looming pension crisis, caused by an ageing population that will have to be supported in retirement by a relatively smaller workforce. Insurance companies and pension funds that formerly had to match investments and liabilities—that is, promised payments to pensioners—in the same currency and country now can operate on a broader European scale. The euro also will have important implications for the international monetary system and Europe's role in maintaining international economic stability. These implications are examined in Chapter 8, which deals with the EU as an international economic power.

THE EURO AND THE FUTURE OF EUROPEAN INTEGRATION

Turning to the two questions posed at the beginning of this chapter—is the euro economically sustainable and able to deliver the economic benefits promised, and will the EMU project propel the EU forward toward political union—it is possible to draw an initial assessment of the implications of EMU for the future of European integration. The answer to the first question would seem to be a "yes," but in a tentative and preliminary way. Many of the anticipated benefits of the single currency were apparent already during its first year. Although it is difficult to judge which effects are attributable to EMU and which to other factors, economic growth accelerated and unemployment continued to fall in the euro area in 1999. Price transparency in markets improved, helping to hold down inflation. The expected restructuring of financial markets took hold, as companies (including U.S. companies operating in Europe) issued a huge volume of euro-denominated stocks and bonds. Public acceptance appeared to be growing, laying a solid basis for the introduction of the currency at the retail level in 2002.

Nonetheless, the puzzling spectacle of the euro's almost continuous fall against the dollar surprised most economists, causing concern in the ECB and focusing attention once again on underlying problems in basic economic performance. The euro area was running a large trade surplus with the rest of the world that should have bolstered the new currency's value. But statistics showed that companies were diverting investment away from the euro area, thereby depressing demand for the currency. This in turn provoked new questions about the competitive situation of the EU in the global economy, and led back to the debate about reform. EMU could hold out great economic benefits for Europe, but only, as the ECB and others repeatedly warned, if the Union and the member states continue with the structural reforms and other changes needed to meet the challenges of globalization, an ageing population, unemployment, and other policy issues.

In sum, the politically driven project of EMU was starting to deliver its promised economic benefits, but the single currency was by no means a panacea for all economic problems. Like other regions, Europe will need to adapt and reform on an almost continuous basis in order to prosper in the highly competitive world of twenty-first-century capitalism.

With regard to the second question, the jury is still out. Definitive conclusions about the political implications of the euro will not be possible until after European citizens have used the euro for a while and "forgotten" their national currencies. At least initially, however, there does not seem to be much evidence that EMU in itself constitutes a decisive step toward political integration. It is an important step, but one that must be seen in the context of the continued primacy of national politics, of intergovernmental decision-making in the Union, and of other projects in the EU that also are intended to propel the integration process forward. Indeed, the renewed emphasis on several of these projects (notably a stronger CFSP and closer cooperation in justice and home affairs) at the end of the 1990s and into the new century was perhaps the clearest if still tacit admission that EMU alone cannot transform the Union. One of the most important of these new projects, the development of what the EU calls "a new area of freedom, justice and security," is the subject of the next chapter.

Notes

1. Pierre Jacquet, "European Integration at a Crossroads," *Survival* 38, no. 4 (Winter 1996–97), 91.

2. Accounts of monetary diplomacy in the 1960s by participants include Robert Solomon, *The International Monetary System 1945–1981* (New York: Harper & Row, 1986); and Paul Volcker and Toyoo Gyohten, *Changing Fortunes: The World's Money and the Threat to American Leadership* (New York: Times Books, 1992).

3. *Interim Report on the Establishment by Stages of Economic and Monetary Union: "Werner Report,"* Supplement to Bull. EC 7–1970.

4. Tsoukalis, *The New European Economy Revisited*, 138–142.

5. Tsoukalis, *The New European Economy Revisited*, 18, citing OECD.

6. Patrick McCarthy, "France Fears Reality: Rigeur and the Germans," in David P. Calleo and Claudia Morgenstern, *Recasting Europe's Economies* (Lanham, Md.: University Press of America, 1990), 25–78.

7. Solomon, *The International Monetary System, 1945–1981*, 25; 384–385.

8. Robin Bladen-Howell, "The European Monetary System," in Artis and Lee, *The Economics of the European Union*, 332–336, based on European Commission, "One Market, One Money: An Evaluation of the Potential Benefits and Costs of Forming an Economic and Monetary Union," *European Economy* 44 (1990), Table 2.4.

9. Ibid., 334.

10. Moravcsik, *The Choice for Europe*, takes an alternative view, and argues that Delors had much less to do with EMU than Kohl and Mitterrand. It seems fair to say that all three men agreed on the principle (if not the details) of EMU, and can claim a share in the credit.

11. Michael Emerson, et al., *One Market, One Money: An Evaluation of the Potential Benefits and Costs of Forming an Economic and Monetary Union* (Oxford: Oxford University Press, 1992).

12. Bull. EC 6–1989, 11.

13. Robert Mundell, "A Theory of Optimum Currency Areas," *American Economic Review* 51 (September 1961): 657–665.

14. Cliff Walsh, Horst Reichenbach and Roderick Meiklejohn, "Fiscal Federalism and Its Implications for the European Community," *European Economy* 5 (1993): 3–20.

15. Peter Kenen, *Economic and Monetary Union in Europe: Moving Beyond Maastricht* (New York: Cambridge University Press, 1995), 88–89.

16. Barry Eichengreen and Charles Wyplosz, "The Unstable EMS," *Brookings Papers on Economic Activity* 1 (1993): 51–124.

17. "Resolution of the European Council on the Stability and Growth Pact," Bull. EU, 6–1997, 17–18; and IMF, *World Economic Outlook*, October 1997, 58–59.

18. "Appointment of the Members of the Executive Board of the European Central Bank," and "Oral statement by Mr. Duisenberg, President of the European Monetary Institute," *Council of the European Union, meeting in the composition of Heads of State or Government*, C/98/124.

19. Article 2.

20. European Commission, "1999 Broad Economic Policy Guidelines," IP/99/204, Brussels, March 30, 1999.

21. ECB, *Monthly Bulletin* (January 1999): 7.

22. "Chronology of monetary policy measures of the Eurosystem," ECB, *Monthly Bulletin* (January 1999): 37–38.

23. Martin Wolf, "Not the Right Way," *Financial Times*, June 16, 1999.

Suggestions for Further Reading

De Grauwe, Paul. *The Economics of Monetary Integration*. Oxford: Oxford University Press, 1994.

Gros, Daniel and Niels Thygesen. *European Monetary Integration: From the European Monetary System to European Monetary Union*, 2nd ed. London: Longman, 1997.

Jones, Erik. *The Politics of Economic and Monetary Union*. Lanham: Rowman and Littlefield, 2000.

Kenen, Peter B. *Economic and Monetary Union in Europe: Moving Beyond Maastricht*. New York: Cambridge University Press, 1995.

Solomon, Robert. *Money on the Move: The Revolution in International Finance since 1980*. Princeton: Princeton University Press, 1999.

Ungerer, Horst. *A Concise History of European Monetary Integration: From EPU to EMU*. Westport: Quorum Books, 1997.

CHAPTER 7

The Citizen's Europe
A NEW AREA OF FREEDOM, JUSTICE, AND SECURITY

Western Europe emerged from World War II committed not only to restoring peace and economic prosperity, but to safeguarding civil and political rights and the rule of law—values that had been trampled upon by the Nazi and fascist dictatorships in the 1930s and that again were being denied by the communist authorities in central and eastern Europe after 1945. These values were enshrined at the national level in the new postwar constitutions of France and Italy and in the Basic Law of the Federal Republic of Germany, adopted when that state was founded in 1949. At the European level, they were reflected in the statute of the Council of Europe, also signed in 1949 as an outgrowth of the Hague conference of European federalists.

Unlike the ECSC that was founded several years later, the Council of Europe was not endowed with supranational powers and strong central institutions. It worked and continues to work on the basis of conventions adopted by its member states, the earliest and most important of which was the November 1950 European Convention for the Protection of Human Rights and Fundamental Freedoms.[1] The convention set certain basic standards that all members of the Council of Europe were pledged to observe. Along with several follow-on agreements, it also established mechanisms for addressing human rights abuses: a European Commission of Human Rights to investigate alleged breaches of the convention submitted to it by states and individuals and a European Court of Human Rights (established in 1959) to adjudicate cases sent to it by the human rights commission.

In contrast, the ECSC, the EC, and Euratom were set up as essentially economic organizations, albeit ones that reflected the long-term political aspirations of the founding fathers. As such, they did not directly concern themselves with civil and political rights. The Treaty of Rome guaranteed free movement of "workers," but it did not confer a general right upon the citizens of one member state to reside or seek employment elsewhere in the Community. The treaty had a modest social dimension, but it was narrowly focused on economics and the functioning of the single market. It dealt with persons as economic actors rather than as citizens. This meant, for example, that it contained rather strong language about equal pay for equal work for men and women, but it had nothing to say about combating discrimination unrelated to the workplace. This remained a national responsibility, enshrined in different ways in the constitutions and national laws of the member states.

As the EC developed, however, it began to involve itself in matters that touch upon the rights and responsibilities of individuals as citizens: police and judicial cooperation, immigration, asylum and refugee matters, and eventually the citizenship rights granted by the new European Union. Three factors contributed to the growing importance of citizenship and other people-related issues in the integration process: (1) the need to address the potentially negative consequences of the lowering of intra-European borders, especially as it related to the free movement of people; (2) the growth in the Union's social dimension and the links between the economic and social rights of EU citizens and their civil and political rights; and (3) the need to address the "democratic deficit" in the Union and the link between political rights and citizenship.

EU involvement in citizenship and related issues has developed in stages. In the 1970s the EC member states began to cooperate among each other on an intergovernmental basis, initially mainly to deal with the transnational problem of terrorism. In the 1980s, largely under the impetus of the single market program, they started to negotiate formal agreements among each other making cooperation on justice and home affairs matters mandatory, albeit still on an intergovernmental basis outside the formal structures of the Community. In 1992 they concluded the Maastricht Treaty, which established an EU citizenship and the EU's third pillar, thereby formally bringing citizens' rights and certain aspects of justice and home affairs under the purview of the Union. In 1997, the EU member states agreed in the Treaty of Amsterdam to a more extensive transfer of responsibility for matters relating to justice and home affairs to the first pillar of the EU, thus giving the Union's supranational institutions a major role in shaping and executing policy in these areas. A new section in the treaty entitled "Freedom, Security and Justice" reiterated provisions on fundamental rights and nondiscrimination contained in other EU documents and called for the progressive establishment of an EU-wide area of freedom, security, and justice.

The 1970s

Cooperation among the EC member states on police and judicial matters began in 1975 with the agreement to establish, under the auspices of European Political Cooperation, the Trevi Group (named after the fountain in Rome near where the group held its first meeting) of senior officials from justice and home affairs ministries.[2] The mid-1970s were marked by mounting international terrorism emanating both from the Middle East and from home-grown groups such as Italy's Red Brigades and West Germany's Baader-Meinhof gang. The Trevi Group was to serve as a forum for the exchange of information and the discussion of steps to combat terrorism in Europe. As was the case with EPC, the policy issues dealt with by the group were outside the competence of the Community. Coordination took place on an intergovernmental basis, with no role for the European Commission and other central institutions and no basis in the treaties or EC law.

Like the Council of Ministers, the Trevi Group operated on several levels. The ministers met every six months. A group of senior officials met as needed to prepare the agenda for ministerial meetings and to monitor the progress of the working groups, which dealt with cooperation among national authorities to combat terrorism, for example by sharing information about known terrorist organizations. Cooperation at these three levels helped to lay the basis for future cooperation among the member states on other matters with judicial implications, including combating narcotics trafficking and illegal immigration.

As the member state governments increased their cooperation on police and judicial matters, often through working-level links that attracted little public attention, more public moves were afoot to add a citizenship dimension to European integration. The December 1975 Rome European Council, the same meeting that called for the first direct elections to the European Parliament, reached agreement in principle on creating a uniform passport for citizens of all EC member states. In the same month, Belgian Prime Minister Leo Tindemans presented his report to the European Council arguing the need to make Europe more relevant to the everyday needs of citizens and outlining a series of proposals concerning citizenship.[3] Little was accomplished along these lines, however, until the relaunch of the 1980s.

The 1980s and the Single European Act

CITIZENSHIP ISSUES

The 1980s saw continued slow progress toward a de facto Community citizenship. In June 1981 the member state governments reached agreement on the introduction of an EC passport. On January 1, 1985, the first such passports were issued in most member states. At the June 1984 Fontainebleau summit, the European Council set up a committee chaired by Italian politician Pietro Adonnino to develop ideas for a "people's Europe." The Adonnino committee presented its report to the European Council the following year. Entitled *Citizen's Europe*, it recommended a list of measures that would have immediate practical benefit for citizens, including simpler border controls, mutual recognition of diplomas and qualifying examinations, and measures to allow citizens of one member state to live and work in other member states. The Adonnino report was largely forgotten, but some of its recommendations were subsumed under the 1992 program.

Under Delors, the Commission began to promote a sense of European patriotism and identity.[4] In May 1986 the Commission raised the new European flag—the familiar ring of yellow stars on a blue background—to the strains of Beethoven's famous "Ode to Joy," which had been proclaimed the European anthem. For the most part, however, the big story of the 1980s was not citizenship but borders: the progressive dismantling of the internal borders of the Community, various attempts to strengthen its external borders, and the political and institutional implications of these attempts.

SCHENGEN AND THE SINGLE MARKET

The renewed interest in the 1980s in completing the single market—for labor, capital, and services as well as for goods—had important implications for European cooperation in justice and home affairs. On the one hand, it stimulated efforts by the member states, in bilateral and multilateral forums, within the Community and outside of it, to accelerate the removal of border checks and other frontier-related measures that still impeded the functioning of the internal market. On the other hand, it led to new efforts among governments to cope with the anticipated negative side effects of the elimination of border controls through closer cooperation. To some extent there was a tension between these two responses to the single market program, as the search for controls at the European level on occasion complicated implementation of the free market provisions of the Single European Act that they ostensibly were intended to advance.

In July 1984 France and Germany concluded an agreement on the gradual elimination of border checks between the two countries. The Franco-German agreement was an important precursor to both the Schengen Agreement and the SEA. In June 1985, Belgium, France, the Federal Republic of Germany, Luxembourg, and the Netherlands concluded the Schengen Agreement on the elimination of border controls among these five countries.[5] Named for the town in Luxembourg where it was negotiated, the agreement was to enter into force on January 1, 1990. It was concluded as an intergovernmental accord outside the framework of the EC, but its intent was to give effect, in a part of the Community, to the provisions on free movement that were in the Treaty of Rome and that were expected to be included in the single market program then under discussion. In addition to eliminating border controls among the signatory states, it called for establishing common rules in the Schengen area for visa and asylum policies and comprehensive cooperation among the national authorities on such matters as combating trafficking in drugs and weapons, combating terrorism and illegal immigration, and hot pursuit by police across national borders. A key element of the implementation plan was to be the development of a Schengen Information System (SIS), a database established and maintained by the Schengen country governments to help police track aliens, individuals wanted for extradition, suspected terrorists, and certain other categories of persons whose movement across borders was of interest to the authorities.

Schengen was followed by the signature, in January 1986, of the SEA, which provided for an area in which the free movement of persons was to be ensured. As an annex to the treaty, the member states adopted a "Political Declaration by the Governments of the Member States on the Free Movement of Persons," in which they agreed to cooperate on immigration matters and the combating of terrorism, crime, and traffic in drugs and illicit trading in works of art and antiques. As with other aspects of the single market program, however, the lowering of barriers to cross-border movement did not flow automatically from the language of the treaty. Member states had to adopt implementing directives at the Community level and to transpose these directives into national legislation. This they did with great difficulty. Britain, Ireland, and Denmark took the position that the free movement provisions of the SEA should apply only to citizens of Community countries, and not to third-country nationals. The other nine member countries (all actual or prospective signatories of the Schengen Agreement) took the view that any individual, having legitimately entered the Community, had the same right of movement throughout the Community as nationals of the member state. (Thus under the majority position, for example, an Indian citizen living in Germany on a student visa should be free to travel to Belgium, Italy, or any other EC country, much as if he were a German; under the minority position, the student would have to obtain a visa to travel to another EC country, much as if he were coming directly from India.) This issue was important not only—or even primarily—for the third-country individuals concerned, but because the British position implied the maintenance of intra-EC border controls that would affect EC citizens as well, as continued checks of everyone crossing the national border was the only way to police the movement of third-country nationals.

These agreements to open the EC's internal borders were paralleled by moves to strengthen controls at the Community's external frontiers through expanded cooperation in the Trevi process. In 1985 Trevi set up a working group to coordinate action against international drug trafficking and other forms of serious international crime. This was followed, in 1986, by establishment of an Ad Hoc Group on Immigration to work on migration-related issues associated with the lifting of border controls.

The Ad Hoc Group on Immigration was instrumental in negotiating two intergovernmental conventions that addressed issues relating to migration from outside the Community. The Dublin Convention on Asylum, concluded by the twelve EC member states in June 1990, established common rules for dealing with asylum seekers. It set criteria by which to determine which country was responsible for examining an asylum seeker's application and, if warranted, for granting that individual's request under the terms of the 1950 European Convention for the Protection of Human Rights and Fundamental Freedoms and the 1951 Convention Relating to the Status of Refugees. If a country decided to admit an individual, this decision would be accepted by all other member states. A second agreement, the July 1991 Convention on the Crossing of EC External Borders (also known as the External Frontiers Convention), was modeled on the Schengen Agreement but was intended to apply to all member states. It provided for drawing up a common list of countries whose nationals would or would not require visas for entry into the Community. Neither the Dublin Convention nor the External Frontiers Convention proved easy to implement, however, as the national governments dragged their feet on putting these agreements into effect. The External Frontiers Convention was not signed, owing to Britain's refusal to remove its intra-EC border controls. The Dublin Convention ran into opposition from Ireland and the UK, which were concerned about its security implications.

IMMIGRATION AS A POLICY PROBLEM

The Dublin and External Frontiers conventions and the provisions of the Schengen Agreement dealing with visa and asylum policies were all responses to the rising saliency of immigration as a policy problem. The European countries traditionally saw themselves as countries of *emigration*, not *immigration*. During the economic boom years lasting from the late 1950s to the early 1970s, industry in West Germany, France, and the Benelux countries suffered shortages of labor that they alleviated by importing "guest workers" from abroad. Many of these workers came from southern Italy, and thus were citizens of a Community country covered by the free movement provisions of the Treaty of Rome. Others came from Yugoslavia, Spain and Portugal (still not members of the EC), Turkey, and North Africa. When the economic recession of 1974–1975 occurred, many of the West European countries hoped that these migrants would return to their home countries. By this time, however, many of these people had put down roots in their adopted countries and had no wish to return to where they or in many cases their parents had originated. With the Turks and North Africans especially, Western Europe was confronted with large numbers of people who were not fully integrated into European society but who also had little prospect of return to their countries of origin. This resulted in educational, crime, and other social problems with alienated immigrant youth, particularly in large cities, and in a racist and xenophobic backlash in a part of the local population.

The late 1980s and early 1990s again became a time of rapidly expanding legal and illegal immigration into the Community, as migrants from the developing world were attracted to Western Europe by strong economic and employment growth, political and economic turmoil in many parts of the developing world, and as borders in eastern Europe began to break down. Once inside one member country, an illegal immigrant could make his or her way to other countries in the Community. Requests for political asylum also exploded, initially as a result of political and ethnic upheavals in the developing world, and later as a consequence of the civil war in the former Yugoslavia.

By the early 1990s it was estimated that there were some 14.1 million resident aliens living in the twelve member states of the Community. Some 4.9 million of these people were citizens of one EC country living in other member states, but over 9 million were nationals of third countries, for example Turkey, Yugoslavia, and many African, Asian, and Latin American countries.[6] In 1991 alone, Eurostat reported the immigration of 1.24 million non-EC nationals into the member states. Emigration of non-EC nationals was just over 500,000, leaving a net inflow of over 700,000 people, more than half of whom settled in Germany.[7] Apart from the numbers of people involved, there was, as is shown in Table 7.1, a confusing array of different legal categories of migrants, all of which were covered by different national laws and in some cases international treaties.

PROBLEMS WITH IMPLEMENTATION

The upsurge of immigration in the late 1980s coupled with the dismantling of internal borders in connection with the 1992 program led to intensified efforts within the Community to strengthen external borders and to upgrade police and

Table 7.1   Categories of Cross-Border Movements

Category	Applicable Laws and Treaties
Citizens	Different national laws on citizenship apply
	Being native born does not necessarily confer citizenship
	Different naturalization procedures
	All citizens of a member state also EU citizens (TEU)
Citizens of EU countries resident in another EU country	Right to move and reside throughout the territory of the Union as EU citizens (TEU)
	Can vote in municipal and EP elections
Non-EU country nationals on temporary stays	EU to draw up common visa list, set standard visa procedures (TOR, as amended by Amsterdam)
Legal immigrants from non-EU countries	EU to draw up common immigration policies, set standard visa procedures (TOR, as amended by Amsterdam); exceptions for UK and Ireland
Illegal immigrants	EU to draw up common immigration policies, set standard visa procedures (TOR, as amended by Amsterdam); exceptions for UK and Ireland
Asylum seekers	Dublin Convention; Common European Asylum System (in progress)
Refugees and displaced persons	Convention Relating to the Status of Refugees; Common European Asylum System

judicial cooperation, both in the Trevi process and among the subset of countries that had signed the Schengen Agreement. As the member states moved closer toward true cross-border mobility of persons and capital, governments became increasingly concerned that organized crime would be among the main beneficiaries of the single market. Member states were dismantling their national controls but they had not put in place at the Community level common policies on the control of external borders or procedures for sharing information about organized crime, illegal immigration, and other cross-border matters. Within Trevi, permanent and ad hoc groups were set up to deal with the policing implications of the reduction in border controls (Trevi '92), the possible establishment of a European Criminal Police Office, and judicial cooperation on such matters as extradition, legislation against fraud, and the mutual recognition of court decisions.

But the slow pace of progress in Trevi and, more importantly, problems with implementing Schengen soon revealed how politically difficult it was for governments to dismantle their external borders and to entrust key aspects of internal security to untested European mechanisms. Many governments were looking to preserve or even strengthen their national border controls. This was especially the case for Ireland and the UK, island countries that still found it relatively easy to control the entry of foreigners, but it was true even for some of the continental countries committed to Schengen. As the January 1990 deadline approached, the Schengen signatory states began backpedaling on implementing the agreement, citing a number of issues including unresolved matters relating to the movement of migrant workers from third countries, technical deficiencies in the SIS, as well as certain matters completely unrelated to immigration, such as differences between the Netherlands and Luxembourg over bank secrecy laws and their implications for the fight against tax and fiscal fraud.

In an attempt to resolve these differences, the five countries reopened negotiations in early 1990. In June of that year they finally concluded the Schengen Implementing Convention that spelled out detailed arrangements for the free movement of persons, particularly with regard to asylum policy, visa regime harmonization, hot pursuit by police across borders, and the SIS.[8] Italy acceded to the Schengen Agreement and the implementing convention in 1990, Portugal and Spain in 1991, Greece in 1992, and Austria in 1995. However, differences among member states and continuing problems with the Schengen database led to further postponements in actually putting the agreement into effect, and it was not until April 1, 1995, that six countries—Belgium, Luxembourg, Germany, the Netherlands, Portugal, and Spain—declared the complete elimination of border controls in what the press quickly dubbed "Schengenland." The other signatory states, including France, were not yet ready to put the agreement into effect on their territories. France claimed to be upset with the liberal drug policies in the Netherlands and was unwilling to open its borders until the Dutch cracked down on policies that made soft drugs freely available for possible transport to other European countries. In reality, the French government was caught off guard by a strong domestic political backlash against the opening of borders, and seemed to be using the drugs issue as a way to defer fulfilment of its Schengen obligations.

Full implementation of Schengen, the most ambitious of the 1980s initiatives in justice and home affairs, thus was pushed off until well into the 1990s. The Dublin and External Frontiers conventions encountered a similar fate. The Dublin Convention finally was ratified by all member states and went into effect on September 1, 1997. The External Frontiers convention still had not been ratified at the time of the Amsterdam IGC, owing to a dispute between Spain and the UK over Gibraltar.

The Maastricht Treaty

The Maastricht Treaty was significant in bringing into a single structure—the new European Union—many of the mechanisms for cooperation on citizenship and justice and home affairs that had developed in past decades on an ad hoc basis, mostly outside the formal structures of the EC. Germany was the strongest proponent of expanding immigration and police cooperation, both because it faced the most immediate problems in these areas caused by the collapse of communism and the rise of instability in central and eastern Europe and because it preferred to "Europeanize" certain issues that, given Germany's past, were politically difficult to handle in a purely domestic context. Dissatisfaction with the pace of development in Trevi and with implementation of the Schengen Agreement were important considerations in German thinking.

The treaty introduced three major changes. First, it introduced human rights and fundamental freedoms into the treaty structure, albeit mainly by linking the EU to agreements concluded earlier under Council of Europe auspices. The treaty stipulated that "the Union shall respect fundamental rights, as guaranteed by the Convention for the Protection of Human Rights and Fundamental Freedoms . . . and as they result from the constitutional traditions common to the member states, as general principles of Community law."[9] Second, it established EU citizenship. Third, it established cooperation in justice and home affairs as the Union's third pillar. As with the second pillar (CFSP), the establishment of a separate pillar was a compromise between two competing sentiments: on the one hand, the desire of the member states for closer and more effective cooperation on matters that increasingly defied national treatment, especially with the elimination of border controls under the SEA, and on the other the requirement of the member states, and especially Britain, to retain sovereignty in these areas. As with CFSP, the intergovernmental pillar was a means to reconcile increased cooperation at the EU level with the continued maintenance of the national veto.

EU CITIZENSHIP

Citizenship issues had become increasingly prominent in the Community in the 1980s, after the first direct elections to the European Parliament in 1979 and in response to concerns about a "democratic deficit" in an EC that seemed to be acquiring ever more influence over the everyday lives of European citizens. The Maastricht Treaty established citizenship as an aspect of the political union. All persons who are citizens of a member state also are citizens of the Union. EU citizenship supplements but does not replace national citizenship. The establishment of an EU citizenship removed a lingering ambiguity about whether free movement of persons in the Union is an economic right, linked to the functioning of the single market, or a civil right rooted in the very essence of citizenship. The treaty takes the latter interpretation, specifying that "every citizen of the Union shall have the right the move and reside freely within the territory of the member states."[10] However, as was seen in Chapter 4, it makes the exercise of this right subject to limitations and conditions set by the member states.

As a practical matter, EU citizenship conferred very few real new rights upon individuals, who for the most part seemed satisfied with the rights they enjoyed as citizens of EU member states. Nationals of one member state residing elsewhere in the Union have a right to vote or be a candidate in elections for the European Parliament and for municipal offices. They have the right to diplomatic and consular assistance from the representatives of other EU member states when traveling or living in a third country where their own country has no embassy or consular offices. They have the right to correspond with the institutions of the Union in any of its official languages, and they may petition the European Parliament and the Ombudsman according to certain procedures. The latter position, established in the Maastricht Treaty, was set up to hear citizen complaints about maladministration by EU institutions and offices.

THE THIRD PILLAR

The third pillar provisions of the Maastricht Treaty defined nine areas to be of common interest among the member states of the newly established Union: (1) asylum policy; (2) rules governing the crossing of external borders; (3) immigration policy, including conditions of entry, conditions of residence, and combating unauthorized immigration, residence, and work by nationals of third countries on the territory of EU member states; (4) combating drug addiction; (5) combating fraud on an international scale; (6) judicial cooperation in civil matters; (7) judicial cooperation in criminal matters; (8) customs cooperation; and (9) police cooperation for the purposes of preventing and combating terrorism, unlawful drug trafficking, and other serious forms of international crime. The list did not extend to ordinary crime, which remained the responsibility of national and local authorities.

In addition to these nine areas, the Maastricht Treaty specified one policy area—visas—that was to be handled as a first-pillar matter and made subject to decision-making by the EU's supranational institutions. A new article inserted into the Treaty of Rome called upon the Commission to draw up proposed lists of countries whose nationals required a visa to cross the external borders of the Union for approval by the Council of Ministers. Beginning in 1996, the Council was empowered to act by qualified majority voting with regard to visa policy. This provision was important not only because it helped to establish a unified EU visa policy, but also because it established a precedent for handling other matters relating to justice and home affairs in the first pillar.

To facilitate cooperation in the nine areas listed in the third pillar, the Maastricht Treaty established an intergovernmental decision-making process that more or less corresponded to the one set up for the second pillar. The Trevi Group was abolished and its responsibilities turned over to the new K.4 committee (named after the relevant treaty article), whose job was to prepare the work of the Council of Ministers in the nine areas of common interest. Apart from day-to-day cooperation at working levels between the appropriate national ministries and departments (justice and home affairs, customs services, tax authorities, and so forth), the treaty specified three ways in which the member states were to work together in the third pillar: (1) by adopting joint positions; (2) by adopting joint actions; and (3) by drawing up conventions among all or some of the member states for specific purposes. In this way, agreements already negotiated, such as the Dublin Convention and the External Frontiers Convention, could serve as building blocks for cooperation under the third pillar.

Conventions, long used in the Council of Europe, establish a certain kind of law of general or partial application in the Union. In the first pillar, laws passed by the Council or by the Council and the Parliament either apply directly or they must be transposed into national law in all of the member states. The ECJ has jurisdiction over such laws and can levy fines against member states for failing to transpose or enforce Community law. Conventions, in contrast, are adopted voluntarily by the member states, albeit under the umbrella of the third pillar. The Maastricht Treaty further stipulated that implementing measures for such conventions could be adopted by the Council of Ministers by a two-thirds vote of the signatory states and that the signatories could stipulate in these conventions that the ECJ had jurisdiction over their interpretation. In this way, the method of harmonization long used in the intergovernmental Council of Europe was incorporated into the largely intergovernmental third pillar of the new EU. It was a looser form of cooperation than that used on economic and related matters in the first pillar, but it represented an important interim step towards creating an EU-wide area for justice and home affairs.

EUROPOL

Police cooperation had been developing since the 1970s under the auspices of the Trevi Group, but it received a strong new impetus from Germany in the early 1990s. At the June 1991 Luxembourg summit, Chancellor Kohl called for the establishment of a new European central criminal investigation office. What the

Germans had in mind was something like a full-fledged European Federal Bureau of Investigation (FBI), which could investigate serious crimes and help to enforce law at the European level. In August 1991 an Ad Hoc Working Group on Europol was set up within the Trevi process. Building upon the work of Trevi, the Maastricht Treaty identified as an area of common interest police cooperation for the purpose of preventing and combating terrorism, unlawful drug trafficking, and other serious forms of international crime. It called for organizing a Union-wide system of exchanging information within a European Police Office—otherwise known as Europol—but left establishment of this body to further negotiation and the conclusion of a separate convention among the member states.

Consistent with the mandate in the Maastricht Treaty, the member states began drafting a Europol convention. Progress was slow, however, owing to differences over the organization's powers and activities and over whether the Court of Justice should be granted jurisdiction over Europol actions. Germany, with its long borders and heavy exposure to crime and instability in central and eastern Europe, was the strongest proponent of EU-level police cooperation, while France and the UK, traditionally jealous of their national prerogatives, were skeptical about the need for a strong Europol. As an interim step, in June 1993 the member states agreed to establish a European Drugs Unit as a precursor to Europol. Located in the Hague, it became operational in 1994. Its initial tasks were to collect and analyze information from national police forces about drug trafficking. However, it did not have the power to conduct criminal investigations or to maintain files on individuals.

The fifteen reached agreement on and signed the Europol Convention in July 1995, but only after a long delay caused by a dispute about the role of the ECJ that pitted Britain against the other fourteen member states.[11] The latter supported an article in the draft Europol Convention stipulating that the ECJ would be given the responsibility to resolve any dispute among the member states concerning the interpretation or implementation of the convention that the Council was unable to solve in a six-month period. The Netherlands, concerned about the power of the large states and about upholding the rule of law, insisted on such a provision; the UK, determined to maintain the strictly intergovernmental role of Europol and to preserve the autonomy of the British courts, refused to accept the article. The impasse finally was broken through an "opting in" provision reminiscent of the Social Protocol to the Maastricht Treaty. All member states except the UK stated in an appended declaration that they would refer cases concerning the interpretation or implementation of the Europol convention to the ECJ, which is not explicitly referred to in the convention.

By June 1998 all fifteen member states had ratified the Europol Convention, and Europol formally became operational on October 1, 1998, absorbing the activities of the European Drugs Unit and acquiring new responsibilities to combat illicit trafficking in nuclear and radioactive substances, human beings, and vehicles as well as drugs, and money laundering related to these activities. It began with a staff of 155, including 41 European Liaison Officers representing different law enforcement agencies from all fifteen member states. The staff is projected to grow to 350 by 2003. For the present, Europol remains primarily a coordinating mechanism for the sharing of data and experience, including through the Europol Computer System. It does not have the legal jurisdiction to conduct criminal investigations or to bring prosecutions, but must work through the national authorities. This does not preclude the possibility, however, of future agreements among the member states to set up multinational operational units or special commissions to fight particular international crimes.

THE EXTERNAL DIMENSION

Police cooperation in the EU also has an important foreign policy dimension. The most immediate threat to the security of the EU member countries no longer comes from conventional or nuclear attack, as was the case when the Warsaw Pact existed and the Soviet Union stationed hundreds of thousands of troops in the heart of Europe. External threats now come from illegal smuggling of people, weapons, and drugs and the spread of nuclear, biological, and chemical materials that could be used to develop weapons of mass destruction. Rampant corruption, organized crime, and the breakdown of order in neighboring states make dealing with these problems especially difficult. As is discussed in Chapter 9, Italy and several other EU member states organized an intervention force for Albania in 1997 following the collapse of law and order that was precipitated by a political crisis and near civil war linked to massive fraud in the financial sector. Elsewhere in the Balkans, one of the most pressing challenges following the end of the wars in Bosnia and in Kosovo was to establish strong, effective, and noncorrupt local police forces that could replace NATO peacekeeping forces and provide security against ethnic killing as well as combat the corruption that stifles economic revival. Crime in Russia and Ukraine also poses a threat to the EU.

In response to these threats, EU external policy places a growing emphasis on police and judicial cooperation. The Europe Agreements that are being used to help the candidate countries prepare for membership provide for expanded cooperation and technical assistance in these areas. The common strategies toward Russia and Ukraine adopted by the European Council in 1999 call for expanded cooperation between their law enforcement authorities, Europol, and national police forces in the EU member states. Police and judicial cooperation also has increasing importance in relations between the United States and the EU, as both sides work together to address money laundering, cyber-crime, drug trafficking, and other crimes with a strong international character.

The Amsterdam Reforms

The justice and home affairs provisions of the Maastricht Treaty did not work very well. In the first eighteen months in which the third-pillar provisions were in effect, the Council did not adopt a single common position. It adopted joint actions in only two cases, one dealing with Europol and one on a decidedly secondary issue—travel facilities for school pupils from nonmember countries resident in a member state. It also had adopted the text of a convention on simplified extradition procedures, but one that dealt only with cases in which the subject of the extradition agreed with the procedure. This convention was in any case not yet ratified and put into effect by the member states.[12]

The dismal performance of the EU with regard to third-pillar cooperation led to calls for reform. In its review of the treaty prepared for the reflection group that began work on the Amsterdam Treaty, the Commission noted the second and third pillars used essentially the same intergovernmental decision-making procedures, but that "the two fields are utterly different. Foreign policy mainly has to deal with fluid situations, whereas justice and home affairs frequently involve legislative action which, because it directly affects individual rights, requires legal clarity."[13] The approaching enlargement to central and eastern Europe provided additional arguments to strengthen cooperation in justice and human home affairs, as the EU faced the prospect of incorporating new member states with weak traditions and administrative and judicial infrastructures in criminal and civil law, and of managing long and possibly unstable borders with Russia, Ukraine, and the Balkans.

The Amsterdam Treaty instituted two major reforms, both essentially procedural: it incorporated the Schengen Agreement into the structure of the EU, making it part of the *acquis*, and it effectively "communitized" the areas of asylum and immigration, judicial cooperation in civil matters, and police and judicial cooperation in criminal matters by moving them out of the intergovernmental third pillar and introducing into the Treaty of Rome, by way of amendment, a new title called "Visas, Asylum, Immigration and Other Policies Related to the Free Movement of Persons." Much of what had been the EU's third pillar was moved to the first pillar, becoming subject to stronger and more uniform decision-making processes and to the binding jurisdiction of the ECJ.

With the entry into force of the Treaty of Amsterdam, the Schengen Agreement has now become the Schengen Protocol to the treaty.[14] Decisions about immigration and movement of peoples now are made by the EU's institutions—the Commission, Council, and Parliament—rather than in a separate structure outside the Union. There are still some anomalies, however. Ireland and the UK remain exempt from the Schengen Protocol and there are special arrangements for Denmark, while Iceland and Norway, non-EU member countries that long have had free movement arrangements with fellow Nordic countries Sweden, Denmark, and Finland, are part of the Schengen area and participate in the Schengen Information System.

The "communitarization" of formerly third-pillar matters was accomplished in a cautious manner that reflected the lingering reluctance by member state governments to surrender national powers in an area of political sensitivity. The new provisions (amendments to the Treaty of Rome introduced by the Treaty of Amsterdam) included derogations, long phase-in periods, and complex decision-making procedures that weakened the effect of the reforms. As with Schengen, Ireland and the UK secured the right to opt out of the provisions on asylum and immigration policy. In addition, the treaty divided implementation of the provisions on immigration, asylum, and police and juridical cooperation into two periods. During a transitional phase lasting five years from the entering into effect of the treaty (i.e., from May 1, 1999, to April 30, 2004) the Commission and the member states both have the right to submit legislative proposals, the European Parliament's role is limited to consultation, and, most importantly, member states will have to agree unanimously on all decisions. After this period, the Commission will have the exclusive right to introduce legislation, and the member states may decide, on a unanimous basis, to adopt decisions relating to immigration and the free movement of persons on the basis of QMV and EP co-decision.

In addition to these important procedural reforms, the Amsterdam revisions included several changes intended to strengthen the rule of law and to bolster the rights of citizens. A new article inserted into the Treaty of Rome stipulated that the Council, acting unanimously on a proposal by the Commission and after consulting the EP, "may take appropriate action to combat discrimination based on sex, racial or ethnic origin, religion or belief, disability, age, or sexual orientation."[15] Although this sweeping, high-profile language signaled a new determination on the part of the member states to combat discrimination, it too was essentially procedural; it did not in itself guarantee rights or combat discrimination in any way. This will have to be done through secondary legislation that most likely will take the form of directives that will have to be transposed into national law. The unanimity requirement sets a high barrier for passage of such legislation.

The Amsterdam Treaty also adopted a new procedure for dealing with a serious and persistent breach by a member state of the principles of freedom and the rule of law. At the 1996–1997 IGC some member states floated the idea of a mechanism for expelling human rights violators from the Union. This was rejected as too severe and possibly helping to establish a legal basis for secession from the Union. Instead, the treaty stipulates that a member state may lose certain rights, including voting rights in the Council, if the other member states unanimously condemn its human rights practices. Under the procedure, the Commission or one-third of the member states may propose a measure condemning a member state. The measure must be approved by a two-thirds vote in the Parliament, and then unanimously by the Council, meeting in the composition of heads of state and government. The country being singled out in the proposal does not vote. If the Council decides that the breach exists it may, acting by qualified majority, suspend certain rights under the treaties.[16]

These provisions apply to all member states, but they clearly were adopted by the fifteen at Amsterdam with an eye toward enlargement to the former communist countries. As will be seen, the controversy in early 2000 over the formation in Austria of a coalition government including the far-right Freedom party of Jörg Haider led to calls for a review and possible strengthening of sanctions on member states perceived as not meeting the standards set in the treaties.

RACISM AND XENOPHOBIA

The new anti-discrimination provisions of the Treaty of Amsterdam reflected a growing sensitivity in the EU to issues of tolerance and equality in an increasingly multicultural Europe. With the upsurge of immigration in the early 1990s, Western Europe saw a growing number of racially and religiously motivated attacks on foreigners and immigrants. Anti-foreigner sentiment also was rampant in the applicant countries of central and eastern Europe, where it was fueled by high unemployment. While seeking to stem the flow of new migrants, member state governments and the institutions of the Union also felt compelled to take action to combat anti-immigrant and other forms of violence and discrimination.

In 1995 the Commission presented a communication on racism, xenophobia, and anti-semitism that was intended to initiate discussion in this area. This was followed by a decision in principle by the European Council, at the June 1996 Florence summit, to establish a European Monitoring Center on Racism and Xenophobia. The EU also designated 1997 as the European Year Against Racism, and in March 1998 the Commission issued an Action Plan Against Racism that contained concrete proposals aimed at changing public attitudes through education and other programs.[17] The action plan also was intended to start a debate on legislative action, which the Commission would be empowered to propose once the Treaty of Amsterdam went into effect.

The European Monitoring Center on Racism and Xenophobia was formally established in June 1997.[18] By decision of the Council, it was based in Vienna—an ironic and perhaps unfortunate choice given the rise of the Austrian Freedom party with its pronounced anti-foreigner and anti-immigration program. The center's mandate is to provide objective, reliable, and comparable information on racism and xenophobia and to engage in research and documentation that will assist in formulating policies in these areas. It pursues these efforts in part through its own activities in Vienna, but also through a European Racism and Xenophobia Network linking universities and research centers in the member states.

Implementation and the Tampere Summit

The experience of recent decades suggests that implementing the provisions of the Treaty of Amsterdam to create a genuine "area of freedom, security, and justice" will take time and will be fraught with controversy over many legal and practical details. Looking to the pending entry into force of the Amsterdam Treaty, in 1998 the Council and the Commission drew up an action plan of concrete steps to realize this area. The European Council endorsed the plan and scheduled a special session, to be held in October 1999 in Tampere under the Finnish presidency, to evaluate progress in justice and home affairs cooperation.

At the Cologne summit in June 1999 the European Council further agreed to work toward adoption of a Charter of Fundamental Rights of the European

Union by the end of 2000.[19] This proposal, pushed heavily by Germany, was designed to repair what was seen as a missing piece of the Maastricht and Amsterdam treaties, which affirmed human rights and freedoms already codified in national law and in Council of Europe conventions but that did not codify any rights specific to the citizens of the Union.

The Tampere summit emphasized the importance of security and justice for citizens as a counterpart to the economic achievements of the Union (see Box 7.1), as well as made some concrete progress on implementation of the Amsterdam commitments. But Tampere also showed that completing the area of freedom, justice, and security is likely to be a long-term process and that there may even be inherent limits to how far the EU member states can go in harmonizing their systems of law and justice given their deep-seated historical and cultural differences. At Tampere, the European Council established an ad hoc body responsible for drafting the EU Charter of Fundamental Rights. Composed of fifteen representatives of the member state governments, one representative of the Commission president, sixteen members of the EP, and thirty members of national parliaments (two from each national parliament), this body was not given a firm deadline to complete its work.[20]

The most concrete achievement at Tampere was an agreement to establish a Common European Asylum System, the elements of which will include a shared understanding of the method for determining the member state responsible for examining an asylum application, common standards for a fair and efficient asylum procedure, common minimum conditions of reception for asylum seekers, and the approximation of rules on the recognition and content of refugee status. The leaders also agreed to look into the question of providing financial compensation from EU sources to member states affected by sudden and unexpected influxes of refugees. Countries such as Germany and Austria that were likely to be

Box 7.1   The Challenge of Amsterdam

From its very beginning European integration has been firmly rooted in a shared commitment to freedom based on human rights, democratic institutions and the rule of law. These common values have proved necessary for securing peace and developing prosperity in the European Union. They will also serve as a cornerstone for the enlarging Union.

The European Union has already put in place for its citizens the major ingredients of a shared area of prosperity and peace: a single market, economic and monetary union, and the capacity to take on global political and economic challenges. The challenge of the Amsterdam Treaty is to ensure that freedom, which includes the right to move freely throughout the Union, can be enjoyed in conditions of security and justice accessible to all. It is a project which responds to the frequently expressed concerns of citizens and has a direct bearing on their daily lives.

(Source: Presidency Conclusions: Tampere European Council, October 15–16, 1999.)

affected by refugee surges generally favored compensation, while the UK was opposed.

Tampere also made some progress on the issue of third-country nationals resident on the territory of the EU member states. The European Council endorsed efforts to approximate national laws on this matter, and endorsed the principle that "long-term legally resident third country nationals be offered the opportunity to obtain the nationality of the member state in which they are resident."[21] Recognizing that third-country nationals (many from Africa, Asia, the Middle East, and the Caribbean) are often targets of discrimination, the European leaders again called for stepping up the fight against racism and xenophobia, based on the Commission's 1998 action plan.

The summit achieved more modest results with regard to the establishment of "a genuine European area of justice," a relatively new area for concentrated EU action. The Commission and some member states were in favor of approximation of laws covering serious crimes, but this met with strong resistance from the UK and other member states. The European Council endorsed mutual recognition of judicial decisions as the cornerstone of judicial cooperation on civil and criminal matters, with approximation of laws to be pursued where necessary. In civil matters, for example, the European Council endorsed as a first step automatic recognition in other EU member states of national or local court decisions regarding small claims and family litigation (e.g., child support, visiting rights for parents). In the criminal sphere, they called for mutual recognition of court orders concerning search and seizure and measures to ensure that evidence lawfully gathered in one member state would be admissible in the courts of other member states. Implementation of mutual recognition in the judicial sphere will not be automatic, however. It will require measures at the EU and the national levels before the principle can be applied and integrated into judicial practice in the courts.

Finally, Tampere gave new impetus to longstanding efforts to improve cooperation in the fight against organized and transnational crime. The European Council called for measures to strengthen Europol and to broaden its areas of responsibility, as well as agreed to the establishment of a EUROJUST network composed of national prosecutors, magistrates, and high police officials that would help to coordinate the work of national investigators and prosecutors in actions against organized crime. Like most of the other measures agreed at Tampere, establishing EUROJUST will require further legislative action by the Council of Ministers.

Enlargement

If completing the area of freedom, justice, and security proclaimed in the Treaty of Amsterdam is likely to be a protracted process, extending this area to the candidate countries seeking to join the Union will take even longer and present more formidable difficulties. One of the criteria for accession adopted by the European Council in 1993 specifies that "membership requires that the candidate country has achieved stability of institutions guaranteeing democracy, the rule of law, human rights and respect for and protection of minorities."[22] In its July 1997 opinions on the level of preparation of the candidate countries for accession, the Commission concluded that all but one of the candidate countries met this criterion. The sole exception, Slovakia, subsequently improved its performance in this area following the elections of September 1998 that resulted in a more democratic government. The European Council recognized Turkey as a candidate for membership at the December 1999 Helsinki summit, but it was not asked to begin negotiations alongside the other twelve candidate countries, precisely because it did not meet the political and human rights criteria.

While the twelve countries that began negotiations in 1998 and 2000 were judged to have met the basic standard set by the Copenhagen criteria, they are being pressed by the EU to make further progress in this area. Traditions of rule of law in many of these countries are less developed than in Western Europe and were disregarded under communist rule. There are also shortages of trained judges, lawyers, and officials able to administer and enforce the law. In its reports on the progress of the candidate countries toward accession, the Commission has singled out these factors as well as continued discrimination against the Roma (Gypsy) minority in many countries, protection of minority language rights (e.g., of Russians in Estonia and Latvia), and safeguards against governmental interference in radio and television.

During the 1990s membership in the Council of Europe played a role in helping the candidate countries to prepare their legal structures for EU membership. The EU's PHARE program of assistance for the candidate countries since has made justice and home affairs one of four priority areas for pre-accession work in central and eastern Europe. PHARE-funded projects include strengthening border police and customs administration through training and provision of equipment, help in preparing for Schengen implementation, including establishment of the requisite information systems, training for judges and administrators in dealing with asylum and migration issues in accordance with EU norms, and projects to strengthen the capacity of justice ministries and other institutions to combat corruption and organized crime. Most of these projects involve twinning arrangements with border guards, police forces, court systems, and other counterpart institutions in EU member states.[23]

Beyond the need to anchor democracy and the rule of law in the candidate countries themselves, the pre-accession process must prepare these countries to deal with immigration, international crime, and related problems in Russia, Ukraine, and other NIS countries which, with enlargement, will become the eastern neighbors of the Union. The current members of the EU are insisting that the candidate countries tighten their own borders with non-EU countries as a condition of membership. With Schengen now a part of the *acquis*, the candidate countries will be required to adopt the Schengen rules and become part of the Schengen Information System. They also will be required to adopt the EU's uniform visa policy. This will mean, for example, that Poland will have to require visas for visitors from Russia and Ukraine, something that is not required today. Critics argue that extending the justice and home affairs provisions of the EU treaties to the new member countries will draw new lines in Europe and contribute to the isolation of countries such as Russia and the other Newly Independent States (NIS) that may be unlikely ever to join the Union. Proponents answer that secure external borders are a necessary concomitant to the single market and the free movement of peoples in the Union, and that new member states can only expect to reap the gains of the latter by accepting the former.

Jörg Haider and the Future of the Union

Even as the bureaucracy pressed ahead with preparations for enlargement, closer to home the EU was hit by an unexpected crisis that raised questions about the future of the Union as "a new area of freedom, justice and security." It began in October 1999 when the Freedom Party of Austria (FPÖ) scored 27 percent of the vote in the national elections. The Christian Democratic and Social Democratic parties that had ruled the country throughout the postwar period negotiated to form a coalition government, but failed to come to terms over more than three months of wrangling. Early the following year Christian Democratic leader Wolfgang Schüssel turned to Haider's party, forming a government that included four FPÖ members. Haider, who in addition to holding his party post served as governor of the province of Carinthia (and as a member of the EU's Committee of the Regions), was not a member of the government, but he was the lightning rod that touched off a storm of protest in Europe and beyond. A young and telegenic politician known for his flashy suits and passable English, Haider had accused foreigners of "swamping" Austria and "stealing our jobs." Most controversially, he had made favorable references to Hitler's labor policies, described the Nazi death camps as mere "punishment" camps, and stated that the Waffen SS contained fine individuals and should not be judged collectively. Polls suggested that most Freedom party voters were not attracted by his anti-immigrant sentiment and still less by his statements about the Nazi era, but were registering a protest against a corrupt and stagnant situation in Austrian politics, in which the two leading parties not only had a permanent lock on power, but used their power to apportion jobs and favors in the bureaucracy and state-owned industry. Still, revulsion against Haider's views on race and immigration was not strong enough to deter them from supporting his party for other reasons.

When it became clear that the Christian Democrats were planning to form the coalition, the other fourteen member states of the Union took the unprecedented step of announcing sanctions that they would take against Austria if its government included the FPÖ. In a statement issued in Lisbon on behalf of the fourteen, the Portuguese presidency declared that the other member states would not promote or accept any bilateral official contacts at political level with the Austrian government, not support Austrian candidates seeking positions in international organizations, and receive Austrian ambassadors in EU capitals only at the technical level.[24] From a purely practical perspective, shunning Austria in this way was not easy, given the fact that in the EU system some group of ministers is almost always meeting in the composition of the Council. Nonetheless, the fourteen were determined to show their resolve. At the first Council session after the sanctions decision was announced (a meeting of social affairs and employment ministers in Lisbon), the Portuguese hosts canceled all social events surrounding the ministerial, several ministers did not show up, and the French and Belgian ministers walked out as their Austrian colleague prepared to speak.[25] In an attempt to defuse the controversy, Haider offered to resign his post as FPÖ leader, and followed through on this pledge on May 1. He remained an influential force in Austrian politics, however, and the other member states vowed to maintain the sanctions until their demands for exclusion of the FPÖ were met.

These sanctions provoked indignation in Austria and a wide-ranging debate in the Union about their wisdom and effectiveness. The decision to shun Austria was a political act by fourteen member governments that did not involve the Commission or the other institutions of the Union. It was not made in reference to the new provisions of the Amsterdam Treaty relating to a serious and persistent breach by a member state of the principles of freedom and the rule of law. The procedures in the relevant article were not followed, and no one alleged that such breach had occurred. The Austrians and some in Europe criticized the EU for heavy-handed interference in what after all was the result of a free election in a democratic country. These criticisms were made on the basis both of democratic principle and practical political effectiveness. There was little indication that harsh external criticism was doing anything other than bolstering Haider's popularity and making Christian Democratic leader Schüssel more determined to proceed with his coalition plan. Some also argued that party politics were behind the action by the other member states, since most of their governments were socialist or social democratic and thus ready to take sides against the political right, even in collusion with the Austrian social democrats.

Defenders of the action argued that the EU had to take a stand and that it could not permit business as usual with a country that elected, no matter how democratically, a government with neo-fascist members. To act otherwise would be to encourage far right groups in other member states and to send the wrong signal to the candidate countries of central and eastern Europe, which were being told by the EU to improve their records on human rights and democracy to qualify for admission.

Two principles were in conflict. On the one side was the right of the Austrian people to choose their representatives in free elections and of political leaders to form a government from among these representatives. On the other side was the claim, voiced repeatedly by EU and national political leaders throughout the cold war and beyond, that the Community and the Union were more than economic groupings and that "Europe" was not just a geographical expression but a community of values. How this conflict plays out goes to the heart of the identity of the Union and will shape its future.

Article 6 of the TEU (as amended by the Treaty of Amsterdam) states that "the Union is founded on the principles of liberty, democracy, respect for human rights and fundamental freedoms, and the rule of law, principles which are common to the Member States." The treaty is unclear as to whether this passage is intended as a statement of fact—that the member states are by definition democratic—or as a criterion which member states need to meet through constant action and performance. The fact that the treaty also provides for sanctions in the event of serious breaches of these principles suggests in the view of some legal scholars that the latter interpretation is correct. It is noteworthy that the controversy over Haider—which also almost exactly coincided with the launch of the post-Amsterdam IGC—led to calls for a strengthening of the "policing" functions of the EU. The government of Belgium, for example, announced that it would use the IGC to try to amend the founding treaties to permit the expulsion of states that breached principles of freedom and respect for human rights.

Changes in this direction would be controversial and could backfire, however. Politicians such as Haider already have been quite skillful in portraying themselves as elected voices of the people ranged against the "bureaucrats" of the EU—even though, of course, it has been other politicians elected by other voters that have objected most strongly to Haider, not the appointed officials of the Commission or other Brussels-based bodies. At a minimum, the popular appeal of politicians such as Haider as well as Jean-Marie Le Pen in France and right-wing anti-EU campaigners in other countries shows the difficulties the EU faces in selling the idea of an area of freedom, justice, and security to the proverbial man or woman in the street. The EU argument is that the forces that generate crime, immigration, refugees, and drugs that threaten local, national, and European values are global and that as such they demand responses from a Europe that is strong and unified enough to confront those forces, within Europe and internationally.

While this argument may be true up to a point, the average voter can just as easily see the EU as the unwelcome bearer of those unwelcome global forces, rather than as his or her protection from them. It will be the EU, after all, that will bring some measure of free movement of Polish, Romanian, and eventually even Turkish workers into Austria and other member states; the EU that imposes rules on trade, agriculture, the environment, many of them negotiated in remote forums such as the WTO. To successfully complete the area of freedom, justice, and security proclaimed in the treaties, the EU will have to convince a skeptical public that it is not just another manifestation of globalization, but a reasonable and effective European response to globalization and its dark sides. This will be no easy task, especially as enlargement proceeds.

Notes

1. Text in Mark Janis, Richard Kay and Anthony Bradley, *European Human Rights Law: Text and Materials* (Oxford: Clarendon Press, 1995), 468–482.

2. John Benyon, "Policing the European Union: The Changing Basis of Cooperation on Law Enforcement," *International Affairs* 70, no. 3 (1994): 507–509.

3. *Tindemans Report on European Union to the European Council*, EC Bull. Supplement 1/1976.

4. "A people's Europe: Final Report of the *ad hoc* Committee," Bull. EC 6–1985, 21–23.

5. *Agreement between the Governments of the States of the Benelux Economic Union, the Federal Republic of Germany and the French Republic on the gradual abolition of controls at the common frontiers*, June 14, 1985.

6. Rey Koslowski, "Intra-EU Migration, Citizenship and Political Union," *Journal of Common Market Studies* 32, no. 3 (September 1994): 369.

7. European Commission, *Communication from the Commission to the Council and the European Parliament: On Immigration and Asylum Policies*, COM(94) 23, February 23, 1994, Tables 1B and 1D.

8. *Convention implementing the Schengen Agreement of June 14, 1985 between the Governments of the States of the Benelux Economic Union, the Federal Republic of Germany and the French Republic on the Gradual Removal of Controls at Common Frontiers*, 1990, *EEUL*, v. 2, 11–0016–11–0078.

9. Article 6 TEU, ex Article F.2.

10. Article 18 TOR, ex Article 8a.

11. *Convention based on Article K.3 of the Treaty on European Union, on the establishment of a European Police Office (Europol Convention)*, Brussels, July 26, 1995, O.J. C316/2.

12. European Commission, *Intergovernmental Conference 1996: Commission Report for the Reflection Group*, 51.

13. Ibid.

14. "Protocol integrating the Schengen *acquis* into the framework of the European Union," *Treaty of Amsterdam*, 93–96.

15. Article 13, TOR.

16. Article 7 TEU; Article 309 TOR.

17. European Commission, *Communication from the Commission: An Action Plan Against Racism*, COM(1998) 183 final, Brussels, March 25, 1998.

18. Council Regulation (EC) No. 1035/97, June 2, 1997, O.J. L 151, June 6, 1997.

19. "European Council Decision on the Drawing Up of a Charter of Fundamental Rights of the European Union," Annex IV, *Presidency Conclusions: Cologne European Council, 3 and 4 June 1999*, SN 150/99 CAB, 43.

20. *Presidency Conclusions, Tampere European Council, October 15 and 16, 1999*, SN 200/99, Brussels, October 16, 1999.

21. Ibid.

22. *The European Councils, 1992–1994*, 86.

23. "Annex 3—Twinning Projects 1988–1999," in European Commission, *Regular Report from the Commission on Progress towards Accession by Each of the Candidate Countries: Composite Paper, 1999*, IP/99/751, October 13, 1999. This and other reports on the progress toward enlargement are available on europa.eu.int.

24. "Statement from the Portuguese Presidency of the EU," Lisbon, January 31, 2000.

25. Neil Buckley and Peter White, "Haider Casts a Shadow over Lisbon," *Financial Times*, February 12–13, 2000.

Suggestions for Further Reading

Anderson, Malcolm, et al., eds. *Policing the European Union*. Oxford: Clarendon Press, 1995.

Meehan, E. *Citizenship and the European Community*. Newbury Park, CA: Sage, 1993.

Robertson, A. H. and J. G. Merrills, eds. *Human Rights in Europe: A Study of the European Convention on Human Rights*. Manchester: Manchester University Press, 1994.

Springer, Beverly. *The European Union and Its Citizens: The Social Agenda*. Westport, CT: Greenwood Press, 1994.

CHAPTER 8

Europe as a Global Actor
TRADE AND FINANCE

The EU accounts for about 20 percent of all world trade in goods, not counting trade within the Union, which no longer can be considered truly international (Table 8.1). It is the world's largest exporter of goods, and ranks second to the United States in total imports. Unlike the United States, with its large and chronic trade deficits, the EU in recent years has had substantial trade surpluses with the outside world. Along with the United States, it is also the world's leading exporter and importer of commercial services. The size of the EU market has grown as successive enlargements have transformed once important external trading partners into member states. The projected enlargement of the EU to central and eastern Europe will continue this process. For all practical purposes it will mean the consolidation of the entire European continent—excluding most of the former Soviet Union—into a single trading entity.

The key instrument that makes the EU an international trading power is the common external tariff. Established by the Treaty of Rome and fully put in place by July 1, 1968, the tariff helped to consolidate the common internal market by eliminating the need (although not entirely, as was seen in Chapter 4) for internal border checks to ensure that imported goods were not trans-shipped from low to high tariff countries within the Community. The common external tariff also

Table 8.1   Leading Exporters and Importers, World Merchandise Trade, 1998 (Billions of Dollars and Percentage)

Exporters	Value	Share	Importers	Value	Share
European Union	813.2	20.1	United States	944.4	22.3
United States	682.5	16.8	European Union	800.7	18.9
Japan	387.9	9.6	Japan	280.5	6.6
Canada	214.3	5.3	Canada	206.2	4.9
China	183.8	4.5	Hong Kong	186.8	4.4
Hong Kong	174.9	4.3	China	140.2	3.3
South Korea	132.3	3.3	Mexico	129.0	3.0
Mexico	117.5	2.9	Taiwan	104.2	2.5
Singapore	109.9	2.7	Singapore	101.6	2.4
Taiwan	109.9	2.7	South Korea	93.3	2.2

Source: World Trade Organization.

increased the EC's bargaining power in international trade negotiations, since six countries began to negotiate as a unit. The member states remained members of GATT, but the European Commission, as the executive arm of the Community, took over international trade negotiations for the six, both with individual countries and in the periodic multilateral trade talks carried out under the auspices of the GATT. With each enlargement, new member countries have had to give up their old tariff schedules to adopt the common external tariff. They also have had to adopt the Common Agricultural Policy, which has important implications for international trade. These enlargements have increased still further the relative weight of the EU in the GATT system and its international power to bargain.

The 1961–1962 Dillon Round of the GATT and the 1964–1967 Kennedy Round took place as the Community was establishing the common external tariff and were particularly important for setting the pattern of the Community's trade relations with the outside world. Customs unions can cause both trade creation and trade diversion, and the United States and the other EC trade partners were concerned that establishment of the customs union and the common external tariff proceed in tandem with external liberalization to minimize its trade-diverting effects. By playing a positive role in these negotiations, the Community laid to rest the worst fears in Washington and other capitals about trade diversion. In the Dillon round, the EC agreed to lower the planned external tariff by 20 percent. The Kennedy round was even more ambitious, and reduced tariffs worldwide an average of 35 percent, with tariffs on some industrial goods reduced by as much as 50 percent.

Nevertheless, in its formative years the Community still had many difficulties in its trade relations with the rest of the world. The most problematic issue tended to be agriculture. Other countries regarded the Common Agricultural Policy as highly protectionist and a major source of international trade tensions. The Community insisted that agriculture be kept off the table at the Kennedy Round, and it was not until the completion of the Uruguay Round in late 1993 that the EU reached an uneasy accommodation with its main trading partners over the issue of its agricultural subsidies and protection. Agriculture remains a bone of contention between the EU and its trading partners, however, as was seen in disputes in the 1990s over hormone-treated beef and genetically modified organisms.

Other countries were concerned about the EC's widespread use of preferential trade and cooperation agreements that were concluded outside the framework of the GATT and that ran against the spirit, if not always the letter, of the MFN principle. The Treaty of Rome provided for "the association of overseas countries and territories with the Community with a view to increasing trade and pursuing jointly their effort towards economic and social development."[1] This provision was included at the insistence of France, which in the mid-1950s still had a large African empire in which it hoped to preserve a special role. When most of the overseas colonies became independent in early 1960s, the Community revamped its association relationships with these countries, concluding the 1963 Yaoundé

Convention with eighteen independent African countries, all but one of which were former French, Italian, or Belgian colonies. The convention provided these countries with preferential trade access to the Community market as well as access to grants and loans. In recent years the EU has tried to tone down its use of preferential agreements, but reliance on them remains a source of international trade tension and lies at the heart, for example, of the 1998–1999 U.S.-EU dispute over banana imports.

In the 1970s the EC also began to make heavy use of subsidies and non-tariff barriers (NTBs). By that time successive rounds of GATT negotiations had lowered tariffs worldwide, but they failed to arrest the growth of such barriers, including quotas, voluntary export restraints (VERs), and aggressive use of anti-dumping measures. The industrial countries increasingly resorted to these measures as the level of tariff protection fell and domestic industries were exposed to the full brunt of import competition. Many of these measures were directed against low-cost imports from the newly industrializing countries, especially in Asia.

The most significant NTB agreement was the Multi-Fibre Arrangement (MFA) that the EC, the United States, and the developing countries concluded in 1974. It limited textile imports to the industrial countries by a rigid system of bilaterally negotiated quotas. The MFA originally was justified as a temporary measure to assist threatened industries while they adjusted to competition, but it was repeatedly renewed in the 1970s and 1980s and expanded to include more categories of textiles as well as clothing, thus becoming a semi-permanent feature of the international trading system. The EC was a strong proponent of the MFA system, and adopted a tough line in negotiations with such leading textile and clothing exporters as Hong Kong, South Korea, and Taiwan.

Cars are another area in which the EC adopted a high degree of non-tariff protection, mainly against Japan. Italy had a national quota of only 2,500 cars per year that could be imported from Japan. France set a limit of 3 percent of its national market for direct imports from Japan. Spain and the UK also set national limits on market share—the UK a relatively generous 11 percent of the total market, Spain a derisory 1,000 units per year. These national limits—along with an EC-wide tariff on cars that was negotiated in the GATT—were allowed to persist in the common market until 1993, when they were abolished as incompatible with the single market. They were replaced by a voluntary export restraint agreement concluded by Japan and the EC in July 1991, under which the Japanese agreed to an overall annual quota of 1.23 million cars and light trucks by 1999, after which the quotas were to be abolished.

As will be seen, many of these EC trade practices were regarded as incompatible with the GATT, and they have been the subject of hard negotiations in the successive GATT rounds and the subject of disputes in the new World Trade Organization (WTO) that was established to supersede the GATT in 1995.

GATT and the Uruguay Round

Because of the sheer magnitude of its exports and imports, the EU has been, along with the United States, the major protagonist in the shaping of the international trading system in recent decades. The basic outlines of that system were established in 1947 by the GATT. There have been eight rounds of tariff reduction and trade promotion talks within the GATT, four of which took place in the late 1940s and 1950s before the EC was established. The first six GATT rounds dealt mainly with reductions in tariffs, which at the time were perceived as the main barriers to trade in goods. The last two rounds of trade talks—the 1973–1979 Tokyo Round and the 1986–1993 Uruguay Round—were concerned with tariffs as well, but they also began to deal with NTBs and, at Uruguay, new subjects such as services and investment. At Seattle in December 1999 the WTO failed to launch a new round of trade talks, as the member states were deeply divided over the agenda and as anti-WTO demonstrators disrupted the proceedings. Governments vowed, nonetheless, to launch a new millennium round early in the next century.

The Tokyo Round took place in the mid- and late 1970s, a time of worldwide economic crisis and rising protectionism linked to concerns in many countries about unemployment and recession. Its main proponent was the United States, which saw a new set of talks as a way to head off the drift to protectionism. Washington also wanted to repair the damage to its interests caused by the exclusion of agriculture from the Kennedy Round, and it entered the negotiations prepared to press the EC hard on this issue. The results of the round were mixed, however. The members of the GATT negotiated another 33 percent reduction in tariffs on industrial goods. By the end of the round, the tariffs of GATT-member industrialized countries had fallen to 4.5 percent, down from an average of 40 percent in the early 1950s.[2] The Community's tariff on some 9,500 items was a weighted average of 6.5 percent. In the end, however, the EC again refused to yield on agriculture, even though many other countries sided with the United States on this issue.

The Tokyo Round also produced nine non-tariff codes on such issues as standards and technical barriers to trade, subsidies and anti-dumping measures, public procurement, import licenses, and civil aircraft exports in connection with government subsidies to industry. These codes were largely toothless and did not fundamentally alter the nature of the international trading system. However, they pointed to a growing recognition on the part of the GATT members that further tariff reductions in themselves were not enough to sustain world trade. In this respect, the Tokyo negotiations foreshadowed the Uruguay Round, which were to focus on establishing means to ensure that trade was free in fact as well as on paper.

Taking its name from the resort city of Punta del Este where the talks where launched in September 1986, the Uruguay Round lasted more than seven years before concluding, in December 1993, with some 26,000 pages of agreements, including a 550-page final act that was signed at a special ceremony in Morocco in April 1994. The Uruguay Round agreements went into force on January 1, 1995.

The round completed the work begun at Tokyo and resulted in a major revamping of the international trading system. Its most politically visible result was the establishment of a new institution, the WTO, to replace the GATT. The new organization ties together the various trade agreements negotiated over the years under GATT auspices, including the Tokyo Round codes and the agreements negotiated in the Uruguay Round itself: the 1994 GATT agreement on trade in goods, a new General Agreement on Trade in Services (GATS), the Agreement on Trade-Related Aspects of Intellectual Property Rights (TRIPs), various agreements relating to dispute resolution and regular review of national trade policies, and four plurilateral agreements (operating under WTO auspices but not accepted by all WTO members) dealing with civil aircraft, government procurement, and trade in meat and dairy products. A separate agreement covers Trade-Related Investment Measures (TRIMS).[3] These agreements provide the framework in which the EU conducts its international trade policy.

The Uruguay Round covered four major areas affecting trade: (1) trade liberalization and market access; (2) trade rules; (3) new issues; and (4) institutional issues and dispute settlement.[4]

TRADE LIBERALIZATION AND MARKET ACCESS

Like previous GATT rounds, the Uruguay agreement improved market access for industrial goods by lowering tariffs. The EU reduced its external tariff an average of 37 percent for all goods from GATT member states and obtained roughly comparable tariff concessions from its main trading partners. For all products, developed country tariffs after the completion of the round fell to an average of just 3.9 percent. For some sectors—construction equipment, agricultural equipment, medical equipment, steel, beer, distilled spirits, pharmaceuticals, paper, toys, and furniture—the industrialized countries agreed to eliminate tariffs altogether. Under the 1994 agreement, the EU's average tariff on manufactures was scheduled to fall by 2000 to 3.7 percent.[5]

Unlike previous GATT rounds, the Uruguay negotiations dealt with agriculture. The United States, scarred by its experience in the Tokyo Round and backed by a coalition of developing and developed country agricultural exporters, insisted that the negotiations address this sector and that they result in real changes in how CAP affects world markets. This was a very difficult issue for Europe, and one on which the Commission negotiators were on the defensive almost to the very end of the round. In the Blair House agreement of November 1992 the United States and the EU reached a bilateral deal that became the basis for the overall agreement accepted by all partners in the GATT. The EU was able to make concessions only because it was already committed to the MacSharry reforms aimed at drastically lowering the level of EU farm subsidies and at shifting from market intervention to direct income support.

The Uruguay agreement called for the phasing out of non-tariff import charges—such as the CAP's long-established system of variable levies—and their replacement with fixed import tariffs similar to those on industrial goods. For the "tariffied" items, the EU introduced duties based on the differences between internal and external prices in the base period 1986–1988. The actual tariff levels were still so high that they resulted in little actual trade liberalization, but with "tariffication" the EU could claim that its farm policies for the first time were fully compliant with its external obligations under the GATT and WTO agreements. Along with the United States and the other developed country signatories of the WTO Agreement on Agriculture, the EU was further committed to a 36 percent reduction in average agricultural tariffs by July 1, 2001. The EU also agreed to cut the level of its export subsidies over six years by 36 percent and to reduce the volume of subsidized exports by 21 percent over the same period.

The Uruguay negotiations also agreed finally to do away with the MFA for textiles and clothing. This was another awkward issue for Europe, albeit one that tended to unite it with the United States against the negotiators from the developing world. The developing countries entered the round insisting on ending a system that subjected their exports to strict country-specific quotas. They made clear that without satisfaction on this issue they would not respond to industrial country pressures for market opening in the industrial and service sectors. The developing countries eventually prevailed on this issue, as the round concluded with agreement to phase out all quotas and to dismantle the MFA system over a ten-year period ending in 2005. Even though many of the most restrictive quotas were to remain in place until the very end of the phase-out period, this measure proved controversial and pitted member states such as Portugal that were still dependent on textile and apparel production themselves against more advanced EU countries such as Germany. Apart from the obvious benefits for European consumers, the textile provisions of the Uruguay agreement were also helpful to EU exporters of textiles and apparel (mostly high-priced goods made in countries such as Italy and Germany) by opening markets for their products.

In addition to the main areas of tariffs, agriculture, and phasing out of the MFA, the Uruguay Round promoted trade liberalization in the area of government procurement. The WTO Agreement on Government Procurement strengthened the provisions of a previous GATT undertaking on government purchases, requiring its signatories (which included the United States, the EU, and Japan, but not most major developing countries) to make market access commitments for goods, services, and construction contracts by central governments, subcentral governments (e.g., states, provinces and cities), and public utilities.

TRADE RULES

Building upon a start made in the Tokyo Round, the Uruguay agreements addressed trade rules and the circumstances under which countries are permitted to block imports for domestic economic reasons or to protect themselves from unfair practices in other countries. These rules cover anti-dumping, subsidies and countervailing measures, and safeguards.

The GATT allows countries to restrict imports that are dumped on their home market, that is, priced at "less than their normal value," when such imports cause harm to domestic industry. This is done by imposing a temporary anti-dumping duty that raises the final price of the imported good, usually by the margin of dumping. All countries agree in principle on the need for anti-dumping rules, but they vary widely in their views on what constitutes dumping and how these rules should be applied. Newly industrializing countries seeking to establish industries see nothing wrong with aggressive pricing aimed at establishing a market presence, while the EU, the United States, and other developed countries increasingly have resorted to anti-dumping measures, especially against imports from Asia, to protect domestic industries that claim to be the victims of unfair pricing.

In response to developing country complaints that anti-dumping cases were being used as a disguised form of protectionism, the Uruguay Round tightened the rules for applying anti-dumping duties, set new requirements for how authorities calculate dumping margins, and introduced a sunset clause requiring that anti-dumping measures be reviewed periodically and that they expire automatically after five years to prevent temporary relief for domestic industry from evolving into a permanent form of protectionism.

The Uruguay Round also tightened existing GATT rules on the use of subsidies to gain unfair trade advantages. It provided a precise definition of what constitutes a subsidy and banned all nonagricultural subsidies explicitly linked to the promotion of exports. As in the anti-dumping provisions, the Uruguay agreement allows countries adversely affected by subsidized exports, either in their home or third-country markets, to take countervailing measures, such as the imposition of duties, to neutralize the effect of the subsidy. The Uruguay agreement also was noteworthy for specifying precisely which government subsidies are permitted under international trading rules. These include support for research and development that does not contribute directly to the development of products traded on national and world markets, general aid to regions suffering high unemployment or where per capita income is less than 85 percent of the national average, and subsidies to help existing plants meet stricter environmental requirements. These exemptions are all important for the EU, in that they permit EU research, regional assistance, and environmental policies to go forward without leading to problems on the international trade front.

The original GATT agreement of 1947 included various safeguard provisions allowing member countries to take temporary action against imports that cause "serious injury" to domestic industry or that result in general balance of payments problems. These provisions were much abused over the years, both by developed and developing countries. In the 1970s and 1980s the EU and the United States resorted to so-called "voluntary export restraint" agreements under which exporters in particularly sensitive industries "voluntarily" agree to hold down the level of their sales to another country to provide relief to its domestic industry.

The Uruguay Round banned such voluntary agreements, which meant that the EU had to phase out its VER agreement with Japan relating to automobiles within a four-year period, or by the end of 1999. The agreement also tightened the definition of "serious injury" and provided for the phasing out of safeguards after eight years, thereby preventing such measures from turning into permanent instruments of protection.

NEW SUBJECTS

The Uruguay Round tackled a long list of new subjects that had only been touched upon in the supplemental codes negotiated in the Tokyo Round. Like other developed economies, the EU derives an increasing share of GDP, employment, and trade from services, a sector that was almost completely unregulated in the international trading order before 1994. Along with the United States, the EU pressed for and achieved, largely in exchange for concessions on textiles and other matters, the conclusion of a General Agreement on Trade in Services (GATS) as a natural complement to the GATT for goods. In theory, the GATS extends the MFN principle to trade in all commercial services. In practice, the GATS includes many exemptions, exceptions, and long phase-in periods. Many issues, including basic telecommunications, maritime transport services, and financial services were left to subsequent negotiations carried out after the completion of the round. Nonetheless, the agreement was an important breakthrough into a whole new area of market opening that resulted in specific commitments by the signatory states to open up markets in professional services (accounting, auditing, management consulting, and computer services), value-added telecommunications (e.g., electronic mail, voice mail, database retrieval), and tourism.

Besides services, the Uruguay Round opened up two other areas—foreign direct investment and intellectual property—for negotiation. A separate agreement on Trade-Related Investment Measures (TRIMs) limited the ability of states to enact national laws relating to investment that restrict or distort trade. Requirements that investors include a certain percentage of locally produced components in their manufactures or that they export a certain percentage of their production were banned. However, as in many other areas of the Uruguay package, the TRIMs accord was only a first step that included a large number of exemptions, long phase-in periods for the developing countries (five and seven years, depending on level of national income) and no mechanism for follow-on negotiations or sanctions against violations of the agreement.

Intellectual property rights are an important issue for the EU, as for the United States. Such property includes patents for pharmaceutical and chemical products, integrated circuit designs, sound recordings, films, books and computer programs, and even famous luxury good labels like Gucci or the names of unique wines and cheeses. Claiming that they lost hundreds of millions of dollars each year from pirated and counterfeited goods produced mainly—although by no means exclusively—in the developing countries, EU businesses pressed for action in this area. The Uruguay Round resulted in the conclusion of a separate agreement on Trade-Related Intellectual Property Rights (TRIPs) that strengthens protection for patents, copyrights, and industrial designs and that obliges countries to crack down on piracy and counterfeiting.

DISPUTE SETTLEMENT

As trade agreements have become more comprehensive, uneven enforcement of domestic and international trade rules and the lack of redress with countries perceived as violating their international obligations have become pressing problems for many trading powers, including the EU and the United States. Partly at the urging of the EU, the Uruguay Round addressed these concerns by establishing new dispute settlement procedures within the context of the WTO. Under the Uruguay agreements, a government involved in a trade dispute is not permitted to resort to unilateral retaliatory action but is required to take the dispute to the WTO for resolution. The WTO establishes impartial panels of governmental and nongovernmental experts to rule expeditiously on particular disputes. There is also an appellate body that can review and overturn panel findings. If a country is found to be violating its trade obligations, the WTO can ask it to comply with those obligations or ask that it compensate those countries that are damaged by its noncompliance. If the country fails to act in this way, an injured country can request and receive permission for trade retaliation. The EU was a strong proponent of these more rigorous dispute settlement procedures, both because it shared with the United States a desire to crack down on rampant disregard of trade obligations in many developing countries and because it wanted additional leverage over the United States, which from the EU perspective has had a tendency to resort to unilateralist responses to trade disputes. As will be seen, however, in recent years the EU has been on the losing end of a number of WTO rulings and has had internal difficulties in bringing some of its trade practices into compliance with international trade agreements.

Key Trade Partners

In addition to participating in the global trading system, the EU has developed special trade relations with important economic and political partners, including the United States, the former European colonies known as the ACP countries, and many countries on the southern and eastern periphery of the EU. In developing these special relationships, the EU has faced a certain tension between adherence to the universal MFN principle and a desire, for economic, political, and historical reasons, to offer preferential treatment to particular countries or regions. In this respect the conflict between regionalism and universalism that was present already in early post–World War II discussions of the international economic order persists, albeit in a different form.

THE EU'S NEAR ABROAD

EFTA and the EEA. Close ties between the EU and its European neighbors go back to the 1960s, when the original EC of the six constituted only a substantial portion of European economic output, but did not include such important industrial countries as Britain and Sweden or the Iberian countries. Britain declined to join the EC, and in 1960 organized an alternative trade organization, EFTA, that included Austria, Denmark, Norway, Portugal, Sweden, and Switzerland. Britain and the Scandinavian countries disliked the special, preferential approach of the six, and had tried to head off the establishment of different trading blocs in Europe by proposing an industrial free trade area to include the six and all other interested West European countries. This approach foundered on opposition by the governments of the six, which to varying degrees sought the close political and institutional ties called for in the Treaty of Rome, and especially that of France, which was committed to a preferential trade area that would restrict imports of agricultural products from non-European countries—something that was unacceptable to the British, with their close Commonwealth ties to such major agricultural producers as Canada, Australia, and New Zealand.

Over time the EC emerged as by far the stronger of the two organizations. Britain, along with Denmark and Ireland, joined the EC in 1973, largely to overcome trade discrimination by Brussels and to gain a seat at the table of the organization that increasingly set the economic rules and standards on the continent. EFTA continued to exist without its founder and largest member, its ranks later augmented somewhat by the accession of Finland, Iceland, and Liechtenstein.

In 1972–1973 the EC concluded separate free trade agreements with all of the EFTA countries, under which by January 1, 1984 all customs duties and quantitative restrictions affecting bilateral trade were to be removed. In April 1984 the EC and EFTA issued a joint declaration calling for closer economic cooperation and the further elimination of barriers to trade through harmonization of standards, simplification of border procedures, and other measures leading to the creation of what was called a European Economic Space.[6] This agreement notwithstanding, the EFTA countries were in a weak bargaining position vis-à-vis the Community, and became concerned about possible exclusion from the Community's single market program. The EC had less to fear from EFTA, but it had important trade relations with its member countries and a keen interest in the issue of truck and rail transit across the Alpine passes in Austria and Switzerland.

These interests came together in the conclusion, in May 1992, of an agreement to establish a European Economic Area (EEA) on January 1, 1994. The EEA essentially extended the four freedoms of the Treaty of Rome to the EFTA countries, in exchange for which the latter were compelled to adopt EU legislation on standards, competition policy, public procurement, and other matters. The EEA was never satisfactory from the EFTA perspective, however, given its highly asymmetrical character. The EFTA countries were obliged to accept decisions (including future decisions) taken in Brussels but had very little voice in making those decisions.

Voters in Switzerland rejected the EEA agreement in a December 1992 referendum. Austria, Finland, Norway, and Sweden entered the EEA, but decided to press ahead with applications for full EU membership. Voters in Norway rejected EU accession, but the other three countries completed the accession process and became full members of the EU in 1995. The EEA thus operated in its originally envisioned form for only one year—1994. The EEA continues to exist, but only as a relatively minor arrangement that integrates three EFTA countries—Iceland, Norway, and Liechtenstein—into the EU's single market.

Norway remains an important EU trading partner, particularly as a supplier of natural gas. As shown in Table 8.2, it accounted for 4.1 percent of EU imports in 1998 and 3.4 percent of exports, ranking fifth in the world as an EU partner in both categories.[7] As an EEA member, it has full access to the EU market for goods, services, capital, and people and grants reciprocal access to its own market. Free movement of people between Norway and the EU is further underpinned by its adherence to the Schengen Agreement. Given the high degree of integration between Norway and the EU, Norway may at some point revive its application for membership, but only if the government were confident that popular attitudes had changed sufficiently to ensure that there was little risk of a third rejection.

With the 1992 vote against the EEA, Switzerland indefinitely postponed its application for membership. Instead, it sought to develop a bilateral relationship that would preserve access to the EU market and to gain participation in EU research and technology programs. In an arduous process of negotiation that began in December 1994 and took four years to complete, the EU and Switzerland concluded a package of seven bilateral agreements to regulate the movement of persons, transport, technical barriers to trade, research, agriculture, and other issues. Switzerland retained its access to the EU market and its right to participate in many EU programs, but it had to give way on EU demands that it lift a ban on forty-ton trucks from EU countries transiting Switzerland. The Swiss parliament approved these agreements in the fall of 1999, but opponents of closer integration successfully mounted a signature campaign calling for a national referendum on the agreements. In May 2000 the Swiss voters approved the agreements by a surprisingly large margin, signaling a new and more positive attitude toward cooperation with the Union. The agreements still need to be ratified by the EU and its member states before taking full legal effect.

Switzerland ranks a distant second to the United States as a destination for EU exports (some 7.8 percent of the total) and ranks third (6.9 percent) with regard to imports.[8] The EU accounts for just over 60 percent of Switzerland's exports and nearly 80 percent of its imports. Like Norway, Switzerland eventually could join the Union. Swiss business and government elites are worried about isolation in

Table 8.2 EU Trade in Goods, 1998

Rank	Partner	Billion euro	Percent
Major import partners			
	World	709.227	100.0
1	U.S.	150.756	21.3
2	Japan	65.511	9.2
3	Switzerland	49.229	6.9
4	China	41.788	5.9
5	Norway	29.023	4.1
Major export partners			
	World	729.236	100.0
1	U.S.	159.807	21.9
2	Switzerland	56.934	7.8
3	Japan	31.418	4.3
4	Poland	28.066	3.8
5	Norway	24.887	3.4
Major imported products			
	Total	709.227	100.0
1	Electrical machinery	53.565	7.6
2	Office machines	52.204	7.4
3	Oil	46.859	6.6
4	Clothing	40.762	5.7
5	Road vehicles	36.632	5.2
Major exported products			
	Total	729.236	100.0
1	Road vehicles	68.026	9.3
2	Electrical machinery	52.558	7.2
3	General industrial machinery	47.145	6.5
4	Specialized machinery	43.955	6.0
5	Other transport equipment	40.809	5.6

Source: European Commission, "EU trade facts and figures," 1999.

Europe and for the most part favor membership. This remains unpopular with many voters, however, particularly in the German-speaking cantons, and a future referendum on accession might not succeed.

The Mediterranean. With nearly all of the EFTA countries united with the original six in the EU (and with the separate accessions of Ireland, Spain, and Greece), the EU's periphery has moved outward, and now includes central and eastern Europe and the Mediterranean. The EU has concluded or intends to conclude preferential trade agreements with nearly all of these countries. As with the EFTA countries, these agreements are seen in Brussels as useful in their own right, but in many cases they also are regarded as precursors to eventual membership.

The EC concluded an association agreement with Cyprus in December 1972 that came into effect in June 1973 and that provided for the establishment over a ten-year period of an EC-Cyprus customs union. Turkey's invasion of the island in 1974 delayed implementation of the agreement, however, and in 1990 the Greek Cypriot government applied for full membership. Malta and the EC concluded an association agreement in 1970, which also led to extensive trade integration and an application for membership in 1990.

Turkey and the EC signed an association agreement in September 1963, similar to the 1962 agreement between the Community and Greece that helped to pave the way to eventual membership of that country. The 1963 agreement referred to "the accession of Turkey to the Community at a later date."[9] It was followed in 1970 by the conclusion of an additional protocol to the 1963 agreement that came into effect in January 1973 and that stipulated that the two sides were to establish a customs union within a 22-year period, or no later than the end of 1995.

Despite deteriorating political relations between the two sides over human rights and other issues, Turkey and the EU finally concluded a customs union in March 1995, along with an accompanying package of ECU 375 million in financial aid for Turkey. The EP threatened to disapprove ratification of the agreement over Turkey's human rights record, but under heavy prodding from the Commission and member state governments, finally approved it in December 1995, allowing the customs union to begin on January 1 of the following year.[10] The customs union does not extend to trade in services or agricultural goods, the latter an area in which Turkey is well-placed to compete in EU markets.

Apart from its economic shortcomings, Turkey and the EU have differed over the long-term political significance of the customs union. Many in Western Europe saw the 1995 agreement as a substitute for EU membership, which Turkey applied for in 1987. Turkey, in contrast, regarded the customs union as a step toward EU membership, which remained a key Turkish objective. These differences were at least partially resolved in December 1999, when the European Council affirmed that Turkey was a candidate for EU membership. This is at best a long-term prospect, however, which means that the customs union agreement will govern Turkish-EU trade relations for the foreseeable future.

EU policy towards Cyprus, Malta, and Turkey is part of a broader set of trade and cooperation arrangements with the countries of North Africa and the Middle East. The EC began to forge special trade and cooperation links with many of these countries already in the 1970s. It concluded cooperation agreements with Israel in 1975, Algeria, Morocco, and Tunisia in 1976, and Egypt, Jordan, and Syria in 1977. In 1978 the Community began to provide direct financial assistance to the Mediterranean countries in the form of grants from the Community budget and loans from the EIB.

With the coming into effect of the Maastricht Treaty and the start of the CFSP, the EU attempted to revitalize its policies toward this region by launching, at a special summit in Barcelona in November 1995, a new Euro-Mediterranean Partnership. Twelve countries of North Africa and the Middle East signed the partnership agreement. In the economic sphere, it called for the progressive establishment by 2010 of a free trade area and for other measures to promote economic growth in the Mediterranean region, including financial aid and EIB loans.

The Mediterranean basin as a whole accounts for 11.6 percent of EU exports and 8.5 percent of imports, substantially more than trade with such groupings as the four Asian "tigers" (Hong Kong, South Korea, Singapore, and Taiwan), ASEAN, or Latin America.[11] Many of the countries of this region remain unhappy with EU trade practices, however, which from their perspective concentrate on opening markets for EU manufactured goods while restricting access for agricultural products, cut flowers, fish, and textiles that these countries have to sell.

Central and Eastern Europe. With the collapse of communism in 1989–1991, central and eastern Europe was transformed from a region that had modest and highly regulated trade involvement with the Community into a rapidly growing extension of the EU market. In August 1990 the European Commission proposed the conclusion of what it called Europe Agreements between the Community and Hungary, Poland, and Czechoslovakia. The key economic provision of the Europe Agreements was the establishment, within a ten-year period, of free trade arrangements between the Community and the signatory countries (also known as associated countries). Expanded market access was controversial in some of the Community member states, where protectionist lobbies sought to maintain tight quotas on the import of iron and steel, textiles, and agricultural goods—the very items these countries had to sell. At one point Hungary and Poland threatened to suspend the negotiations unless they received a better offer from the Community negotiators. The offer was improved, and in December 1991 these two countries and Czechoslovakia concluded the first of the Europe Agreements. (The agreement with Czechoslovakia later was replaced, following the breakup of that country in 1993, by separate agreements with the Czech Republic and Slovakia.) Europe Agreements subsequently were concluded with Romania (February 1993); Bulgaria (March 1993); Estonia, Latvia, and Lithuania (June 1995); and Slovenia (June 1996).

The agreements are asymmetrical, in that they provided for faster dismantlement of trade barriers on the Community than on the associated country side. With the exception of textiles and clothing and iron and steel products, all quantitative restrictions on the import of industrial goods to the Community were eliminated from the date of entry into force of the trade provisions of the agreements.[12] Market access for agricultural products was enhanced, although quantitative restrictions remained in place. The agreements also called for the progressive approximation of legislation in the central and east European countries to Community norms and adoption of Community competition rules.

Under the liberalizing effect of the Europe Agreements and in response to broader changes in the region, trade in central and eastern Europe has been rapidly redirected toward the EU market. The region has become one of the EU's largest trade partners, accounting for 10.2 percent of exports and 8.1 percent of imports in 1996. It was also the fastest-growing EU export market of the 1990s, increasing by over 80 percent in the three-year period from 1993 to 1996 alone.[13] (As seen in Table 8.2, by 1998 Poland alone had surpassed Norway as the fourth-ranking export market for EU goods.)

The ten Europe Agreement countries all have applied for full EU membership and are engaged in a pre-accession process designed to prepare them for membership, a topic that is discussed in detail in Chapter 10. The Europe Agreements and trade integration are key instruments of the pre-accession process. For the less developed countries of the region whose accession could be delayed for many years, the agreements will provide preferential trade access short of membership for an indefinite period.

Russia and the NIS. Russia, Ukraine, and the other Newly Independent States of the former Soviet Union can be considered as the furthest extension of the EU's periphery. These countries are not considered potential candidates for EU membership, but they are becoming extensively integrated with the EU market and could at some point become part of a broader European trade area. The EU has concluded Partnership and Cooperation Agreements (PCAs) with these countries that include many of the trade benefits of the Europe Agreements but that are not intended to lead to eventual membership. PCAs were signed with Russia and Ukraine in June 1994, Moldova in November 1994, Belarus and Kazakhstan in early 1995, and all but two of the remaining non-Baltic Soviet successor states by the end of 1996.

Under the trade provisions of the EU-Russia PCA, trade is in theory free of most restrictions. In practice, trade in steel, textiles, and nuclear fuels is governed by special regimes, and Russia has been subject to actual or prospective antidumping measures for a variety of products. The situation with regard to Ukraine is similar. Trade is free of most restrictions, but imports of textiles and steel are subject to special arrangements and EU anti-dumping actions are common. Even with the existing restrictions on trade, the EU accounts for a growing share of trade with the NIS. In all, the EU accounts for about 40 percent of Russia's total foreign trade. Russia exports primarily oil, gas, and ferrous and nonferrous metals to the Union, and imports machinery, equipment, consumer products and foodstuffs, and unprocessed agricultural products. Ukraine's trade is still heavily oriented toward Russia and its former Soviet partners, but the EU accounts for over 12 percent of its exports, a figure that should grow if economic reform accelerates.

The EU-Russia and the EU-Ukraine PCAs both provide for the eventual establishment of free trade areas. Both agreements stipulated that reviews were to take place in 1998 to determine whether negotiations toward free trade areas should begin. Given the poor economic conditions in both countries and the fact that as of 1998 neither had yet been admitted to the WTO, these reviews did not produce significant results. Indeed, it is unlikely that free trade areas will be created soon—if ever. Nonetheless, the EU will remain the most important international market for these countries and a key factor in their economic development.

THE LOMÉ AREA AND OTHER DEVELOPING COUNTRIES

The oldest of Europe's preferential trade arrangements is with the former colonies of the original six member countries. The early years of European integration coincided with the great wave of post–World War II decolonization. To some extent these processes were linked, as European countries that previously had focused their political and economic energies on their empires redirected their attention to Europe. Even as they granted or were forced to grant independence to their colonies, however, the European powers sought to retain a degree of political and cultural influence in these countries, as well as preferential access to their markets. This was especially the case with France, which established the French Community of French-speaking countries in Africa. The Treaty of Rome provided for the association of the French, Belgian, and Dutch overseas colonies and territories with the original Community. An annex to the treaty established a European Development Fund (EDF) financed by member state contributions to assist with economic and social development.

As the largest and most important colonies became independent countries, their relations with the EC were revamped in the 1963 Yaoundé Convention, which provided preferential access to the European common market and continued access to aid from the EDF. With the accession of Britain to the Community in 1973, many former British colonies were made eligible for the same basic arrangement. In February 1975 the EC and 46 African, Caribbean, and Pacific (ACP) countries signed the first Lomé Convention. Named after the capital of Togo where the agreement was signed, the convention provided for a mix of trade concessions, development aid, and institutional association with the Community, including an ACP-EC council and a joint parliamentary assembly that meets once each year. Under the leadership of the largest ACP member, Nigeria, the ACP countries organized themselves into a loose grouping to negotiate collectively with the Community.

The first Lomé Convention ran for five years (1976–80), and was followed by Lomé II (1980–84), Lomé III (1985–89), and the ten-year Lomé IV (1990–99).[14] The number of ACP countries increased from the original 46 to a total of 71. The EDF grew from ECU 581 million ($726 million) in its first five-year period to ECU 14.625 billion ($18.3 billion) for the 1996–2000 funding cycle.[15] This, along with bilateral assistance from the member states and other assistance provided from the EU budget (e.g., disaster relief and help in combating AIDS), make the Union and its member states by far the largest source of aid for the African and other ACP states, as well as their leading trade partner.

Despite this commitment of resources and the institutional continuity of the Lomé process, the Lomé conventions have been severely criticized in the EU and the ACP countries on a number of grounds. Other countries criticized the Community for the preferential aspect of the Lomé agreements, which could divert trade from other partners. (The preferences are incompatible with the MFN provisions of the GATT, and have required a waiver that is granted by a vote of the

GATT signatories.) The EU defends these preferences as justifiable for development reasons, but critics point out that the ACP countries have been less successful than the East Asian and Latin American countries in industrializing and exporting manufactured products. In any case, the EU-ACP relationship has become relatively less preferential as the EU has developed special relations with its own periphery and as global trade barriers have come down.

When the European Commission sat down with the ACP countries in September 1998 to negotiate "Lomé V," the EU hoped to achieve radical changes in the next agreement. It proposed splitting Lomé into six regional agreements and favored a gradual phasing out of ACP trade preferences. The EU also wanted to include provisions in the new agreements relating to human rights, political freedom, and "good governance"—issues that figure prominently in the EU's relations with its Mediterranean and European peripheries but that were not originally an element of its relations with the ACP countries. The ACP countries, many still among the poorest in the world, resisted these proposals. They were afraid that they would lose negotiating leverage in a regional approach, concerned about a perceived decline in their importance relative to central and eastern Europe and Mediterranean, and wary of attempts to introduce political and human rights conditionality into longstanding trade and aid arrangements.

After nearly eighteen months of negotiation, in February 2000 the EU and the ACP countries reached a new, 20-year trade, development, and political package that reflected a compromise between these positions. Scheduled to be signed in Fiji in May 2000, the new agreement extended the major provisions of the Lomé IV agreement for another eight years. It also stated that the EU and the ACP countries will negotiate, by 2008 at the latest, a set of regional trade agreements phasing out all barriers to trade. These agreements may include 12- to 15-year transition periods, however, in which the ACP countries will retain their preferences. The regional agreements will encompass 33 of the largest and most economically advanced ACP countries. The 38 poorest members of the group will not participate in these agreements, but will gain market access to the EU for "substantially all" of their products by 2005. The Fiji Convention, as the new agreement was called, also contained a new aid package of 13.5 billion euros for the first five years of the agreement. The EU also managed to secure language on human rights and good governance, the latter a code phrase for efforts to combat corruption.[16]

Preferential trade relations and aid thus can be expected to remain a factor in EU-ACP relations, but their relative importance for both sides most likely will decrease. For both economic and political reasons the EU is looking to its own periphery and to larger markets in Asia and Latin America. For their part, the ACP countries understand that over the long run they must rely more on their own resources and look to new markets (including the United States) and to global organizations such as the IMF, World Bank, and WTO to speed economic development.

For countries that are not members of the ACP, the EU participates in the UN-sponsored Generalized System of Preferences, under which developed countries grant tariff concessions to developing countries on a nonreciprocal basis. The EU has been unwilling, for commercial reasons, to extend participation in the Lomé agreements to certain large countries that are former European colonies, including India, Pakistan, and, more recently, South Africa after the establishment of black majority rule. It has been open to separate, less preferential agreements with these countries.

The 1995–2000 negotiations with South Africa toward such an agreement illustrate the difficulties the EU has had in reconciling its complex internal decision-making processes and its deep-seated agricultural protectionism with its attempts to use trade agreements to serve broader economic and political objectives. Negotiations on a bilateral free trade agreement began in 1995, after EU leaders promised President Nelson Mandela expanded cooperation in support of the post-apartheid transition, but they quickly bogged down. While pressing for expanded access to the South African market for European manufactured goods and for a dismantling of South Africa's extensive system of state aid for industry, the EU was willing to allow only 62 percent of South African agricultural exports to enter the Union duty-free after a ten-year phase-in period—up substantially from the 18 percent at the start of the talks, but short of what the South African negotiators were demanding in exchange for concessions in other areas.[17] As with other trading partners, the EU also took a very tough line on South Africa's use, in exports to Europe and in third markets, of product names originating in Europe for wines and spirits, demanding that it stop using such names.

The talks were not completed until October 1999, when the two sides concluded an agreement that even then several EU member states threatened to veto. Product labels remained a sticking point to the very end. South Africa provisionally agreed to phase out the use of the terms "port" and "sherry" on any of its products, but it balked at EU attempts to claim exclusive use of more than 150 "traditional expressions," including such terms as "ouzo," "grappa," "tawny," and "vin de pays."[18] For their part, the five major EU wine-producing countries—France, Greece, Italy, Portugal, and Spain—threatened to block the agreement if Pretoria did not yield. In the end, the difficult and protracted negotiating process left many in the South African government embittered against the EU and its tactics, thereby calling into question the very purpose of an agreement that was intended originally by the EU as a gesture of support for the new black majority government.

ASIA AND LATIN AMERICA

Until the global financial crisis of 1997–1998, East Asia and Latin America were the world's most economically dynamic regions and the fastest-growing potential market for European exports. U.S. and Japanese companies were active in both regions, and throughout the 1990s American political leaders frequently alluded to the shift in global economic power from the Atlantic to the Pacific and the resulting shift in U.S. foreign policy priorities. In 1993 the Pacific rim countries, including the United States, Canada, Chile, and the most important Asian countries, established a new forum, Asia Pacific Economic Cooperation (APEC), that met for the first time in Seattle. The EU was not invited to participate. At the time, APEC was widely seen as part of a U.S. strategy to prod the EU into taking a more positive stance in the then-stalled Uruguay Round.

Determined not to lose economic opportunities and political influence, the EU stepped up its own diplomacy toward these regions. The first Euro-Asian summit took place in Thailand in early 1996, and brought together the fifteen EU member states and the European Commission with the leaders of China, Japan, South Korea, and the Association of Southeast Asian Nations (ASEAN) countries to address an agenda that included trade, energy, and security. These meetings were institutionalized on a biannual basis. A second Euro-Asian summit took place in Britain in 1998 under the UK presidency, and a third was scheduled for Seoul in 2000. The EU also intensified its bilateral diplomacy with China and India, and continued its series of annual summit meetings with Japan in accordance with a joint declaration signed in 1991. Much of the focus of EU policy and that of the member states in Asia has been on the expansion of trade and investment through such initiatives as the Asia-Europe Investment Promotion Action Plan, the Asia Europe Business Forum, and the Asia-Europe Environment Technology Center, all of which were agreed at the Bangkok meeting.

While the EU was criticized by European businesses and Asian governments in the early 1990s for seemingly not doing enough to ensure Europe's participation in the great East Asian boom, by 1997–1998 it was being castigated by many observers for not doing enough to help the Asian economies struck by the world financial crisis. Both cases confirm the obvious: that Europe and Asia are rather distant from each other and that for the foreseeable future the EU will be less engaged in Asia than in more adjacent regions. The sheer weight of the EU in the world economy will mean, however, that its actions will be felt in Asia and that it will come under pressure from the United States and the Asian countries themselves to adjust its policies to developments in this region.

Along with the United States, the EU will play the key role in determining the timing and conditions of China's accession to the WTO. The East Asian countries have borne the brunt of EU anti-dumping suits and other protectionist measures, and they can be expected to continue calls for Europe to open its markets to their exports. The euro is certain to heighten monetary interaction between the two regions. Along with the European countries themselves, the East Asian countries are the major holders of currency reserves, mostly in the form of dollars. They are expected to shift a large portion of their holdings from dollars to euros, a move that will further confirm the EU's increased international economic stature, but one that will only occur if the euro proves to be a strong and stable currency and the ECB wins the confidence of Asian governments and investors.

Latin America is an important market for the EU, and a region that is culturally linked to Europe through Spain and Portugal, the former imperial powers.

The region accounts for 5.7 percent of EU exports and 6.9 percent of imports. However, there is a danger that the EU could lose out in trade with this region as the United States and Canada go forward with initiatives such as NAFTA (which includes Mexico) and the Free Trade of the Americas initiative while the EU concentrates on its near abroad. The EU thus has stepped up its trade diplomacy with the region.

The EC concluded cooperation agreements with Mexico in 1975 and with the Andean Pact (Bolivia, Colombia, Ecuador, Peru, and Venezuela) in 1983. It launched the San José process with the Central American countries in 1984, and has since had regular meetings with the five members of the Central American Common Market and Panama to discuss trade and other issues. In late 1995 the EU concluded a Framework Agreement on Trade and Cooperation with Mercosur, the Latin American trade grouping of Argentina, Brazil, Paraguay, and Uruguay that to some extent is modeled on the original EC.

At the instigation of the EU, the first-ever summit of EU heads of state and government and their counterparts from Latin America and the Caribbean countries took place in Rio de Janeiro in June 1999. One of its results was an agreement between the EU and Mercosur to begin negotiations on tariff negotiations in July 2001, leading to a possible bilateral free trade agreement. In November 1998 the EU and Mexico began negotiating a free trade agreement. The two sides reached a tentative accord a year later, under which all tariffs on bilateral trade are to disappear by 2007. Mexico will grant EU suppliers improved chances to compete for public procurement contracts, better investment opportunities in financial services and telecommunications, and stronger protections for intellectual property.

The EU-Mexico and other agreements with Latin America are seen in Europe as helping to secure access for EU exporters and investors to a region in which U.S. influence has increased in recent years, owing to NAFTA and other trade arrangements. As with many other parts of the world, however, EU protectionism remains a powerful brake on improved trade relations. The EU is insisting that agriculture be excluded from any deal with Mercosur. Skeptics in Mercosur note that their trade surplus of $7.9 billion with the EU in 1990 had turned into a trade deficit of $6.5 billion in 1997 and are wary lest an agreement simply exacerbate the current deficit.[19]

THE UNITED STATES

The United States is the EU's largest economic partner, accounting for over 21 percent of EU exports and imports, as well as by far the largest share of foreign direct investment in and from the Union. Apart from their interactions in the WTO, the United States and the EU have a special bilateral relationship that reflects the intensity of economic flows across the Atlantic and the special transatlantic political and security relationship. This bilateral relationship began to develop in the early 1990s, as Washington recognized the growing importance of the EC in the post-cold war world and the relative decline of NATO's centrality.

In November 1990 the United States and the EC signed their first general bilateral agreement, the Transatlantic Declaration.[20] It called for improved cooperation and consultations in both the political and the economic spheres, the latter in the context of joint efforts to strengthen the multilateral trading system. The agreement was short on specifics, however, and was overshadowed by the sharp disputes between the two sides in the early 1990s over completion of the Uruguay Round. In December 1995 the United States and what by then had become the EU concluded a second agreement, the New Transatlantic Agenda (NTA), that contained a more detailed blueprint for economic cooperation, including the establishment of what was called the New Transatlantic Marketplace.

At the time, there was growing concern on both sides of the Atlantic that in the absence of a unifying threat Europe and America were beginning to drift apart. To counter these concerns, leading politicians in Europe and North America were calling for a grand gesture to breathe new life into the transatlantic relationship. One of the most frequently heard proposals was for the creation of a Transatlantic Free Trade Agreement (TAFTA) on the model of the North American Free Trade Agreement concluded in 1993 by the United States, Canada, and Mexico.[21] While governments agreed that action of some kind was necessary, they rejected the TAFTA proposals as premature and unrealistic. Both sides were suffering from trade liberalization fatigue following the stormy conclusion of the Uruguay Round and feared that a new set of negotiations might do more harm than good by stirring up controversies over such unresolved issues as audiovisual products and agriculture. Instead, the NTA called for progress on an economic agenda that was more modest but more concrete and achievable over the short run. The two sides agreed to carry out a joint study of ways to facilitate trade in goods and services and to further reduce or eliminate tariff and nontariff barriers.

In May 1998 the United States and the EU launched a new bilateral framework, the Transatlantic Economic Partnership (TEP). It includes three elements: near-term market access for goods, services, and agricultural products, promotion of multilateral and bilateral trade liberalization in the WTO and other forums, and the deepening of transatlantic dialogue between representatives of nongovernmental, parliamentary, and governmental organizations on trade and investment issues. This was followed, in late 1998, by adoption of an EU-U.S. action plan for the TEP outlining a program of bilateral and multilateral negotiations with specified target dates for completion in nineteen areas, including, for example, dispute settlement, tariffs, intellectual property, investment, procurement, trade and environment, and core labor standards.[22]

An important element of the EU-U.S. economic relationship is the Transatlantic Business Dialogue (TABD), a regular conference of U.S. and European business leaders that was launched in Seville, Spain, in November 1995. The TABD has become a powerful lobby for business interests favoring further trade liberalization. It is organized into four working groups, Business Facilitation, Global Issues,

Small and Medium-Sized Businesses, and the Transatlantic Advisory Committee on Standards and Regulatory Reform. The latter group played an important role in facilitating conclusion, in June 1997, of the first EU-U.S. Mutual Recognition Agreement (MRA), a framework document covering technical and safety standards for certain electrical and electronic equipment, pharmaceutical products and certain medical devices, and the safety of recreational boats. Other MRAs are under discussion.

Notwithstanding the effort by both sides to embed EU-U.S. relations in a stable institutional framework and to identify areas in which to cooperate on a systematic basis, the United States and the EU continue to clash with some frequency on economic and political issues and to view the world through somewhat different perspectives. Economic disputes have flared up over beef hormones, genetically modified organisms, banana imports, aircraft noise, and other issues.

The banana dispute goes back to 1993, when the EU, acting to create a uniform import regime consistent with the single market, eliminated tariff-free access for Latin American-produced bananas to the German market and extended the preferences given to former European colonies to the whole of the single market. The United States and four Latin American countries complained to the GATT. Two GATT panels found that EU import restrictions were in violation of GATT rules, but under the old dispute resolution procedures the EU was able to block adoption of the panel report by the GATT Council.[23]

The United States and its Latin American partners brought another case against the EU in 1996, after the Uruguay agreements had gone into effect and the WTO, with its much tougher dispute resolution provisions, had been established. In May 1997 a WTO panel found against the EU regime. The EU appealed the finding, but it was upheld by the WTO Dispute Settlement Body in September 1997. A WTO arbitrator gave the EU until January 1, 1999, to make significant changes in its banana import regime, but the EU continued to make only cosmetic changes that did not address the underlying complaint. In December 1998 the United States announced that it was planning to take retaliatory action against the EU for failing to implement the WTO decision and issued a list of EU export products totaling some $500 million on which it would impose punitive import duties on EU suppliers.

Although much derided in the press, the banana dispute was a crucial test of the WTO and its powers of enforcement. For the United States, it was essential to establish that the EU and other trade partners could not string out indefinitely the WTO compliance process with delays, appeals, and technical changes in the policy followed by more appeals, thereby frustrating the original WTO design for binding dispute resolution provisions and effective action against protectionist practices. The EU, in contrast, claimed that the readiness of the United States to impose unilateral sanctions was itself a violation of WTO rules.

The dispute finally was resolved in April 1999 when the WTO formally authorized the United States to impose sanctions on EU imports as compensation for the latter's failure to comply with the ruling on bananas—although only on

$191.4 million of imports rather than the $500 million originally claimed. The United States hailed the decision as a victory for the WTO and its enforcement mechanisms. The EU announced that it would not appeal the ruling, and began work on a new banana import scheme that would still give preferences to the ACP countries but that would be consistent with WTO agreements.

The beef hormone dispute has some similarities with the banana case, in that it deals with enforcement of WTO rules. The EU has long banned the import of beef raised using growth-promoting hormones—a widespread practice in the United States and Canada. WTO rules allow signatories to block imports for reasons of health and safety, but only if there is valid scientific evidence showing that health and safety concerns are legitimately grounded and not an excuse for protection. The GATT and subsequently the WTO have ruled against the EU ban. The EU has refused to comply with these rulings, in part because hormones and other aspects of high-technology agriculture are politically unpopular in Europe, but also because European producers benefit from the ban. The EU instead has commissioned numerous lengthy scientific studies, none of which has been able to substantiate harm to human health. The WTO granted the EU a "reasonable period"—defined as by May 13, 1999—to bring its regulations on beef hormones into conformity with the WTO Sanitary and Phytosanitary Agreement. The EU claimed that it could not comply with this deadline, and suggested several alternative solutions, one of which was to admit that it could not comply and to pay compensation through trade concessions, as in the banana dispute. The genetically modified organism (GMO) dispute is similar to these other cases, in that it concerns EU bans on biotechnology products (certain hybrid seeds, for example) that are widely used in North American agriculture and that are not seen as posing a risk to human health. More generally, the EU would like to see stronger legal recognition of the validity of the "precautionary principle" in consumer safety matters, under which products can be banned on the basis of suspicions about possible harm to health or the environment. The United States is skeptical of the precautionary approach, at least as it is interpreted in the EU, seeing it as a license to block trade not on the basis of scientific evidence but of pressures from interest groups that sometimes are reacting to fear and rumor.

Aircraft have long been a flashpoint in EU-U.S. trade relations. Specific areas of contention have included European government subsidies to the European consortium Airbus Industrie and what the EU sees as comparable subsidies to U.S. manufacturers, and the Boeing-McDonnell Douglas merger, which the EU competition authorities were initially hesitant to approve. A more recent dispute concerned aircraft noise. In late 1998 the European Parliament voted to ban hush kits from use in European airports. These kits are a way of retrofitting older jets to dampen the noise that they produce. The United States saw this as less an environmental measure than a potential strike at Boeing, which planned to sell such kits to keep the fleet of older, European-owned Boeing jets in operation. This dispute was defused, at least temporarily, when the EU delayed the imposition of the new restrictions in exchange for a U.S. pledge to try to negotiate new international aircraft noise restrictions in the International Civil Aviation Organization (ICAO), the international body with the authority to set noise standards. It flared up again in early 2000 when the EP refused to shelve legislative action limiting the use of hush kits from April 2002 and the United States signaled that it would pursue a complaint against the EU in ICAO. The dispute is noteworthy for showing the competing claims of environment and free trade and for reflecting the EP's growing activism on issues that affect international trade and its decreasing willingness to defer to the Commission and national governments on such matters. (In this regard, the EP is becoming more similar to the U.S. Congress.)

On the political level, the United States has taken a harder line than the EU on so-called rogue states—Cuba, Iran, Iraq, Libya, and North Korea—that support international terrorism or that flaunt global regimes to control the spread of nuclear, chemical, and biological weapons. In 1996 the Congress passed legislation—the Cuban Liberty and Democracy Solidarity Act and the Iran Libya Sanctions Act (known respectively as the Helms-Burton and the D'Amato acts after their main Congressional sponsors)—that seeks to punish non-U.S. companies that trade with or invest in these countries. One of the key factors underlying Helms-Burton was the expropriation, by the Castro regime in the 1960s, of property owned by U.S. firms and citizens. The law threatened to cripple European and Canadian investment in Cuba by giving U.S. nationals the right to file suit against foreign companies with assets in Cuba and to impose U.S. entry restrictions on executives and shareholders of third-country firms "trafficking" in Cuba. The EU protested these acts, arguing that their extraterritorial reach was illegal under WTO treaties and contrary to general principles of international law. In October 1996 it filed a case in the WTO against the Helms-Burton Act.

In April 1997 the EU temporarily suspended its complaint in the WTO in exchange for concessions by the United States on both Helms-Burton and ILSA. Both laws remained on the books, but the Clinton administration promised to waive the right for its nationals to file suit against foreign companies under provisions of the Helms-Burton Act. For its part, the EU agreed to address the expropriation issue, pledging to work with the United States on the development of disciplines that would inhibit investment in countries that had illegally expropriated assets. The United States and the EU extended and reinforced their understanding at the May 1998 London summit.

Sanctions remain an unresolved issue in U.S.-EU relations, however, with the EU continuing to deplore the U.S. use of extraterritorial and unilateral measures, while the United States, and in particular the Congress, is determined to reserve its right to use broad economic sanctions for political and security objectives. These perspectives in turn can be traced to a certain difference of outlook between the United States and the EU regarding the relationship between politics and trade. The Europeans tend to be more commercially oriented, unwilling to let political and security considerations interfere with export sales. The United States traditionally has given greater weight to such factors. The U.S. Congress is also highly responsive to ethnic and religious groups with strong interests in particular foreign policy issues, and reluctant to concede the primacy of international obligations over domestic law. These differences can be managed by dialogue and compromise, but they are likely to flare up again as future foreign policy crises emerge.

Future Trade Issues

In looking to the future, and in particular to a new Millennium Round of trade talks that is expected to be launched early in the 21st century, the EU faces a number of key questions, the resolution of which will have major effects on the international trading order and the economic and political makeup of the EU itself. First, the EU and its member states will confront important institutional questions about how they conduct trade negotiations and make decisions on trade deals. These questions will become more pressing as the EU enlarges and as trade negotiations continue to expand into new, nontraditional areas such as services and investment.

Second, the EU will continue to face the old tension between globalism and regionalism in its trade policies. Along with the United States, it is one of the two major pillars of the world trading system based upon the MFN principle. As has been seen, however, the EU has built a network of preferential agreements with countries and groups of countries with which it has or seeks to build special ties. Within the EU itself there continues to be a certain tension between trade creation and trade diversion and a temptation to resort to a Fortress Europe approach over some issues. How the EU balances the competing claims of globalism and regionalism will have deep and lasting implications for the international system, especially in view of enlargement and the emergence of the euro as a global currency.

Third, the EU, like all regions and countries, faces political and philosophical questions about the competing claims of an open international trading order and the pursuit of certain noneconomic, societal values. In principle, the EU favors open international trade in goods, services, information, and technology. In practice, the EU, its member states, and important constituencies within the member states are committed to other values—the maintenance of the countryside and a rural way of life, protection of European languages and culture from the "invasion" of American films and television shows, or protection of privacy through limits on transborder flows of commercial data—that conflict with free trade, or at least with free trade as practiced by other partners, and that provide ready-made excuses for discrimination against its trading partners for a wide range of products and services. How the EU balances the competing demands of international markets and domestic society thus will be another crucial issue for the twenty-first century.

INSTITUTIONAL ISSUES

The EU's authority to negotiate trade agreements goes back to Article 113 (Article 133 in the Amsterdam renumbering) of the Treaty of Rome, which made the European Commission responsible for developing recommendations for the EC's negotiating policies for submission to the Council of Ministers. Once the Council approves the Commission's negotiating mandate (which is done by QMV), the Commission is empowered to conduct negotiations directly with third powers. The individual member states refrain from direct participation in international trade negotiations that might give the appearance that they are conducting a national trade policy in contravention of EC law. (G-7 consultations with the United States, Canada, and Japan on trade matters, for example, take place in a G-4, or "Quad," in which the European members of the G-7—Germany, France, Italy, and the UK—are replaced by the European Commissioner responsible for trade.) Article 133 also provides for the establishment of a special committee appointed by the Council that oversees the work of the Commission as negotiations proceed. Consisting of senior officials from trade ministries of the member states, the 133 Committee has played an active but behind-the-scenes role in all trade negotiations, ensuring that any agreement negotiated by the Commission on behalf of the Union is acceptable to the member states.

These procedures for negotiating trade agreements can be cumbersome and have provoked complaints from both within and outside the Union. Prominent EU trade negotiators have argued that the Union has been unable to take a leadership role in world trade negotiations and unable to respond swiftly enough in bargaining situations because of its slow-moving decision-making process.[24] Countries that have negotiated with the EU often complained about a rigidity in its negotiating positions that results from the need to seek agreement among the member states. The position presented by the Commission in international forums such as the GATT inevitably is the result of hard-fought compromises among the member states in the 133 Committee. The Commission finds it difficult to change its position in the course of a fast-moving international negotiation, especially since any change in the international negotiating position may alter the balance of gains and losses accruing to the member states from any particular trade agreement.

The Uruguay Round's push into new areas of negotiation and developments in global trade in general raised new institutional questions for the EU. Because so many new subjects—services, intellectual property, investment—were included in the Final Act, the member states claimed that it was a mixed agreement, subject both to EU and member state competence. The Commission argued that the Treaty of Rome made it the sole external negotiator on trade issues, and that these topics were covered under the Commission's trade mandate. In April 1994, just before the scheduled signing of the Marrakesh document, the Commission requested an opinion from the ECJ on the subject of competence as it related to the new issues. Although in the past the Court had frequently strengthened the central powers of the Union by its decisions, it did not uphold the Commission's view. In its opinion, delivered in November 1994, the Court held that the exclusive right of the Commission to negotiate agreements on trade in goods did not extend to the full range of subjects covered in the Uruguay Round.[25] Authority over certain key aspects of trade policy—including many that are of growing importance in the services and investment-driven global economy—thus remains divided between Brussels and the member states. In the 1996–1997 IGC on institutional reform the Commission urged an amendment of Article 133 of the Treaty of Rome to extend its authority over these issues, arguing that the EU's international negotiating position was undercut by this situation of dual competence. The member states were unwilling, however, to surrender permanently their negotiating authority in these areas. Instead, they added a paragraph to Article 133 stating that the Council, acting unanimously on a Commission proposal, could extend Commission competence to international negotiations and agreements on services and intellectual property.

International aviation affords perhaps the best example of the struggle between the Commission and the member states over competence in new areas of trade. Beginning with the Netherlands in 1995, the United States has concluded bilateral "open skies" agreements with most of the member states of the Union. These agreements give U.S. carriers the right to pick up passengers in one European country for subsequent transport to other destinations, in exchange for giving European carriers similar rights in the United States. The Commission claims that such agreements adversely affect the EU's internal market for aviation and distort competition between airlines and airports. It also claims that the EU would have a stronger negotiating position with the United States if it were to negotiate as a unit, with the Commission conducting the talks. In March 1998 the Commission initiated legal action against eight member states for their bilateral aviation treaties with the United States, sending a reasoned opinion to these countries stating the Commission's case that they are in breach of EU law. Barring a negotiated solution, these cases will end up in the ECJ, which again will have an opportunity to decide where member state powers leave off and those of the Commission, acting on behalf of the Union, begin.

GLOBAL TRADE, THE INTERNAL MARKET, AND ECONOMIC REGIONALISM

A recurrent question in the history of European integration has been whether the elimination of barriers within Europe would lead to higher barriers—either in relative or absolute terms—against the outside world. Would trade creation in Europe mean trade diversion from elsewhere, or would the development of an open European market contribute to broader trade liberalization that would benefit the United States, Japan, and the developing countries? In the late 1940s and early 1950s the United States actually *encouraged* the European countries to discriminate in favor of each other's products and against imports from the United States as a way of promoting economic revival. This was a temporary measure, however, designed to cope with the postwar economic crisis. By the early 1960s, the United States and other countries were concerned about the trade-diverting potential of the common market, to which they responded by convening the Dillon and Kennedy rounds of the GATT. The single market program of the 1980s also led to widespread concerns in the United States about a "Fortress Europe" that would be liberal internally but closed to non-EC exporters and investors.

As in the 1960s, these fears proved to be overstated, as completion of the single market program proceeded almost in parallel with the Uruguay Round and dealt with many of the same sectors and issues. For the most part, internal and external trade liberalization tended to complement and reinforce each other. As European countries dismantled barriers to trade and investment with other EU countries, they found it easier to take the same steps with regard to non-EU members. Conversely, the requirements of global trade liberalization pressed on the EU by the international community in the Uruguay Round helped to break down longstanding intra-EU barriers to the single market.

The single market program made it easier, for example, for the EU to negotiate away the MFA in the Uruguay Round, since implementing the MFA entailed assigning national quotas within the EU market and maintaining border checks and other controls to ensure that textiles and clothing imported under one country's national quota were not shipped to and sold in another member state—all of which was incompatible with the internal market provisions of the Single European Act. French, Italian, and Spanish quotas on the import of cars from Japan also had to be abolished as incompatible with the single market, thereby making it easier for the EU to accept the ban on VERs in the Uruguay Round. Similarly, it is difficult to see how the EU could have agreed to the liberalization of services such as banking and telecommunications within the Uruguay Round had its member states not first achieved a certain degree of liberalization within the EU itself. In this case, regional liberalization proved to be a precursor to global liberalization.

Nevertheless, there are cases in which the lowering or elimination of barriers to intra-European trade is accompanied by the raising of new or higher barriers to trade with the rest of the world. The well-known banana dispute between the United States and the EU in part grew out of such a case. Prior to 1993, bananas from Latin America (produced and sold by U.S. companies) entered Germany tariff free. To comply with an EU decision establishing a uniform regime for bananas, Germany subsequently imposed tariffs on so-called dollar bananas and joined its EU partners in giving preference—tariff-free import—to higher cost, lower quality fruit from Europe's former colonies.

In other cases the EU has tried to develop a European market by discriminating against products from outside. The EU's television directive, *Television without Frontiers*, was put into effect in October 1991, ostensibly to ensure equal access throughout the EU market for EU productions. The most controversial element of the directive, however, was a provision stipulating that member states "shall ensure where practicable and by appropriate means, that broadcasters reserve for European works . . . a majority proportion of their transmission time."[26] Clearly directed at limiting imports of American television programs and giving a boost to the EU's own industry, this provision resulted in EU-U.S. friction over audiovisual trade. In the closing stages of the Uruguay Round the two sides in fact agreed to set aside audiovisual products for future resolution, as they were unable to reach a compromise within the GATT.

As globalization of the European economy proceeds, and especially as the largest and most successful EU multinationals come to rely increasingly on their exports to and investments in the world outside the EU, a Fortress Europe approach may become even less politically feasible or economically attractive than in the past. Even traditionally protectionist countries such as France, Italy, and, in nonmanufacturing sectors, Germany are opening up to world markets. On the other hand, the sheer size of the EU market, the capacity of the EU to use this market to favor domestic suppliers or firms in countries that have preferential arrangements with the EU, and the political backlash in some quarters against globalization may increase the temptation toward some kind of economic regionalism on the part of the EU. Agriculture and audiovisual products already fall in this category; armaments also are becoming an area in which pressure to buy European (as discussed in the next chapter) is growing. The Commission has shown interest in developing EU technical standards as a way of challenging U.S. influence in the standard-setting process and perhaps of giving European firms advantages in home and global markets.

Whether such trends develop to the point that global trade is threatened by a more inward-looking Europe will depend on whether trade liberalization moves forward in the WTO or is reversed in a backlash against globalization. It also will depend on the evolution of attitudes in the Union. EU officials and supporters frequently argue in favor of closer integration to a skeptical public by characterizing the Union as Europe's response to the inexorable forces of globalization. What this means in practice will need to be defined on a case-by-case basis. It could mean that the EU will use its enormous leverage in the international economic system to shape rules that will allow Europe to reap the benefits of globalization, but to shift as many as possible of its costs onto other countries. This could be done through a selective approach to globalization that would entail aggressive pursuit of market opening in sectors where European firms have competitive advantages and protectionism or regional solutions in those sectors where they do not.

MARKETS AND SOCIETY

A last future trade issue, closely related to globalization and EU responses to it, concerns the competing claims of markets and society in the international economic system. Historically, dismantling barriers to trade has been politically controversial, pitting powerful domestic constituencies against each other. In the early days of the EC, for example, French industrialists were wary of opening up their domestic market to competition from German industry. France sought and achieved in return for industrial trade liberalization preferential access to other European markets for its farm products. But French (and other) industry still had to go through a process of rationalization and restructuring in which there were losers as well as winners.

The same kinds of domestic tradeoffs still occur in Europe in response to globalization and the effects of completing the single market and, more recently, the introduction of the euro. But some experts believe that these tradeoffs are becoming harder to manage politically. National governments have less latitude than in the past to "buy off" the victims of increased competition and industrial restructuring through generous social welfare and other aid programs. After the fiscal excesses of the 1970s and 1980s, governments came under heavy pressure to cut spending and taxes, both for reasons of macroeconomic stability and in order to attract and retain international investment, which has become increasingly mobile and can threaten to migrate to countries or regions with lower taxes, lower wage costs, and less onerous regulation.

Within the EU, Britain's refusal, in 1991–1997, to adhere to the social charter led to charges of "social dumping," especially after a Swedish company announced that it was closing a plant in France and shifting production and jobs to Scotland to take advantage of lower costs. ("Europe can have the social charter. We shall have employment. . . . Let Jacques Delors accuse us of creating a paradise for foreign investors; I am happy to plead guilty," was how Prime Minister Major responded to this discussion.)[27] Fear of lower labor costs and standards also explains some of the political resistance in the EU to enlargement to central and eastern Europe, although as a practical matter trade with this region is already free of most trade restrictions and it could be argued that workers in the existing Union would be better off having these countries as members and subject to costly EU regulations.

Charges of "social dumping" are heard even more often in relation to trade with the developing world. Trade unions in France, other European countries, and the United States argue that imports from developing countries are competitive in world markets only because employers in many less developed exporting countries pay such low wages with minimal social benefits. They are demanding that the WTO begin to fashion rules on labor standards. The developing countries are vehemently opposed to the "linkage" approach, which in their view runs counter to the whole idea of free trade and is an attempt to negate the natural advantage that poor countries enjoy from having lower labor costs. Similar arguments are made with regard to "environmental dumping," under which some countries are said to gain advantage in world markets by adopting low environmental standards. Here again, developing countries reject this position, arguing that high environmental standards are a luxury that wealthy countries can afford and that they in any case should not be used to interfere with trade.

The clash between markets and society also can be seen in the cultural field, although there the United States rather than the developing world is the main protagonist. As culture, services, and intellectual property are increasingly traded and as trade in these areas is subject to negotiation in the WTO system, all countries face choices between protecting certain national values and interests and participating in the new global information order with its own rules and regulations (or lack thereof). European countries are concerned, for example, about the privacy implications of cross-border electronic commerce and would like to impose restrictions that U.S. firms regard as protectionist. Some European governments argue that culture, including movies, television shows, and popular music, should not be regarded just as commodities to be bought and sold like any others, but that they should be subject to restrictions (such as in the EU's television directive) designed to uphold certain nonmarket values.

Culture is likely to remain a troubled issue for the international trading order. For the United States, the aggressive pursuit of expanded markets for movies and television is one of the highest international trade policy priorities—a fact that can be explained in part by the importance of Hollywood and the entertainment industry as a contributor to political campaigns. The EU is likely to resist U.S. pressures, given the attitude of member states such as France, but it will have difficulty in forging a cultural trade policy that has positive content of its own and that can command the support of all member states in the Union. The EU is not a cultural entity. Citizens in European countries may understand efforts to protect and subsidize *national* cultural products, but it is not self-evident why, for example, Dutch television viewers should be pressured to watch a French or Italian movie in lieu of an American product, or why Danish radio should have to broadcast Greek or German songs in place of U.S. (or other non-EU country) offerings. Indeed, the blurring of cultural identities and boundaries within the EU has at times been contentious, as, for example, when direct satellite broadcasting has undermined the state television broadcasting regimes in place in EU member states. Over time, new technologies such as direct broadcasting and the Internet (with its growing capacity to transmit music and film) will further complicate efforts to develop trade rules for culture and intellectual property, which are likely to remain items on the world trade agenda for years to come.

SEATTLE AND THE MILLENNIUM ROUND

The saliency of these issues—the institutional complexities of EU decision-making, the dynamic between the global order and economic regionalism, and the tension between trade and the protection of social and cultural values—were very much in evidence as the EU prepared for the WTO ministerial meeting scheduled to begin in Seattle on November 30, 1999. Under the terms of the Uruguay Round General Agreement on Trade in Services (GATS), the WTO member states were committed to entering successive rounds of negotiations, "with a view to achieving a progressively higher level of liberalization," beginning no later than five years after the entry into force of the GATS, or by January 1, 2000, at the latest. Under the terms of the Agreement on Agriculture, they also were committed to launching a new round of talks on agricultural trade by the same date. In addition to these built-in agenda items, many WTO members were keen on launching a new Millennium Round of talks that, like the Uruguay Round, would cover the entire range of trade issues.

While the United States was lukewarm about a comprehensive new round (after a skeptical Congress refused to grant the Clinton administration "fast track" negotiating authority), the EU was one of its strongest proponents—in part because the Commission was eager to seize a leadership position on international trade issues, but also for tactical reasons. With the EU once again on the defensive for its agricultural protectionism, it preferred a forum in which agriculture would blend into a broader setting with other issues, rather than be singled out in a separate negotiation. This would allow tradeoffs among other issues—enabling the EU in effect to win acceptance of some agricultural protectionism by making concessions in other areas and perhaps facilitating EU concessions on agriculture by creating a domestic political constituency for a broader agreement covering manufactured goods, services, market access, and new trade rules for investment and competition policy that would benefit many industrial sectors. Critics of EU negotiating tactics took a more skeptical view, suspecting the EU of planning to thwart any real liberalization of agriculture by tying up the WTO in endless negotiations on issues such as competition policy that would be almost impossible to resolve in the 135-country forum.[28]

As the Seattle meeting approached, the Council of Ministers struggled to settle on a negotiating mandate for the Commission. Member states agreed on the desirability of pressing for a broad agenda and a comprehensive round, but were divided on two important issues, the so-called cultural exception and labor rights. France wanted to sustain the position, extracted from the United States in the last-minute compromise that saved the Uruguay Round, that audiovisual trade be exempted from discussion in the new round. Other member states were sympathetic to the French view, but thought that pressing for such a blatant exclusion would undermine the EU's position in favor of a comprehensive round. On labor rights, Germany, with some support from other member countries, took a strong line on the need to establish a WTO working group on labor rights—a position vigorously opposed by the developing countries, which believed that discussion of such issues in the WTO context would be the opening wedge of a drive by the developed countries to use charges of "social dumping" to block imports from poor countries with lower wages and labor standards, thereby blunting the developing world's main advantage in the global economy. On agriculture, the fifteen had little trouble uniting behind a position declaring agriculture a "multifunctional" activity that fulfils social and environmental as well as economic roles. The EU wanted to see "multifunctionality" written into the Seattle ministerial statement that would set the agenda for the Millennium Round—a position that was opposed by the United States and the Cairns group of agricultural exporters, which rightly saw this as providing a thinly disguised justification for continued high levels of protection.

After months of wrangling, the Council finally adopted a mandate that the Commission could take to Seattle and to preparatory bilateral talks in the United

States (see Box 8.1). On labor rights, the EU ministers agreed to call for a "joint standing working forum" on globalization and worker rights, to be set up by the International Labor Organization (ILO) and the WTO. It was hoped that this position would be acceptable to the developing countries. On culture, the fifteen declared that the EU would "maintain the possibility to preserve and develop their capacity to define and implement their cultural and audiovisual policies for the purposes of preserving their cultural diversity."[29] This stopped short of the complete exception demanded by France, but left the Commission with limited room for negotiation.

The difficulties in agreeing to the Commission's mandate were just a foretaste of the problems that would be encountered in Seattle. Once the meeting got underway, thousands of protestors, many of them violent, disrupted the proceedings, preventing delegates from reaching the official sessions and causing millions of dollars in damage to the downtown business district. The positions voiced by the protestors were confused and self-contradictory, but they reflected the degree to which nongovernmental organizations representing environmental, labor, human rights, and other concerns had made the WTO the focal point of protest against the perceived evils of globalization. On the one hand, the protestors accused the WTO of being like a secretive world government, reaching deals behind closed doors that affected the lives and livelihoods of ordinary citizens. On the other hand, the same protestors seemed to be castigating the WTO for *not* acting more like a world government—for not imposing stronger labor and environmental standards, especially on the developing countries. WTO secretary General Mike Moore and others sought to counter the protestors with the argument that the ministers in Seattle were from democratically chosen governments and that the nongovernmental organizations in the streets could not arrogate to themselves the

---

Box 8.1   The Millennium Round

Required Agenda Items
   Agricultural trade liberalization
   Services trade liberalization

Optional Items Favored by the EU
   A "comprehensive" round
   Industrial tariff reductions
   Recognition of the "multifunctionality" of agriculture
   Recognition of core labor standards
   Enhanced WTO-ILO cooperation to promote labor standards
   Greater transparency in the dispute settlement process
   Integration of environmental considerations into trade policy
   Recognition of the precautionary principle in health and consumer safety issues

(*Source:* European Commission, *The EU and the Millennium Round.*)

right to represent the public. President Clinton took a more sympathetic line, stating that the WTO process should be opened up "to all those that are demonstrating on the outside."[30] In what was widely seen as a move to placate organized labor on the eve of an election year, Clinton infuriated the developing countries by stating that he might support sanctions in the WTO framework for countries that abused labor standards.

Inside the conference center, things did not go much better. Developing country ministers complained about their inability to influence the proceedings, which were dominated by the major trading powers, above all the EU and the United States. For their part, Brussels and Washington failed to make significant progress on the issues that divided them. In the end the meeting broke down, as the ministers headed home having failed to adopt a mandate to launch the much-heralded Millennium Round. The debacle in Seattle showed the inadequacies of the trade system established less than a decade earlier in the Uruguay Round and led to calls for reform in the direction of greater openness and transparency. EU trade commissioner Pascal Lamy was among the most prominent voices in this discussion, calling for the possible establishment of a WTO parliamentary arm. The developing countries were disturbed that the proceedings seemed to have been hijacked by the wealthy countries, both inside and outside the conference hall, leaving little time to focus on their agenda of trade access, development, and debt relief.

The Seattle meeting also again showed the complexities and rigidities inherent in the EU's trade decision-making process, as U.S. and other negotiators complained about how little room for genuine negotiation the Commission was accorded by the member states in Brussels. At one point in the proceedings, the Council of Ministers forced the Commission to reverse an agreement that it had made with the United States to establish a working group to discuss biotechnology in the WTO framework. While some Europeans admitted the shortcomings in their own decision-making processes, they also could and did point to a difficult situation in the U.S. side, reflected in the absence of fast-track authority and in the pre-election pandering to domestic interest groups by the Clinton administration.

The failure of the Seattle meeting also dealt at least a temporary blow to the goal of a truly open international system based on MFN, perhaps giving new impetus to the system of regional preferences that have been central to EU trade policy from its inception and delaying the start of talks on agriculture and services. The conclusion of the February 2000 Fiji Agreement between the EU and the ACP countries derived at least in part from the failure of the Seattle meeting.

Perhaps most ominously for the future of the world trading system, the Seattle meetings highlighted the intense conflict between the competing claims of markets and society. The fact that "society"—or those purporting to speak in its name—protested so strongly against the claims of markets may encourage governments in all parts of the world to dig in their heels against forms of liberalization that cut across the wishes of powerful domestic interest groups. This would be a particular danger in the EU, where such claims are already a key element of the Commission's negotiating posture.

In its *Strategic Objectives 2000–2005*, drafted in the shadow of Seattle, the Commission called for the EU to seize the initiative in the globalization debate and work to shape the globalization process in ways that will minimize its negative effects on culture, labor, and the environment (see Box 8.2).

But these positive-sounding generalities are likely to ring hollow to those countries that have been on the receiving end of EU protectionism. Many of these countries will be tempted to conclude that the EU pursues a one-sided vision of trade in which it uses multilateral and bilateral trade policy instruments to batter down impediments to exports of the medium-technology and luxury products in the manufacture of which it excels (and to secure investment opportunities for the surpluses and profits earned by these exports), while invoking an array of arguments based on cultural, environmental, societal, and other criteria in order to close EU markets to much of what *other* countries would like to export.

Agriculture must be protected, the EU argues, because of its "multifunctional" contributions to the environment and culture. Fishing is subsidized and protected to preserve the traditional way of life in European fishing villages. High technology must be supported to prevent the United States from achieving monopolies. Films, television, and other cultural products should be excluded from international markets to protect Europe from Hollywood's influence. The environment, labor standards, and violations of competition norms could provide the rationale for further exceptions to the norms of free trade.

To point out the inconsistencies in EU trade policy is not to argue that the EU is necessarily wrong on these issues or to argue that the inevitable logic of globalization will force it to change its policies. Many people outside Europe—including in the United States—also are concerned about the negative effects of

---

Box 8.2 The Commission on Globalization

Globalisation opens up new prospects for trade, investment and technological development. But it does have certain negative side-effects. The process has turned out to be exclusive rather than inclusive and has widened the inequalities between countries and between social categories and regions within them. Moreover, the emergence of global actors with global strategies can have the effect of marginalising democratic mechanisms and jeopardising policies for sustainable development.

Europe's objective must be to make globalisation compatible with the common interest of society. . . .

The Union must work to secure greater coherence in the management of the world economy, gradual integration of the developing countries, sustainable development and the definition of new "ground rules", which are essential if the fruits of globalisation are to be divided fairly and benefit the largest number of people possible. Minimum levels should be established for competition, social and environmental standards and investment.

(*Source:* European Commission, *Strategic Objectives 2000–2005*, 8.)

free trade, disturbed by the homogenization of culture around the world, and convinced that a better balance needs to be struck between the competing demands of the market economy and other values. If, however, the EU persists with what other countries perceive as a one-sided approach to trade, the effects on the world trading system will be profound. The EU will be less able to play a leadership role in the world economy than its relative weight would suggest that it should and the course of globalization, so triumphantly proclaimed by its advocates, is likely to be marred by harsh international trade disputes pitting the EU against its partners, and above all the United States.

The International Implications of the Euro

THE EURO AND THE DOLLAR

The launch of the euro on January 1, 1999, added a new dimension to the EU's role as a global economic actor. With EMU, many experts predicted that the world monetary system will evolve into an effective duopoly, with the dollar and the euro rivaling each other as the leading currencies and the ECB becoming a player in international monetary affairs at or nearly at the level of the U.S. Federal Reserve.

The argument for the euro rests heavily on an analogy with trade. As has been seen, the United States and the EU are the dominant players in the WTO, as they were in the previous GATT system. Without agreement between Washington and Brussels on key trade issues, global agreement is not possible. The situation in the world financial system has been quite different. Although as economic actors the United States and the EU are roughly comparable in size (Table 8.3), the share of the dollar in international transactions has been far greater than that of the EU currencies, and larger than would be predicted based on U.S. shares of real economic activity. The dollar is the dominant currency held by central banks and ministries of finance in their official foreign exchange reserves, in international lending, and in the conduct of international trade (Table 8.4). It is common for

Table 8.3 Basic Economic Indicators

	United States	EU	Euro-11
Population (millions)	268.0	374.2	290.5
GDP (share of world)	21	20	16
Economic Growth (Annual average percentage, 1990–1999)	2.4	2.0	2.1
Share of world exports (1998)	16.8	20.1	—
Share of world imports (1998)	22.3	18.9	—

Source: European Commission; IMF.

countries and firms that have no direct connection with the United States to use the dollar in private or governmental transactions—for example when a Swiss bank lends money to an Asian country or when a Mexican firm exports a product to Africa. A key question is whether in the future more of these transactions will be carried out in euros, and what implications this might have for the EU, the United States, and the international system.

The effects of the euro most likely will be seen first in international trade. World trade in some commodities, for example oil and jet aircraft, generally is priced in dollars. Traders may begin to use euros for some of these transactions, particularly in countries or regions that conduct a high proportion of their trade with the EU. This will eliminate the currency risk that European firms now face and put them on a par with U.S. competitors.

Over a longer time-frame, some public and private portfolio rebalancing is expected to occur. As can be seen in Table 8.4, dollars account for nearly two-thirds of all official foreign exchange reserves held by central banks and finance ministries. The euro is likely to develop as an official reserve currency, as countries diversify their holdings from dollars to euros. One expert predicts that eventually the dollar and the euro each may account for about 40 percent of reserves, while the yen and other currencies account for the remainder.[31] Developing country governments that now tend to issue their debt in dollars may begin to borrow in euros.

What effects these shifts will have on the EU and U.S. economies are as yet unclear. European financial centers and companies may reap some benefits from the euro at the expense of New York– and other U.S.-based firms. European and other borrowers who earn the money to repay their debts mainly in euros will be better protected against rapid appreciation of the dollar that can increase their dollar debts (in real terms) overnight. Conversely, exporters of commodities that are priced in euros will be protected from real declines in the prices of their products caused by dollar depreciation.

Officially, the U.S. government and Federal Reserve have welcomed the cre-

Table 8.4 Currency Shares in Global Finance (Percent)

	$ U.S.	All EU currencies	Japanese Yen
Official foreign exchange reserves (1996)	64.1	21.2	7.5
Denomination of world exports (1992)	47.6	33.5	4.8
International private assets	37.9	33.5	12.4
International note and bond markets (1997)	50	28	12
International bank lending (1997)	45	17	4

Source: C. Fred Bergsten, Weak Dollar, Strong Euro? The International Impact of EMU (London: Centre for Economic Reform, 1988), 14.

ation of the euro, which they note could help to make Europe a more dynamic and rapidly growing economy with better opportunities for U.S. exporters and investors. Nonetheless, loss of dollar hegemony could have some negative implications for the United States. A relative decline in the dollar's role might even make it more costly for the United States to borrow internationally. As a result of its chronic balance of payments deficits, the United States is the world's largest debtor country. Most of the money lent by foreigners to U.S. public and private entities is denominated in the United States' own currency, the dollar. But as international lenders have more opportunities to lend in euros, the rates at which the United States can borrow may increase.

European officials have been quick to argue that the euro will not challenge the dollar and (somewhat contradictorily) that the emergence of a second major reserve currency will have beneficial effects for the world economy and by extension for the United States as well. Nonetheless, even under the best of circumstances the euro could encourage a European attitude of benign neglect toward the international system as a whole that could have negative implications for other countries. Throughout much of the postwar period, European leaders often accused the United States of ignoring the international implications of its domestic economic policies. Such complaints often were exaggerated, but they contained an element of truth. Given the special status of the dollar and with its huge internal market relatively immune to international influences, the United States could afford to make economic policy in relative isolation. Such an approach was not possible for the small and medium economies of Western Europe, for which trade comprised 50 percent or more of economic activity.

With the completion of the single market and the introduction of the euro, the EU as a whole has become very much more like the United States, a continental economy that for economic reasons at least need not be overly concerned about the international consequences of its policies. The openness ratio (defined as total exports and imports divided by GDP) of the United States in fact now exceeds that of the EU. If the EU tends to ignore the broader implications of its policies, this could lead to tensions with the United States and have harmful effects on weaker countries in the international economy. It is for this reason that institutional issues—the question of how the EU, the ESCB, and the ECB relate to the broader international financial system—have come to the fore and represent a key part of the EMU story since 1999.

INSTITUTIONAL ISSUES

Institutionally, the euro will transform how Europe relates to the international financial system. Ever since the 1970s, the finance ministers and heads of central banks of France, Germany, Italy, and the UK have been represented in the G-7. With a single currency and monetary policy, it would be logical to expect the emergence of a G-3 comprised of the United States, the EU, and Japan. For the moment this is not happening, however, since fiscal and other economic policies (not to mention the many political issues dealt with by the G-7) are still partly or entirely decided at the national level.

Assuming that something like a G-3 does emerge, a key question will be whether this will hinder or facilitate EU-U.S. harmony and promote better, less crisis-prone management of the international financial system. On the surface it would seem that a directorate of three would be more workable than a larger grouping of more disparate powers. In practice, however, it is unclear how effective G-3 coordination would be compared with the pre-1999 system. With its cumbersome decision-making processes, the ECB could have difficulty in reacting to a worldwide financial crisis that required immediate attention.

The Maastricht Treaty also contains certain ambiguities relating to international monetary policy that could hinder decision-making. The treaty stipulates that the EU can conclude formal agreements on an international exchange rate system in which the euro participates only with the unanimous agreement of the member states in the Council, acting on a recommendation from the ECB or the Commission. In the event that the international community wanted to overhaul fundamentally the post-Bretton Woods monetary system, the treaty sets a very high hurdle to EU participation. Such a case is unlikely, given the technical and political difficulties associated with moving back to anything like a system of fixed exchange rates, but over the long term it cannot be dismissed altogether.

More relevant to current and medium-term policy are the treaty's provisions on exchange rate policy in the existing system and on the negotiation of ad hoc or informal currency arrangements, such as the Plaza and Louvre accords negotiated by the G-7 in the 1980s to bring down the value of the dollar. The treaty stipulates that the Council—in this case ECOFIN—will formulate "general orientations" for exchange rate policy based on recommendations from the Commission or the ECB, and always after consultation with the ECB. The Council may act by QMV. This raises the specter of conflict between political leaders and the central bank over exchange rate policy at the European level, as frequently occurred at the national level prior to EMU.

The treaty is especially vague on the question of how the EU can negotiate informal or ad hoc monetary agreements. It leaves the question of who is to negotiate on behalf of the EU to a future decision by the Council, acting by QMV on a Commission recommendation after consultation with the ECB. The treaty merely specifies that "these arrangements shall ensure that the Community expresses a single position."[32] This provision could come into play if, for example, the political leaders of the EU wanted to establish "target zones" for the euro in relation to the dollar and the yen. This idea was floated by the German finance minister in late 1998, but resisted by the ECB and in any case rejected by the United States, which would have to agree to such a scheme.

The treaty also is not definitive on the question of representation of the ECB and the Eurosytem in international forums. It states only that the Council should decide this question by QMV. As the start of the euro approached, the EU not surprisingly sought to avoid tough choices by proposing additional seats in international forums for the institutions of EMU, rather than the consolidation of national positions into a single EU representation. In November 1998 the Commission proposed that the single currency be represented in the G-7 meetings of finance ministers and central bank governments by a triad of the Commission, the ECB, and the finance minister of the country holding the rotating presidency of the euro-11 (if this was not France, Germany, or Italy), in addition to the existing national representations (finance ministers and central bank governors) of these three countries. (The UK, a non-euro country but still an EU member, also would be represented on the G-7.) This approach threatened to worsen what is already an absurdly over-represented position for Western Europe in the G-7, and was rejected by the United States. Under a compromise worked out in early 1999, the national central bank governors of the euro countries do not attend the first half of G-7 finance meetings, when purely monetary issues are addressed. They do join the second part of the meeting, however, when the agenda is broader.[33] The EU presidency country (or the chair of the euro-11, if the presidency is held by a non-euro country) also attends these meetings.

EMU AND THE GLOBAL ECONOMY

While institutional issues as they relate to global economic affairs are important, it could be argued that the more important question for the international system is internal to the EU: how and for what purpose will it pursue a unified economic and monetary policy? In particular, how will the ECB manage the possible trade-offs between price stability and the pursuit of other economic objectives such as higher growth and lower unemployment. As a newcomer to the international financial system, the ECB clearly sees a need to establish its credibility as a successor to the Bundesbank by fulfiling its Maastricht Treaty commitment to maintaining price stability. As ECB president Duisenberg told a Washington audience in September 1999, "the most important task and challenge of the Eurosystem is to build up a track record of actual price stability in the euro area. Action speaks louder than words. Showing in practice that we are capable of providing stable prices is what really counts. We have to ensure that European citizens are confident that the euro is a currency which can sustain its value over time, and that the ECB is an institution which they can trust. The ECB should be perceived as an institution that says what it does and does what it says."[34]

But whether this continued very heavy emphasis on price stability is warranted remains a matter of debate, both in Europe and internationally. During Stage 2 of EMU, Europe experienced relatively slow economic growth, in part because governments were forced to rein in spending in order to meet the Maastricht criteria and as central bankers kept interest rates relatively high to combat lingering inflation in the system. With the euro launched, the trade unions and some left-wing political leaders expressed a desire see the ECB and the Eurosystem take measures to stimulate economic growth. Even in Washington there was concern that the ECB might have a tendency to pursue tight-money, slow-growth policies that could impart a further deflationary impulse to the world economy. U.S. officials expressed a hope that economic growth in Europe would accelerate so that it could absorb more imports from the crisis-ridden developing countries. As the euro moved toward and ultimately fell below parity with the dollar in early 2000, U.S. Secretary of the Treasury Lawrence Summers spoke out against what he called the "complacency of diminished expectations" in Europe and Japan that resulted in acceptance of continuing slow rates of economic growth and of growth based largely on exports rather than increased domestic demand.[35] The U.S. trade deficit ballooned to a record $270 billion in 1999, while the euro area and the EU as a whole registered huge surpluses.

While sensitive to concerns about growth, the ECB continued to stress the primacy of the inflation-fighting imperative, particularly as the euro continued to drop, bringing with it the prospect of higher inflation caused by increasing import prices. Equally important, the ECB joined many national governments in stressing that monetary policy alone was not a solution to Europe's economic problems and that what Europe really needed was increased dynamism linked to structural reform. This was clearly the sentiment behind the March 2000 Lisbon summit which, as discussed in Chapter 11, set new strategic economic goals for the EU up to 2010, with a heavy emphasis on the Internet economy and on overtaking the United States as the most dynamic and productive region of the world economy.

Notes

1. Article 3.

2. Paemen and Bensch, *From the GATT to the WTO*, 27.

3. The texts of all of these agreements can be found on the web page of the WTO, at http://www.wto.int.

4. These categories and much of the analysis that follows is based on Jeffrey J. Schott, *The Uruguay Round: An Assessment* (Washington: Institute for International Economics, 1994); and European Commission, *The Uruguay Round*, Background Brief 20, Brussels, March 14, 1994.

5. World Trade Organization, Trade Policy Review Body, *The European Union: Report by the Secretariat—Summary Observations*, July 1995, on http://www.wto.int/reviews.

6. Bull. EC 4–1984, 9–10.

7. Eurostat data for 1998, in European Commission, "EU trade facts and figures," *European Union Millennium Round Information Packet*, November 1999.

8. Ibid.

9. *Agreement establishing an association between the European Economic Community and Turkey*, Ankara, September 12, 1963, O.J. 3687 (1964).

10. *Decision I/95 (96/142/EC) of the E.C.-Turkey Association Council on implementing the final phase of the Customs Union*, O.J. L35/1 (1996).

11. Eurostat data for 1996, in European Commission, "EU trade facts and figures," *European Union World Trade Information Packet*, November 1998.

12. Bartlomiej Kaminski, "The Significance of the 'Europe Agreements' for Central European Industrial Exports," *Policy Research Working Paper* (1314), The World Bank, June 1994.

13. European Commission, "EU trade facts and figures," November 1998.

14. *Fourth ACP-EEC Convention*, Lomé, December 15, 1989, O.J. L229/3 (1991).

15. Christopher Piening, *Global Europe* (Boulder, CO: Lynne Rienner, 1997), 184.

16. European Commission, EU-ACP Negotiation, Information Memo No. 10, "Conclusions of the Brussels ministerial conference held on 2 and 3 February," Brussels, February 4, 2000.

17. Caroline Southey, "Compromise sought as talks break down," *Financial Times*, October 21, 1998.

18. Victor Mallet, "Pretoria condemns EU wine policy," *Financial Times*, November 5, 1999.

19. Richard Lapper and Michael Smith, "Europe's farmers stand in way of Mercosur Deal," *Financial Times*, June 28, 1999.

20. European Commission, *Transatlantic Declaration on EC-US Relations*, Brussels, November 23, 1990.

21. Bruce Stokes, ed., *Open for Business: Creating a Transatlantic Marketplace* (New York: Council on Foreign Relations, 1996).

22. "Transatlantic Economic Partnership Action Plan," November 9, 1998, http://europa.eu.int/comm/dg01/1109tep.htm.

23. Christopher Stevens, "EU Policy for the Banana Market: The External Impact of Internal Policies," in Wallace and Wallace, eds., *Policy-Making in the European Union*, 325–351.

24. Paemen and Bensch, *From the GATT to the WTO*, 93.

25. Opinion 1/94, *Competence of the Community to conclude international agreements concerning services and the protection of international property*, ECR I-5267-I-5422 (1994–11/12).

26. Philip R. Schlesinger, "Europe's Contradictory Communicative Space," in *Daedalus* 123, no. 2 (1994) (*Europe Through a Glass Darkly*), 31.

27. Stephan Leibfried and Paul Pierson, "Semisovereign Welfare States: Social Policy in a Multitiered Europe," in Leibfried and Pierson, *European Social Policy*, cited in Dani Rodrik, *Has Globalization Gone Too Far?* (Washington: Institute for International Economics, 1997), 39.

28. Michael Smith et al., "Anything but agriculture," *Financial Times*, November 19, 1999.

29. Neil Buckley, "EU agrees position for trade talks," *Financial Times*, October 25, 1999.

30. Francis Williams, "Clinton is sympathetic to concerns," *Financial Times*, December 1, 1999.

31. C. Fred Bergsten, *Weak dollar, strong euro? The international impact of EMU* (London: Centre for European Reform, 1999), 15.

32. Article 111(3) TOR, ex Article 109(3).

33. I wish to thank C. Randall Henning for clarifying this point.

34. "The Past and Future of European Integration: A Central Banker's Perspective," 1999 Per Jacobsson Lecture, Washington, DC, September 26, 1999.

35. Stephen Fidler and Gillian Tett, "Summers urges more structural reforms," *Financial Times*, January 22–23, 2000.

Suggestions for Further Reading

Hayes, J. P. *Making Trade Policy in the European Community*. New York: St. Martin's Press, 1993.

Henning, C. Randall. *Cooperating with Europe's Monetary Union*, Washington: Institute for International Economics, May 1997.

Paemen, Hugo and Alexandra Bensch. *From the GATT to the WTO: The European Community in the Uruguay Round*. Leuven: Leuven University Press, 1995.

Peterson, John. *Europe and America: The Prospects for Partnership*. New York: Routledge, 1996.

Piening, Christopher. *Global Europe*. Boulder, CO: Lynne Rienner, 1997.

CHAPTER 9

Europe as a Global Actor
FOREIGN POLICY AND DEFENSE

The EU's emergence as a global economic power inevitably raises questions about its potential as a political and military power, able to defend its political and security interests with the same level of commitment and unity that it brings to the economic sphere. In the heady days after the collapse of communism, there was great optimism that following decades of security dependence on the United States, Europe could again become the master of its strategic destiny. The Maastricht Treaty established the Common Foreign and Security Policy as the second pillar of the EU and called for the creation of a European Security and Defense Identity.

For the most part, however, progress in the second pillar has been a disappointment to advocates of a stronger and more integrated Europe. The EU failed to resolve the crisis in the former Yugoslavia in the early 1990s and ended the decade still mired in Balkan conflicts. It was unable to arrest the economic crises in Russia and Ukraine, and it still plays only a limited role in the Middle East and other world regions. Recognition of the failures of CFSP led to reforms in the Amsterdam Treaty and to the development of new political and military structures that are intended to give the EU an autonomous capacity for military action. It remains unclear, however, whether institutional tinkering alone will be able to narrow the disparity between the EU's economic role and its political weight on the world scene. The EU member states continue to have different approaches to many international problems and have been unwilling so far to spend the money needed to develop the kinds of sophisticated military forces that the United States has maintained into the post-cold war period.

The Cold War Legacy

One of the reasons why the EU has had such difficulty in developing a strong CFSP is the legacy of the cold war and the long period of security dependence on the United States. Acceptance of this dependence was not foreordained. As was seen in Chapter 1, after World War II the West European countries took a number of steps toward political and security integration that did not involve the United States. In March 1947 Britain and France concluded the Treaty of Dunkirk in which they pledged to come to each other's defense if either was attacked by Germany. In March 1948 Britain, France, and the three Benelux countries signed the Treaty of Brussels that also contained a mutual defense clause and that provided for a standing consultative council of foreign ministers. In September of that year the five formed a Western Union Defense Organization to coordinate military planning. One objective of the Brussels treaty was to create a collective European framework that would encourage the United States to take a more active role in European security (much the way the OEEC facilitated American economic involvement in early postwar Western Europe), but it also served as a possible fallback against American disengagement.

At the time it was unclear whether the West European countries would be forced to fend for their own security or whether they would succeed in forming an alliance with the United States. The United States had withdrawn most of its troops from Europe after World War II and initially had no plans to depart from its long tradition of "no entangling alliances" by concluding a peacetime military alliance with its wartime allies. As the cold war deepened, however, views in Washington shifted. In April 1949 the United States, Canada, and nine European countries signed the Washington Treaty establishing the North Atlantic Alliance. The key provision of the treaty, Article 5, stated that an attack on one or more signatory states "shall be considered an attack against them all" and that in the event of such an attack the members would take actions deemed necessary, including the use of armed force. The treaty also provided for establishment of a council of member states and for regular consultations on issues of common concern.[1]

Communist North Korea's attack on the South took place in June 1950—a month after Schuman made his bold proposal for what became the European Coal and Steel Community—and led to three further developments that shaped the security order in Europe. First, fearing that war in Europe was imminent, the United States decided to rearm West Germany and to include it in some way in the Western alliance. Second, the alliance established the permanent peacetime command structure that became known as the integrated NATO military command and that took over the responsibilities of the Western Union Defense Organization. Third, in order to deter against a possible Soviet attack, the United States dramatically increased its military presence in Western Europe. General Dwight D. Eisenhower was appointed the first allied supreme commander and by 1952 the United States had raised its troop strength in Europe to 346,000 from a postwar low of 145,000.[2]

With the United States committed to the defense of Europe and to the rearming of West Germany, a key question became how to integrate a reviving German power in the Western alliance system. Initially, there was some hope that the structures of the ECSC could be extended and adapted to the defense realm. Had this hope been realized, Western Europe would have had a defense component from the very beginning of its integration process in the early 1950s. But Europe was unable to realize the plans for a European defense community at this time. As a result, NATO became the dominant security organization for the remainder of the cold war era. It was not until the Maastricht Treaty of the early 1990s that the European states again tackled the question of adding a security dimension to European integration.

Although the Korean War led many in the West to conclude that West German manpower was needed if there was to be a chance of stopping a Soviet attack in Europe, there was still great reluctance, especially in France, to see Germany rearm so soon after World War II. As in the case of the ECSC, French leaders saw integration as a way of tapping into German resources while ensuring that Germany would not emerge as an independent threat in the heart of Europe. In October 1950 French Prime Minister René Pleven proposed the establishment of a European army whose forces would be drawn from the six ECSC states. The Pleven Plan as such was not adopted, but it led to a follow-on proposal for a European Defense Community (EDC) with the same membership as the ECSC. Like the ECSC, the EDC was to be a supranational organization with its own common institutions and budget. A council of member states would oversee a supranational executive. The EDC and the ECSC would share the same parliamentary assembly. National military units would be retained up to the division level, but they would be commanded by an integrated general staff. The EDC would develop common equipment and infrastructures. The proposed European army would constitute the military contribution of the six powers to NATO and would operate within the NATO framework.

In May 1952 the six ECSC countries signed a treaty establishing the EDC and a European army. It soon became apparent, however, that the EDC was too ambitious for the Europe of the 1950s. Misgivings about the plan arose in all of the signatory states, but were strongest in France, where the Gaullists on the right and the communists on the left opposed submerging their national army in a supranational organization. In August 1954 the French National Assembly voted not to ratify the EDC treaty, effectively killing the project.

The collapse of the EDC project caused consternation in Bonn, Washington, and other Western capitals and led to a frantic search for an alternative security arrangement that would satisfy U.S. interest in German rearmament, French concerns about a revival of German power, and West Germany's own insistence on rough equality of status in the Western alliance. Adopting a proposal by British Prime Minister Anthony Eden, the West European governments agreed to a new arrangement under which West Germany and Italy acceded to the 1948 Brussels Treaty, making both countries members of a modified Western European Union (WEU). Under the terms of their accession to the WEU, both countries agreed to accept limits on their production of certain sophisticated conventional weapons and to forswear the development and possession of nuclear, chemical, or biological weapons. West Germany also became a member of NATO, and pledged to place its armed forces entirely under the NATO integrated command.

The WEU thus served as a legal mechanism for integrating West Germany into Western security structures. However, the WEU lost its original operational significance. The West European powers effectively abandoned their efforts to create a distinctly European military organization with a European military force. Military integration went ahead under NATO rather than European auspices, with the dominant role played by the United States. Security integration in Europe thus developed on a separate track from the intensive economic integration that had been launched by the six in the ECSC and that was soon followed by the EC and Euratom.

The Quest for a European Pillar

The failure of the six founding members of the ECSC to establish a European defense organization led back to a focus on economics and thus indirectly to the founding of the second and the third European Communities, the EC, and Euratom. Scarred by their experience with the EDC, the founding members steered clear of foreign and defense matters in the treaties of 1957. Indeed, Article 223 of the Treaty of Rome specifically exempted production and trade in arms, munitions, and war material from the strictures of the common market.[3]

To be sure, elements of a Community foreign policy were implicit in the Treaty of Rome. The treaty established a European Development Fund and provided for the conclusion of association agreements between the Community and third countries. Over time, the Community became involved in a wide range of activities with international implications, including trade and development assistance, humanitarian aid, international environmental matters, international transport and telecommunications policies, and, in Euratom, the implementation of safeguards against the spread of nuclear technologies to non-nuclear states. But these were all examples of what political scientists call "low politics"—spillovers from the Community's involvement in day-to-day economic life. Fundamental issues of war and peace, or "high politics," remained the province of the member states rather the Community.

The member states pursued rather different foreign policies, especially after de Gaulle's return to power in 1958. France became critical of American policy toward Europe and the global economy, and eventually withdrew from the NATO integrated command in 1966. West Germany and the other member states continued to align their foreign policies more closely with that of the United States. The Community and its member states thus faced what many saw as an increasingly anomalous situation: in some international forums, for example the GATT, the EC spoke with one voice, whereas in others the member countries went in different policy directions. While each member state preserved its diplomatic freedom of action, the EC as a whole lacked influence on the global stage because of its failure to develop a common foreign policy.

EUROPEAN POLITICAL COOPERATION

Prospects for foreign policy cooperation brightened in the late 1960s after de Gaulle's departure from politics and as the Community looked toward its first enlargement. At the Hague summit in December 1969 the leaders of the six asked the Community foreign ministers to prepare a report on progress towards "political unification." The foreign ministers concluded that "efforts ought first to concentrate specifically on the co-ordination of foreign policies in order to show the whole world that Europe has a political mission."[4] To that end, they recommended the launch of what became known as European Political Cooperation (EPC). They agreed to "consult on all questions of foreign policy" and where possible to undertake "common actions" on international problems. They further agreed that the Community foreign ministers would meet at least every six months and that a committee of political directors (the highest-ranking civil servants in each foreign ministry) would meet at least four times each year to prepare the ministerial meetings.

EPC took place outside the federal structures and institutions of the Community. The member states agreed as sovereign states to consult and if possible to arrive at common positions. They did not agree to pool sovereignty or to delegate decision-making authority to supranational institutions. The Commission and the Court of Justice thus did not have competence in foreign policy matters, making EPC a much weaker form of cooperation than that established in the economic sphere by the Treaty of Rome. It also did not extend to the security sphere. Countries such as West Germany, the Netherlands, and, after its accession in 1973, the United Kingdom were staunchly Atlanticist and wary lest any assertion of a European security identity be misconstrued in Washington and lead to a weakening of NATO. In addition, Ireland, which also joined the EC in 1973, was a neutral country certain to resist any move by the Community into the security sphere.

Externally, the member country holding the rotating presidency of the Council of Ministers became the official representative for EPC. To ensure continuity and to bolster the status of EPC when smaller member countries held the presidency, the EC developed the troika system, under which three countries jointly represented the Community: the presidency country and the countries that had previously held and that were next in line for the presidency. This meant, for example, that when the Community decided under EPC to deliver a protest over human rights or some other issue to a foreign government, the ambassadors from the three member states in the troika would go as a group to that country's foreign ministry to deliver the protest.

EPC led to some practical results in the 1970s. The governments of the six and later the nine member states issued joint statements on Cyprus, southern Africa, the Middle East, and other international problems and crises, thereby establishing a higher international political profile for Europe. EPC was used to coordinate member state policies in the thirty-five–nation Conference on Security and Cooperation in Europe (CSCE) that convened in 1973. It also was used to launch a Euro-Arab dialogue with the twenty member countries of the Arab League. Perhaps most important, EPC led to the development of a "European reflex" in national decision-making. Confronted by an international crisis or a new policy issue, member state foreign ministries learned to look to the other member states to share information and to ascertain how they intended to react.

Nonetheless, the results of EPC were in many ways disappointing. Most EPC actions were purely verbal—statements deploring or praising international developments—but without the economic, political, and military follow-up that is essential to translate words into foreign policy results. The troika system was useful in ensuring continuity in a system without a central decision-making body, but it tended to confuse foreign governments unable to deal with a single EPC representative. Moreover, major international crises tended to confirm that Europe remained divided over foreign policy matters. In the Arab-Israeli war of October 1973 and the ensuing Arab oil embargo, for example, the European states could not agree on a common policy, as each country scrambled to protect its own interests and its access to oil. The 1979 Soviet invasion of Afghanistan had similar results as, for example, West Germany followed the U.S. lead in boycotting the 1980 Moscow Olympics while the other member states chose to participate.

REFORM IN THE 1980s

Dissatisfaction with the results of EPC led to efforts in the 1980s to strengthen foreign policy coordination. In a report adopted at their meeting in London in October 1981, the EC foreign ministers called for EPC to become more anticipatory in its approach—to work towards shaping the international environment in desired directions rather than to react to crises after they occurred. They also agreed to extend the subject of EPC to "certain important foreign policy questions bearing on the political aspects of security."[5] This very cautious step into what traditionally had been the exclusive domain of NATO reflected a growing sense on the part of the member states that Europe needed to take greater responsibility for its own security.

The conclusion, in 1986, of the Single European Act marked a further step forward. Although best known as the agreement that launched the single market program, the act introduced important institutional reforms into the Community, one of which was the establishment of the EPC on a treaty basis. With its entering into force, the member states were bound by legal agreement rather than just a political commitment to consult together in the foreign policy sphere and to seek to develop common actions. The act did not, however, change the essentially intergovernmental nature of EPC. Responsibility for foreign policy remained with the member states and there was no transfer of decision-making powers to the central institutions of the Community.

The other major development of the 1980s was the partial revival of the WEU. As has been seen, the WEU played an important role in the 1940s in establishing security cooperation among the West European democracies and in the mid-1950s in integrating West Germany into NATO. However, once the United States became the dominant player in West European security affairs the WEU lost its original rationale. The Brussels Treaty remained in effect, but the WEU as an organization was virtually moribund by the 1970s. In October 1984 the seven members of the WEU, all of them also members of the Community and participants in EPC, decided to activate the WEU as a forum for discussion of security issues. They agreed to hold meetings of foreign and defense ministers every six months and to work to harmonize member state views on defense questions, arms control, East-West and transatlantic relations, and European armaments cooperation. An important advantage of the WEU, as seen by those countries most interested in developing a European defense identity, was that it did not include Denmark, Greece, and Ireland, EC member countries that had been most resistant to adding a security dimension to EPC. In October 1987 the WEU adopted the Hague Platform on European Security Interests. In 1987–1988 the WEU coordinated European participation in mine-sweeping operations in the Persian Gulf associated with the Iran-Iraq War. Portugal and Spain became members of the organization in 1988, strengthening its Mediterranean dimension and making WEU and EC membership nearly coterminous. In late 1991 and early 1992 the WEU helped to coordinate the enforcement by European naval units of UN sanctions in the Gulf following Iraq's seizure of Kuwait. After Greece announced its decision to join in 1992, Denmark (where WEU membership was complicated by the country's complex relations with Germany) and neutral Ireland were the only EC members that were not also members of the WEU.

CFSP

Despite the developments in EPC and the WEU, most of the member states remained dissatisfied with the level of cooperation Western Europe had managed to achieve in the realm of foreign and security policy. The Community's weaknesses in this area left it particularly badly positioned to try to shape the changes that were sweeping the communist world at the end of the 1980s. Foreign policy cooperation thus was high on the agenda of the 1991 IGC on political union.

France favored radical reforms that would allow the proposed Union to act independently of the United States if it chose to do so. Britain was satisfied with the level of foreign policy cooperation mandated in the SEA and was opposed to any "Europeanizing" of security that might offend the United States and damage NATO. As a neutral country, Ireland also was wary of introducing security into the European integration process. Germany tended to lean toward the French position, although like Britain it was cautious about damaging NATO and offending the United States.

The conference eventually hammered out a set of compromises among these different views. The Maastricht Treaty abolished EPC and replaced it with the CFSP, which became the second pillar of the new European Union. CFSP in turn was linked to the European Security and Defense Identity (ESDI) and a new and formal relationship between the EU and the WEU. The treaty specified five very general objectives for the CFSP: safeguarding the common values and interests of the Union; strengthening its security; preserving peace and strengthening international security in accordance with the principles of the UN Charter; promoting international cooperation; and developing and consolidating democracy and the rule of law and respect for human rights and fundamental freedoms.

Decision-making in the second pillar was to be largely intergovernmental, but the treaty broke new ground in giving the central institutions of the Union a role in foreign policy. The Commission was given the right to suggest actions under CFSP, although not a sole right of initiative as in the first pillar. The member states were given a co-equal right to make proposals under CFSP. CFSP decisions were not made subject to the jurisdiction of the Court of Justice. The treaty also stipulated that the EC budget could be used to underwrite CFSP actions by the Union. The European Council was charged with formulating general guidelines for the CFSP. On the basis of the guidelines, the Council of Ministers was expected to take decisions on concrete actions, generally by consensus. Externally, the presidency country was charged with representing the Union and the troika system was retained.

The EU member states were to pursue the objectives of CFSP by establishing a "systematic cooperation" in the field of foreign policy and by adopting joint actions in areas of common interest. The Maastricht Treaty thus built upon the provisions on EPC in the SEA, but it created a stronger legal commitment on the part of the member states to develop a common foreign policy. The member states were to consult with each other on matters of mutual interest and to ensure that national policies were in conformity with common positions of the Union. Following the practice already begun in EPC, they were to coordinate their positions in the UN and other international forums.

In what was potentially its most far-reaching change, the Maastricht Treaty stipulated that the CFSP "shall include all questions related to the security of the Union, including the eventual framing of a common defence policy, which might in time lead to a common defence."[6] This cautious and somewhat vague wording reflected a compromise among the member states. It left open the question of how long the "eventual" framing of a defense policy would take and whether this policy "in time" would be followed by a real common defense. The treaty further stated: "The Union requests the Western European Union (WEU), which is an integral part of the development of the Union, to elaborate and implement decisions and actions of the Union which have defence implications."[7] In a separate "Declaration on the Western European Union," the WEU member states identified specific ways in which the WEU would work with the EU (and with NATO) and outlined concrete steps that the WEU would take to upgrade its operational capabilities.[8] These included the establishment of a WEU planning cell, work towards the creation of a European armaments agency, establishment or designation of military units answerable to the WEU, and possible establishment of a European Security and Defense Academy.

The WEU Council of Ministers met again in Petersberg, Germany in June 1992 and issued a three-part declaration further clarifying the role of the WEU in

European security. The ministers reaffirmed the WEU's role as the defense component of the EU and as the strengthened European pillar of the Atlantic Alliance, called for further practical steps to improve coordination among the WEU, EU, and NATO, and declared that the WEU would be prepared to make forces available for conflict prevention or crisis management, such as peacekeeping activities of the UN or the CSCE.[9] Military measures short of collective defense against an external attack, including peacekeeping, rescue, and humanitarian relief missions, subsequently became known as the "Petersberg tasks," and were designated as an area in which Europe should be prepared to take full responsibility, if necessary without assistance from the United States.

These changes took place just as the EU was preparing to start enlargement talks with four EFTA countries, three of which—Austria, Finland, and Sweden—were neutral countries that were not members of NATO or the WEU. This raised concern on the part of some EU member states about an increased diversity of security outlooks in an enlarged Union and about these countries' neutrality becoming perhaps a permanent obstacle to the further development of the CFSP. These concerns were put to rest, at least for the time being, in November 1993, when the Belgian presidency, acting on behalf of the twelve, negotiated with the applicant countries a joint declaration on CFSP that was later annexed to their accession treaties. It stated that "the acceding states will from the time of their accession be ready and able to participate fully and actively in the CFSP," and that they accept without reservation the provisions of the Maastricht Treaty establishing the second pillar.[10] This meant that they accepted the WEU as "an integral part of the development of the Union," even though like existing EU member states Denmark and Ireland they were not members of this organization.

In January 1993 the seat of the WEU Council and Secretariat was transferred from London to Brussels to facilitate cooperation with the EU and NATO. A WEU Planning Cell staffed by about forty personnel headed by a general officer became operational in April 1993, following a formal decision by the WEU ministers in October 1992. A Center for the Interpretation of Satellite Data began operations at Torrejon, Spain in April 1993, following a decision by the WEU Council at the June 1991 ministerial meeting.[11] Little by little the EU was acquiring, through the WEU, its own defense identity and structures.

This process was slow and controversial, however, and was to be found wanting in the first great security crisis of the post-cold war era, the war in the former Yugoslavia. Already at Maastricht the member state governments recognized that many of the awkward compromises contained in the second pillar would have to be reevaluated and possibly renegotiated in the next intergovernmental conference. For this reason, the Maastricht Treaty contained specific language requiring the Council to review the security provisions of the treaty in a report to be presented in 1996 and identified the security-related aspects of CFSP as an item to be addressed in the IGC scheduled to convene in that year.

THE AMSTERDAM REFORMS

The weaknesses of the CFSP and above all the failure of the EU to deal with the crisis in the Balkans led to increasing pressures for reform as the post-Maastricht IGC approached. One of the key themes of the conference adopted by the European Council became "a strengthened capacity for external action of the Union."[12] When the conference convened in March 1996, much of the discussion focused on ways to strengthen the operational capabilities of the Union, an area in which CFSP had proven to be especially inadequate. France, Germany, and most of the other member states favored the complete merger of the EU and the WEU, but this was opposed by Britain and those EU countries that were not members of the WEU. The discussion also focused on the slow and cumbersome decision-making processes in CFSP and on the absence of a single individual who could represent EU policy to the outside world.

In response to these weaknesses, the Treaty of Amsterdam introduced several organizational reforms in the second pillar. In addition to the principles and general guidelines already mentioned in the Maastricht Treaty, the treaty added a clause giving the European Council the responsibility to decide on common strategies for the Union in areas where the member states have important interests in common. It did not bring about the merger of the EU and the WEU, but it strengthened the links between the two organizations and reemphasized the latter's role as the operational arm of the Union in CFSP. The treaty sharpened the language on the circumstances under and procedures by which the member states might adopt a common defense. In place of the vague and open-ended wording in the Maastricht Treaty, it stated that the European Council was empowered to decide upon the "progressive framing" of a common defense policy, in which case the member states would have to adopt "such a decision in accordance with their respective constitutional requirements."[13] The European Council was formally given the right to establish policy guidelines for the WEU. All member states agreed to participate as necessary in EU and WEU military actions relating to humanitarian and rescue tasks, peacekeeping, and crisis management or peacemaking operations. This was particularly significant for Austria, Finland, and Sweden, relatively new member states that as neutrals were not members of the WEU or NATO, but that had a long history of involvement in UN peacekeeping and humanitarian missions.

The most significant reform was the introduction of a new article on decision-making that was intended to stop the near paralysis on some foreign and security policy issues by providing a mechanism by which "coalitions of the willing" could take action under the EU umbrella using EU and WEU resources, but not necessarily involving all of the EU states. The treaty revisions still formally respected the unanimity procedures of the Council of Ministers in the CFSP, but member states were allowed to abstain and abstentions could not prevent a measure from being carried. A state that abstains can declare that it is not required to apply the decision—which might entail, for example, supplying troops or equipment to a particular military mission—but it must recognize the Union's commitment to the decision and is obliged, "in a spirit of mutual solidarity," to refrain from steps that conflict with or impede action by the Union. This new procedure should make it possible for the EU to act in crisis situations by sidestepping the unanimity problem that has long complicated decision-making in this area.

To address the problem of weak and disparate voices articulating the CFSP, the Amsterdam Treaty established a new post, High Representative for the CFSP, to be exercised by the secretary-general of the Council. The deputy secretary-general of the Council was made responsible for day-to-day tasks, including domestic affairs, while the High Representative is to function as the EU counterpart to the secretary-general of NATO or the UN. The treaty also abolished the old troika system and replaced it with a new troika consisting of the High Representative, the Council presidency (assisted by the country next in line), and the Commission.

In June 1999, a month after the Amsterdam Treaty went into effect, the member state governments selected Javier Solana, the then Secretary-General of NATO, to become the first CFSP High Representative. Solana assumed his post in October of that year. In the fall of 1999 he also was named the new Secretary-General of the WEU, a move that presaged the expected merger of that organization with the EU.

Defense in Europe

REFORMING NATO

The establishment of the CFSP took place more or less at the same time as the collapse of communism in Europe, and thus could not be separated from a parallel debate about the future of NATO that arose as the alliance's cold war rationale disappeared. As has been seen, one of the major points of contention at Maastricht was how far the EU should go in creating a defense identity that might be seen as an alternative to NATO. This debate soon was followed by another discussion about whether NATO should enlarge—and if so to which countries—and how the enlargement of NATO should relate to that of the EU.

When the Soviet alliance system began to fall apart, Moscow let it be known that it preferred to see both NATO and the Warsaw Pact dissolved or to have both organizations subsumed in a pan-European entity such as the CSCE. The West European states were intent on preserving their more than forty-year-old alliance with the United States and Canada and unanimously rejected such proposals. But even they had differences among themselves about the role of NATO once the Soviet threat had disappeared. As has been seen, France preferred to see a drastic downgrading of NATO's role relative to the EU and the WEU, while Britain took the opposite position. For its part, the United States was determined to preserve NATO through reform, adaptation, and ultimately expansion. As the 1990s unfolded, the failure of the EU to cope with the Yugoslav crisis on its own and the desire of the central and east European states to join NATO as insurance against a possible resurgence of Russian power helped to preserve the political centrality of NATO. Over the long run, however, its future remains uncertain. How far and how fast the EU goes in developing a security identity apart from the alliance with the United States remains unsettled.

The reform of NATO began at the June 1990 London summit, when the leaders of the alliance declared that NATO was prepared to turn to the countries of central and eastern Europe and "extend to them the hand of friendship." At the November 1991 Rome summit the members of the alliance agreed to a new strategy document that eliminated all references to a specific enemy in the east and identified instability as the new danger confronting the alliance. These changes were part of the diplomatic maneuvering that preceded the unification of Germany, and were designed to make the membership of a united Germany in NATO (and the concomitant loss of the GDR from the Soviet security sphere) more palatable to Soviet leader Gorbachev and his domestic critics.

While NATO undertook these initial reforms, U.S. officials kept a wary eye on the security discussions in the IGC on political union. At one point in the negotiations, the U.S. Department of State sent a demarche to the eleven NATO members of the EC in which it indicated that the United States supported a stronger European foreign and security policy but that it opposed the formation of a European caucus within NATO that would present the United States with a unified European position. From the European perspective, the U.S. intervention was heavy-handed and self-contradictory, since it was difficult to see how a European pillar could be formed within NATO without the Europeans being able to concert their policy outside the NATO forum. In the end, the United States professed to be satisfied with the Maastricht arrangements, and the CFSP provisions of the treaty contained a passage stating that EU policy would respect "the obligations of certain Member States under the North Atlantic Treaty and be compatible with the common security and defence policy established within that framework."[14]

Nonetheless, tensions between the EU and the United States, and especially between Paris and Washington, ran high in the early 1990s as both sides seemed to pursue different and incompatible visions of Europe's future security order. In the end, what helped to save the alliance and to defuse these tensions was the crisis in the former Yugoslavia. The prolonged and bloody impasse with Serbian President Slobodan Milosevic convinced the European powers that they needed more rather than less U.S. involvement in the security affairs of the continent, while it helped to convince the United States of the advantages of a stronger European security organization that could take responsibility for crises in Europe in which the United States might not want to become involved. The humanitarian and peacekeeping operations in the former Yugoslavia also gave NATO, the EU, WEU, OSCE, and national bureaucracies concrete tasks that helped to divert attention from and defuse abstract debate over the relative importance of European versus transatlantic security institutions.

Following up on the WEU's June 1992 Petersberg Declaration, the leading West European powers began reconfiguring their military forces so that they could operate either under WEU or NATO command (or both). In January 1994 NATO further agreed to the concept of the Combined Joint Task Force (CJTF), under which NATO equipment and infrastructure could be used for certain non-NATO missions.[15] In June 1996 the allies took a further step toward resolving transatlantic defense tensions by agreeing, in the Berlin communiqué, that NATO might in future facilitate WEU military operations by making NATO assets available for approved WEU operations.[16]

The other major development that bolstered the relevance of NATO in the late 1990s was enlargement. The central and east European democracies began pressing for NATO membership soon after the collapse of Soviet power. Along with admission to the EU, they saw membership as a way of bolstering their own internal reforms and of gaining insurance against a possible resurgence of Russian power. The United States and its allies initially were reluctant to expand the alliance, which was seen as unnecessarily provocative to the Russians and in any case irrelevant to the primarily economic and political problems of transition facing these countries. In 1994 the United States proposed—and NATO quickly adopted—a Partnership for Peace (PfP) program under which non-NATO member countries could cooperate with the alliance on military activities ranging from joint training exercises, exchanges of personnel, and various other forms of cooperation. At least initially, PfP was seen by many as a way for NATO to reach out to the central and east European countries without offering membership.

But under pressure from domestic lobbies and leaders such as Czech President Vaclav Havel and President Lech Walesa of Poland, the United States as the leading power in the alliance gradually moved toward embracing full membership for at least a subset of the former Warsaw Pact countries.[17] This decision provoked controversy in Europe and the United States, as politicians and experts debated the timing and sequencing of EU and NATO enlargement and the relationship between these two processes. Two days before the December 1994 Essen European Council meeting at which the EU outlined its pre-accession strategy for central and eastern Europe, outgoing Commission president Delors characterized early NATO enlargement as "premature and ill-timed."[18] According to Delors, "I would have advised the United States not to propose an enlargement of the Atlantic Alliance now as this will, I believe, complicate firming relations between the United States, the European Union, and Russia." Delors was expressing a view heard in some parts of Europe that NATO expansion was not the real answer to the security problems of the continent and explainable largely in terms of U.S. domestic politics and perhaps a desire by the United States to undercut the EU by redirecting attention to NATO and the transatlantic security dimension. Such views were by no means universally shared, however, and there was little desire in European capitals to resist Washington on this matter. In Germany, in fact, Defense Minister Volker Ruehe strongly supported the integration of especially Poland and the Czech Republic into NATO, which would mean that the United

States would guarantee Germany's eastern neighbors, thereby ending once and for all the front-line status that Germany had occupied throughout the cold war.

At the 1997 Madrid summit the sixteen NATO members invited three countries—Poland, Hungary, and the Czech Republic—to negotiate treaties of accession to the alliance. These countries formally acceded to the Washington Treaty in March 1999, just in time for the NATO 50th anniversary celebrations in Washington the following month. NATO also developed agreements and instruments, including special charters with Russia and Ukraine and a continuation of the PfP program, to facilitate cooperation between the alliance and those former communist countries that were not yet—and might never be—members of the alliance, even as it reaffirmed its commitment to further enlargement involving new candidate countries.[19] But the question of how far and how fast enlargement would proceed remained unanswered at the time of the Washington celebrations, and was in any case soon overshadowed by a new crisis in the Balkans and intensified discussions over the extent to which the EU needed to develop its own security mechanisms, linked to but outside the NATO framework.

ESDI

The WEU declaration on CFSP attached to the Maastricht Treaty stated: "WEU Member States agree on the need to develop a genuine European security and defense identity and a greater European responsibility for defense matters."[20] ESDI subsequently became a general phrase to denote the envisioned defense arm of the EU, to be constructed through successive phases by the WEU. Genuine progress toward ESDI was painfully slow, however, chiefly as a result of three factors: (1) lingering differences among the EU and WEU member states about the role of NATO and cooperation with the United States and about how far Europe should go in asserting an identity separate from the United States; (2) differences among the member states about the use of force in international politics—in effect different views about the fundamental rationale for a defense identity; and (3) limited financial and material resources to actually give substance to an ESDI. In the course of the 1990s the first two of these obstacles seemed to diminish, as attitudes in the member states about transatlantic relations and the use of force converged. The third obstacle—inadequate resources—loomed as large as ever at the end of the decade, as European countries continued to cut military expenditures and to miss out on the high-technology "revolution in military affairs" underway in the United States.

As has been seen, Britain long opposed defense cooperation in Europe that took place outside the NATO framework and that might give offense to Washington. France pursued the opposite policy, consciously seeking to build a European defense identity as a way of diminishing NATO's role and U.S. influence on the continent. The other EU countries were ranged between the British and French positions. These differences narrowed in the course of the 1990s, as France moderated its stance under the pressure of events in the former Yugoslavia and as the United States itself came to embrace a stronger and more autonomous European defense identity. Most importantly, the British government under Prime Minister Tony Blair modified its previous position on ESDI, coming to accept a strong European defense component as important for British national interests and compatible with a strong NATO.

The crisis in the former Yugoslavia pointed up the persistence of different national traditions with regard to the use of force in international relations. France and Britain are former great powers with long military traditions and residual global territories and interests. They have not been averse to using force overseas to protect those interests, as Britain showed in the 1982 Falkland Islands war and France demonstrated over the years by its repeated interventions in Africa. But most of the other European countries have faced stronger domestic constraints on their ability to use force as an instrument of foreign policy. In Germany, several of the major political parties long took the view that the Federal Republic's constitution, adopted after World War II to ensure a peaceful Germany, banned the deployment of German troops outside the country.

But just as the crisis in the former Yugoslavia helped to unify the key EU states on the need to develop a stronger European defense identity, it contributed toward a certain convergence of views on the use of force for political ends by propelling Germany into an active military role. In December 1996 the German parliament finally broke the taboo on Bundeswehr participation in out-of-area operations by voting overwhelmingly to contribute 3,000 German troops to the NATO-led stabilization force in Bosnia. A little more than two years later, Germany was a major contributor to the 1999 NATO war against Yugoslavia, as German Tornado aircraft joined those of France, the UK, and the United States in attacking targets in Serbia and Kosovo. Italy and the Netherlands also contributed to the war effort. The non-NATO members of the Union did not participate in the war, but they did not oppose NATO or EU policy, and they contributed to the postwar peacekeeping activities that fall under the rubric of the Petersberg tasks.

There was less progress in the 1990s on overcoming the third major obstacle to a stronger European defense component, inadequate military resources. The crisis in the former Yugoslavia highlighted Western Europe's military weaknesses and demonstrated that without U.S. help the EU could not mount large-scale military operations even in its own backyard, much less in more distant regions such as the Persian Gulf. EU countries spent too little on defense, and much of what they did spend contributed little to the capabilities needed to make ESDI a reality. In the late 1990s the EU member states had over 2.4 million personnel in their armed forces compared with some 1.45 million in the United States. Collectively they allocated some $173 billion each year to defense, or about 60 percent of the U.S. total.[21] But too large a share of this spending was for manpower and not enough for purchasing new equipment or for effective research and development. Defense industry was fragmented, resulting in wasteful duplication of effort across defense establishments. A large share of French and UK defense spending went to maintaining national nuclear weapons capabilities.

During the cold war, NATO forces were directed against the threat from the Warsaw Pact. They were relatively stationary, tank-heavy armies designed to counter an armored attack from the east. To respond to new challenges and to give Europe a capability to act independently of the United States, the European powers need to invest in reconnaissance satellites, strategic airlift, and other capabilities that either were not needed or that were provided by the United States during the cold war. Restructuring Western Europe's military forces and buying new mobility-enhancing capabilities proved difficult in the 1990s, however, as overall levels of defense spending declined as governments and parliaments responded to a reduced perception of threat and as the EU countries concentrated on meeting the EMU convergence criteria for budgetary discipline.

THE COLOGNE AND HELSINKI DECISIONS

The Kosovo crisis, the new British attitude toward European defense under Blair, and the entering into effect of the Treaty of Amsterdam with its strengthened security provisions all combined in the first half of 1999—under the German EU and WEU presidency—to produce new momentum toward a strengthened CFSP with a real security component. Britain signaled its long-awaited shift on CFSP at the informal European Council meeting in Pörtschach in late October 1998, at which Blair called for "fresh thinking" on European defense cooperation and mentioned different institutional options, including possible full merger of the WEU into the EU, a step previously opposed by the UK. In early December Blair and French President Chirac issued their pathbreaking "Declaration on European Defense" at their meeting in St. Malo. It stated that the EU "must have the capacity for autonomous action, backed up by credible military forces, the means to decide to use them and a readiness to do so in order to respond to international crises."[22] It stressed "full and rapid implementation of the Amsterdam provisions on CFSP," including "the responsibility of the European Council to decide on the progressive framing of a common defence policy in the framework of CFSP."

The first-ever meeting of EU defense ministers occurred in November 1998 during the Austrian presidency. It was followed in early December by the first-ever meeting between an EU Council president, in this case Austrian Foreign Minister Wolfgang Schüssel, and the NATO Secretary-General. At its Vienna session in December, the European Council welcomed the St. Malo developments and called upon the Council to develop specific proposals for operationalizing the provisions in the Treaty of Amsterdam regarding closer EU-WEU cooperation, to be examined at the Cologne summit in June 1999.

The Kosovo crisis subsequently added a sense of urgency to the preparations for the Cologne decisions. At their Bremen meeting in May 1999 the WEU defense ministers set an informal 18-month deadline for concrete progress toward a

European defense identity, meaning that key decisions could be taken under the French presidency at the end of 2000. Incoming Commission president Romano Prodi told interviewers that a "logical next step" for CFSP would be the creation of an EU army, and suggested that the alternative would be "to be marginalised in the new world history."[23] Meeting in Brussels at the end of the month, the EU foreign ministers finalized many of the details concerning the eventual absorption of the WEU by the EU.

The Cologne European Council adopted the report prepared by the foreign ministers, endorsing the general goal of abolishing the WEU by the end of 2000 and transferring its capabilities to the EU.[24] Under plans to be worked out by the member state governments and incorporated in subsequent agreements, the EU was set to establish a permanent, Brussels-based political and security committee and an EU military committee consisting of military representatives that would make recommendations to the political and security committee. It also would convene regular and ad hoc meetings of defense ministers and would take over the WEU planning cell, situation center, and satellite center. The WEU treaty containing mutual security obligations among the signatory states would remain in effect, but the WEU itself would cease to exist as an organization.

With the WEU set to disappear, NATO also began to define itself more directly in relation to the EU. Its revised strategy document issued at the April 1999 Washington summit declared NATO's readiness "to define and adopt the necessary arrangements for ready access by the European Union to the collective assets and capabilities of the Alliance, for operations in which the Alliance as a whole is not engaged militarily as an Alliance."[25] The North Atlantic Council was tasked with finding ways to provide assured EU access to NATO planning capabilities, ensuring the availability to the EU of pre-identified capabilities and common assets, and further adapting NATO's defense planning system to prepare for possible EU-led operations. The United States endorsed the developments in the EU, but there was lingering concern in Washington about a too-independent European defense stance, its possible effects on NATO, and its implications for the two non-EU European NATO members, Norway and Turkey.

Notwithstanding the concerns expressed in Washington and the unresolved issue of how the European countries, most of which continued to cut defense budgets, would pay for the improved capabilities, as the decade ended the EU pressed on with plans to create a more autonomous military stance. At the December 1999 Helsinki summit the European Council adopted a report by the Finnish presidency calling for the establishment of a 50,000–60,000 person military force that would be able, by 2003, to deploy within sixty days and be sustained for at least one year, capable of carrying out the full range of Petersberg tasks.[26] To ensure the necessary political guidance and strategic direction for EU-led operations, the summit called for the establishment, as envisioned in the Cologne decisions, of new political and military bodies that would operate within the framework of the Council of Ministers. They included a standing Political and Security Committee (PSC) in Brussels, a Military Committee, and a Military Staff. These bodies were established on an interim basis in February 2000, pending a possible revision of the treaties to define their place in the EU institutional framework. (The role of the various EU institutions in making foreign political and economic policy is summarized in Box 9.1.)

At Helsinki and in subsequent declarations, the EU and its member states emphasized that the new Common Policy on Security and Defense (or CPSD as it was dubbed, replacing the old ESDI) was not a threat to NATO—that EU-led military operations in response to international crises would be launched only when NATO as a whole was not engaged, that unnecessary duplication of forces would be avoided, and that modalities would be developed for full consultation and cooperation between the EU and NATO. There could be little doubt, however, that the Helsinki decisions represented a real effort by the EU to acquire options independent of the United States—something that did not go unnoticed in Washington and that was disturbing to those U.S. policy circles that remained deeply attached to NATO as the chief means by which the United States had related to Western Europe during the cold war.

CAPABILITIES AND COSTS

With the EU moving toward closer defense cooperation based on new institutions and decision-making processes, the most important remaining obstacle to Europe's developing as a serious defense community with autonomous capabilities is its low level of defense spending, especially as it relates to procurement and research and development. As one defense expert noted, "unless defense expenditure is allowed substantially to increase, the build-up of a serious defense capability will remain the stuff of communiqués."[27]

In 1985, when the Soviet military threat was still very real, the European members of NATO devoted an average of 3 percent of GDP to defense, compared with 6.5 percent by the United States. By 1998, spending as a share of GDP had fallen to just over 2 percent, with Germany sinking to just 1.5 percent.[28] U.S. defense spending also had declined, but from a much higher base and with far greater restructuring to save on costs. Moreover, while U.S. spending turned up again at the end of the decade, European defense budgets continued to shrink as EU countries struggled to meet the fiscal criteria of the Maastricht Treaty and the Growth and Stability Pact.

The Cologne and Helsinki decisions did not address the problem of defense expenditures and will not in themselves ensure that Europe buys the requisite equipment and forces needed to make the CPSD a reality. Incorporating defense into the EU could make it easier for member states to maintain and perhaps increase their national defense spending, particularly if the EU adopts convergence criteria for such spending modeled on the successful convergence process that preceded the launch of the euro. Led by France, several member states have endorsed such an approach.

Box 9.1   EU External Policy—Who Does What (Economics and Politics)

European Council

Defines principles and general guidelines for CFSP; decides on common strategies to be implemented by the Union.

Council of Ministers

Meeting usually as the *General Affairs Council* (the foreign ministers), the Council of Ministers adopts joint actions and common positions and takes other decisions necessary to implement the CFSP on the basis of general guidelines.

Meeting as *ECOFIN*, the Council formulates general guidelines for exchange rate policy affecting the euro.

The Council authorizes the Commission to conduct negotiations on trade and other matters covered by the Common Commercial Policy. The *133 Committee* oversees these negotiations on a continuous basis.

The *Presidency country* presents EU CFSP positions to other governments and in international organizations and at international conferences.

The *Secretary-General of the Council, High Representative for CFSP* assists the Council in the development of CFSP, assists the Presidency with external representation, and formulates and prepares CFSP position papers.

The *Political and Security Committee* (PSC) is composed of national representatives at senior or ambassadorial level, permanently based in Brussels. It deals with all aspects of CFSP, including political control and strategic direction of military operations under the control of the Council.

The *Military Committee* is composed of chiefs of defense, represented by military delegates. It provides military advice and makes recommendations to the PSC, as well as provides military direction to the Military Staff.

The *Military Staff* provides military expertise and support to the CSDP. It performs early warning, strategic assessment, and strategic planning for the Petersberg tasks.

Commission

The Commission has the exclusive right of initiative on first-pillar legislative matters, including those with international implications. It shares a right of initiative with the member states with regard to CFSP.

The *Commissioner for External Affairs* coordinates the external relations activities of the Commission. This includes interfacing with the General Affairs Council and the High Representative for CFSP. The commissioner oversees the External Relations Directorate, which handles the Commission's involvement in bilateral relations with countries around the world and the Commission's involvement in CFSP, oversees the 120 Commission offices outside the EU, and administers EU aid to the countries of the Balkans and the former Soviet Union.

The *Commissioner for Trade* is responsible for multilateral trade negotiations in the WTO and OECD (under Council of Ministers mandate and with oversight by the 133 Committee), and for trade policy instruments such as anti-dumping and anti-subsidy measures.

(Continues)

(Continued)

The *Commissioner for Enlargement* oversees the Enlargement Directorate, which helps to prepare the candidate countries for membership, administers PHARE and other pre-accession aid, and assists the Council of Ministers and the Presidency with the enlargement negotiations.

The *Commissioner for Development and Humanitarian Aid* oversees development cooperation with the African, Caribbean and Pacific (ACP) countries, EU overseas territories, and South Africa; oversees EU humanitarian and disaster relief aid distributed by the European Community Humanitarian Organization (ECHO).

Other Commissioners have primarily intra-EU reponsibilities, but often make decisions with international implications (e.g., the Commissioner for Transport with regard to international aviation agreements; the Competition Commissioner concerning anti-trust cases involving U.S. multinationals; the Commissioner for Environment regarding UN climate-change conventions.)

European Parliament

Approves budgetary allocations for external action; approves association agreements; approves admission of new member states.

European Central Bank

Responsible for foreign exchange operations involving the euro; represents euro-area in G-7, IMF, and other international fora.

Fundamentally, however, there are powerful external and internal factors working against a shift toward substantially higher military expenditure. Externally, the EU does not face a military threat comparable to that posed by the Warsaw Pact during the cold war. Instability in the Balkans and the former USSR constitutes a threat, but it is of a lesser order and in any case calls as much for economic and political interventions as military responses. Europe could face more serious threats from a resurgent Russia or from weapons of mass destruction in the Middle East, but these are longer-term dangers that politicians are reluctant to highlight and that in any case could lead as much to a revitalization of NATO and a tendency to lean more on the United States as to a stronger push for an EU defense capability.

Internally, the EU member states lack the political motivation to make defense a high priority. France values its autonomy and has a long tradition of seeking to assert its independence from the United States, but such sentiments find little political resonance in most other European countries, where publics seem content with the status quo and where pacifist, anti-military sentiment is strong. The outlook for a major upsurge in defense spending thus is quite limited, absent the appearance of an immediate external threat that might galvanize Europe into action.

DEFENSE INDUSTRY

The question of costs and capabilities cannot be separated from the fate of defense industry in Europe. European leaders have argued that by consolidating defense industry on a European scale to make it more efficient and cost effective, Europe may be able to achieve economies of scale that will result in greater defense capabilities at current or only modestly increased levels of funding. They also argue that a stronger European defense industrial base will help to sustain a domestic political constituency for defense spending. European governments also have renewed their longstanding calls for the establishment of a genuine "two-way street" in which Europe will sell far more defense hardware to the United States than it does at present.

Throughout the cold war, European countries cooperated with each other on some weapons projects, but they also were free to pursue purely national solutions to armament needs or to buy U.S. weapons. Efforts at defense industrial collaboration were marked by high overhead costs, inefficiency, and delays caused by differences among the collaborating countries about the specifications of particular weapons systems. There were a few notable successes, such as the Tornado combat aircraft built by Germany, Italy, and the UK, but they came at high financial cost. One of the main sources of inefficiency in European defense projects has been the strict application of *juste retour*—the principle that shares of development and production work on a particular aircraft or ship or missile must be apportioned to the various national industries according to how much of the project is paid for by each partner. This meant loss of time in haggling over which company was responsible for what subsystems and components and often resulted in firms being chosen to develop and produce subsystems or components not because they were the best qualified, but as the result of political maneuvering. It also tended to stifle competition, as national firms were guaranteed a share of work on collaborative projects regardless of their price or technical competitiveness.

European defense ministries and firms observed with alarm the post–cold war consolidation of U.S. defense industry and the establishment through mergers of a handful of industry giants such as Lockheed Martin and Boeing. In response, they began to strengthen Europe's defense industrial base through cooperation and some modest steps toward consolidation. In December 1992 the WEU member states agreed to establish a Western European Armaments Group (WEAG) within the WEU to strengthen armaments cooperation. In 1995 WEAG established an executive organ, the Western European Armaments Organization, to manage cooperative R&D projects and to promote a common arms procurement policy.

The CFSP provisions of the Amsterdam Treaty also called for stronger cooperation in the field of armaments production. The treaty did not, however, repeal Article 223 of the Treaty of Rome (Article 296 in the Amsterdam renumbering) exempting defense production from the provisions of the treaty, such as the European Commission had proposed. Had the Commission's campaign for repeal of this article been successful, it would have brought defense production under EU trade, competition, research and development, and single market provisions and would have created one path, at least, toward a stronger European defense industry. But this was unacceptable to the larger member states, who were unwilling to surrender so much control over defense industry to Brussels. Instead, the leading military powers in the EU followed the more cautious path of intergovernmental cooperation, both in WEAG and in ad hoc bilateral and multilateral arrangements. In November 1996 France, Germany, Italy, and the UK established a new Joint Armaments Cooperation Agency (JACA) to coordinate development and production of major weapons systems.

Cross-border consolidation at the company level also got underway. In December 1997 the defense ministers of France, Germany, and the UK jointly instructed their leading defense and aerospace companies—British Aerospace, Daimler-Benz Aerospace (Dasa) of Germany, and France's Aerospatiale—to draw up plans to form a unified European defense industry giant. These companies (along with Casa of Spain) were the partners in the Airbus Industrie consortium that manufactures civilian aircraft and thus already had much experience in working together on high-technology projects. The privately owned British and German groups were reluctant to cooperate with the state-owned Aerospatiale, but this obstacle to pan-European cooperation was partly removed when the French government announced plans to sell the majority of its holdings in the company to private investors. Aerospatiale subsequently merged with a non-state-owned French missile and defense company, Matra, to form Aerospatiale Matra. Leading companies in Italy, Spain, and Sweden also announced that they hoped to become part of a new, Europe-wide aerospace and defense company.

British Aerospace subsequently opted out of the pan-European merger by purchasing the defense division of another British company to become BAe Systems, an all-British company with strong subsidiaries in the United States. But in October 1999 Aerospatiale Matra and Dasa (by that time DaimlerChrysler Aerospace, following the merger of Chrysler and Daimler-Benz) merged to form a new company, the European Aeronautics, Defense and Space Company (EADS). In December of the same year, Germany, France, and Spain signed an agreement under which Casa also was merged into EADS. The political and commercial motivation for forming this new defense giant was to create a firm that could compete as well as partner with the leading U.S. defense companies. With annual revenues of over $22 billion and capabilities in aircraft, helicopters, missiles, space, and defense electronics, EADS is the world's third-largest defense company, after Lockheed Martin and Boeing.

The success of the new company will depend on how well it does in integrating its component firms into a more cost-efficient and technologically stronger whole. Equally important, its success and that of the other remaining European defense firms will depend on the funding environment in which they operate. If defense spending in Europe continues to fall as it did in the 1990s, it is difficult to see how even highly streamlined and efficient European firms will be able to secure the level of orders needed to sustain the R&D and production capabilities for the next generations of military equipment. Contrary to the arguments advanced by political leaders, low defense spending is a cause of weakness in the European defense industry sector, not its result. Nor is the "two-way street" a panacea for Europe's defense dilemmas. The Pentagon is unlikely to reverse fundamentally its longstanding opposition to dependence on foreign firms for critical weapons systems. Moreover, U.S. officials argue that precisely because the United States has continued to invest heavily in defense, U.S. firms are more capable and produce more sophisticated equipment. Further defense industry consolidation—including even transatlantic mergers and acquisitions—can be expected, but in themselves these industrial reshufflings will not eliminate the need to spend more money to acquire added capability.

CFSP in Action

The discussion so far has focused on the debate among the European powers over the need for a common foreign policy, the modest progress they have made in achieving such a policy, and the parallel debate on security and defense and the even more limited progress that they have made in that area. Critics of the EU have grown weary of the seemingly endless discussion of institutions and have asked fundamental questions about the purpose of EU policy. What must or should the EU try to accomplish internationally that requires it to have a CFSP? What, in other words, should be the substance rather than the institutional form of a foreign and security policy?

Since Maastricht, the EU itself has attempted to answer these questions. The Maastricht Treaty established five objectives for the CFSP that are repeated, in slightly modified form, in the Treaty of Amsterdam. These objectives are very general, however, and do not offer guidelines for specific foreign policy actions. European political leaders recognized this already at the time of the 1991 Maastricht summit, where they asked the Council of Ministers to prepare, for the June 1992 Lisbon session of the European Council, a report identifying regional priorities for the CFSP.

The Lisbon report singled out two groups of countries as priority regions for EU foreign policy: the formerly communist countries of central and eastern Europe and the Maghreb and the Middle East.[29] In other words, it recommended that the emphasis in CFSP be on the arc of instability to the east and south of the EU. Following the pattern already partly established under EPC, it suggested that the EU become more active and anticipatory toward these regions—that it work to head off political and economic crises with potential implications for EU security by dealing with such underlying problems as poverty and unemployment, intraregional ethnic and religious tensions, environmental decay, and the absence of democratic institutions and guarantees of civil and political rights. The ministers' report was formally adopted by the European Council in Lisbon and became the main operational guideline for the CFSP in its formative years. With some modifications and shifts in emphasis, the Lisbon priorities have remained the basis for the CFSP and are reflected in the common strategies adopted by the EU under the new provisions of the Treaty of Amsterdam.

Following the June 1993 Copenhagen decisions on enlargement, policy toward those countries of central and eastern Europe that were eligible for EU membership increasingly was subsumed under the pre-accession strategy aimed at preparing them for membership—a subject that is discussed in the next chapter.

CFSP as such thus came to focus on three other regions—the Balkans, the Newly Independent States (NIS) of the former Soviet Union, and the Mediterranean countries of North Africa and the Middle East. In addition to the Lisbon priority areas, CFSP has enabled the EU to pursue a more active policy toward more distant regions, including the United States, East Asia, Latin America, and sub-Saharan Africa.

The Balkans

THE BREAKUP OF YUGOSLAVIA

Policy toward the former Yugoslavia was the first major test for the CFSP and one that most European political leaders acknowledge that it failed. The crisis in this region erupted in June 1991 when two of the six Yugoslav republics, Slovenia and Croatia, declared independence from the Serbian-dominated federation. The Yugoslav army moved into Slovenia, provoking clashes between federal forces and the Slovenians. Austria, which shares a common border with Slovenia, called for CSCE intervention. Throughout the summer of 1991 there were further clashes involving federal and Croatian forces and ethnic Serbs living in Croatia and the newly formed Croatian army.

At the time, the governments of the twelve EC member states were preoccupied with negotiating the Maastricht Treaty and still digesting the implications of German unity, as well as concerned about developments in the USSR, where Gorbachev was losing his grip on power and ethnically based tensions were mounting. Nevertheless, this was a time of great optimism for Western Europe. The soon-to-be-formed European Union appeared set to play a new role on the world stage and perhaps the decisive role in European affairs. In June 1991 Luxembourg Foreign Minister Jacques Poos, representing the Council of Ministers, made his famous statement, "This is the hour of Europe, not the hour of the United States."[30]

In the summer of 1991 the Community seized the initiative on the Yugoslav crisis, jointly convening with the UN the Hague conference on Yugoslavia to discuss a negotiated ceasefire and a compromise peace plan for an association of sovereign Yugoslav republics. The twelve sent observers to the region and pressured the Serbs to accept the EC peace plan or to face economic sanctions. At the request of the European Council, the WEU began drawing up plans for a possible peacekeeping operation involving European troops. The United States supported these efforts, but it was unwilling to become involved directly in the crisis.

Over the course of the next several years the EU was much chastened by events in the former Yugoslavia, as it failed to impose a peace settlement and at times was unable to maintain its own unity in the face of the escalating conflict. The EU ultimately emerged from the Yugoslav crisis with its self-confidence damaged, its credibility as a foreign policy actor eroded, and with a much more sober view of its ability to act decisively to resolve international crises—even on its own periphery. The first major disagreement among the member states was over whether to recognize Croatia and Slovenia following their unilateral declarations of independence. Germany, which had close historic ties with Croatia and a large Croatian minority living inside its borders, pressed for immediate recognition. France and Britain traditionally had had closer ties with Serbia and were concerned that recognition of the post-Yugoslav states would inflame rather than dampen the conflict. At the December 1991 meeting of the Council of Ministers, the Community foreign ministers collectively decided to establish diplomatic relations with the two new states, but this was largely in response to German pressure and because they knew that Germany, CFSP commitments notwithstanding, was prepared to act unilaterally.[31]

Meanwhile, fighting intensified as Serbian forces besieged the Croatian cities of Zadar, Dubrovnik, and Vukovar and bombed the capital Zagreb—actions that were widely seen on European television and demonstrated to the public both the brutality of the conflict and the apparent failure of Europe's diplomatic efforts. As tensions mounted, the international community agreed to establish the UN Protection Force (UNPROFOR) to help maintain peace and later to provide security for the relief efforts directed at the growing number of refugees and displaced persons. The EU countries provided half of UNPROFOR's 25,000 soldiers, with the largest contingents supplied by France and Britain. The United States did not commit ground forces, which soon became a point of contention within the Atlantic alliance.

THE WAR IN BOSNIA

As stability returned to Croatia and Slovenia in the course of 1992, the focus of the conflict shifted to Bosnia-Herzegovina, the most ethnically and religiously diverse of the six former Yugoslav republics. After Bosnia declared independence from Yugoslavia in March 1992, the Serbian minority in the country declared its independence from Bosnia and formed its own mini-state, closely allied with Serbia proper, and an army that was heavily supported by the Yugoslav federal (i.e., Serbian) army. The Bosnian Serbs then began a program of "ethnic cleansing" in which non-Serbian citizens were killed or driven out of their villages. By the end of 1992 the self-styled Republic of Srpska, covertly assisted by the Yugoslav army, had seized 70 percent of the territory of Bosnia and had established a blockade of the capital of Sarajevo. Over a million Bosnians fled their homes to avoid the fighting. Most found refuge in camps located elsewhere in Bosnia or in other parts of the former Yugoslavia, but many made their way to Western Europe. Germany alone took in over 200,000 Bosnian refugees and displaced persons in the course of the conflict.

The EU countries (along with the United States) recognized Bosnia in April 1992, even as they continued to press for a diplomatic solution to the conflict among the Serbs, Croats, and Muslims living in Bosnia. In August 1992 the EU and the UN convened another peace conference, this time in London under the UK presidency, aimed at finding a negotiated solution to the Bosnian crisis. Following detailed discussions among the warring parties throughout the fall of 1992, in January 1993 the EU and UN mediators, David Owen and Cyrus Vance, put forward a peace plan based on a confederal solution. Bosnia would be divided into three autonomous regions—Muslim, Serb, and Croat—which would be loosely united in a single state. All three parties rejected this solution, however, and the war continued, punctuated by televised atrocities, usually although not exclusively linked to the Serbs, that increased worldwide revulsion to the conflict. As the war dragged on, UNPROFOR was increasingly discredited.[32]

In May 1995 NATO aircraft, acting under a UN Security Council mandate, struck Bosnian Serb targets in an attempt to halt an offensive. The Bosnian Serbs took UN soldiers hostage and chained them to likely military targets as a defense against further air strikes. The UN had established six safe areas where civilians could seek refuge from the conflict, but UNPROFOR proved unable to protect the zones. In July 1995 Bosnian Serb forces captured Srebrenica and committed numerous atrocities against the civilian population seeking refuge in the town. The following month, a Bosnian Serb–fired mortar shell fell into a marketplace in Sarajevo, killing thirty-seven civilians.

Prompted by the continued fighting and convinced that only decisive U.S. action would end the conflict, the United States, acting through NATO, finally became more directly involved. During the two-week period from August 30 to September 17, NATO planes flew some 800 combat missions against Bosnian Serb targets. The United States also became more involved in efforts to find a diplomatic solution. A U.S. team led by Assistant Secretary of State for Europe Richard Holbrooke used shuttle diplomacy to broker a ceasefire that took effect in October. In November, the United States invited all of the parties involved to continue the negotiations at Wright-Patterson Air Force Base near Dayton, Ohio. After three weeks of intense discussions, Holbrooke managed to broker a settlement that was signed by the presidents of Serbia, Croatia, and Bosnia in a ceremony in Paris the following month. All parties recognized that Bosnia would remain a unified state, but it was to be composed of two distinct entities, the Bosnian-Croat Federation and the Republika Srpska, the former with 51 percent, the latter with 49 percent, of the country's territory.[33]

UNPROFOR forces were withdrawn, and replaced by a new Implementation Force (IFOR) under NATO command that was charged with enforcing the peace agreement. IFOR's 60,000 troops included units from the United States, Western Europe, central and eastern Europe, Russia, and Ukraine. Pending the reestablishment of Bosnian democratic institutions capable of standing up to pressures from the country's ethnic groupings, all of which remain highly suspicious of each other, civilian administration in Bosnia was assigned to an Office of the High Representative, which could call on NATO forces to deal with potential threats to the peace and to assist with postwar reconstruction. In the Dayton negotiations, the EU representatives insisted that the High Representative be a European, both to counterbalance the fact that the NATO IFOR commander was to be an American and in recognition of the EU's predominant role in financing reconstruction of the country. The first High Representative for Bosnia was former Swedish Prime

Minister Carl Bildt, later succeeded by former Spanish Foreign Minister Carlos Westendorp.

Reestablishing a viable Bosnian state has proven to be a daunting task, and there is no guarantee that fighting will not resume in the future, especially after foreign peacekeeping forces are withdrawn. Recognizing the stakes involved, the Western powers devoted money, manpower, and diplomatic energies to ensuring the success of the Dayton accords. IFOR was supposed to be withdrawn after a year, but it was replaced by a smaller Stabilization Force (SFOR) that was seen as necessary to preserving the peace. Along with the World Bank and other international organizations, the EU and the United States provided massive aid to help restore the battered Bosnia economy. Progress in reviving the economy was extremely slow, however, with little evidence of self-sustaining growth even several years after Dayton. Corruption was rampant, refugees were unwilling to return to their native villages, and businesses reluctant to invest. Bosnia thus remained in effect a dependency of the Western community, and a reminder of the difficulty of restoring peace and economic viability after the failure of the international community and the Yugoslavs themselves to halt the slide into war at the beginning of the 1990s.[34]

MACEDONIA AND ALBANIA

Elsewhere in the western Balkans, Macedonia and Albania were additional flashpoints that confronted EU policy in the 1990s. Macedonia was among the smallest and the poorest of the ex-Yugoslav republics seeking full independence after 1991, and desperately in need of outside economic and political assistance. But EU policy toward Macedonia initially was paralyzed by a dispute with Greece over the country's name. As long as Macedonia was a constituent republic of the Yugoslav federation, Greece had no objection to its name. But Macedonia is also the name of Greece's northernmost province, redolent with history going back to Alexander the Great. The Greeks claimed that the use of the name by an independent state reflected a latent desire to seize Greek territory. Athens managed to block recognition by the other EU member states of the new republic and in the summer of 1992 it imposed a blockade of petroleum deliveries to Macedonia in an effort to pressure the government to change the country's name. The issue was defused somewhat when Greece agreed, in February 1993, to accept recognition of the country under a name to be decided by international arbitration. The arbitrators proposed that pending a final settlement of the issue, the country be called the Former Yugoslav Republic of Macedonia (FYROM), and it was under this slightly absurd name that this small, impoverished, and landlocked country was admitted to the UN in April 1993. All other EU members (but not Greece) recognized the FYROM, as did Russia and the United States.

Greece continued its hard line, however, and in early 1994 it closed the port of Thessaloniki to shipments to and from Macedonia as well as blocked rail and road links to the country. The other EU members were appalled at Greece's behavior and worried at the damage being done to the fragile, post-communist economy of the new state. The European Commission initiated legal proceedings against Greece in the ECJ, contending that it was in violation of obligations under the Treaty of Rome that limited member state competence with respect to foreign trade. Interestingly, the Court, which often can be counted on to take a pro-integration position against recalcitrant member states, ruled in favor of Greece on the grounds that national security and foreign policy matters, upon which Athens based its actions, were not within the purview of the treaty.[35] There is still no definitive solution to the Greece-Macedonia imbroglio, but in 1995 the two countries reached a modus vivendi under which the FYROM changed its flag and amended certain portions of its constitution regarded as offensive by the Greeks, in exchange for which Greece agreed to lift the economic blockade. Trade between Greece and the FYROM soon burgeoned and Greek businesses became major investors in the country, helping to stabilize its weak economy.

One of the factors working in favor of a rapprochement between Greece and the FYROM was the deteriorating situation in Albania, which borders both countries and which has ethnic ties with Kosovo, Macedonia, and Greece. The collapse of the communist regime in early 1991 led to rising economic and political disorder in the country, causing ethnic Greeks to flee southward and an exodus by boat of more than 20,000 Albanians to Italy. The Italian authorities clamped down on illegal migration in August 1991 and began to repatriate many of the refugees, but only after Western Europe had been given a vivid example of how instability on its doorstep could quickly spill over onto its own territory.

Albania appeared to make some economic and political progress in the early 1990s, but fraudulent elections in 1996 followed by a financial crisis in early 1997 led to a breakdown of law and order and civil war between the government of President Sali Berisha and rebel forces seeking his overthrow. Concerned about another massive influx of refugees, Italy took the lead in organizing a multinational force of peacekeeping troops that supervised food distribution and other humanitarian tasks and managed to restore order in the country. Italy contributed 2,500 troops to the 5,915-member Multinational Protection Force, France 1,000, and smaller contingents came from Greece, Spain, Romania, Austria, and Denmark. It was significant, however, that the force was an ad hoc body, endorsed by the UN Security Council and involving the OSCE, but not formally under the EU or the WEU.

KOSOVO

Kosovo, formally a province of Serbia but with a 90 percent ethnically Albanian population, was the scene of violence between Serbs and Albanians beginning in the early 1980s. In March 1989 the Serbian parliament voted to suspend the autonomy that the province had enjoyed for much of its history as part of the Yugoslav state, leading to a further escalation of tensions. The older generation of leaders in Kosovo counseled nonviolence and looked to the international community for support. As Serb oppression continued, however, and after the international community failed to address the issue of Kosovo in the Dayton accords, the underground Kosovo Liberation Army (KLA) emerged as the province's leading political force. Smuggling weapons into Kosovo from neighboring Albania, the KLA established military control over large parts of the country and became more assertive in pressing its demand for a completely independent state. The international community did not support the demands of the KLA, but it also warned the Serbs about overreacting to the KLA threat and continued to call for a peaceful solution to the tensions based on a restoration of the province's autonomy, perhaps as a third republic in a Yugoslav federation, along with Serbia and Montenegro.

Ignoring Western warnings, in early 1998 military and police units operating from Serbia struck the province hard, destroying villages and driving out their populations in what Belgrade said was a legitimate campaign against KLA terrorists. Once again, European and American audiences could see on television the violence and the streams of refugees on Western Europe's Balkan doorstep. Using the threat of NATO air strikes as leverage, in October 1998 the United States managed to broker a ceasefire between the Serb authorities and the Kosovo separatists, to be followed by talks on a political settlement and the return of refugees. Serbian leader Milosevic agreed to the dispatch of 1,500 OSCE observers to monitor the ceasefire and NATO deployed an "extraction force" of troops in Macedonia to be prepared to come to the rescue of the unarmed observers should they come under attack from either side. The EU as such was not involved in the Kosovo crisis, although member states committed personnel and equipment to the OSCE and NATO missions.

The October 1998 agreement failed to resolve the crisis, however, and a continuing deterioration of conditions in the province led to open war between Serbia and NATO in the spring of 1999.[36] In an effort to halt the escalating violence in the province, in February 1999 the Western powers convened a peace conference in Rambouillet, France, at which they essentially presented the Yugoslav government with an ultimatum, demanding that it withdraw its forces from Kosovo and allow NATO peacekeeping forces to enter the province or face allied air strikes. Belgrade refused, and on March 24 NATO began attacks against Serb targets in Kosovo and Serbia proper. This accelerated the campaign of ethnic cleansing by the Serbs, as almost the entire Kosovar population fled their homes to escape Serb military and police forces engaged in widespread killing and burning of whole villages. Some 800,000 people crossed the borders into Macedonia and Albania, threatening the economic and political stability of these countries, while many more were displaced inside Kosovo.

Despite doubts among critics about the wisdom of NATO strategy and the skill with which the United States and its allies had conducted the pre-war diplomacy, NATO was able to maintain support for its bombing campaign for 78 days, causing widespread destruction to Yugoslav forces, industry, and infrastructure. Milosevic finally accepted a UN- and Russian-brokered peace agreement that met the essence of NATO's demands: that Serb forces withdraw from the province and that Kosovo be occupied by a NATO-led peace force that would allow the refugees to return home in relative safety. Known as KFOR, this force of 40,000 troops deployed to Kosovo in June, with the EU countries providing most of the manpower and equipment.

The Kosovo crisis had two important implications for the Union. First, it created a new argument for the EU to begin strengthening its own defense capabilities. The war highlighted the gap in military capabilities between the United States and its European allies and led to calls from Blair and other European leaders to strengthen the European defense pillar, not just by revamping institutions but also by acquiring real military capabilities. Whether European governments actually will follow through and make the necessary investments to build such capabilities remains uncertain for the reasons discussed above, but there can be little doubt that Europe's weak performance in the spring of 1999 was a major contributor to the decision later that year to form a 60,000-person EU peacekeeping force able, if necessary, to operate independently of NATO in a future crisis. Second, the war created a huge problem of postwar reconstruction and redevelopment for which the EU assumed primary responsibility. This in turn affected thinking in the EU about the broader problem of enlargement and the integration of the whole of Europe into a stable economic and security order.

BALKAN STRATEGY AFTER KOSOVO

The crisis in Kosovo and its spillover effects on other countries in the region compelled the EU to concentrate more seriously than in the past on its Balkan policy and the future of the region. In theory, all of the countries of the region could become members of the Union. Slovenia, a former Yugoslav republic that does not consider itself a Balkan country, was included in the first wave of accession negotiations that began in 1998. Romania and Bulgaria were second-wave countries that began such negotiations in early 2000.

In 1995 the EU began preliminary discussions with Croatia, the country in the subregion that is culturally and geographically closest to the heart of Europe, about a Europe Agreement that would have made it eligible to prepare for accession talks. This was a logical extension of the approach that had begun with Slovenia in which the most promising countries of the region were drawn toward the EU on a one-by-one basis. In May 1996, however, the EU suspended negotiations with Croatia following adoption by the Council of a new regional approach to the former Yugoslavia—Slovenia excepted. The EU announced that henceforth it would not negotiate separate agreements with the four countries involved (Croatia, Bosnia-Herzegovina, the Serb-Montenegrin federation of Yugoslavia, and Macedonia) but would insist that they work together on a regional approach to integration. The new policy was adopted in part to head off a repeat of the 1991 situation, when different member states followed different approaches towards Slovenia and Croatia, thereby helping to precipitate the wider war.

On balance, however, EU policy toward the region was one of relative neglect, as the Balkans seemed to drift further away from the European mainstream. The war in Kosovo injected a new sense of urgency into EU thinking about the region and led to development of a new strategy backed by new resources. This strategy had several components. First, it included large-scale financial assistance for rebuilding and resettlement of refugees. The EU was prepared to contribute half of the 1.0–1.5 billion euros needed each year for three years to rebuild Kosovo. Over the longer term, it was prepared to contribute much larger sums to regional development, including EIB loans. To coordinate its assistance effort, it established a special Europan Agency for Reconstruction in Kosovo, headquartered in Thessaloniki, Greece. Second, the EU adopted a proposal, first put forward by Germany, for a special Stability Pact for South-Eastern Europe intended to enhance cooperation among countries in the region. Bodo Hombach, a close aide to Chancellor Schroeder, was named special coordinator for the stability pact. Third, the EU revisited its approach to bilateral agreements with the countries of the region. It was not yet ready to conclude Europe Agreements with them in a way that would put them firmly on a path toward membership, but it recognized the need for new, in effect pre-pre-accession arrangements that would draw these countries closer to the Union and hold out better prospects for eventual membership.

The experience of the international community in Kosovo after the war soon proved, however, how difficult it was to translate expressions of support into stability and economic growth. Ethnic Albanians returned to Kosovo from refugee camps in Albania and Macedonia, but many ethnic Serbs fled the province, fearful of Albanian reprisals. The KLA resisted attempts by NATO to disarm, and pressed for full independence. Corruption was rampant, and the EU itself failed to deliver in a timely fashon the aid that it had promised for reconstruction. Combined with the difficulties encountered in Bosnia, these developments suggested that at best it would be many years before the countries in this region become members of the Union. At worst, the western Balkans could become a pocket of semi-permanent instability in the underbelly of Europe that will stand as a monument to the policy failures of the 1990s.

The Newly Independent States

The breakup of the Soviet Union in late 1991 caught Western governments by surprise, leaving the EC and its member states largely unprepared to deal with the postcommunist governments and transition economies that emerged in Russia, Ukraine, and the other former Soviet republics. Overnight, the Soviet superpower fragmented into fifteen independent countries, ranging from the Russian Federation with nearly 150 million people and still the largest land area of any country in the world to tiny Estonia with its population of under 1.5 million.

With the accession of Finland in 1995, the EU acquired its first common border with the former Soviet Union—a 1,000-kilometer stretch where Finland's relative prosperity confronts the poverty and environmental degradation of Russia's northwestern provinces. With enlargement to central and eastern Europe, the EU will gain even longer borders with Russia as well as with Belarus, Ukraine, and Moldova. What happens in these countries thus will be of increasing interest for the EU.

EU policy toward the NIS has roots in the late Soviet era, when President Gorbachev, abandoning the earlier Soviet policy of shunning the EC and seeking to undermine West European integration, turned to Brussels for support for his reforms. In November 1989 the USSR and the EC concluded their first trade and cooperation agreement. Because the Soviet Union was still a nonmarket economy in which domestic prices were set by administrative decision rather than by market signals, the EC did not grant it MFN status. As with other nonmarket economies, the EC limited trade by establishing quotas for each major category of good that the Soviet Union wished to sell in the EC market.[37]

With the breakup of the Soviet Union at the end of 1991, the terms of the EC-USSR agreement were transferred to Russia and the other successor states. The 1989 agreement did not, however, provide an adequate basis for cooperation with these states as they began moving, some more rapidly than others, to create market economies and multiparty political systems. The EU thus offered to conclude Partnership and Cooperation Agreements (PCAs) with the NIS that would establish a framework for more comprehensive relations based on trade, financial aid, regular political dialogue, closer cultural ties, and efforts to work together to harmonize legislation in important areas such as anti-trust. Like the Europe Agreements then being negotiated with the countries of central and eastern Europe, the PCAs are mixed agreements, signed and ratified both by the EU and its member states, so as to provide for relations both in areas such as trade where Brussels has policy competence and those such as culture and foreign policy where competence lies mainly with the member states. As noted in Chapter 8, the PCAs with Russia and Ukraine liberalize trade and could lead to future free trade agreements. For now, however, trade is held back by restrictions on the EU side and economic weakness in Russia and Ukraine.

The EU also established a Technical Assistance to the CIS (TACIS) program as a counterpart to the PHARE program of aid for central and eastern Europe. Beginning with ECU 396 million in committed funding for 1991 and rising to ECU 536 million in 1996, TACIS funded nuclear reactor safety projects, the development of private enterprise, food production and distribution, and transport and telecommunications infrastructure. Russia and Ukraine received the lion's share of the aid, but smaller amounts were apportioned to all of the NIS, including the Caucasus and Central Asia. In December 1999 the Council renewed TACIS for another seven years, with funding set at 3.138 billion euros for 2000–2006.[38] The EU coordinates its overall assistance toward the NIS with the other leading Western states in the G-7 as well as works through multilateral institutions such as the World Bank, the IMF, and the EBRD.

The effectiveness of EU policy toward Russia has been a matter of debate. The EU points to the level of TACIS aid and the large volume of trade with Russia, but Russian officials are less impressed. They complain about a lack of openness to Russian exports. Russia has been the target of frequent EU anti-dumping actions which have severely curtailed sales of steel, aluminum, and other products that Russian firms are able to sell on the European market. TACIS also is criticized as being slow and bureaucratic, with much of the money flowing back to high-priced EU-based consultants and contractors.

Throughout the 1990s Russia made progress toward creating a market economy and a political democracy by, for example, privatizing most of its economy, holding relatively free and fair elections at the national, regional, and local levels, and developing a vigorous and independent press. But Russia continued to be plagued by political instability and frequent changes of government under President Boris Yeltsin, pervasive corruption, and poverty and low incomes in much of the population. A short-lived economic boom came to a crashing end in August 1998, when a financial crisis forced the Russian government to devalue the rouble and to postpone repayment of some public and private debt. Some foreign investors abandoned the Russian market, and the small Russian middle and entrepreneurial class was in danger of being thrust into poverty.

Like the IMF, World Bank, and other Western institutions involved in Russian economic transformation, the EU stressed that Russia had to save itself—that external help could not pull it out of crisis if it failed to reform outdated structures and crack down on corruption. But the EU also mobilized itself to assist the Russians with the short-term crisis and over the longer haul. The December 1998 Vienna European Council decided on the preparation of a common strategy for Russia, to be ready by the end of the German presidency in the first half of 1999. Adopted at the Cologne summit, the common strategy reaffirmed the goal of a "stable, democratic and prosperous Russia, firmly anchored in a united Europe free of new dividing lines."[39] The EU set four goals for its Russia strategy: consolidation of democracy, the rule of law, and public institutions; integration of Russia into a common European economic and social area; cooperation to strengthen stability and security in Europe and beyond; and meeting common challenges on the European continent (e.g., energy and nuclear safety, environment, and the fight against organized crime and drugs). It also outlined a long list of instruments and mechanisms for pursuing these objectives and stressed that the key to implementation of the common strategy was effective coordination of exchange and assistance programs run by the EU itself and the fifteen member states. Under the terms of the Amsterdam Treaty, the member states can act by qualified majority voting when taking implementing actions on the basis of the common strategy. Implementation of the common strategy began in the second half of 1999, but was hampered by the brutal war in Chechnya, which the EU criticized, and by uncertainty about the democratic credentials and reform course of Yeltsin's chosen successor, Vladimir Putin.

With a population the size of France and territorially the second-largest country in Europe after Russia, Ukraine is an important factor in the future stability of Europe and a key country for EU interests. Relations between the EU and Ukraine have been complicated, however, by corruption and the slow pace of economic reform in Ukraine, the dispute over the shutdown of the Chernobyl nuclear power plant, and differences over trade and development. The Ukrainians have long complained about what they see as an ongoing neglect of their interests by the Union and a refusal by Brussels and the member states to accelerate the integration of Ukraine into Europe. For its part, the EU has stressed the effect that corruption and political deadlock in Ukraine have had in deterring foreign investment and the development of trading links. Officials in Brussels argued that the EU could only do so much to help a country that did not do more to help itself.

The EU adopted its common strategy for Ukraine at the Helsinki summit of December 1999. Like the strategy for Russia, it stresses economic reform, measures to fight corruption, democratization, and nuclear safety. While Ukraine welcomed the increased attention that the common strategy indicated, over the long run its ambition is to be recognized as a candidate country for EU membership. The EU refused to place Ukraine in this category, and argued that Ukraine should continue with its internal reforms and exploit the full potential offered by the EU-Ukraine PCA, rather than focus on the at this point rather remote prospects of joining the Union.

Over the long term, membership or at least some form of close association between Ukraine and the EU cannot be ruled out. For now, however, there is a divide between Ukraine and the countries of central and eastern Europe that are negotiating to become members of the Union. This divide could deepen as these countries achieve membership and begin to apply to Ukraine the EU's common external tariff and the Schengen principles on the movement of people into the Union.

The Mediterranean

The Mediterranean long has been an area of focus for West European economic and foreign policy. Morocco and Tunisia were French protectorates until the 1950s, and Algeria a French colony that achieved independence in 1962 after a bitter struggle with France. Libya was an Italian colony before World War II, and Egypt a British protectorate—in large part because of the strategic importance of the Suez Canal. Western Europe also had a special if complex relationship with Israel.

In the 1970s, the EC concluded economic cooperation agreements with most of the countries of the region. The enlargements of the 1980s brought the Community more directly into contact with the region and created new incentives for policies that would help to narrow the wide economic and cultural differences between Europe and its southern neighbors. Per capita GNP in the countries of the Middle East and North Africa is only around $1,800 per year compared with more than ten times that level in the affluent countries of Western Europe. The countries on the southern littoral of the Mediterranean are expected to increase their populations by some 85 million between 1995 and 2015, which could result in higher levels of legal and illegal immigration into Europe as young entrants to the labor force are unable to find jobs in their own countries.[40] The European countries also are concerned about the rise of Islamic radicalism in countries such as Egypt and

Algeria, which is fueled by difficult economic conditions and which could spill over into Europe itself, where substantial numbers of immigrants from these countries already live and work. The situation is further complicated by the fact that Europe obtains much of its oil and gas from this region, by tanker and by gas pipelines that cross the Mediterranean from Algeria to Italy and from Algeria to Spain via Morocco.

The EU's overall strategy towards the region was launched with the 1995 Barcelona Euro-Mediterranean Partnership. The driving force on the European side behind the partnership was the Mediterranean countries of the Union, and especially France and Spain. With the fall of communism and the new focus on enlargement and the stabilization of Russia, they were concerned about an eastward tilt in EU foreign and development policy that in their view was inspired mainly by Germany and that most served German interests. While stabilization of the EU's eastern borders was important, dealing with instability to the south deserved equal attention.

The Barcelona partnership was based on expanded cooperation in three spheres: political; economic; and social, human, and cultural. As was seen in Chapter 8, in the economic area it called for the progressive establishment by 2010 of a free trade area and for other measures to promote economic growth in the Mediterranean region, including financial aid and EIB loans. In the political sphere, the Barcelona agreement called for respect for human rights and the rule of law, joint efforts to prevent the spread of chemical, nuclear, and biological weapons, and other measures aimed at building confidence in the region. In the social and cultural area, the agreement provided for the development of direct contacts between nongovernmental organizations, educational and cultural institutions, and local and regional authorities on both sides of the Mediterranean.

The partnership was underwritten from the EU side by a major financial commitment. At the Cannes summit in June 1995 the European Council reached agreement on the division of grant aid between the countries of central and eastern Europe (both the NIS under TACIS and the accession candidates under PHARE) and the Mediterranean countries for the period 1995–1999. ECU 4.685 billion was allocated to the Mediterranean, less than the ECU 6.693 billion earmarked for the former communist countries, but a substantial sum nonetheless—especially when viewed on a per capita basis. The EIB also was asked to increase its lending to the non-EU Mediterranean countries. The Vienna European Council called for the preparation of an EU common strategy for the Mediterranean, again very much at the instigation of Spain and other Mediterranean countries.

U.S.-EU Relations

Relations with the United States are probably the most important focus of CFSP other than the EU periphery. Since its development in the early 1960s, the U.S.-EC relationship had a heavy focus on trade. The EC as such had no competence for political and security issues, and Washington in any case preferred to deal with

Europe on these issues in NATO and through its bilateral relations with such key allies as Britain and West Germany. Economics and trade remain the focal point of the U.S.-EU relationship, and Washington continues to look to NATO as its preferred vehicle for political and security dialogue with Europe. However, since the early 1990s the United States and the EU have developed a separate dialogue and a pattern of cooperation that reflects the Union's broader responsibilities under CFSP and its important role in issues of concern to the United States, such as Turkey, the future of Russia, and the crisis in the Balkans.

The impetus for the new relationship came initially from Washington, which recognized the growing significance of the EC/EU under post–cold war circumstances. In a speech in Berlin in December 1989, some two months after the opening of the Berlin Wall, Secretary of State James Baker acknowledged the need to develop stronger ties between the United States and the EC in the political as well as the economic spheres, and proposed that the two sides "work together to achieve, whether in treaty or some other form, a significantly strengthened set of institutional and consultative links."[41] This proposal was greeted warily in some European capitals (notably Paris), where the United States was suspected of wanting to gain a seat at the EC table as the importance of NATO diminished. These concerns were overcome in negotiations that followed Baker's proposal, and the United States and the EC eventually concluded the Transatlantic Declaration institutionalizing U.S.-EC consultations at the summit, ministerial, and working levels. The declaration called for cooperation in such areas as combating terrorism, fighting narcotics trafficking and international crime, and preventing the spread of nuclear, chemical, and biological weapons.[42]

The December 1995 New Transatlantic Agenda expanded the range of U.S.-EU dialogue and cooperation on issues going beyond the traditional economic agenda. In addition to the trade and economic provisions of the NTA discussed in the previous chapter, it called for expanded cooperation in three other areas: promoting peace, stability, democracy, and development worldwide; responding to global challenges; and building bridges across the Atlantic. Unlike the 1990 agreement, which was negotiated during a period of tension between the United States and France over the future of NATO and which contained only a perfunctory affirmation of the Atlantic Alliance, the NTA contained a strong and more explicit affirmation of NATO as the "centerpiece of transatlantic security" as well as of the emerging ESDI as an element strengthening the European pillar of the alliance.[43] It thus reflected a certain convergence of views on security issues, with the United States coming to embrace a stronger European identity while the Europeans, including France, explicitly recognized the enduring role of NATO.

In Europe, the United States and the EU pledged to work to implement the peace in the former Yugoslavia, to strengthen democratic and market institutions in central and eastern Europe, to build a European framework including Russia, Ukraine, and the other NIS, to promote Turkey's further integration into the transatlantic community, and to work toward a resolution of the Cyprus question. Beyond Europe, they affirmed the global nature of their partnership, and pledged "to act jointly to resolve conflicts in troubled areas, to engage in preventive diplomacy together, to coordinate our assistance efforts, to deal with humanitarian needs and to help build in developing nations the capacity for economic growth and self-sufficiency."[44] With regard to global issues, the agreement called for cooperation in combating the proliferation of weapons of mass destruction and common efforts toward international disarmament. It also expanded upon the commitments made in the 1990 declaration for mutual cooperation in responding to global challenges covered by the EU's third pillar: the fight against organized crime, terrorism, drug trafficking, and immigration and asylum matters.

On the basis of the 1990 and 1995 agreements, the EU and the United States have a bilateral summit every six months, usually in June or December at the end of each EU presidency. The EU is represented by the Commission president and the prime minister of the EU presidency country. There are also regular ministerial and working level consultations on global, regional, and bilateral issues, and a Senior Level Group of diplomats from both sides that prepares a report on progress in the relationship for each summit. The EU-U.S. dialogue has resulted in commitments to joint actions and positions in many areas, as reflected, for example, in the Joint Statement on Ukraine (December 1997), the Declaration of Nonproliferation (May 1998), the Declaration on the Middle East Peace Process (December 1999), the EU-U.S. Summit Statement on Chechnya (December 1999), and the EU-U.S. Statement of Common Principles on Small Arms and Light Weapons (December 1999).

Other Regions and Global Issues

While the focus of CFSP is on regional issues and efforts to shape events on the eastern and southern peripheries of the EU, this does not mean that it entirely lacks a broader global dimension. As was seen in Chapter 8, the EU has launched regular processes of dialogue with Asia and Latin America. The focus of these dialogues is on trade and the promotion of EU exports and investment, but they also have a political dimension, which is reflected in such actions as EU support for democracy and human rights in Burma, involvement in the East Timor dispute in Indonesia, and financial backing for the Korean Peninsula Energy Development Organization (KEDO), an international effort that also involves the United States, Japan, and Korea that is intended to encourage North Korea to abandon its nuclear weapons program by developing alternative sources of energy.

Growing out of the colonial heritage of several of its member states, the EU also remains heavily involved in sub-Saharan Africa. The EU is also the world's largest provider of humanitarian aid, which it administers through the European Community Humanitarian Office (ECHO) to regions as diverse as Kosovo, Central America (especially in the wake of 1998's Hurricane Mitch), and southern Africa.

Global issues cut across particular regions, and include international environmental disasters, the fight against international crime, terrorism, and trafficking in drugs, international migration, proliferation of weapons of mass destruction, and rapid outbreaks of deadly contagious diseases such as the Ebola virus. These are seen by many experts as the real security threats of the 21st century. As such, they are likely to become an increasing focus of CFSP and other areas of EU policy. For the most part, however, the EU is likely to develop chiefly as a regional power, mindful of its relations with the United States, seeking trade and investment opportunities in East Asia, Latin America, and elsewhere, but concentrating the bulk of its resources on the stabilization of its immediate periphery.

Notes

1. http://www.nato.int/docu/basictxt/treaty.htm.

2. Richard L. Kugler, *Commitment to Purpose: How Alliance Partnership Won the Cold War* (RAND: Santa Monica, 1993), 54.

3. This provision remains in effect as Article 296 of the renumbered treaty.

4. "First Report of the Foreign Ministers to the Heads of State and Government of the Member States of the European Community (Luxembourg Report)," in *European Political Co-operation (EPC)*, 4th ed. (Bonn: Press and Information Office of the Federal Government, 1984), 30.

5. Bull. EC 10–1981, 55–56.

6. Article J.4. This language is found in amended form in Article 17(1) of the amended TEU.

7. Ibid.

8. *EU: Selected Instruments Taken from the Treaties*, Book I,1, 80–85.

9. WEU Council of Ministers, "Petersberg Declaration," June 19, 1992.

10. "Joint declaration on the CFSP annexed to the Accession Treaties," quoted in Fraser Cameron, *The Foreign and Security Policy of the European Union* (Sheffield: Sheffield Academic Press, 1999), 104.

11. *Western European Union: History, Structures, Prospects* (Brussels: WEU Press and Information Service, June 1995).

12. *Presidency conclusions: Turin European Council, 29 March 1996*, in *The European Councils: Conclusions of the Presidency 1996* (Luxembourg: OOPEC, 1997), 7.

13. Article 17.

14. Article J.4.4.

15. *NATO Press Communiqué* M-1(94)3, "Declaration of the Heads of State and Government, Ministerial Meeting of the North Atlantic Council, Brussels," January 11, 1994; Jeffrey Simon and Sean Kay, "The New NATO," in Ronald Tiersky, ed., *Europe Today* (Lanham: Rowman and Littlefield, 1999), 369–399.

16. *Final Communiqué*, NAC-1(96)63, Ministerial Meeting of the North Atlantic Council, Berlin, June 3, 1996.

17. James M. Goldgeier, *Not Whether but When: The U.S. Decision to Enlarge NATO* (Washington, DC: Brookings Institution Press, 1999), 77–107.

18. Paris AFP, December 7, 1994, in Foreign Broadcast Information Service, *West Europe Report*, December 8, 1994.

19. "Charter on a Distinctive Partnership between NATO and Ukraine" and "Founding

Act on Mutual Relations, Cooperation and Security between NATO and the Russian Federation," *NATO Review*, No. 4, 1997.

20. "Declaration on the Western European Union," *European Union: Selected Instruments*, 80.

21. IISS, *The Military Balance 1998/1999* (London: Oxford University Press, 1999), 295–300.

22. "Declaration on European Defense," UK-French summit, St. Malo, December 3–4, 1998, http://www.fco.gov.uk.

23. Peter Norman and Andrew Parker, "Common EU army the 'logical next step'," *Financial Times*, May 10, 1999.

24. "Presidency Report on Strengthening of the common European policy on security and defence," *Presidency Conclusions (Cologne)*, Annex III, 36–42.

25. "An Alliance for the 21st Century," Washington Summit Communiqué, http://www.nato.int/docu/pr/1999/p99–064e.htm.

26. "Presidency Progress Report to the Helsinki European Council on Strengthening the Common European Policy on Security and Defence," *Presidency Conclusions (Helsinki)*, Annex IV.

27. IISS director John Chipman, quoted in Alexander Nicoll, "European leaders found wanting when it comes to putting up cash for defence," *Financial Times*, October 22, 1999.

28. IISS, *The Military Balance, 1999–2000* (London: IISS, 1999), 300.

29. "Report to the European Council in Lisbon on the likely development of the Common Foreign and Security Policy (CFSP) with a view to identifying areas open to joint action vis-à-vis particular countries or groups of countries," *The European Councils, 1992–1994*, 16–20.

30. Quoted in Grant, *Delors*, 192.

31. Hanns W. Maull, "Germany in the Yugoslav Crisis," *Survival* 37, no. 4 (Winter 1995–96): 99–130.

32. See David Owen, *Balkan Odyssey* (New York: Harcourt, Brace, 1995).

33. Richard Holbrooke, *To End a War* (New York: Random House, 1998).

34. *Promoting Sustainable Economies in the Balkans: Task Force Report* (New York: Council on Foreign Relations, 2000), 9–15.

35. *Commission v. Greece*, ECR I-3037–3068 (1994–6).

36. Tim Judah, "Kosovo's Road to War," *Survival* 41, no. 2 (Summer 1999): 5–18.

37. John Van Oudenaren, *Détente in Europe: The Soviet Union and the West since 1953* (Durham: Duke University Press, 1991), 275–282.

38. "New TACIS Regulation enters into force," IP/00/66, Brussels, January 21, 2000.

39. *Common Strategy of the European Union on Russia of 4 June 1999*, Annex II, *Presidency Conclusions: Cologne*, 14–32.

40. Russell King, "Labour, Employment and Migration in Southern Europe," in John Van Oudenaren, ed., *Employment, Economic Development and Migration in Southern Europe and the Maghreb* (Santa Monica: RAND, 1996).

41. Text in *New York Times*, December 13, 1989.

42. European Commission, *Transatlantic Declaration on EC-US Relations, November 23, 1990* (Brussels: European Commission, Directorate General for External Relations, 1991).

43. "The New Transatlantic Agenda," *Presidency Conclusions (Madrid)*, Annex X, in *The European Councils, 1995*, 77.

44. "Joint EU-US Action Plan," Madrid, December 16, 1995.

Suggestions for Further Reading

Buchan, David. *Europe: The Strange Superpower*. Aldershot: Dartmouth, 1993.

Cameron, Fraser. *The Foreign and Security Policy of the European Union*. Sheffield: Sheffield Academic Press, 1999.

Gasteyger, Curt. *An Ambiguous Power: The European Union in a Changing World*. Gütersloh: Bertelsmann, 1996.

Grilli, Enzo. *The European Community and the Developing Countries*. New York: Cambridge University Press, 1993.

Macleod, I., I. D. Henry and Stephen Hyett. *The External Relations of the European Communities: A Manual of Law and Practice*. Oxford: Clarendon Press, 1996.

Nuttall, S. *European Political Cooperation*. Oxford: Clarendon Press, 1992.

Regelsberger, Elfriede et al., eds. *Foreign Policy of the European Union: From EPC to CFSP and Beyond*. Boulder: Lynne Rienner, 1996.

CHAPTER 10

The Next Enlargement

At the time of the third enlargement in January 1986, few EC country politicians would have predicted that within six years they would be debating membership for ten candidate countries from central and eastern Europe, three of which were then still part of the Soviet Union. It was assumed that with the accession of Portugal and Spain, the Community more or less had reached the limits of its expansion in Western Europe and that the challenge of the future was to deepen rather than widen to new members. By mid-1993, however, the then twelve member states had taken a decision in principle to admit those countries just emerging from the shadow of more than forty-five years of communism. As the EU concentrated during the remainder of the 1990s on implementing the Maastricht Treaty and especially its provisions on EMU, the candidate countries embarked on an arduous pre-accession process designed to prepare them for membership early in the twenty-first century. For both the candidate countries and the EU, enlargement will be a crucial test—one that will determine whether the model of European integration that brought peace and prosperity to Western Europe in the cold war era can be extended under post-cold war conditions to the whole of the continent.

The Collapse of Communism

The initial groundwork for enlargement was laid in the late 1980s, after Gorbachev abandoned the previous Soviet policy of trying to undermine the EC by refusing to deal with it and the Community began to develop its relations with central and eastern Europe. In June 1988 the EC and CMEA signed an agreement according each other diplomatic recognition and pledging to cooperate in such areas as the environment, harmonization of standards, and science and technology. This was followed by the conclusion of bilateral trade and cooperation agreements between the EC and the CMEA member countries, beginning with a ten-year trade and cooperation agreement with Hungary signed in June 1988.

These first-generation agreements soon were rendered obsolete, however, by the accelerating pace of change in the communist world. In June 1989 partially free elections took place in Poland, resulting in a resounding victory for the opposition Solidarity movement. In the same month, roundtable talks between government and opposition began in Hungary aimed at fundamental change in the political system. By mid-1989 there was reason to hope that at least these two countries were on a path that would lead to the establishment of market economies and pluralist political systems. Western governments sought to respond to these signs of change and to support them with external aid. At the July 1989 Paris summit, the G-7 issued a declaration of support for economic and political reform in eastern Europe and called for an international conference to coordinate Western aid to Poland and Hungary. In December 1989 the Council of Ministers approved PHARE (*Pologne et Hongrie: Actions pour la Reconversion Économique*), a Community-funded program of technical assistance to encourage the development of private enterprise and the building of market-oriented economies.[1]

Once again, however, within a short time the West European governments found themselves playing catch up with rapid change. In September 1989 Hungary opened its border with Austria, allowing thousands of East German citizens to travel to West Germany. After months of mass demonstrations in Leipzig, Dresden, and other cities, on November 9 the Berlin Wall was thrown open by an East German government that could no longer control its borders. In November and December opposition rallies led to the ouster of the communist regime in Czechoslovakia. In December, roundtable talks between government and opposition began in Bulgaria. For the most part these revolutions were peaceful, but they culminated in late December with bloody fighting in Romania between opposition and security forces and the execution, on Christmas Day, of former dictator Nicolae Ceausescu and his wife Elena. By 1990, the communist regimes in central and eastern Europe all had been swept away.

The most immediate political challenge facing Western governments as a result of these upheavals was German unification. Chancellor Kohl quickly seized the initiative on this issue, putting forward, in November 1989, a ten-point plan for creation of a German confederation. The United States supported unification, but Britain and France were skeptical. The Soviet Union had taken a hands-off attitude toward the changes in eastern Europe, but it declared itself opposed to unification. The Soviet Union still had several hundred thousand troops in the GDR, and as a World War II victor power it had certain legal rights in Germany. In the GDR itself it was initially unclear whether the voters would opt for rapid absorption by West Germany or whether they would seek to maintain some kind of separate identity within a German confederation. By the fall of 1990 these uncertainties were resolved. In July, Kohl and Gorbachev met at a Soviet retreat in the Caucasus and reached agreement on the external aspects of German unity. Germany would remain in NATO, Soviet troops would be withdrawn, and a special bilateral treaty of friendship and cooperation between Germany and the Soviet Union would be signed. On August 31 the two German states signed a treaty on unification, and on September 12 the four victor powers concluded a treaty on the "final settlement with regard to Germany." On October 3, less than a year after the breaching of the wall, Germany was united. The five states of the former GDR automatically became part of the Community and immediately qualified for aid from the structural funds.

Europe's Initial Response

PHARE, THE EBRD, AND EARLY DISCUSSION OF ENLARGEMENT

While focusing on the immediate question of Germany, the Community and its member states took up the broader challenge of stabilization in central and eastern Europe as a whole. At an extraordinary session of the European Council in November 1989, French President Mitterrand proposed the establishment of a special bank to help finance economic transition in the central and east European countries. The other member states embraced Mitterrand's idea, which led to the founding of the European Bank for Reconstruction and Development (EBRD) the following year.

In July 1990 the Community extended its PHARE program to Bulgaria, Czechoslovakia, Yugoslavia, and East Germany. Assistance to Romania was temporarily delayed, owing to the post-Ceausescu government's suppression of student demonstrations in the spring of 1990, but in 1991 Bucharest became eligible for PHARE grants. Following the breakup of the Soviet Union, PHARE was extended to Estonia, Latvia, and Lithuania, an early indication that the EU was determined to treat the three Baltic countries as part of central and eastern Europe, rather than lump them with Russia and the Commonwealth of Independent States.[2]

Almost immediately after assuming power, the post-communist leaders of central and eastern Europe began to suggest that their countries should be admitted to what soon was to become the EU, as well as NATO. These suggestions evoked an ambivalent response in Western Europe. On the one hand, political leaders were concerned about instability emanating from the region and its potential implications for the EU: the spread of ethnic conflict such as had erupted in the former Yugoslavia, surges of refugees and migrants, environmental disasters, and political extremism. Membership in a strengthened EU was probably the only way to ensure, over the long term, that instability and reversion to dictatorship were banished from the continent. In addition, many in Western Europe felt a strong sense of obligation to the peoples of central and eastern Europe and especially to those who had led the fight against communism. Welcoming these people into the European family was clearly the right thing to do.

On the other hand, the costs and complications of enlargement promised to be enormous, and could well derail the ambitious plans of the early 1990s to deepen—to create a Union with a single currency, a common foreign and security policy, and increased powers for the Union's central institutions. There was also the difficult question of where to draw the line: even if the decision in principle to admit former communist countries was taken, it was still necessary to decide which countries, how many, and according to what criteria. It was not too difficult to envision Germany's eastern neighbors, Poland and the Czech Republic, becoming members, but what about the countries in the unstable Balkans? The question of membership became even more acute when, at the end of 1991, the Soviet Union dissolved into fifteen constituent states, raising the prospect that the Baltic countries or Ukraine or even Russia might apply.

Initially, there was some discussion about alternative arrangements to membership, such as the proposal for a European confederation advanced by Mitterrand in his 1989 New Year's Eve speech, or in the various proposals for a Europe of "concentric circles" in which the EU would form an inner core, the EEA, perhaps expanded to include the more advanced countries of central and eastern Europe, would form a second circle, and Russia and the other countries of the former Soviet Union would form the outermost circle. None of these schemes had enduring appeal, however, especially to the countries of eastern and central Europe, which continued to press for nothing less than full EU membership.

THE EUROPE AGREEMENTS

In addition to PHARE, the most important element in the EU's response to the changes in central and eastern Europe was the Europe Agreements, so named to distinguish them from the association agreements that the Community had concluded with many countries in other parts of the world. These agreements established a legal framework for the expanding economic, commercial, and human contacts between the Union and countries that were rapidly emerging from communism. They also were an interim response to the requests from the countries of the region for rapid admission to the Union. By establishing a form of association that would help to prepare these countries for membership as well as provide concrete and symbolically important links to the Union, the EU hoped to put off the question of membership. The preambles to the Europe Agreements noted the aspirations of the signatories to join the Union, but they stopped short of guaranteeing that membership was assured.

Because the Europe Agreements deal both with economic matters that are the responsibility of the EU as a unit and with political and cultural matters that are the shared or exclusive responsibility of the individual member states, they are mixed agreements, concluded by the European Communities (EC, ECSC, and Euratom) and the member states. They thus required a lengthy ratification process involving the European Parliament, each of the EU member state national parliaments, and the parliament of the associated country. In order to facilitate trade and investment during the ratification process, the Commission put into effect Interim Agreements with each associated country covering just those areas—trade and commerce—reserved for Community competence. All of the associated countries thus were able to benefit from expanding trade and investment with the EU even before the Europe Agreements went into effect.

As was seen in Chapter 8, the trade and investment provisions of the Europe

Agreements established a de facto free trade area between the EU and the candidate countries. Through approximation of legislation and other means, they went a long way toward extending the four freedoms of the single market to the candidate countries well in advance of actual membership. The one major exception was the free movement of people, the part of the single market that also was weakest in the existing EU. Reflecting the concern in Western Europe about possible surges of immigrants from the economically distressed central and east European countries, the agreements were very cautious with regard to the movement of workers. Their main contribution was to improve the lot of workers already in EU countries rather than to facilitate new flows of people.

In addition to their trade and economic provisions, the Europe Agreements provided for expanded political dialogue and cultural cooperation. They called for regular meetings of foreign ministers and other high officials to discuss topics of common interest with the aim of achieving convergence in foreign policy positions. In the cultural sphere, the central and east European countries became eligible to participate in many EU and member state cultural and educational programs. To monitor implementation, each Europe Agreement provided for the establishment of an Association Council consisting of representatives of the EU (i.e., the Commission), the member states, and the associated state. These councils were to meet at the ministerial level at least once each year to review progress and to take decisions regarding further action.

OTHER INSTITUTIONS

While attempting to slow the momentum toward EU membership, the West European countries, supported by the United States, encouraged the gradual integration of the former communist countries into other Western economic and political institutions, notably the Council of Europe and the OECD. Hungary joined the Council of Europe already in 1990, Poland in 1991, Bulgaria in 1992, and the Czech Republic, Estonia, Lithuania, Romania, Slovakia, and Slovenia in 1993. In 1990 the OECD established a Center for Cooperation with European Economies in Transition. The following year the Czech and Slovak Federal Republic, Hungary, and Poland became special OECD Partners in Transition. The Czech Republic became a full member of the OECD in 1995, followed by Hungary and Poland in 1996.

The Copenhagen Decisions

The debate on enlargement simmered throughout the early 1990s. British Prime Minister Thatcher and her successor, John Major, were among the most enthusiastic proponents of enlargement. They tended to favor the earliest and broadest possible expansion. As Thatcher later wrote, "having democratic states with market economies, which were just as 'European' as those of the existing Community, lining up as potential EC members made my vision of a looser, more open Community seem timely rather than backward."[3] At one point in the discussion Major even suggested that Russia might become a member.

At the other end of the spectrum were federalists such as Delors who, while they recognized that something had to be done for central and eastern Europe, were concerned that a broader and more diverse membership would undermine progress toward a more cohesive Union. Delors was skeptical about the admission of even the EFTA countries and warned that it would take fifteen to twenty years before the ex-communist countries were ready for membership.[4] In the end the most decisive voice in the debate was that of Kohl, who favored enlargement to central and eastern Europe—including the three Baltic states—but ruled out membership for Russia, Ukraine, and other states of the former Soviet Union. Kohl's position was somewhere between that of the British, who were accused by many of favoring indiscriminate and hasty enlargement, and that of Delors and many in the southern European countries, who sometimes were suspected of wanting to postpone enlargement indefinitely. The German view therefore tended to emerge as the consensus position.

Enlargement became a matter of "not whether but when" at the June 1993 Copenhagen European Council. This was the first occasion on which the EU member states formally declared enlargement as an explicit goal of the Union. Although they did not set a timetable, the EU leaders stated that accession would "take place as soon as an associated country is able to assume the obligations of membership by satisfying the economic and political conditions required."[5] The associated countries were those countries with which the Union had concluded or planned to conclude Europe Agreements. Poland, Hungary, Czechoslovakia, Romania, and Bulgaria had already signed such agreements, and the European Council had signaled its intention to negotiate Europe Agreements with the three Baltic states and Slovenia.

The European Council further specified four criteria for determining whether an associated country was ready for membership: (1) stability of institutions guaranteeing democracy, the rule of law, human rights, and respect for and protection of minorities; (2) the existence of a functioning market economy; (3) capacity to cope with competitive pressures and market forces within the Union; and (4) the ability to take on the obligations of membership, including adherence to the aims of political, economic, and monetary union—that is, the *acquis communautaire*. Recognizing that the *acquis* itself was expanding as EMU was established and other policy areas continued to develop, the European Council did not insist that the new members meet all standards and participate fully in all areas of integration from day one of membership. They were not, for example, expected or required to adopt immediately the Union's single currency. But they had to commit to eventual participation in EMU. Similarly, they were expected to participate in the Common Foreign and Security Policy, to cooperate in the development of a European Security and Defense Identity, and to join the WEU as the future defense arm of the EU.

While it was up to the applicants to meet these political and economic criteria, the European Council established one condition for the EU itself to meet, stipulating that "the Union's capacity to absorb new members, while maintaining the momentum of European integration, is also an important consideration in the general interest of both the Union and the candidate countries." This condition later was interpreted to mean that negotiations regarding the admission of additional candidates would not begin until at least six months after the completion of the IGC that was scheduled to convene in 1996. The EU ultimately stuck to this timetable, taking the decision to begin negotiations with five central and east European countries and with Cyprus in December 1997, exactly six months after the signing in Amsterdam of the new treaty that resulted from the IGC.

Meeting the Criteria

PRE-ACCESSION STRATEGY

With the Copenhagen decision, the EU had committed itself to admitting ten countries with a combined population of 105 million. Measured at purchasing power standards, per capita GDP in the region was less than one-third the EU average. In addition to its relative poverty, the central and east European region is highly diverse, with different languages, religions, and historical traditions. The magnitude of the enlargement challenge facing the Union thus called for an effective pre-accession strategy to prepare the candidates for membership, but also for an overhaul of the Union's own policies and institutions that would make it capable of functioning with a larger and more diverse group of members.

The main instruments used to help the candidate countries get ready for membership were the Europe Agreements and PHARE. Proposed at first in part to deflect demands for membership, the Europe Agreements soon became the key means to advance the pre-accession process. In addition to helping to redirect trade from what had been the CMEA to the EU market, the agreements provided a framework for the alignment of candidate country laws and regulations with EU norms and a mechanism, through the Association Councils, for regular bilateral dialogue.

Initially established in 1989 to promote the transition from communism, PHARE was also expanded and adapted to serve the needs of a longer-term pre-accession process. PHARE money provided technical and financial assistance for aligning legislation with EU norms, dealing with environmental and nuclear safety problems, and developing the telecommunications and transport infrastructure needed to speed integration into the European and world markets. PHARE was allocated ECU 4.2 billion for the period 1990–1994, an amount that was increased to ECU 6.693 billion for 1995–1999.

The candidate countries also benefitted from U.S. aid under the Support for East European Democracy (SEED) Act, technical assistance programs mounted by the OECD, and loans from the EBRD and World Bank. U.S. aid tapered off over time, however, as it became clear that the integration of these countries into the West was the primary responsibility of the EU. This left PHARE as by far the largest source of assistance for the region. Not all of this money was spent efficiently, however, and much of it ended up in the coffers of EU-based consultants.

THE ESSEN DECISIONS

Although the European Council took the decision in principle to enlarge in June 1993, at first there was little real momentum behind the enlargement effort. There were delays in putting into effect the Europe Agreements. The unexpectedly difficult Maastricht ratification process preoccupied the twelve through much of 1993, and was followed by the complex task of finalizing the accession agreements with Austria, Finland, and Sweden. The EU was widely criticized in the United States and in the candidate countries for a perceived lack of seriousness about the accession process. This in turn helped to strengthen the rationale for the NATO enlargement that was discussed in the previous chapter.

The stage finally was set for more rapid progress at the June 1994 Corfu European summit, at which the Greek presidency prepared to turn its responsibilities over to Germany, which had announced that it intended to make enlargement a priority of its presidency in the second half of 1994. The European Council invited the Commission to make specific proposals for the further implementation of the Europe Agreements and the Copenhagen decisions. On the basis of this request, the Commission produced several documents that became the basis for the pre-accession strategy adopted by the European Council at Essen in December 1994.

The Essen Council reviewed all of the areas in which progress was needed to prepare the candidate states for accession and singled out and began to address several issues that were expected to be especially difficult and that had the potential to derail the admission of the candidates. These issues included the internal market, agricultural policy, and the structural funds. The European Council approved the comprehensive strategy developed by the Commission after Corfu, the key element of which was a clear focus on the internal market. As discussed in Chapter 4, the European Council instructed the Commission to prepare a detailed white paper on the internal market that was to serve as a guide for the candidate countries to the EU-level legislation that they needed to transpose into national law and be prepared to implement and enforce. The European Council also called for the Commission to prepare a paper on agriculture policy as it related to enlargement and that could serve as the basis for tackling this sensitive area.[6]

The most noteworthy institutional innovation at Essen was the establishment of the Structured Dialogue. Unlike the Association Councils, which brought each associated country together with the Council in a 1 + 15 format, the Structured Dialogue would bring together all of the Europe Agreement states and all of the EU member states—in effect prefiguring future Council sessions in an enlarged

Union. Under the St...   ...rs, economics ministers,
and ministers of trans...   ...ther specific areas began
to meet with their EU...   ...e on policy convergence
and other forms of cc...

The Accession

THE LEGAL BAS...

The formal procedu...   ...in Article 49 of the Treaty
of European Union,...   ...am (see Box 10.1). It stipulates that any Eur...   ...tic principles and the rule
of law may apply to...   ...ferences to political rights
and political freedo...   ...article governing enlargement, Article O of...   ...oration by the 1996–1997
IGC reflected heigl...   ...ituation in formerly communist countries ar...

The first step ir...   ...o the Council of Ministers,
which is done by s...   ...ying documentation to the
government of the...   ...residency of the Council.
After it receives an...   ...mmission to offer an opinion on the candid:...   ...sed on these opinions, but
exercising its ultin...   ...the Commission's opinion,

Box ...   nlargement

Article 49, Trea...

Any European S...   ...t in Article 6(1) may apply
to become a me...   ...application to the Council,
which shall act u...   ...ission and after receiving the
assent of the E...   ...an absolute majority of its
component mer...

The conditions...   ...Treaties on which the Union
is founded whic...   ...ject of an agreement between
the Member Sta...   ...nt shall be submitted for ratification by all t...   ...heir respective constitutional
requirements.

Article 6(1)

The Union is founded on the principles of liberty, democracy, respect for human
rights and fundamental freedoms, and the rule of law, principles which are common
to the Member States.

the Council then must take a unanimous decision whether or not to begin accession negotiations with a candidate country.

The member states then conduct what are in effect separate intergovernmental conferences with each candidate country aimed at concluding treaties of accession. While the member states are the formal parties to these negotiations, in practice the EU presidency country, assisted by the Council secretariat and the Commission, undertakes much of the work. The draft treaty of accession then must be approved by the European Parliament by an absolute majority and by the Council unanimously. Following formal signature, the treaty must be ratified by all fifteen member state parliaments and by the parliament of the applicant country. Once this is accomplished, the accession process is complete and the candidate country can take its place as a full member.

Since the 1993 Copenhagen decisions, the EU has gone step-by-step in accordance with the procedure outlined in Article 49. Beginning with Hungary in March 1994 and concluding with Slovenia in June 1996, all ten associated countries formally applied for membership. (Turkey had already applied in 1987; Cyprus and Malta in 1990.) Having in principle already decided at Copenhagen to proceed with enlargement, the Council of Ministers instructed the Commission to begin work on opinions for each of the ten candidate countries shortly after receiving their applications. The prospective members were asked by the Commission to complete long and detailed questionnaires to determine how much convergence with EU norms and legislation had been achieved and to identify remaining problem areas. Because accession negotiations could not begin until after completion of the 1996–1997 IGC, the Commission decided to withhold the formal issuing of any opinions until after the signature of the Amsterdam Treaty.

AGENDA 2000

At its December 1995 Madrid session the European Council asked the Commission to prepare a composite paper that would include opinions on all ten candidate countries as well as a review of the Cyprus candidacy, noting that "this procedure will ensure that the applicant countries are treated on an equal basis."[7] In addition to asking the Commission to look at all of the applicants at the same time and in the same general framework, the Madrid European Council directed the Commission to examine the likely effects of enlargement on the Union, particularly with regard to agricultural and structural policies, but also in relation to the long-term budgetary outlook for the Union. The budgetary question was particularly important, given the fact that new members were expected to be, at least initially, a substantial drain on the EU budget and that the EU itself needed to adopt a new seven-year budget plan in 1999.

The Madrid request was the basis for *Agenda 2000: For a Stronger and Wider Union*, which the Commission delivered in July 1997, a little less than a month after the Amsterdam summit closing the IGC. Running to some 1,300 pages, the report consisted of three parts: an analysis of EU policies and the expected effect of enlargement on the EU, the detailed assessment of each of the eleven candidate countries requested by the Council and required under the enlargement provisions of Article 49, and the new financial framework proposals that were discussed in Chapter 3. In judging the preparedness of the candidate countries for enlargement, the Commission referred explicitly to the political and economic criteria established by the European Council at Copenhagen.

As measured against these criteria, the Commission recommended that five countries were ready to begin accession negotiations: the Czech Republic, Estonia, Hungary, Poland, and Slovenia. In addition, it reiterated an earlier opinion that Cyprus was ready to start accession talks. It rejected one applicant—Slovakia—for political reasons, namely the lack of democracy and respect for human rights under Prime Minister Vladimir Meciar. It concluded that four other countries— Bulgaria, Latvia, Lithuania, and Romania—needed to make greater progress with economic transformation before accession negotiations could begin. (The twelfth candidate country, Malta, had temporarily suspended its application, for reasons that are discussed below.)

The Commission opinions were controversial with the five countries being left behind in the next step of the enlargement process and with some member state governments. Latvia and Lithuania complained that Estonia had been singled out for special treatment in the Baltic region and appealed to their traditional backers, the Nordic countries, for inclusion in the first round of talks. Slovakia argued that its political situation had been misunderstood by the Commission, while Bulgaria and Romania warned that instability might arise if they were excluded both from NATO and the EU. As the Council prepared for the December 1997 session at which it was expected to approve the start of accession negotiations (a decision requiring the support of all the member states), these countries lobbied hard for the Council to disregard the Commission's opinion and include them in the next stage of the enlargement process.

THE LUXEMBOURG DECISIONS

Agenda 2000 triggered a broad debate among EU experts and political leaders about how to manage enlargement. There were very real concerns about timing and sequencing. Bringing some countries in ahead of others might, it was feared, divert investment from or contribute to political demoralization in those countries that were left behind, possibly encouraging them to drift back into the Russian sphere of influence. There were also practical considerations. Bringing the Czech Republic into the Union ahead of Slovakia would be difficult to reconcile with the existing Czech-Slovak customs union, while admitting Hungary but not Romania could create hardships for ethnic Hungarians living in Romania and used to traveling freely across the border. On the other hand, maintaining the credibility of the enlargement process and keeping the pressure on laggard countries to improve their performance required some degree of differentiation. Economic performance in Romania and Estonia was so widely disparate that it was difficult to justify treating both in the same group.

The question of Turkey also arose to complicate the enlargement discussion. Privately, many European politicians argued that Turkey was too culturally and economically different from Europe ever to become a member of the Union. Even those in Europe who believed that Turkey some day might join had concluded that it was by no means ready for accession negotiations—or even a serious pre-accession strategy. For its part, the Turkish government accused the EU member states of an anti-Islamic bias and was especially incensed that the Commission had recommended that the EU begin accession negotiations with Cyprus—meaning in effect the Greek Cypriot government in Nicosia that was boycotted by the Turkish minority on the island.

The various currents in the enlargement debate confronted the EU governments as they gathered in Luxembourg in December 1997 to take their decision on a first wave of accession negotiations. In the main, the EU heads of government endorsed the Commission's recommendation in favor of Cyprus and five central and east European countries, but they also put in place certain mechanisms intended to minimize any sense of exclusion on the part of the other five transition candidates. They announced that the accession process would begin on March 30, 1998, at a twenty-six–member meeting in London. The participants in the meeting would be the fifteen EU member states, the ten associated states, and Cyprus. This meeting would set the overall framework for accession talks with the candidates and symbolically underline that all eleven had the same status and the same theoretical chance to achieve membership. Within this framework, the EU proposed to establish an "enhanced pre-accession strategy" based on a new mechanism, the "accession partnership," and to begin the first accession negotiations. The EU stressed that those countries not asked to begin negotiations in 1998 were not necessarily being left permanently behind: they could catch up by improving their economic and, in the case of Slovakia, political performance. The Commission was asked to make annual reports to the Council of Ministers and to recommend when additional countries were ready to begin accession negotiations.[8]

In addition to these mechanisms involving the candidate countries, the European Council proposed the convening of an annual European Conference consisting of the fifteen EU member states, the eleven candidates, and Turkey. The conference was described as "a multilateral forum for political consultation, intended to address questions of general concern to the participants and to broaden and deepen their cooperation on foreign and security policy, justice and home affairs, and other areas of common concern, particularly economic matters and regional cooperation."[9] In reality, the conference was little more than a consolation prize for Turkey: a forum in which it could participate with the current and prospective EU member states, but one that was not in itself a part of the enlargement process. The Turkish government denounced this arrangement as confirming Turkey's "third-class" status in EU eyes, and chose not to participate in the conference when it took place in London the following March.

As decided by the Luxembourg meeting, the negotiations with the first six candidate countries were to begin in parallel with the implementation of an enhanced pre-accession strategy for all eleven of the applicant countries. This strategy was based on existing mechanisms—the Europe Agreements, PHARE, and the Structured Dialogue—along with the new instrument, the accession partnerships that were to be negotiated bilaterally between the Union and each of the candidate countries. Each partnership was to consist of a detailed program aimed at helping the candidate country adopt as much of the Union *acquis* as possible in the run-up to accession. PHARE aid was to be conditioned on how well the candidate countries did in implementing their accession partnership programs. The EU also pledged to increase the overall level of its pre-accession aid and opened certain programs (e.g., in education and training and research) to the applicant countries even before they became members. This was intended to give the candidates experience in EU working methods and to provide opportunities for students, teachers, business people, and academics from the candidate countries to cooperate on joint projects with counterparts from EU member states.

Negotiations

THE FIRST WAVE

Negotiations with the first six candidate countries began in March 1998. Based on the four previous enlargements and the situation in the candidate countries, most experts predicted that the first enlargement negotiations and the ensuing ratification process would take three to five years. The most advanced countries could expect to become members by 2001 at the earliest, with 2003 probably a more realistic target. Many in central and eastern Europe questioned why the enlargement negotiations should take so long.

In principle, a country joining the EU is asked to accept the *acquis communautaire*. There thus would not seem to be all that much to negotiate. In practice, however, candidate members usually seek to negotiate transition periods for phasing in Union rules and policies on their territory and in some cases to secure permanent derogations from certain EU policies or legal provisions. In the case of the enlargement to central and eastern Europe, the EU itself is attracted to phase-in periods for some EU treaty provisions and policies, for example free movement of people and support payments for agriculture.

Apart from these especially sensitive areas, the member states and even more so the Commission generally prefer to minimize the use of derogations and to keep transition phases relatively short so as to preserve the unity and coherence of the Union and especially its single market. The acceding countries, on the other hand, are under political pressure from domestic interest groups—farmers, fishermen, or property owners, for example—to seek exceptions and delays.

The first stage of the accession negotiations was an elaborate screening process carried out for thirty-one chapter headings. As shown in Table 10.1, the process covers both first-pillar matters and CFSP and Justice and Home Affairs issues reserved for the EU's second and third pillars. Screening began with relatively straightforward and uncontentious areas, such as small and medium-sized enterprises, science, education, and external relations, and then only later proceeded to the more difficult areas, such as agriculture, competition policy, and free movement of persons.

Following a series of multilateral meetings at which experts from the Commission presented their understanding of the *acquis* for each of these areas, the Commission undertook bilateral meetings with each of the six applicants to determine how far they had come in accepting the *acquis* for each chapter. The candidate countries were asked whether they were prepared to accept all of the EU legislation and regulations for a given chapter and if so whether they had adopted the

Table 10.1   Chapter Headings of the Screening Exercise

1. Free movement of goods
2. Freedom of movement for persons
3. Freedom to provide services
4. Free movement of capital
5. Company law
6. Competition policy
7. Agriculture
8. Fisheries
9. Transport policy
10. Taxation
11. Economic and monetary union
12. Statistics
13. Social policy and employment
14. Energy
15. Industrial policy
16. Small and medium-sized enterprises
17. Science and research
18. Education and training
19. Telecommunications and information technologies
20. Culture and audiovisual policy
21. Regional policy and coordination of structural instruments
22. Environment
23. Consumers and health protection
24. Cooperation in the fields of justice and home affairs
25. Customs union
26. External relations
27. Common foreign and security policy
28. Financial control
29. Financial and budgetary provisions
30. Institutions
31. Other

Source: European Commission.

necessary domestic laws and established the requisite administrative structures to implement those laws and regulations. This was also the stage at which the candidate countries declared whether they intended to request transitional arrangements for some chapters. Screening of some chapters was complete by the fall of 1998, and was followed by the start of actual negotiations for those chapters. The screening process as a whole was completed by the summer of 1999.

The results of the screening exercise were perhaps predictable. For some countries and some areas, acceptance of the *acquis* presented relatively little problem. For others, the transition periods requested were so long as to render almost meaningless the concept of an *acquis*. In the environmental area, for example, several applicant countries suggested that they would be ready to comply with EU drinking water directives only by 2017.

PROGRESS REPORTS AND THE SECOND WAVE

In November 1998 the Commission issued the first of the reports detailing how well the candidates were preparing themselves for enlargement. As mandated by the Luxembourg European Council, the reports covered both the six countries already engaged in accession talks and the others that had been placed on hold. For the former, the reports drew heavily on the initial results of the screening process.

The overall assessments were blunt and somewhat surprising. Of the six leading countries already involved in negotiations, Estonia and Hungary were given high marks for continuing to make progress on accepting the *acquis*, while Poland was given a more mixed report for its delays in addressing standards, state aids, the environment, agriculture, and administrative capacity. The Czech Republic and Slovenia, two frontrunners at the top of the per capita income scale in the region, were castigated for making almost no progress since the Commission opinions of July 1997.

On the other hand, several of the countries in the second tier were praised for real progress on reform. Latvia in particular was singled out as nearing the point where it might be ready to join the first tier and begin the actual negotiation process.[10] The report thus was mixed, suggesting that in some leading countries the pre-accession process was bogging down, but that the overall EU strategy of trying to narrow the gap between the first and second tiers was working, at least in some cases.

The Commission issued its second regular report on the progress of the candidate countries in October 1999, after the six leading countries had completed the screening process and after the six other candidate countries had had the benefit of nearly two years of intensified pre-accession assistance. The Commission again was upbeat about the economic performance of Hungary, Latvia, and Bulgaria and about the turn to democracy in Slovakia. It noted that in Poland delays in transposing EU directives into national law were accumulating, and was again critical of the Czech Republic. It expressed continuing concern about the disastrous economic situation in Romania, where reform still lagged.

The 1999 report also tackled the question of transition periods that had come up in the screening process and that was emerging as an important issue in the negotiations. Some of the candidate countries were asking for postaccession transition periods of a decade or more for EU urban waste water directives, the drinking water directive, and various other environmental laws, arguing that they did not have the resources to bring their performance up to EU standards except over the very long term. The EU had begun the negotiations with the position that transition periods be limited to no more than five years, but gradually showed a greater willingness to grant the candidate countries more time and latitude in nonmarket areas of the *acquis*—while still driving a hard bargain on the internal market. In the 1999 progress report the Commission for the first time made explicit this differentiation in the *acquis*, recommending a new approach to transition periods that distinguishes between areas linked to the functioning of the single market and matters such as environment, energy, and infrastructure. Such a differentiation was already implicit in the December 1994 decision to single out the internal market as a special area for attention through the commissioning of a white paper, but it was not spelled out until second progress report.

Despite the somewhat mixed assessment in the 1999 report, the Commission recommended that the Council authorize the start of accession negotiations with all of the candidate countries left out in 1997 and that it elevate Turkey's status to that of a formal candidate. This gave rise to some concern among the member states that the Commission was rushing the enlargement process (the European Council refused, for example, to back Prodi's call for the setting of a firm timetable for the first accessions), but at the Helsinki summit in December 1999 they endorsed the recommendations in the October 1999 progress report. In February 2000 negotiations got underway with six additional countries: Bulgaria, Latvia, Lithuania, Malta, Romania, and Slovakia. The Commission began by screening chapters of the *acquis* with each of the candidate countries: eight with Latvia, Lithuania, Malta, and Slovakia, six with Bulgaria, and just five with Romania, which remained the laggard of the integration process.[11]

Cyprus and Malta

Although most of the focus in the current enlargement round has been on central and eastern Europe, Cyprus and Malta, two small Mediterranean island countries with historic ties to Europe, are also part of this process and present some special difficulties. The population of Cyprus—about 770,000—is approximately 80 percent ethnically Greek, with the remainder Turkish Cypriot. Under the 1960 constitution, power was apportioned between the Greek and Turkish communities. However, Cyprus has been partitioned since the 1974 invasion of the island by

Turkey. The northern part of the island has declared itself to be an independent state, which the international community does not recognize. The Turkish Cypriots do not participate in the legally recognized government in Nicosia, which is effectively in the hands of the Greek majority.

Prompted by Greece's admission to the EC in 1981 and Cyprus's own economic interests, in July 1990 the Cypriot government applied for membership. In June 1993 the Commission issued a favorable opinion on the application, noting the relative strength of the Cypriot economy and the progress that Cyprus had made in using its association agreement with the EU to align itself with many EU laws and practices.[12] Both sides began preparing for accession negotiations, but it was not until the June 1994 European Council in Corfu that the member states confirmed that the next phase of the enlargement process would include Cyprus (and Malta), a decision that was taken under pressure from Greece. It meant that the European Council was pledged not to proceed with any eastward enlargement without also taking up the Cypriot application, either simultaneously or beforehand. The Cyprus candidacy thus was at least tacitly linked with those of the central and east European countries.

In response to these developments, Turkey argued that any move to incorporate Cyprus into the EU would run counter to the 1960 Treaty of Guarantee that was signed by Greece, Turkey, and Britain and that bars Cyprus from joining any international organization of which Greece and Turkey are not both members. The Turkish government further warned that if the Greek Cypriot government joined the EU against its wishes, it would incorporate the northern part of the island into Turkey. The EU rejected this interpretation of the 1960 treaty and argued as a matter of principle that Turkey could not wield a veto over the actions of the legally recognized government in Nicosia. As a practical matter, however, the EU was concerned about the implications of proceeding with enlargement in the face of Turkish opposition and bringing a still-partitioned island into the Union. Incorporation of the northern zone into Turkey would be particularly problematic, as it would mean the occupation of a part of EU territory by a non-EU power.

In the 1990s, EU policy toward Cyprus appeared to rest on a vague hope that the prospect of EU membership would soften the differences between the Greek and Turkish communities, much the way EU membership for Ireland and the UK helped to defuse conflict over the status of Northern Ireland, thereby contributing to the April 1998 Belfast agreement. Per capita income in the Turkish sector of Cyprus is only one-third the level of that in the south, and the Turkish minority stands to benefit enormously from the structural aid and market access that would come with enlargement.

By the time the EU began accession talks with Cyprus in March 1998, however, there was still little sign that this approach was working. The Turkish community turned down an invitation to participate in the talks and repeated its threats to accept an offer to merge with Turkey. Although it did not attempt to block a start of talks, France vowed to block actual accession if the negotiations concluded before a solution to the partition of the island was achieved. For its part, Greece threatened to veto any enlargement to central and eastern Europe if Cyprus was not accorded membership as well. The elevation of Turkey to candidate status in December 1999 helped to ameliorate the tension over the island, but did not in itself provide an answer to the question of whether a divided Cyprus could be admitted to the Union.

The accession of Malta, a relatively prosperous country with a population of just over 360,000, does not present major difficulties for the EU, but the Maltese themselves have been somewhat ambivalent about joining the Union. After achieving independence from Britain in 1964, Malta was for many years governed by the neutralist Labor party, which opposed closer ties with Western Europe. The Nationalist Party took power in 1987 and adopted a pro-integration position. Following the lead of Cyprus, in July 1990 the Nationalist government applied for EC membership.

In June 1993 the Commission issued a favorable opinion on Malta's candidacy and in June 1994 the European Council pledged that Malta could participate with Cyprus in the next wave of enlargement negotiations.[13] However, after the October 1996 elections the Labor party returned to power and promptly suspended Malta's application. Malta thus was left out of the key decisions about enlargement that were made at the 1997 Luxembourg European Council.

The Nationalist party returned to power in the elections of 1998 and quickly sought to reactivate Malta's bid for membership. The December 1998 Vienna European Council welcomed this decision and asked the Commission to undertake an update of its 1993 opinion. But the EU did not rush into enlargement negotiations, lest the domestic political situation change once again. Malta ultimately was included in the list of countries approved for the start of accession negotiations by the December 1999 Helsinki European Council, and negotiations began in February 2000.

Malta presents the EU with little in the way of economic and financial difficulties, but its small size compounds the political and institutional challenges of enlargement. After Luxembourg, it would be the second mini-state in the Union and its accession would exacerbate the problems of small-country over-representation in the EP and the Council. Like other small countries, Malta would have to strain its diplomatic resources to manage the rotating EU presidency. Malta thus provides the Union with added reason to undertake institutional reforms in advance of the next enlargement.

Turkey

As noted above, Turkey was accorded the status of formal candidate for EU membership at the December 1999 Helsinki European Council. This was only the latest step in a long and complex relationship between Turkey and Western Europe. A country of 64 million people, most of whom are Muslim, Turkey was a recipient of Marshall Plan aid and thus a founding member of the OEEC/OECD. It has been a member of the Council of Europe since 1949 and of NATO since 1952. Since Kemal Attaturk's reforms of the 1920s, it has been a secular republic in which people are free to practice their religion but in which Islam is given no special political status. Turkey thus considers itself a European power that should be welcome in all European bodies, including the EU.

But Turkey also faces economic, political, and security problems that distinguish it from the rest of Europe. Its economy suffers from high inflation and budget deficits in the 7–8 percent of GDP range. Economic growth has been strong, but from a low base. Per capita GDP is only one-third the EU average. Turkey's population is young and growing and according to current projections will surpass even that of Germany by 2015, which would make Turkey the largest country in the Union were it to become a member.

Internally, Turkey faces a severe political challenge from its Kurdish minority in the southeastern part of the country. The struggle with the Kurdish independence movement has resulted in thousands of deaths and harsh criticism in Western Europe about violations of human rights by the Turkish government and armed forces. Turkey also faces a complex international security situation. It has tense relations with its southern and eastern neighbors, Syria, Iraq, and Iran, as well as disputes with Greece over Cyprus, oil rights under the Aegean Sea, and the ownership of a small island off the Turkish coast.

As noted in Chapter 8, in 1963 Turkey and the EC concluded an association agreement that pointed to eventual full membership. But relations between Turkey and the Community deteriorated in the 1970s, at first over Cyprus and later because of internal developments in Turkey. In order to forestall the annexation of Cyprus by Greece, in July 1974 Turkey invaded the island, occupying its northern part. Some 200,000 Greek Cypriots fled south to escape Turkish rule. The United Nations adopted resolutions calling for the removal of foreign troops and the return of refugees, but over the years the division of the island hardened and became a permanent irritant in Greek-Turkish and EC-Turkish relations. In 1983 authorities in the Turkish sector unilaterally proclaimed the establishment of the Turkish Republic of Northern Cyprus (TRNC). The international community has never accepted the legality of this action and no state besides Turkey recognizes the TRNC.

These developments were accompanied by a deterioration of economic and political conditions in Turkey. In September 1980 a group of Turkish military officers seized power, dissolved the parliament, and suspended the constitution. In January 1982 the EP responded by voting to suspend the Turkey-EC association agreement. The accession of Greece to the Community in 1981 cast a further shadow on the EC-Turkish relationship, as it meant that henceforth there was one member state with strongly anti-Turkish feelings that was able to block all important initiatives toward Turkey under the unanimity provisions of the founding treaties.

Between 1983 and 1987 civilian rule was gradually restored. In April 1987 Turkey formally applied for EC membership, and in September 1988 the suspension of the EC-Turkey association agreement was lifted, resulting in a renewal of economic aid to Ankara. As required by the provisions in the Treaty of Rome governing accession of new members, the European Commission delivered an opinion on Turkey's candidacy for membership in December 1989. It concluded that the Community was not ready to accept any new members until completion of the single market program. It also identified problems specific to Turkey that would have ruled out enlargement negotiations in any case: Turkey's relatively poor record on democracy and human rights, its disputes with Greece, and the failure to find a solution to the Cyprus problem. In the absence of real progress toward membership, the keystone of the EU-Turkey relationship became the 1996 customs union that was discussed in the previous chapter.

Throughout the 1990s, the fact that Western Europe seemed to be backing away from earlier pledges regarding membership contributed to a sense of betrayal in Turkey. Relations with the EU were badly strained as the pre-accession process with the central and east European countries and with Cyprus gathered momentum, leaving Turkey in its wake and suggesting that the West European countries were more ready to accept the formerly communist countries of central and eastern Europe than a country that had been a loyal ally throughout the cold war and in the 1990–1991 Persian Gulf war against Iraq. These tensions came to a head in 1997 with the approach of the crucial Luxembourg decisions about the start of enlargement talks.

The Turks were well aware of how far they needed to go to be ready for membership. But they also had come to believe that the real reasons for rejection by the EU had less to do with their own economic and political problems than with the fact that Turkey is an Islamic country and as such was fundamentally unwelcome in Europe. The European People's Party, the EU-wide grouping of the Christian Democratic parties, issued a statement in 1997 that explicitly rejected EU membership for Turkey. According to Wilfried Martens, former prime minister of Belgium and president of the group, "the EU is in the process of building a civilization in which Turkey has no place." Although not an official policy statement, such remarks were deeply offensive to the Turks.

In *Agenda 2000*, the European Commission reaffirmed Turkey's eligibility for membership but it also drew attention to the same economic, political, human rights, and foreign policy problems highlighted in its 1989 opinion. As has been seen, at Luxembourg the European Council declined to affirm Turkey's candidacy by treating it in the same way as the other twelve candidate countries, but it did propose the ill-fated European Conference, as well as instructed the Commission to draw up a new strategy to prepare Turkey for accession "by bringing it closer to the European Union in every field." The Turks were not impressed with these measures, and instituted a deep freeze in relations with the Union. Some Turkish political leaders even threatened to veto the enlargement of NATO to Poland, Hungary, and the Czech Republic if Turkey was not granted EU candidate status. In the Turkish view, the EU was relegating Turkey to a third-tier status, not only behind the leading candidates such as Poland but also behind relative laggards such as Romania and Bulgaria—countries that in some cases had barely begun the market reforms called for by the end of communism.

The Turks were especially critical of Germany, which they saw as the main opponent of Turkish membership. Turkey subsequently declared that it was ready to join the European Conference, but only if the EU improved its treatment of Turkey's application. The UK, traditionally among the more pro-Turkish member states, sought to use its January–June 1998 presidency to set a new tone in EU-Turkish relations. The Commission's "Strategy for relations between Turkey and the European Union," drawn up in response to the Luxembourg request, repeated familiar proposals for closer cooperation in various fields and tacitly called for Greece to lift its veto on the approval of special funds for Turkey previously promised in connection with the customs union agreement.

Despite such gestures and the election in September 1998 of a new German government that was widely seen as more sympathetic to Turkey and to Turkish immigrants in Germany, the impasse in relations persisted. Indeed, a new crisis broke out in late 1998 over the request of alleged Kurdish terrorist Abdulah Ocalan for political asylum in Rome and Italy's subsequent refusal of Turkey's request that he be extradited to Turkey to stand trial. Ocalan eventually was seized by Turkish agents in Kenya and flown to Turkey, where in June 1999 he was convicted and sentenced to death by a Turkish court. His seizure defused a budding crisis in Turkish-EU relations, but his sentencing only seemed to underscore the deep cultural and political gap between the Turks and the Union. (EU countries do not use the death penalty.)

Relations finally took a dramatic turn for the better in December 1999, when the European Council, endorsing the recommendation in the Commission's October 1999 progress report, formally upgraded the status of Turkey to candidate member. The heads of state and government declared that "Turkey is a candidate state destined to join the Union on the basis of the same criteria as applied to the other candidate states." To lend substance to this claim, the EU agreed to develop a pre-accession strategy for Turkey and to conclude an accession partnership agreement on the same basis as those negotiated with the other candidate countries. Turkey also was granted the right to participate in certain EU programs and in multilateral meetings among the EU member states and the candidates for membership. In response to the positive steps on the EU side, the Turks deferred the execution of Ocalan and vowed to step up the pace of economic and political reform.

Given the plethora of internal and external problems that Turkey faces, many experts and political leaders in Europe argue, privately if not in public, that the EU would be extremely foolish to accept Turkey as a member. To do so would be to internalize these problems, dramatically increase the numbers of poor in the Union, and give it extended borders with several unstable Middle Eastern countries. Others in Europe, generally supported by the United States, have stressed that the door must be kept open for Turkey and that EU membership holds out the best prospect for overcoming many of these problems. With the December 1999 decision, the EU seems to have embraced the latter position, stressing that Turkey *is* welcome in Europe and placing the onus on Turkey to meet the same Copenhagen criteria that apply to central and eastern Europe. Actual membership is likely to be at best a long-term prospect, however, and one that may provoke renewed political controversy in the Union.

Prospects

More than a decade after the unraveling of communism in central and eastern Europe, the region gradually is "returning" to Europe. Trade has been reoriented away from the former market in the east to the Union. Foreign direct investment by EU firms in the candidate countries continues to rise, as West European firms establish factories to take advantage of lower labor costs and to create businesses close to new customers in the region.

But progress toward full integration is uneven and, in the view of many in the region, painfully slow. For the next several decades, the EU and the candidate countries face several difficult tasks. First, they must complete the integration of these countries into the EU and into NATO. To succeed in this task, these countries will have to maintain domestic political support for the painful transitions and adaptations needed to prepare for membership. They also will need to win over public and parliamentary support in the EU member countries.

Second, the EU and the more advanced central and east European countries will need to work to ensure that an initial enlargement to perhaps a few countries (especially since the initial enlargement of NATO was confined only to three countries) does not reopen a damaging divide in Europe, leaving the less advanced countries to slip behind into economic hardship and political instability.

NATO's 1999 war with Yugoslavia over Kosovo and the ensuing refugee and economic crises in neighboring countries further complicated the enlargement picture, bringing both setbacks and opportunities. On the one hand, the war damaged economic prospects in the Balkans, making it harder than ever for Bulgaria and Romania to close the gap with the more advanced countries or for Albania and Macedonia (not to mention Serbia itself, where the post-Milosevic transition was just beginning) to reach a level of economic and political stability that would enable them to conclude Europe Agreements that would put them on the road to membership.

On the other hand, the war brought renewed attention from the EU and a new influx of aid. Albania and Macedonia asserted a moral claim to rapid NATO and EU membership based on their support for the war and their taking in of the Kosovar refugees. The Western countries did not formally acknowledge this claim as valid, but the Balkan stability pact and new bilateral partnerships with the countries of the region launched by the EU were a tacit response to the Albanian and Macedonian positions. Although the medium-term economic, political, and security environment in the Balkans is unfavorable, the logic of geography and of previous EU positions suggests that these countries eventually will conclude Europe Agreements and become candidates for membership.

As enlargement proceeds, the European continent will be transformed. In the vision for the future propounded by the Union, all countries from the Atlantic to the Baltic–Black Sea belt will be members of a single union that is democratic, committed to freedom and human rights, and increasingly prosperous. This union will be linked to the United States through an expanded NATO and the U.S.-EU dialogue, and open to the outside world through the Union's commitment to free trade. The central and east European countries will have returned to a Europe that has not existed since the rise of the nation-state in the late Middle Ages, and that perhaps has never truly existed except as a dream of philosophers and visionaries. For this vision to be translated into reality, however, the EU and the applicant countries face years of hard work and difficult economic, political, and institutional adaptation. The challenges ahead and their implications for the citizen are discussed in the next and concluding chapter.

Notes

1. Council Regulation (EEC) 3906/89 on economic aid to the Republic of Hungary and the Polish People's Republic, December 18, 1989.

2. Council Regulation (EEC) 2698/90, September 17, 1990; Council Regulation (EEC) 3800/91, December 23, 1991.

3. *The Downing Street Years*, 769.

4. Grant, *Delors*, 143.

5. *The European Councils, 1992–1994*, 86.

6. "Report from the Council to the Essen European Council on a strategy to prepare for the accession of the associated CCEE," *Presidency Conclusions, 1992–1994*, 155–162.

7. *The European Councils, 1995*, 48.

8. *Luxembourg European Council, 12 and 13 December 1997: Presidency Conclusions*, Brussels, SN 400/97.

9. Ibid.

10. "The new bogeymen," *Business Central Europe*, December 1998/January 1999, 46–47.

11. Michael Smith, "Brussels plots course of EU entry," *Financial Times*, March 19, 2000.

12. *The challenge of enlargement: Commission opinion on the application by the Republic of Cyprus for membership*, Bull. EC Supplement 5/93.

13. *The challenge of enlargement: Commission opinion on Malta's application for membership*, Bull. EC Supplement 4/93.

Suggestions for Further Reading

Avery, Graham and Fraser Cameron. *The Enlargement of the European Union*. Sheffield: Academic Press, 1998.

European Commission. *Agenda 2000: For a stronger and wider Union. Bulletin of the European Union*, Supplement 5/97.

European Bank for Reconstruction and Development. *Transition Report, 1999*. London: EBRD, 1999.

Redmond, John and Glenda B. Rosenthal, eds. *The Expanding European Union: Past, Present, Future*. Boulder: Lynne Rienner, 1998.

CHAPTER 11

Conclusion: Europe and the Citizen—A United Europe?

As the new millennium begins, the EU faces a daunting array of policy challenges, of which three in particular stand out: employment and the economic challenges of globalization, institutional reform, and enlargement. How the EU addresses this agenda will have important implications for citizens. It will affect jobs, the fight against crime, the environment, immigration, taxes, pensions, culture, and potentially even matters of war and peace. Conversely, how citizens regard the EU—whether they see it as part of the solution to the challenges of the new century or as itself a problem—will in part determine the future direction and ultimate objectives of the European integration process. In short, uniting Europe will affect and involve citizens. It will do so in ways that are perhaps obvious, but that are worth highlighting in this concluding chapter.

A New Economic Strategy

THE LISBON EUROPEAN COUNCIL

As was seen in Chapter 6, the EU spent the 1990s heavily focused on meeting the Maastricht convergence criteria and the launch of the euro. Many economists argued that convergence had to be accompanied by structural reform at the firm and societal level. There was also a growing debate, especially after the left took power in key countries at the end of the decade, about a "third way" that would combine the best features of the European welfare state and market-driven U.S.-style capitalism. For the most part, however, the focus was on macroeconomic policy and on meeting the Maastricht targets for deficits, debt, and inflation.

With the euro successfully launched, the focus has shifted decisively to structural reform at the microeconomic level. (Structural reform can be defined as "actions, initiatives and measures taken to improve the functioning of national as well as European product, capital and labor markets."[1]) In a symbolically important move, the first session of the European Council in the new century was a special summit in Lisbon, convened at the initiative of Portuguese Prime Minister Antonio Guterres, to adopt a new economic strategy for the Union for the period 2000–2010.

The declared goal of the new strategy is for the Union "to become the most competitive and dynamic knowledge-based economy in the world capable of sustainable economic growth with more and better jobs and greater social cohesion."[2] The European Council predicted that with continued pursuit of sound macroeconomic policies and a new commitment to structural reform, the EU should be able to grow at a rate of 3 percent per year for the next several years, rather than the 2.0 percent annual rate registered in the period 1990–1999. Press accounts characterized Lisbon as the Internet and e-commerce summit, brought about because of a growing perception on the part of political leaders that Europe needed to adjust fundamentally to the new global economy.

To achieve the new strategic goal, Lisbon mandated action in six areas: creating an information society for all, establishing a European area of research and innovation, creating a better environment for starting and developing innovative businesses, furthering economic reforms to complete the internal market, building efficient and integrated financial markets, and coordinating macroeconomic policies of fiscal consolidation.

To promote a new information society, the European Council charged the Commission and the Council of Ministers with drawing up a comprehensive "eEurope Action Plan" by June 2000. It called for further liberalization of telecommunications markets with the objective of reducing the costs of using the Internet in homes and businesses. It also endorsed the passage of legislation needed to stimulate electronic commerce and set a goal of connecting all schools in the EU to the Internet by the end of 2001.

The proposal to establish a European area of research and innovation was based upon the review of research policy undertaken in connection with the Fifth Framework Program (see Chapter 5), but contained new elements. Continuing the trend toward the use of benchmarks and scoreboards already applied with regard to the single market and employment policy, the European Council called for identifying methods to assess the performance of national R&D policies in different fields and mandated the introduction by June 2001 of a European innovation scoreboard. The intent was to shift the focus from quantitative levels of support to actual results—scientific and especially commercial. Other research-related measures endorsed in Lisbon include the establishment of a high-speed European electronic network linking universities and research institutes, further steps to promote the mobility of researchers, and the establishment of an EU-wide patent by the end of 2001.

To improve the environment for new businesses, the European Council launched yet another benchmarking exercise. It called for the Council and the Commission to begin monitoring, across the member states, such issues as the length of time and costs involved in setting up a company, the availability of risk capital, and the performance of the member states in producing business and scientific graduates. Recognizing that small companies are the main engine for job creation, it endorsed the principle of a European charter for small companies and called for the EIB to take a more active role in directing finance toward business start-ups, especially in the high technology sector.

The last three issues tackled by Lisbon—financial markets, the internal market, and macroeconomic policy—were all areas in which the EU had long been active, as was seen in previous chapters. The summit called for continued efforts to monitor and strengthen the single market and accelerated liberalization in the gas, electricity, postal service, and transport sectors. With regard to finance, it endorsed new action plans for financial services and risk capital intended to promote the kind of venture capital markets and start-up funding that are seen as key factors in the success of Silicon Valley and other high-technology regions. In the macroeconomic sphere, Lisbon reiterated the importance of deficit reduction and the stability targets mandated in the Maastricht Treaty and the Stability and Growth Pact, but argued that even "macroeconomic policies should foster the transition towards a knowledge-based economy." This could be done, for example, by redirecting public expenditures from welfare payments toward expenditure on training and education.

In addition to endorsing these policy measures, aimed at accomplishing the strategic goal of world economic leadership by 2010, the Lisbon European Council called for modernizing the European social model "by investing in people and building an active welfare state." At first glance there would seem to be a contradiction between the EU's stated aspirations to lead the world into the "new" knowledge-based economy and its reaffirmation of the "old" welfare state. Risk capital and social inclusion are buzzwords not often found in the same policy documents. But the European leaders were careful to stress that in their view there was no contradiction between a dynamic capitalist economy and a revitalized welfare state. To some extent this was the result of political compromise, as those national leaders, notably Jospin of France, who were somewhat skeptical of trends in global capitalism insisted upon an emphasis on social protection and the continued role of the state to counterbalance the calls for greater economic liberalization.

Apart from the need for political compromise, however, the Lisbon document reflected a genuinely-held view that European systems of social protection must be preserved. Most European political leaders are committed to a social model distinct from that of the United States. While they acknowledge the U.S. record in achieving high economic growth, budget surpluses, and low unemployment, they argue that these achievements have had costs in terms of greater income inequality, less social protection, financial volatility, and massive trade and payments deficits linked to low savings and excessive consumption.[3]

Beyond defending the intrinsic merits of the European economic and social model, the Lisbon European Council proclaimed that the key features of this model, far from being incompatible with a dynamic economy, in fact will provide the basis for superior European competitive performance in the coming years. It claimed that a stepped-up commitment to overcoming social exclusion through increased education and training, along with the continued pursuit of the employment policies discussed in Chapter 5, could raise employment and increase both the market for and the EU's ability to deliver innovative information technology products. The overall goal articulated at Lisbon was to increase the employment rate from today's 61 percent of the population to 70 percent by 2010 and to increase the number of women in employment from the current 51 percent average among the member states to more than 60 percent by the same date. Further measures in the area of social policy were deferred to the expected adoption of a new European Social Agenda at the European Council in Nice at the end of the French presidency in December 2000.

Along with the policy initiatives agreed upon in Lisbon, the March 2000 meeting resulted in a potentially important institutional decision. The assembled heads of state and government agreed that the European Council would hold a special meeting every spring devoted to economic and social issues and to monitoring implementation—by the member states and the institutions of the Union—of the new economic strategy. The European Council thus in effect returned to the situation that obtained at the time of its establishment in 1974, when three meetings per year were envisioned.

PROSPECTS

The decision to meet every spring to review the new economic strategy reflects the seriousness with which member state governments intend to pursue the Lisbon objectives. It is not, however, in itself a guarantee of success. European citizens are certain to see some concrete results from the March 2000 decisions. Connecting all schools to the Internet, for example, is a discrete, readily measurable policy objective that the Union and the member states, once the commitment has been made, should be able to achieve. But whether the EU can become the most dynamic region of the world economy, reconcile the market with a modernized welfare state, or increase employment rates by close to 10 percent is another matter.

Political opposition may prevent member state governments or the Union as a whole from implementing policies of reform—or the policies themselves may prove inadequate given economic uncertainty and the difficulties inherent in long-term forecasting. Many of the economic challenges facing Europe are rooted in broader demographic and social trends, the implications of which are not yet fully understood. One example is the ageing of the population. The number of persons in the EU aged 60 and over will increase from around 80 million in 2000 to 91 million in 2010. Of these people, the fastest growing group will be those aged 80 and over, which will increase from around 13 million in 2000 to 18 million in 2010.[4] These trends will place a growing burden on European pension and health-care systems and could lead to intergenerational strains as younger workers are forced to support the needs of the elderly. But population ageing also could help to alleviate unemployment, increase productivity, and spur political leaders to undertake long-delayed reforms in tax and pension systems.

The implications of globalization and technological change for economic performance are also difficult to predict. While Europe is in many respects well placed to take advantage of increased cross-border economic flows through trade and investment, it could be more vulnerable than other regions to political backlash against globalization. Studies suggest that globalization increases income inequalities within countries, as unskilled workers are exposed to greater competition from lower-paid workers while professional and managerial employees reap the benefits of expanded global markets. (Wealthier and better educated citizens also benefit disproportionately from many *consumption*-related aspects of globalization, for example easier foreign travel and access to imported luxury goods.) If the EU achieves its targeted 3 percent annual growth, rising inequality could be masked by higher overall incomes and lower unemployment. But if growth lags, there could be demands for greater protectionism and subsidies in the EU relative to the outside world or even within the Union itself in contravention of the single market. Either trend would undercut the assumptions upon which the Lisbon goals are based.

The debate over the costs and benefits of globalization is just one aspect of a broader set of issues concerning social and cultural values that will affect and be affected by future economic developments. In 1999, the Forward Studies Unit of the Commission published a study entitled *Scenarios Europe 2010: Five Possible Futures for Europe*, based on contributions from both Commission and outside experts. In the study, the authors developed alternative futures for Europe that were based on how the different "key drivers" of change might evolve. Along with technology, politics, trends outside Europe and many other factors, the key drivers included culture and values.

In one scenario, for example, self-reliance and economic achievement become the most salient values to the European citizenry, while in other scenarios solidarity and social equality are preeminent. Attitudes toward authority, levels of trust in large organizations, and feelings about participation in the political process are all factors that, although impossible to quantify, were seen as playing an important role in Europe's future economic development.

While no one would claim that any of the scenarios are exact predictions of what Europe will look like in 2010, the study is a useful reminder that radically different historical paths are possible. They also reemphasize the links between economic trends and the social and cultural values held by the citizens. What people want and value will condition their behavior as economic actors, just as economic circumstances will shape people's values and interests.

In the "Triumphant Markets" scenario, Europe develops along stereotypically American lines. In another, "Shared Responsibilities," Europe succeeds in achieving something very much like the outcome envisioned in Lisbon: a dynamic economy combined with high levels of social protection and inclusion. In a third scenario, "The Hundred Flowers," Europe is characterized by a relative breakdown of economic and political structures.[5] Reacting to the failure of government policy, increased income inequality, and the negative effects of globalization—but also taking advantage of new technologies such as the Internet and trends toward decentralization underway since the 1990s—Europeans turn away from "old-style government" and the "new economy." Trends such as consumer boycotts and tax evasion become rampant. The economy fragments as people turn to barter, skill exchanges, local self-government, and growing markets for craft products and second-hand goods. "Most of all, new shared values emerge, a somewhat nostalgic blend of local action, good-neighborliness, mutual support and a return to nature."[6]

"The Hundred Flowers" may not be a very probable outcome for Europe, but it is a reminder that the confident predictions of governments and economists can go awry. Indeed, the analysis behind the Lisbon goals is probably too one-dimensional and, despite the rhetoric about social inclusion, still too removed from everyday citizens' concerns to serve as a guidepost to Europe's economic future. Increasing the number of women in the workforce, for example, will have important implications for child rearing and family life, issues on which citizens will have their own strong feelings that may or may not coincide with the general thrust of EU policy.

The bottom line is that economic policy will remain an enormous challenge for the EU, as it will for other regions of the world. While the Union has set certain economic targets and policy directions, the outside world and, as the scenarios suggest, European society may develop in ways that are difficult to predict. The EU may be a force working to shape globalization, or it may be buffeted by or turn away from forces that it is unable to master. Meanwhile, the Union itself will be changing, reforming its institutions, and admitting new members.

Institutional Reform and IGC 2000

The second major issue on the EU agenda is institutional reform. As was noted in previous chapters, at Copenhagen in June 1993 the European Council decided that the Union would admit those central and eastern European countries that met certain economic and political criteria, but that enlargement negotiations would not begin until after the completion of the 1996–1997 IGC, which was expected to result in a thorough-going reform of the Union's institutions. The December 1995 Madrid European Council established a timetable for progress on enlargement, but further emphasized that it would require changes in the structure and workings of the institutions.

As it happened, however, the 1996–1997 IGC made only limited progress on the reforms regarded as essential for effective decision making in an enlarged Union. Preoccupied with domestic politics and the launch of EMU, the member states managed only second-order changes in the treaties. As was seen in Chapter 3, the Treaty of Amsterdam capped the future size of the EP at 700 members, strengthened the powers of the president of the Commission, and extended the co-decision powers of the EP to new policy areas. The treaty also inserted a flexibility clause into the Treaty of Rome that instituted a legal procedure under which subgroups of member states could establish closer cooperation among themselves within the Union. Fundamentally, however, Amsterdam failed to resolve key issues relating to the distribution of power among the member states and the streamlining of decision making in an enlarged Union. Another IGC thus was seen as necessary, with the only question being whether it would occur before the first enlargement or at some point during the enlargement process.

TIMING

The closest the IGC came to fundamental reform was to adopt a legally binding protocol, appended to the Treaty of Amsterdam, that dealt with three issues: the size of the Commission, weighting of votes in the Council of Ministers, and the possible extension of qualified majority voting in the Council. Because these issues were singled out but not resolved at the 1996–1997 IGC, they became known as the Amsterdam "leftovers." The member states recognized that with enlargement the Commission was in danger of becoming too large to be effective and that without reweighting, the relative weight of the large member states in the Council would decline in a way that would be politically problematic. They thus agreed to link these two issues. The protocol stated that as of the first enlargement, the Commission would be comprised of one national from each member state, provided that by that time the weighting of votes in the Council had been modified, "whether by the reweighting of the votes or by dual majority."[7] In other words, the five large member countries agreed to give up the right to nominate two commissioners in exchange for added weight in the Council.

Eliminating the second commissioner for France, Germany, Italy, Spain, and the UK in exchange for a reweighting of votes in the Council could be a temporary measure geared toward an initial enlargement involving a few countries, but it is not a permanent solution for a Union of 28 or more countries. The protocol thus went on to state that at least one year before the membership of the EU exceeds twenty, a new IGC would be convened to carry out "a comprehensive review of the provisions of the Treaties on the composition and functioning of the institutions." It thus held out the theoretical possibility that accession of the first five candidate countries could take place without the convening of another IGC, provided the member states could reach agreement on the reweighting of votes in the Council.

From the outset, however, some member states made clear that they would force the issue of institutional reform long before membership reached twenty. Belgium, France, and Italy issued a separate declaration stipulating their view that "the Treaty of Amsterdam does not meet the need, reaffirmed at the Madrid European Council, for substantial progress towards reinforcing the institutions. . . . Those countries consider that such reinforcement is an indispensable condition for the conclusion of the *first* accession negotiations."[8] By early 1999 there was general support among the member states for the Belgian-French-Italian position, and little desire to proceed with any enlargement without first resolving the institutional issues left over from Amsterdam. At Cologne in June of that year the European Council formally decided to convene the IGC in early 2000 and set the end of the French presidency, December 2000, as the target date for its conclusion.

AGENDA

In addition to setting the timetable, the Cologne European Council reaffirmed that the IGC would address the three Amsterdam leftovers. It also asked the Finnish presidency to prepare the IGC with a report on these and other issues. For the remainder of 1999, there was a lively debate within the Union about the agenda of the forthcoming conference.

The Parliament, Commission, a few member states, and many academic experts favored an IGC with a broad agenda going beyond the Amsterdam leftovers. The Parliament adopted resolutions calling for the initiation of a "constitutional process" that would review all aspects of the Union's functioning and possibly lead to the adoption of a formal EU constitution. Newly installed Commission president Prodi appointed a committee of "wise men" to prepare a report on the institutional implications of enlargement. Chaired by former Belgian prime minister Jean-Luc Dehaene, the wise men presented their report in October 1999, advising that the IGC adopt a "somewhat broader agenda, including a reorganization of the treaty texts in order to avoid constant treaty revisions" and that it "produce a more substantial reform package within the prescribed deadline."[9]

The wise men argued for radical measures focused on avoiding institutional gridlock and on regaining public support for a decision-making process that they saw as remote from and not understood by the citizens. One of the reasons for public confusion, they argued, was that the treaties were undergoing constant revision. In their view it was important to break the cycle of revision—negotiation followed by ratification followed by new negotiations—that had been underway on an almost continuous basis since the mid-1980s.

They therefore proposed a new approach to treaty change—one that would not always involve the convening of an IGC. They called for splitting the main treaty texts into two parts. The first would contain constitutional elements—all provisions relating to basic aims, principles and general policy orientations, citizens' rights, and the institutional framework. In the future, as at present, these provisions could be amended only by unanimous agreement of the member states, acting in accordance with their requisite constitutional procedures. The second part of the treaties would contain all provisions relating to specific policy matters, for example CAP, EMU, social policy, and so forth. These provisions could be amended by a less demanding procedure, such as a decision of the Council of Ministers (on the basis either of unanimity or QMV with a high threshold) and the assent of the Parliament. The object of these changes, as explained in the report, would be to head off a situation in which treaty revision might be needed to permit the development of policy, but almost impossible to achieve given the need for unanimity among 28 or more governments, ratification by the same number of national parliaments, and in certain countries voter referenda.

In the debate over a narrow versus a broad agenda, the member states had the final word. The narrow approach largely prevailed. The report by the Finnish presidency adopted by the European Council in Helsinki in December 1999 reiterated the need to address the leftover issues. It also recommended addressing several institutional issues that were not explicitly mentioned in the Amsterdam protocol but that were closely related to the issues of weighting and intra-institutional balance: the responsibility of the members of the Commission, the allocation of seats in the Parliament and the extension of the co-decision procedure, efficiency-increasing reforms in the operational procedures of the Court of Justice and the Court of First Instance, and amendments regarding the other EU institutions, in particular the Court of Auditors. In the addition, the European Council asked the incoming Portuguese presidency to prepare for the June 2000 session a progress report on the IGC and if necessary to propose additional issues to be taken on, thereby leaving the door open to a broadening of the agenda.

For the most part, however, the member states rebuffed the call for a broad, constitutional approach. Whereas Dehaene and his committee argued that the constant process of treaty revision was confusing the citizens and undermining political support for the Union—and that for this reason the fifteen needed to settle crucial issues "once and for all"—the member state governments concluded that the Union could ill afford a highly divisive debate on such matters as the drafting of an EU constitution. They also were unwilling to open up discussion of issues—amendments not involving an IGC or the adoption of a formal EU constitution—that implied a diminution of member state powers relative to the Union. They thus favored a more incremental approach, particularly in view of the enlargement-driven December 2000 deadline.

THE KEY ISSUES

Of the three leftover issues on the agenda, the most serious to be tackled at the IGC is probably the reform of voting in the Council. Two developments in recent years have pushed this issue to the fore: the extension, since the 1980s, of QMV and successive enlargements involving mainly small states. Even though votes are weighted under QMV, smaller member states tend to be over-represented relative to their share of total EU population, as voting weights do not fully reflect differences in population size. (For example, France, Italy, and the UK have nearly six times the population of Belgium—Germany eight times—but they have only twice as many votes as Belgium in the Council.) The larger member states are concerned that their influence in the Union will be diluted further by the accession of many new and mostly smaller states. France has been most insistent about the need to address this issue. At present, to reach the QMV threshold requires the support of member states accounting for approximately 60 percent of the EU population.

By some estimates this could drop to as low as 47 percent of total population in an EU of 28 member states.[10]

Proposals for reforms that would remedy this situation have centered on either a simple reweighting of votes in favor of the larger member states or the introduction of a dual majority system. Under the latter approach, the QMV threshold would be kept at the traditional 71 percent, but a new provision would require that a majority be comprised of member state governments representing a certain percentage—most likely 60—of the EU's total population. The other approach is simply to change the relative weights of the votes in the Council in favor of the larger states. As new member states are admitted, each member must be assigned a new number of votes and a new QMV threshold must be set. Larger countries would receive their current number of votes multiplied by a certain factor, while smaller countries would receive their current number of votes multiplied by a smaller factor. This would preserve or even increase the relative weight of the larger countries as enlargement proceeds.

While initially there was support in the EU for the double majority approach, during the preparations for IGC 2000 sentiment in many national governments shifted toward a simple reweighting. The double majority would introduce another complexity in EU decision making and cut against the goal of simplification that all member states support in principle. The key to achieving a reweighting, however, will be to set the factors by which member state votes are multiplied—to determine, in other words, by *how much* votes in the Council should be shifted in favor of the larger member states.

Reform of the Commission is the second major institutional issue on the agenda of IGC 2000. As noted, under the institutional protocol to the Treaty of Amsterdam, the EU could admit five new member states while holding the Commission at its current size of twenty. But this would be only an interim measure. If every member state retained the right to nominate even one commissioner, the size of the Commission eventually could increase to thirty or more members—a radical departure from the nine at the time the Community was established. IGC 2000 thus must address the vexing question of whether every member state must always have a commissioner.

Proposals for reshaping the Commission fall into three categories. The simplest approach calls for a straight downsizing of the Commission. The Commission, Court of Justice, and Court of Auditors have always been formed on the basis of at least one member from each member state, but there is precedent for a narrower approach, notably the Executive Board of the ECB, which has only six members for the eleven countries participating in the Eurosystem. A second approach is the UN Security Council model, in which the large member states always would have a right to nominate a commissioner while the smaller countries would rotate. A third approach is that of differentiated status, in which the number of portfolios would be reduced. Each member state would have a commissioner, but there would be in effect junior and senior members of the college, with the latter much more powerful than the former. Such an approach would build upon what is already existing practice in the EU, in which the large member states lay claim to powerful and politically sensitive portfolios such as external trade and competition, leaving health and consumer protection, education and culture, and employment and social affairs to the smaller countries.

The relative merits of these proposals were widely discussed by academics and government officials in the run-up to IGC 2000. As the opening of the conference approached, however, it became increasingly apparent that the small member states would oppose any reform that would do away with the right of each member state to nominate a commissioner or that would create formal hierarchies of power within the Commission. As the Finnish government's background paper for the IGC concluded, "a college with one national from each member state [is] considered the most appropriate way of ensuring the Commission's legitimacy. It is assumed to strengthen citizens' feeling of belonging to a Union and to ensure that expertise of each member state is represented in the Commission."[11]

If all three of the frequently discussed approaches to radical reform are ruled out as politically impractical, the only remaining option will be for the Union to concentrate on internal reform of the Commission (some of which will not require treaty revision) and reforms in the relationship between the Commission and the other institutions designed to preserve its effectiveness. Prodi and Commission vice president for reform Neil Kinnock began to initiate certain changes in the way the Commission operates following the crisis of 1999. Others are under discussion. Changes that would require treaty revision by the IGC include increasing the number of vice presidents, further expanding the powers of the president vis-à-vis the other commissioners, and giving the Parliament the power to dismiss individual commissioners.

The third leftover issue on the agenda of IGC 2000 is the extension of QMV. Decisions currently not subject to QMV include several policy areas and virtually all constitutional questions relating to the institutions, decision making, and membership. Policy areas that remain entirely or partially subject to unanimous voting include matters related to Union citizenship, the free movement of persons, the budget, taxation, policies on industry, culture and the environment, and the services and intellectual property aspects of trade policy. The second and third pillars also operate largely on the basis of unanimous voting. The Commission and some member states argue that in order to avoid decision-making gridlock, all or nearly all of these areas must be made subject to QMV. As Prodi noted in his opening speech to the IGC, "I genuinely believe that, with 28 members, any areas that are still decided by unanimity will be condemned to stagnation."[12]

Some extension of QMV is likely. The British government, traditionally the strongest defender of unanimity voting in the Union, signaled that it was prepared to look at the extension of QMV on a case-by-case basis and that in particular it would look favorably upon its adoption in such matters as Council approval of ECJ rules of procedure and in certain areas of transport policy where unanimity still is used. But London also made clear its view that unanimity must be retained for key issues of national interest, including treaty change, taxation, border controls, social security, defense, and revenue-raising for the EU budget.[13] IGC 2000 thus is likely to fall well short of the ideal of some of near-universal use of QMV. Decision making will be correspondingly more difficult in an enlarged Union—a fact that will be lamented by some, but which in the long run might prevent the Union from taking unpopular steps that could alienate public support for the very enterprise of European integration.

THE BROADER AGENDA

The broader agenda was pushed aside by the member states in the run-up to the IGC, but it is unlikely to go away. Even the member states agree that certain issues beyond the Amsterdam leftovers may need to be addressed in the IGC. As was seen in Chapter 7, the Cologne European Council called for the drafting of a Charter of Fundamental Rights of the Union, a process that was formally initiated at Tampere the following October. The European Parliament and some member states believe that the charter should be incorporated into the treaties, while other member states believe that such a step would undermine national law and weaken the position of their domestic law and courts. They therefore prefer that it stand on its own as a separate political declaration. Incorporation would require approval by the IGC, and thus is a possible agenda item. The further development of the Common European Security and Defense Policy, also pressed by the Cologne and Helsinki European Councils, might also require treaty revision. The formal abolition of the WEU and the establishment of a chain of command from the European Council to the commanders of the planned EU peacekeeping force may need to be clarified in treaty form.

Beyond these issues, there is the broader question of an EU constitution and the workings of the institutions. The large member states were probably correct in their view that an IGC aimed at fundamental revision and restructuring of the treaties would be difficult to manage. Although deceptively simple, the leftover issues are fundamentally about power, and there was no guarantee that even they could be resolved by the December 2000 deadline. But the Parliament and the Commission were also correct to point out that even after the Amsterdam simplifications, the founding treaties remain excessively complex and difficult for the citizens to understand. Decision making could indeed grind to a halt in an enlarged Union. Amending the treaties under the procedures in place since the 1950s will become increasingly difficult as the Union grows, but perhaps more necessary as new policy challenges are encountered. This may well mean that IGC 2000 will be followed by yet another conference devoted to institutional reform sometime during the enlargement process.

Enlargement and Its Implications

The third major issue on the EU's long-term agenda, enlargement, is perhaps the greatest imponderable facing the Union. The mechanics of the enlargement process are well known and were discussed in Chapter 10. But what enlargement will mean for everyday life—for people in the existing and new member countries who will be citizens of the same vast Union—will become clear only with time.

Enlargement may not take the straightforward path often suggested by European Council declarations, Commission progress reports, and association council statements. The parliaments or voters of one or more of the candidate countries may reject accession out of frustration with delay or fear of losing newly won sovereignty. More likely, enlargement could be held up from the EU side, derailed by concerns about costs or the free movement of people or held hostage to a dispute among the member states over Cyprus or institutional reform.

But assuming that enlargement does go ahead as planned, by the period 2015–2020 the EU could have as many as 28 members. The most likely list of countries would include those already in negotiations plus Croatia, although not yet Turkey. At this size, the EU will be a totally transformed economic and political entity. Economically, it will need to close the income and productivity gap between the existing and the candidate and new member countries, preserve the *acquis* in such crucial areas as foreign trade, the internal market, and EMU, and relate enlargement to the strategic economic goals adopted in Lisbon. Politically, it will have to find ways to deal with a greater diversity of outlooks and interests among the member states, streamline decision making, and defuse potentially explosive minority and territorial issues. For both old and new member countries, enlargement will raise questions about what it means to be European and about whether this vast Union of 500 million or more people fulfills the hopeful vision of Monnet and the founding fathers.

ECONOMIC AND POLITICAL CHALLENGES

In 1995, per capita GDP in the poorest candidate country, Latvia, was only 18 percent of the EU average; in the best off, Slovenia, it was only 59 percent.[14] Closing the gap between these countries and their western neighbors will take decades and will require wrenching social and economic changes. In the agricultural sector, for example, many small farms will cease to exist and farm owners or their children will be forced to seek employment in the service and manufacturing sectors.

For the existing member states, enlargement will mean more intense economic competition, but also expanded markets and investment opportunities. Meeting the economic challenges of enlargement will take place against the background of globalization and the shift toward a more information-based economy identified by the Lisbon European Council. At the most superficial level, the costs of enlargement will constitute a drain on the Union as it makes large new investments in economic restructuring and human capital. But enlargement also will mean new markets for EU firms, a larger pool of scientific and technical talent from which to draw, and increased clout for the Union in international trade forums such as the WTO. Perhaps most importantly, the sheer difficulty of enlargement will force political leaders in the Union to keep the focus on their ambitious plans for economic revitalization.

As formidable as the economic challenges of enlargement might appear, they may be less significant over the long term than the broader issues—ethnic and national identity and how they evolve in a larger and more diverse Union. All of the candidate countries have significant minority populations, with the largest (in percentage terms) in Slovakia, Romania, Estonia, and Latvia. As a divided country, Cyprus even defies characterization in simple majority–minority terms. Along with the ethnic Turks of northern Cyprus, two of the most potentially problematic minority situations concern the Roma (Gypsies) and the ethnic Russians. Romania alone has an estimated 1.8 to 2.5 million Roma, a group that has been badly persecuted and that has proven extremely difficult to integrate into the mainstream of society.[15] Ethnic Russians number approximately 485,000 in Estonia and some 900,000 in Latvia.[16] For the most part an unwelcome reminder in these countries of the Soviet past, these people may be among the first minority groups to take advantage of the free movement principles in an expanded Union to head westward.

As the EU and its member states consider how they will respond to ethnic and minority issues that may be "imported" into the Union with enlargement, they have become increasingly aware of problems in the Union itself. As summarized in an April 1999 expert report on the human dimension of enlargement prepared for the Commission:

> Existing member states cannot claim the right to prescribe and monitor the adherence of applicants and new member states to the EU's basic political values and rules without being prepared to subject themselves to the same scrutiny. Avoiding this opens the EU to the charge of hypocrisy and double standards, and could engender a corrosive cynicism about the professed values and standards in the candidate countries. The EU itself suffers from a "democratic deficit," and implementing democracy, the rule of law, human and minority rights is by no means perfect among current member states. Accelerating social and political change calls for innovation in longer-established democracies, as well as in the new democracies.[17]

The Haider phenomenon suggests that anti-immigrant sentiment may be rising in some member countries. Concerns about the influx of workers from the east is causing the EU to go slowly in the enlargement negotiations with regard to the free movement of people chapters of the *acquis*. Further complicating the situation is the fact that many of Western Europe's most sensitive immigration problems have nothing to do with enlargement, but concern the movement of people from North Africa and beyond. In early February 2000, just as the EU was condemning Austria for Haider's participation in the political process, the European public was shocked by news reports of large-scale attacks in southern Spain on immigrant Moroccan workers.[18]

Another aspect of the situation in the EU-15 that could interact with enlargement is the reassertion of nationality issues in many West European countries and the accompanying trend toward regional devolution. In the UK, a strong Scottish Nationalist Party is pressing for full independence for Scotland. The Flemish (Dutch) and Walloon (French) parts of Belgium are at odds over money, language rights, and economic development. In Spain, regions such as Catalonia are asserting autonomy from Madrid. In Italy, the Northern League has called for the secession of a "Northern Nation" from Rome, even though there are no fundamental ethnic or linguistic differences between the north and the rest of the country. The very revival of these regional identities is partly linked to integration, as people seek to come to terms with change by reasserting local customs and traditions and as disillusionment with distant bureaucracies has led to attempts to deal with problems closer to home.

IDENTITY AND VALUES: EUROPEAN, NATIONAL, REGIONAL

If the EU is to serve as an anchor and a model for the less stable regions to the east and south, it will have to manage tendencies toward fragmentation in the current member states as well as work to build a common identity that applies, at least at some minimal level, to the whole of Europe. One of the arguments in favor of enlarging the EU to central and eastern Europe (and to conflict-ridden Cyprus) has been that supranational integration can help to dampen internal conflicts by widening the arena in which economic and social issues are resolved and by enabling people to have multiple identities that blunt the fierce "us versus them" mentality that underlies much ethnic and religious conflict. A person living in Munich can regard himself or herself as a Bavarian, a German, and a European. The coexistence of such multiple identities can help to prevent the emergence of the kind of ethnic conflict that has raged in the Balkans.

But multiple levels of identity and governance also can lead to political maneuvering among the various levels of government and to the nation-state being "squeezed" between more assertive forces at the supranational and the subnational levels. The Scots in the UK, the Flemings in Belgium, and the Catalans in Spain all argue that because so many powers have been transferred to the EU, the nation-state matters less than in the past and is no longer the best vehicle to promote the interests of the citizen. With monetary policy, foreign trade, immigration, and eventually even defense handled largely or partially at the Union level, what justification is there, they ask, to give primary allegiance to the nation-state. Because small countries enjoy more weight in EU decision making than do large regions within large countries, regions also stand to increase their influence by gaining the status of independent member states in the Union.

This growing regionalization of European politics will play a role in shaping the future development of the Union, particularly as it expands to a larger and more diverse set of members. As was noted in Chapter 1, some sense of community and common identity is needed to underpin ambitious public policies. Citizens are willing to fight for each other, share economic burdens, and submit to common laws if they feel a sense of community with and obligation toward each other. Whether such a sense of community and identity will develop in an enlarged Union—particularly given the parallel emergence of stronger regional identities—is a crucial question for the future.

Just as the long-term economic future of Europe will depend in part on the evolution of social and cultural values, enlargement and its longer term effects on the Union will be shaped by values in the existing and new member states. To what extent these values differ between the existing and the candidate member countries is an important question to which studies give conflicting and ambiguous answers. The situation is in any case changing, as the legacy of communism fades and as Western Europe itself evolves in response to globalization, demographic change, and other factors.

One study undertaken for the Commission noted that as early as 1991, attitudes regarding religious beliefs and behavior in three central European countries (Hungary, Slovenia, and Poland) were remarkably similar to those in three original member countries (West Germany, the Netherlands, and Italy). Respondents to surveys in these six countries were more similar in outlook to each other than to respondents in three other countries (the UK, Ireland, and Austria) that were already members of the Union. But other studies show huge differences of outlook on selected issues. On the matter of trust, for example, an important factor in economic and political life, 56.6 percent of Swedes, 47.9 percent of Finns, and 39.9 percent of West Germans answer "yes" to the question of whether "most people can be trusted." The figure for Slovenia, in contrast, is 15.5 percent and for Turkey an astonishingly low 5.5 percent.[19]

While convergence can be expected to occur over time, it would be surprising if cultural values and norms did not continue to vary significantly in an area with so many different historical traditions, religions, languages, and economic circumstances. Differences in attitudes toward authority, money, law, administrative hierarchy, and secrecy already play a role in the politics of the fifteen. According to one commentator, the "real split" in the Union is not between the political parties of the left and right or between the large and small states, but between north and south. The northerners—Germany, the Netherlands, Scandinavia, and the UK—are large net contributors to the EU budget. Compared with the southerners—Portugal, Spain, Greece, and Italy—they are on balance more oriented toward free trade, open government, and transparency, and less tolerant of nepotism and political corruption. The southerners are also the traditionally high inflation, high deficit countries that had the most difficulty in meeting the Maastricht convergence criteria for EMU. "The split is not just about money and goods. It is about attitudes to the very way the EU is run. . . . It is about differing attitudes to strict implementation of EU directives (strict in the north, lax in the south)."[20] In defense of themselves, southerners are often quick to point out that the north has its own scandals and corruption and that the south has many distinctive strengths and values, for example stronger devotion to family and cultural traditions stretching back to ancient Greece and Rome.

Through successive enlargements, the EC/EU has for the most part succeeded in managing the diversity of values in the Union. All European countries share certain core values—commitment to democracy, human rights, and a market economy—on which to build. France has played an especially important mediating role. Itself a Mediterranean country that straddles the north-south divide, it has worked with Germany to provide leadership to the European integration process. It even could be argued that the southern countries are converging over time toward the "northern" model. But the split persists and to an extent was exacerbated with the admission in 1995 of two Nordic countries, Finland and Sweden, that in many respects embody "northern" ideals. As the Union enlarges, it will need to manage its residual north-south split, as well as avoid the emergence of new divisions—east-south, north-east, or north-south-east—that would impair the effectiveness of the Union. Like so much else, its ability to do so will depend in part on the evolution of citizen attitudes in the member states.

THE CHALLENGE OF COHESION

To cope with increasing size and diversity, the Union will need to develop mechanisms that allow it to function and preserve its cohesion. Institutional reform will be required to prevent decision-making deadlock in a Union of 28 or more members. As was seen in the previous section, however, there are limits to how far institutional reform can go in the face of fundamental clashes of economic and political interest. Institutions can be made more efficient by reducing their size, and decision making can be made more effective by use of majority voting and the elimination of vetoes by single member states or small blocking minorities. But such gains are sometimes purchased at a cost: disaffection among voters already inclined to see the Union as a mechanism for pushing through unpopular decisions from above, poor implementation and enforcement by member states of policies lacking broad political support, and perhaps, over the long run, constitutional crisis. A Union that persisted in taking unpopular decisions against the will of its member states would risk secession and even breakup.

A second approach to managing increased size and diversity could be to expand the use of flexibility. The flexibility clause adopted by the Treaty of Amsterdam sets rather narrow criteria for use, and no member state has yet proposed invoking the flexibility clause on a specific measure. A number of European political leaders have suggested that in order to keep the EU from degenerating into a large free-trade zone with lowest common denominator policies, the Union will need to amend the flexibility clause, making it easier to invoke, and to begin using its provisions to pursue deeper integration among subsets of member states in such areas as citizens' rights, taxation, and foreign policy.

A third element of an EU strategy for managing size and diversity will be to stress the importance of subsidiarity and to concentrate on the practical application of this principle. Relatedly, the EU could move toward accepting a more differentiated *acquis* in some policy areas. As noted in the previous chapter, enlargement in particular is stirring a new debate about greater policy differentiation in the Union. There are limits to how far internal differences can extend, however, given the imperatives of the single market and the need to sustain a level playing field.

The EU, and in particular such central institutions as the Commission and the Parliament, also may do more to try to actually overcome divergences in the Union. Internally, a European social model, as outlined in Lisbon, may play a certain unifying and consensus-building role, provided maintaining this model does not lead to bitter divisions among the member states about costs and the sharing of burdens in the EU budget. Regional policies and related measures such as TENs may also play a role in evening out economic and social disparities in the Union.

Finally, European leaders may be tempted to stress the EU's *external* identity as a way of forging unity out of a diverse group of member states. Although this aspect of European integration was rarely emphasized, the development of the EC and later the EU always was directed to some extent against external powers. Integration was a way of bolstering Western Europe against the Soviet threat and increasing its autonomy vis-à-vis the United States, upon which it was dependent for its security. The Soviet threat has disappeared, but the United States has emerged from the cold war as the world's only military superpower and has strengthened its relative position in some economic and technological fields. Right or wrong, it also is identified with the forces of globalization that are threatening to some parts of European society.

These factors, combined with the mundane commercial rivalries and disputes discussed in Chapter 8, may create a temptation in Europe to try to build a wider Europe with a deeper consensus on policies and values *against* the United States. As one U.S. commentator has written, one of most important factors in Europe's integration process "is the aspiration to build a European identity (political, economic, cultural) based on its differentiation from the United States. . . . If the process of shaping a European allegiance remains as difficult as it has been so far, this factor is bound to remain in play."[21] One indirect effect of enlargement thus may be increased tensions between Europe and the United States over some issues. Managing these tensions will be a key challenge for U.S. and EU foreign policy, with broad implications for the international system.

Europe and the Citizen

As has been seen throughout this book, "uniting Europe" has two dimensions: widening and deepening. It means broadening the integration process so that all of Europe participates in the same economic and social space, without sharp dividing lines that could become sources of conflict or impose hardships on citizens on one or the other side of such lines. It also means establishing a level playing field and common or harmonized policies in all countries that are members of the Union.

Widening and deepening are ongoing processes. With regard to the former, the EU faces several decades of hard work and a few key political decisions. It will need to complete the membership negotiations currently underway with twelve candidate countries and ensure that these countries get and stay on a path toward convergence with the rest of Europe. It also will need to decide whether it really intends to admit Turkey and on the long-term future of a few other potential candidates, notably Ukraine and the countries of the Balkans. Fundamentally, however, widening must at some point end, as the EU's external borders are established once and for all.

Deepening is a more complex story—the reason why the question mark continues to hang over "united Europe." How far and in what direction it will develop is harder to judge. The countries, governments, institutions, and citizens of the Union have different views about what "united" does or should mean—different ideas, in effect, about the desired end point of the integration process.

European governments and citizens are almost universally agreed in accepting the single market and policies in related areas such as agriculture and transport. They may disagree over specifics, but the policies themselves are not in question. With some exceptions, the same is true of EMU and the euro. They are less certain about common policies for defense, immigration, and specialized areas such as taxes and the budget. But in all these areas the trend is toward greater integration.

As was pointed out in Chapter 1, however, deepening poses many dilemmas, particularly as it will occur in parallel with an ongoing process of widening that itself raises questions, such as those concerning values and identity that were discussed in the previous section. Size and governance are particularly important issues. With perhaps as many as thirty members and a population of over 600 million, it may be difficult to sustain citizen loyalty or interest in the Union. Whether a European identity can emerge in such a vast entity or, to the extent that it does, provide the underpinnings for effective governance are open questions. Those who favored a broad agenda at IGC 2000 were concerned about precisely these questions. Whether they had answers to them is another matter.

Globalization creates another complicating factor—one that cuts two ways for the Union. When the EC was founded in the 1950s, there were huge barriers, administrative and even physical, to the movement of goods, people, capital, and information within Europe. These barriers have been dismantled, but so have many barriers to world trade. In this sense, one of the very reasons for the establishment of the Community—the common market—has been superseded to an extent by globalization. But because globalization is a threatening process to many, creating uncertainty for workers, citizens, and consumers, it potentially creates a new role for the EU as the guardian of European interests and values in an increasingly open and competitive world.

Looking back, it is hard not to conclude that the endpoint of the European integration process as envisioned by Monnet and his colleagues has changed. The

EU has evolved into a hybrid entity in which intergovernmental bodies such as the European Council coexist with supranational institutions such as the Commission and the Parliament. National governments pursue national interests in and through the Union. The United States of Europe seen by many in the late 1940s and early 1950s will not be achieved, not least because the citizens of Europe have shown that they are not prepared to abandon national and regional identities and loyalties. But most of these same citizens also realize the benefits that integration has brought. Integration thus is likely to continue, unevenly and imperfectly, but with enduring effects for Europe, its neighbors, and the international system as a whole.

Notes

1. Economic Policy Committee, *Annual Report on Structural Reforms 2000: Report Addressed to the Council and the Commission*, Brussels, March 13, 2000, 13.

2. *Presidency Conclusions: Lisbon European Council, 23 and 24 March 2000*, SN 100/00, March 24, 2000, 4.

3. Gerard Baker, "Europe's Illusion about America's Weakness," *Financial Times*, March 28, 2000.

4. Gilles Bertrand, Anna Michalski, and Lucio R. Pench, *Scenarios Europe 2010: Five Possible Futures for Europe* (Brussels: European Commission, Forward Studies Unit, Working Paper, July 1999), 56.

5. The other two scenarios are "Creative Societies" and "Turbulent Neighborhoods." The entire report can be found on europa.eu.int.

6. *Scenarios Europe 2010*, 25.

7. "Protocol on the Institutions with the Prospect of Enlargement of the European Union," *Treaty of Amsterdam*, 111.

8. "Declaration by Belgium, France and Italy on the Protocol on the Institutions with the Prospect of Enlargement of the European Union," ibid., 144 (emphasis supplied).

9. Richard von Weizsäcker, Jean-Luc Dehaene, and David Simon, *The Institutional Implications of Enlargement: Report to the Commission*, Brussels, October 18, 1999, 4.

10. Estimate by Geoffrey Edwards, "The Council of Ministers and Enlargement: A Search for Efficiency, Effectiveness, and Accountability," in John Redmond and Glenda G. Rosenthal, eds., *The Expanding European Union* (Boulder: Lynne Rienner, 1998), 51.

11. *IGC 2000: Contribution from the Finnish Government—Background and objectives in the IGC 2000*, CONFER 4723/00, Brussels, March 7, 2000, 7.

12. Romano Prodi, "Opening of the IGC: General Affairs Council," Brussels, February 14, 2000.

13. *IGC: Reform for Enlargement—The British Approach to the European Union Intergovernmental Conference 2000*, Cmnd. 4595, February 2000, 20.

14. *Agenda 2000*, vol. 2, 59.

15. J. P. Liegois and N. Gheorghe, *Roma/Gypsies: A European Minority*, quoted in Giuliano Amato and Judy Batt, *Final Report of the Reflection Group on the Long-Term Implications of EU Enlargement: The Nature of the New Border* (San Domenico di Fiesole: European University Institute and Forward Studies Union, European Commission, 1999), 78.

16. Estonia has an additional 30,000 Belorussians and 50,000 Ukrainians; Latvia 120,000 Belorussians and 90,000 Ukrainians. Amato and Batt, 82–84.

17. Amato and Batt, 5.

18. Tom Burns, "Spanish Police Quell Race Riot," *Financial Times*, February 9, 2000.

19. On religion, D. Laitin, "Culture and National Identity: the 'East' and European Integration," September 1998; on trust, D. Fuchs and H.-D. Klingemann, "National Community, Political Culture and Support for Democracy in Central and Eastern Europe," September 1998, cited in Amato and Batt, 15, 80.

20. Quentin Peel, "The EU's Real Split," *Financial Times*, February 25, 1999.

21. Peter W. Rodman, *Drifting Apart?: Trends in U.S.-European Relations* (Washington, DC: The Nixon Center, 1999), 55.

Index

About the Author

John Van Oudenaren is chief of the European Division at the Library of Congress and professorial lecturer at the Nitze School of Advanced International Studies, Johns Hopkins University. Prior to joining the Library of Congress, he was a senior researcher at the RAND Corporation. From 1991 to 1995 he was director of RAND's European office in Delft, the Netherlands. He has served on the Policy Planning Staff of the U.S. Department of State and has been a research associate at the Kennan Institute for Advanced Russian Studies, Woodrow Wilson International Center for Scholars, Washington, and at the International Institute for Strategic Studies in London. He received his Ph.D. in political science from the Massachusetts Institute of Technology and his A.B. in Germanic languages and literature from Princeton University. His publications include *Détente in Europe* (Duke University Press, 1991) and numerous reports, articles and chapters on international relations and European and Russian politics.